the
everything store

JEFF BEZOS
AND THE AGE
OF AMAZON

BRAD STONE

CORGI BOOKS

TRANSWORLD PUBLISHERS
61–63 Uxbridge Road, London W5 5SA
A Random House Group Company
www.transworldbooks.co.uk

**THE EVERYTHING STORE
A CORGI BOOK: 9780552167833**

First published in the United States
in 2013 by Little, Brown and Company

First published in Great Britain
in 2013 by Bantam Press
an imprint of Transworld Publishers
Corgi edition published 2014

Addresses for Random House Group Ltd companies outside the UK
can be found at: www.randomhouse.co.uk
The Random House Group Ltd Reg. No. 954009

Penguin Random House is committed to a sustainable future for
our business, our readers and our planet. This book is made from
Forest Stewardship Council® certified paper.

Printed and bound in Great Britain by Clays Ltd, Elcograf S.p.A.

Typeset in 12/13pt Granjon by Falcon Oast Graphic Art Ltd.

For Isabella and Calista Stone

When you are eighty years old, and in a quiet moment of reflection narrating for only yourself the most personal version of your life story, the telling that will be most compact and meaningful will be the series of choices you have made. In the end, we are our choices.

—Jeff Bezos, commencement speech at
Princeton University, May 30, 2010

Contents

the
everything store

Prologue

In the early 1970s, an industrious advertising executive named Julie Ray became fascinated with an unconventional public-school program for gifted children in Houston, Texas. Her son was among the first students enrolled in what would later be called the Vanguard program, which stoked creativity and independence in its students and nurtured expansive, outside-the-box thinking. Ray grew so enamored with the curriculum and the community of enthusiastic teachers and parents that she set out to research similar schools around the state with an eye toward writing a book about Texas's fledgling gifted-education movement.

A few years later, after her son had moved on to junior high, Ray returned to tour the program, nestled in a wing of River Oaks Elementary School, west of downtown Houston. The school's principal chose a student to accompany her on the visit, an articulate, sandy-haired sixth-grader whose parents asked only that his real name not be used in print. So Ray called him Tim.

Tim, Julie Ray wrote in her book *Turning On Bright Minds: A Parent Looks at Gifted Education in Texas*, was 'a student of general intellectual excellence, slight of build, friendly but serious.' He was 'not particularly gifted in leadership,' according to his teachers, but he moved confidently among his peers and articulately extolled the virtues of the novel he was reading at the time, J. R. R. Tolkien's *The Hobbit*.

Tim, twelve, was already competitive. He told Ray he was reading a variety of books to qualify for a special reader's certificate but compared himself unfavorably to another classmate who claimed, improbably, that she was reading a dozen books a week. Tim also showed Ray a science project he was working on called an infinity cube, a battery-powered contraption with rotating mirrors that created the optical illusion of an endless tunnel. Tim modeled the device after one he had seen in a store. That one cost twenty-two dollars, but 'mine was cheaper,' he told Ray. Teachers said that three of Tim's projects were being entered in a local science competition that drew most of its submissions from students in junior and senior high schools.

The school faculty praised Tim's ingenuity, but one can imagine they were wary of his intellect. To practice tabulating statistics for math class, Tim had developed a survey to evaluate the sixth-grade teachers. The goal, he said, was to assess instructors on 'how they teach, not as a popularity contest.' He administered the survey to class-mates and at the time of the tour was in the process of calculating the results and graphing the relative per-formance of each teacher.

Tim's average day, as Ray described it, was packed. He woke early and caught a seven o'clock bus a block from home. He arrived at school after a twenty-mile ride and went through a blaze of classes devoted to math, reading, physical education, science, Spanish, and art. There was time reserved for individual projects and small group discussions. In one lesson Julie Ray described, seven students, including Tim, sat in a tight circle in the principal's office for an exercise called productive thinking. They were given brief stories to read quietly to themselves and then discuss. The first story involved archaeologists who returned after an expedition and announced they had discovered a cache of precious artifacts, a claim that later turned out to be fraudulent. Ray recorded snippets of the ensuing dialogue:

'They probably wanted to become famous. They wished away the things they didn't want to face.'

'Some people go through life thinking like they always have.'

'You should be patient. Analyze what you have to work with.'

Tim told Julie Ray that he loved these exercises. 'The way the world is, you know, someone could tell you to press the button. You have to be able to think what you're doing for yourself.'

Ray found it impossible to interest a publisher in *Turning On Bright Minds*. Editors at the big houses said the subject matter was too narrow. So, in 1977, she took the money she'd earned from writing advertising copy for a Christmas catalog, printed a thousand paperbacks, and distributed them herself.

More than thirty years later, I found a copy in the Houston Public Library. I also tracked down Julie Ray, who now lives in Central Texas and works on planning and communications for environmental and cultural causes. She said she had watched Tim's rise to fame and fortune over the past two decades with admiration and amazement but without much surprise. 'When I met him as a young boy, his ability was obvious, and it was being nurtured and encouraged by the new program,' she says. 'The program also benefited by his responsiveness and enthusiasm for learning. It was a total validation of the concept.'

She recalls what one teacher said all those years ago when Ray asked her to estimate the grade level the boy was performing at. 'I really can't say,' the teacher replied. 'Except that there is probably no limit to what he can do, given a little guidance.'

In late 2011, I went to visit 'Tim' – aka Jeff Bezos – in the Seattle headquarters of his company, Amazon.com. I was there to solicit his cooperation with this book, an attempt to chronicle the extraordinary rise of an innovative, disruptive, and often polarizing technology powerhouse, the company that was among the first to see the boundless promise of the Internet and that ended up forever changing the way we shop and read.

Amazon is increasingly a daily presence in modern life. Millions of people regularly direct their Web browsers to its eponymous website or its satellite sites, like Zappos.com and Diapers.com, acting on the most basic impulse in any capitalist society: *to consume*. The Amazon site is a smorgasbord of selection, offering books, movies, garden tools, furniture, food, and the occasional oddball items, like an inflatable unicorn horn for cats ($9.50) and a thousand-pound electronic-lock gun safe ($903.53) that is available for delivery in three to five days. The company has nearly perfected the art of instant gratification, delivering digital products in seconds and their physical incarnations in just a few days. It is not uncommon to hear a customer raving about an order that magically appeared on his doorstep well before it was expected to arrive.

Amazon cleared $61 billion in sales in 2012, its seventeenth year of operation, and will likely be the fastest retailer in history to surpass $100 billion. It is loved by many of its customers, and it is feared just as fervently by its competitors. Even the name has informally entered the business lexicon, and not in an altogether favorable way. *To be Amazoned* means 'to watch helplessly as the online upstart from Seattle vacuums up the customers and profits of your traditional brick-and-mortar business.'

The history of Amazon.com, as most people understand it, is one of the iconic stories of the Internet age. The company started modestly as an online bookseller and then rode the original wave of dot-com exuberance in the late 1990s to extend into selling music, movies, electronics, and toys. Narrowly avoiding disaster and defying a wave of skepticism about its prospects that coincided with the dot-com bust of 2000 and 2001, it then mastered the physics of its own complex distribution network and expanded into software, jewelry, clothes, apparel, sporting goods, automotive parts – you name it. And just when it had established itself as the Internet's top retailer and a leading platform on which other sellers could hawk their wares, Amazon redefined itself yet again as a versatile technology firm that sold the cloud computing infrastructure known as Amazon Web Services as well as inexpensive, practical digital devices like the Kindle electronic reader and the Kindle Fire tablet.

'To me Amazon is a story of a brilliant founder who personally drove the vision,' says Eric Schmidt, the chairman of Google and an avowed Amazon competitor who is personally a member of Amazon Prime, its two-day shipping service. 'There are almost no better examples. Perhaps Apple, but people forget that most people believed Amazon was doomed because it would not scale at a cost structure that would work. It kept piling up losses. It lost hundreds of millions of dollars. But Jeff was very garrulous, very smart. He's a classic technical founder of a business, who understands every detail and cares about it more than anyone.'

Despite the recent rise of its stock price to vertiginous heights, Amazon remains a unique and uniquely puzzling company. The bottom line on its balance sheet is notoriously anemic, and in the midst of its frenetic expansion into new markets and product categories, it actually lost money in 2012. But Wall Street hardly seems to care. With his consistent proclamations that he is building his company for the long term, Jeff Bezos has earned so much faith from his shareholders that investors are willing to patiently wait for the day when he decides to slow his expansion and cultivate healthy profits.

Bezos has proved quite indifferent to the opinions of others. He is an avid problem solver, a man who has a chess grand master's view of the competitive landscape, and he applies the focus of an obsessive-compulsive to pleasing customers and providing services like free shipping. He has vast ambitions – not only for Amazon, but to push the boundaries of science and remake the media. In addition to funding his own rocket company, Blue Origin, Bezos acquired the ailing *Washington Post* newspaper company in August 2013 for $250 million in a deal that stunned the media industry.

As many of his employees will attest, Bezos is extremely difficult to work for. Despite his famously hearty laugh and cheerful public persona, he is capable of the same kind of acerbic outbursts as Apple's late founder, Steve Jobs, who could terrify any employee who stepped into an elevator with him. Bezos is a micromanager with a limitless spring of new ideas, and he reacts harshly to efforts that don't meet his rigorous standards.

Like Jobs, Bezos casts a reality-distortion field – an aura thick with persuasive but ultimately unsatisfying propaganda about his company. He often says that Amazon's corporate mission 'is to raise the bar across industries, and around the world, for what it means to be customer focused.'[1] Bezos and his employees are indeed absorbed with catering to customers, but they can also be ruthlessly competitive with rivals and even partners. Bezos likes to say that the markets Amazon competes in are vast, with room for many winners. That's perhaps true, but it's also clear that Amazon has helped damage or destroy competitors small and large, many of whose brands were once world renowned: Circuit City. Borders. Best Buy. Barnes & Noble.

Americans in general get nervous about the gathering of so much corporate power, particularly when it is amassed by large companies based in distant cities whose success could change the character of their own communities. Walmart faced this skepticism; so did Sears, Woolworth's, and the other retail giants of each age, all the way back to the A&P grocery chain, which battled a ruinous antitrust lawsuit during the 1940s. Americans flock to large retailers for their convenience and low prices. But at a certain point, these companies get so big that a contradiction in the public's collective psyche reveals itself. We want things cheap, but we don't really want anyone undercutting the mom-and-pop store down the street or the locally owned bookstore, whose business has been under assault for decades, first by the rise of chain bookstores like Barnes & Noble and now by Amazon.

Bezos is an excruciatingly prudent communicator for his own company. He is sphinxlike with details of his plans, keeping thoughts and intentions private, and he's an enigma in the Seattle business community and in the broader technology industry. He rarely speaks at conferences and gives media interviews infrequently.

Even those who admire him and closely follow the Amazon story are apt to mispronounce his surname (it's '*Bay*-zose,' not '*Bee*-zose').

John Doerr, the venture capitalist who backed Amazon early and was on its board of directors for a decade, has dubbed Amazon's miserly public-relations style 'the Bezos Theory of Communicating.' He says Bezos takes a red pen to press releases, product descriptions, speeches, and shareholder letters, crossing out anything that does not speak simply and positively to customers.

We *think* we know the Amazon story, but really all we're familiar with is its own mythology, the lines in press releases, speeches, and interviews that Bezos hasn't covered with red ink.

Amazon occupies a dozen modest buildings south of Seattle's Lake Union, a small, freshwater glacial lake linked by canals to Puget Sound on the west and Lake Washington on the east. The area was home to a large sawmill in the nineteenth century and before that to Native American encampments. That pastoral landscape is now long gone, and biomedical startups, a cancer-research center, and University of Washington School of Medicine buildings dot the dense urban neighborhood.

From the outside, Amazon's modern, low-slung offices are unmarked and unremarkable. But step inside Day One North, seat of the Amazon high command on Terry Avenue and Republican Street, and you're greeted with Amazon's smiling logo on a wall behind a long rectangular visitors' desk. On one side of the desk sits a bowl of dog biscuits for employees who bring their dogs to the office (a rare perk in a company that makes employees pay for parking and snacks). Near the elevators, there's a black plaque with white lettering that informs visitors they have entered the realm of the philosopher-CEO. It reads:

> There is so much stuff that has yet to be invented.
> There's so much new that's going to happen.
> People don't have any idea yet how impactful the Internet is going to be and that this is still Day 1 in such a big way.
>
> Jeff Bezos

Amazon's internal customs are deeply idiosyncratic. PowerPoint decks or slide presentations are never used in meetings. Instead, employees are required to write six-page narratives laying out their points in prose, because Bezos believes doing so fosters critical thinking. For each new product, they craft their documents in the style of a press release. The goal is to frame a proposed initiative in the way a customer might hear about it for the first time. Each meeting begins with everyone silently reading the document, and discussion commences afterward – just like the productive-thinking exercise in the principal's office at River Oaks Elementary. For my initial meeting with Bezos to discuss this project, I decided to observe Amazon's customs and prepare my own Amazon-style narrative, a fictional press release on behalf of the book.

Bezos met me in an executive conference room and we sat down at a large table made of half a dozen door-desks, the same kind of blond wood that Bezos used twenty years ago when he was building Amazon from scratch in his garage. The door-desks are often held up as a symbol of the company's enduring frugality. When I first interviewed Bezos, back in 2000, a few years of unrelenting international travel had taken their toll and he looked pasty and out of shape. Now he was lean and fit; he'd transformed his physique in the same way that he'd transformed Amazon. He'd even cropped his awkwardly balding pate right down to the dome, which gave him a sleek look suggestive of one of his science-fiction heroes, Captain Picard of *Star Trek: The Next Generation*.

We sat down, and I slipped the press release across the table to him. When he realized what I was up to, he laughed so hard that spit came flying out of his mouth.

Much has been made over the years of Bezos's famous laugh. It's a startling, pulse-pounding bray that he leans into while craning his neck back, closing his eyes, and letting loose with a guttural roar that sounds like a cross between a mating elephant seal and a power tool. Often it comes when nothing is obviously funny to anyone else. In a way, Bezos's laugh is a mystery that has never been solved; one doesn't expect someone so intense and focused to have a raucous laugh like that, and no one in his family seems to share it.

Employees know the laugh primarily as a heart-stabbing sound that slices through conversation and rocks its targets back on their heels. More than a few of his colleagues suggest that on some level, this is intentional – that Bezos wields his laugh like a weapon. 'You can't misunderstand it,' says Rick Dalzell, Amazon's former chief information officer. 'It's disarming and punishing. He's punishing you.'

Bezos read my press release silently for a minute or two and we discussed the ambitions of this book – to tell the Amazon story in depth for the first time, from its inception on Wall Street in the early 1990s up to the present day. Our conversation lasted an hour. We spoke about other seminal business books that might serve as models and about the biography *Steve Jobs* by Walter Isaacson, published soon after the Apple CEO's untimely death.

We also acknowledged the awkwardness inherent in writing and selling a book about Amazon at this particular moment in time. (All of the online and offline booksellers of *The Everything Store* undoubtedly have strong opinions about its subject matter. In fact, the French media giant Hachette Livre, which owns Little, Brown and Company, the house that is publishing the book, recently settled long-standing antitrust litigation with the U.S. Department of Justice and regulatory authorities in the European Union stemming from the corporation's dispute with Amazon over the pricing of electronic books. Like so many other companies in so many other retail and media industries, Hachette has had to view Amazon as both an empowering retail partner and a dangerous competitor. Of course, Bezos has a thought on this as well. 'Amazon isn't happening to the book business,' he likes to say to authors and journalists. 'The future is happening to the book business.')

I've spoken to Bezos probably a dozen times over the past decade, and our talks are always spirited, fun, and frequently interrupted by his machine-gun bursts of laughter. He is engaged and full of twitchy, passionate energy (if you catch him in the hallway, he will not hesitate to inform you that he never takes the office elevator, always the stairs). He devotes his full attention to the conversation, and, unlike many other CEOs, he never gives you the sense that he is hurried or distracted – but he is highly circumspect about deviating from well-established, very abstract talking points. Some of these maxims are so well worn that one might even call them Jeffisms. A few have stuck around for a decade or more.

'If you want to get to the truth about what makes us different, it's this,' Bezos says, veering into a familiar Jeffism: 'We are genuinely customer-centric, we are genuinely long-term oriented and we genuinely like to invent. Most companies are not those things. They are focused on the competitor, rather than the customer. They want to work on things that will pay dividends in two or three years, and if they don't work in two or three years they will move on to something else. And they prefer to be close-followers rather than inventors, because it's safer. So if you want to capture the truth about Amazon, that is why we are different. Very few companies have all of those three elements.'

Toward the end of the hour we spent discussing this book, Bezos leaned forward on his elbows and asked, 'How do you plan to handle the narrative fallacy?'

Ah yes, of course, the narrative fallacy. For a moment, I experienced the same sweaty surge of panic every Amazon employee over the past two decades has felt when confronted with an unanticipated question from the hyperintelligent boss. The narrative fallacy, Bezos explained, was a term coined by Nassim Nicholas Taleb in his 2007 book *The Black Swan* to describe how humans are biologically inclined to turn complex realities into soothing but oversimplified stories. Taleb argued that the limitations of the human brain resulted in our species' tendency to squeeze unrelated facts and events into cause-and-effect equations and then convert them into easily understandable narratives. These stories, Taleb wrote, shield humanity from the true randomness of the world, the chaos of human experience, and, to some extent, the unnerving element of luck that plays into all successes and failures.

Bezos was suggesting that Amazon's rise might be that sort of impossibly complex story. There was no easy explanation for how certain products were invented, such as Amazon Web Services, its pioneering cloud business that so many other Internet companies now use to run their operations. 'When a company comes up with an idea, it's a messy process. There's no aha moment,' Bezos said. Reducing Amazon's history to a simple narrative, he worried, could give the *impression* of clarity rather than the real thing.

In Taleb's book – which, incidentally, all Amazon senior executives had to read – the author stated that the way to avoid the narrative fallacy was to favor experimentation and clinical knowledge over storytelling and memory. Perhaps a more practical solution, at least for the aspiring author, is to acknowledge its potential influence and then plunge ahead anyway.

And so I begin with a disclaimer. The idea for Amazon was conceived in 1994 on the fortieth floor of a midtown New York City skyscraper. Nearly twenty years later, the resulting company employed more than ninety thousand people and had become one of the best-known corporations on the planet, frequently delighting its customers with its wide selection, low prices, and excellent customer service while also remaking industries and unnerving the stewards of some of the most storied brands in the world. This is one attempt at describing how it all happened. It is based on more than three hundred interviews with current and former Amazon executives and employees, including my conversations over the years with Bezos himself, who in the end was supportive of this project even though he judged that it was 'too early' for a reflective look at Amazon. Nevertheless, he approved many interviews with his top executives, his family, and his friends, and for that I am grateful. I also drew from fifteen years of reporting on the company for *Newsweek*, the *New York Times*, and *Bloomberg Businessweek*.

The goal of this book is to tell the story behind one of the greatest entrepreneurial successes since Sam Walton flew his two-seat turboprop across the American South to scope out prospective Walmart store sites. It's the tale of how one gifted child grew into an extraordinarily driven and versatile CEO and how he, his family, and his colleagues bet heavily on a revolutionary network called the Internet, and on the grandiose vision of a single store that sells everything.

PART I
Faith

CHAPTER 1

The House of Quants

Before it was the self-proclaimed largest bookstore on Earth or the Web's dominant superstore, Amazon.com was an idea floating through the New York City offices of one of the most unusual firms on Wall Street: D. E. Shaw & Co.

A quantitative hedge fund, DESCO, as its employees affectionately called it, was started in 1988 by David E. Shaw, a former Columbia University computer science professor. Along with the founders of other groundbreaking quant houses of that era, like Renaissance Technologies and Tudor Investment Corporation, Shaw pioneered the use of computers and sophisticated mathematical formulas to exploit anomalous patterns in global financial markets. When the price of a stock in Europe was fractionally higher than the price of the same stock in the United States, for example, the computer jockeys turned Wall Street warriors at DESCO would write software to quickly execute trades and exploit the disparity.

The broader financial community knew very little about D. E. Shaw, and its polymath founder wanted to keep it that way. The firm preferred operating far below the radar, deploying private capital from wealthy investors such as billionaire financier Donald Sussman and the Tisch family, and keeping its proprietary trading algorithms out of competitors' hands. Shaw felt strongly that if DESCO was going to be a firm that pioneered new approaches to investing, the only way to maintain its lead was to keep its insights secret and avoid teaching competitors how to think about these new computer-guided frontiers.

David Shaw came of age in the dawning era of powerful new supercomputers. He earned a PhD in computer science from Stanford in 1980 and then moved to New York to teach in Columbia's computer science department. Throughout the early eighties, high-tech companies tried to lure him to the private sector. Inventor Danny Hillis, founder of the supercomputer manufacturer Thinking Machines Corporation and later one of Jeff Bezos's closest friends, almost convinced Shaw to come work for him designing parallel computers. Shaw tentatively accepted the job and then changed his mind, telling Hillis he wanted to do something more lucrative and could always return to the supercomputer field after he got wealthy. Hillis argued that even if Shaw did get rich – which seemed unlikely – he'd never return to computer science. (Shaw did, after he became a billionaire and passed on the day-to-day management of D. E. Shaw to others.) 'I was spectacularly wrong on both counts,' Hillis says.

Morgan Stanley finally pried Shaw loose from academia in 1986, adding him to a famed group working on statistical arbitrage software for the new wave of automated trading. But Shaw had an urge to set off on his own. He left Morgan Stanley in 1988, and with a $28 million seed investment from investor Donald Sussman, he set up shop over a Communist bookstore in Manhattan's West Village.

By design, D. E. Shaw would be a different kind of Wall Street firm. Shaw recruited not financiers but scientists and mathematicians – big brains with unusual backgrounds, lofty academic credentials, and more than a touch of social cluelessness. Bob Gelfond, who joined DESCO after the firm moved to a loft on Park Avenue South, says that 'David wanted to see the power of technology and computers applied to finance in a scientific way' and that he 'looked up to Goldman Sachs and wanted to build an iconic Wall Street firm.'

In these ways and many others, David Shaw brought an exacting sensibility to the management of his company. He regularly sent out missives instructing employees to spell the firm's name in a specific manner – with a space between the D. and the E. He also mandated that everyone use a canonical description of the company's mission: it was to 'trade stocks, bonds, futures, options and various other financial instruments' – precisely in that order. Shaw's rigor extended to more substantive matters as well: any of his computer scientists could suggest trading ideas, but the notions had to pass demanding scientific scrutiny and statistical tests to prove they were valid.

In 1991, D. E. Shaw was growing rapidly, and the company moved to the top floors of a midtown Manhattan skyscraper a block from Times Square. The firm's striking but sparely decorated offices, designed by the architect Steven Holl, included a two-story lobby with luminescent colors that were projected into slots cut into the expansive white walls. That fall, Shaw hosted a thousand-dollar-a-ticket fund-raiser for presidential candidate Bill Clinton that was attended by the likes of Jacqueline Onassis, among others. Employees were asked to clear out of the office that evening before the event. Jeff Bezos, one of the youngest vice presidents at the firm, left to play volleyball with colleagues, but first he stopped and got his photo taken with the future president.

Bezos was in his mid twenties at the time, five foot eight inches tall, already balding and with the pasty, rumpled appearance of a committed workaholic. He had spent five years on Wall Street and impressed seemingly everyone he encountered with his keen intellect and boundless determination. Upon graduating from Princeton in 1986, Bezos worked for a pair of Columbia professors at a company called Fitel that was developing a private transatlantic computer network for stock traders. Graciela Chichilnisky, one of the co-founders and Bezos's boss, remembers him as a capable and upbeat employee who worked tirelessly and at different times managed the firm's operations in London and Tokyo. 'He was not concerned about what other people were thinking,' Chichilnisky says. 'When you gave him a good solid intellectual issue, he would just chew on it and get it done.'

Bezos moved to the financial firm Bankers Trust in 1988, but by then, frustrated by what he viewed as institutional reluctance at companies to challenge the status quo, he was already looking for an opportunity to start his own business. Between 1989 and 1990 he spent several months working in his spare time on a startup with a young Merrill Lynch employee named Halsey Minor, who would later go on to start the online news network CNET. Their fledgling venture, aimed at sending a customized newsletter to people over their fax machines, collapsed when Merrill Lynch withdrew the promised funding. But Bezos nevertheless made an impression. Minor remembers that Bezos had closely studied several wealthy businessmen and that he particularly admired a man named Frank Meeks, a Virginia entrepreneur who had made a fortune owning Domino's Pizza franchises. Bezos also revered pioneering computer scientist Alan Kay and often quoted his observation that 'point of view is worth 80 IQ points' – a reminder that looking at things in new ways can enhance one's understanding. 'He went to school on everybody,' Minor says. 'I don't think there was anybody Jeff knew that he didn't walk away from with whatever lessons he could.'

Bezos was ready to leave Wall Street altogether when a headhunter convinced him to meet executives at just one more financial firm, a company with an unusual pedigree. Bezos would later say he found a kind of workplace soul mate in David Shaw – 'one of the few people I know who has a fully developed left brain and a fully developed right brain.'[1]

At DESCO, Bezos displayed many of the idiosyncratic qualities his employees would later observe at Amazon. He was disciplined and precise, constantly recording ideas in a notebook he carried with him, as if they might float out of his mind if he didn't jot them down. He quickly abandoned old notions and embraced new ones when better options presented themselves. He already exhibited the same boyish excitement and conversation-stopping laugh that the world would later come to know.

Bezos thought analytically about everything, including social situations. Single at the time, he started taking ballroom-dance classes, calculating that it would increase his exposure to what he called $n+$ women. He later famously admitted to thinking about how to increase his 'women flow,'[2] a Wall Street corollary to *deal flow*, the number of new opportunities a banker can access. Jeff Holden, who worked for Bezos first at D. E. Shaw & Co. and later at Amazon, says he was 'the most introspective guy I ever met. He was very methodical about everything in his life.'

D. E. Shaw had none of the gratuitous formalities of other Wall Street firms; in outward temperament, at least, it was closer to a Silicon Valley startup. Employees wore jeans or khakis, not suits and ties, and the hierarchy was flat (though key information about trading formulas was tightly held). Bezos seemed to love the idea of the nonstop workday; he kept a rolled-up sleeping bag in his office and some egg-crate foam on his windowsill in case he needed to bunk down for the night. Nicholas Lovejoy, a colleague who would later join him at Amazon, believes the sleeping bag 'was as much a prop as it was actually useful.' When they did leave the office, Bezos and his DESCO colleagues often socialized together, playing backgammon or bridge until the early hours of the morning, usually for money.

As the company grew, David Shaw started to think about how to broaden its talent base. He looked beyond math and science geeks to what he called generalists, those who'd recently graduated at the tops of their classes and who showed significant aptitude in particular subjects. The firm also combed through the ranks of Fulbright scholars and dean's-list students at the best colleges and sent hundreds of unsolicited letters to them introducing the firm and proclaiming, 'We approach our recruiting in unapologetically elitist fashion.'

Respondents to the letters who seemed particularly extraordinary and who had high enough grade point averages and aptitude-test scores were flown to New York for a grueling day of interviews. Members of the firm delighted in asking these recruits random questions, such as 'How many fax machines are in the United States?' The intent was to see how candidates tried to solve difficult problems. After the interviews, everyone who had participated in the hiring process gathered and expressed one of four opinions about each individual: strong no hire; inclined not to hire; inclined to hire; or strong hire. One holdout could sink an applicant.

Bezos would later take these exact processes, along with the seeds of other Shaw management techniques, to Seattle. Even today, Amazon employees use those categories to vote on prospective new hires.

DESCO's massive recruitment effort and interview processes were finely tuned to Bezos's mind-set; they even attracted one person who joined Bezos as his life partner. MacKenzie Tuttle, who graduated from Princeton in 1992 with a degree in English and who studied with author Toni Morrison, joined the hedge fund as an administrative assistant and later went to work directly for Bezos. Lovejoy remembers Bezos hiring a limousine one night and taking several colleagues to a nightclub. 'He was treating the whole group but he was clearly focused on MacKenzie,' he says.

MacKenzie later said it was she who targeted Bezos, not the other way around. 'My office was next door to his, and all day long I listened to that fabulous laugh,' she told *Vogue* in 2012. 'How could you not fall in love with that laugh?' She began her campaign to win him over by suggesting lunch. The couple got engaged three months after they started dating; they were married three months after that.[3] Their wedding, held in 1993 at the Breakers, a resort in West Palm Beach, featured game time for adult guests and a late-night party at the hotel pool. Bob Gelfond and a computer programmer named Tom Karzes attended from D. E. Shaw.

Meanwhile, DESCO was growing rapidly and, in the process, becoming more difficult to manage. Several colleagues from that time recall that D. E. Shaw brought in a consultant who administered the Myers-Briggs personality test to all the members of the executive team. Not surprisingly, everyone tested as an introvert. The least introverted person on the team was Jeff Bezos. At D. E. Shaw in the early 1990s, he counted as the token extrovert.

Bezos was a natural leader at DESCO. By 1993, he was remotely running the firm's Chicago-based options trading group and then its high-profile entry into the third-market business, an alternative over-the-counter exchange that allowed retail investors to trade equities without the usual commissions collected by the New York Stock Exchange.[4] Brian Marsh, a programmer for the firm who would later work at Amazon, says that Bezos was 'incredibly charismatic and persuasive about the third-market project. It was easy to see then he was a great leader.' Bezos's division faced constant challenges, however. The dominant player in the space was one Bernard Madoff (the architect of a massive Ponzi scheme that would unravel in 2008). Madoff's own third-market division pioneered the business and preserved its market lead. Bezos and his team could see Madoff's offices in the Lipstick Building on the East Side through their windows high above the city.

While the rest of Wall Street saw D. E. Shaw as a highly secretive hedge fund, the firm viewed itself somewhat differently. In David Shaw's estimation, the company wasn't really a hedge fund but a versatile technology laboratory full of innovators and talented engineers who could apply computer science to a variety of different problems.[5] Investing was only the first domain where it would apply its skills.

So in 1994, when the opportunity of the Internet began to reveal itself to the few people watching closely, Shaw felt that his company was uniquely positioned to exploit it.

And the person he anointed to spearhead the effort was Jeff Bezos.

D. E. Shaw was ideally situated to take advantage of the Internet. Most Shaw employees had, instead of proprietary trading terminals, Sun workstations with Internet access, and they utilized early Internet tools like Gopher, Usenet, e-mail, and Mosaic, one of the first Web browsers. To write documents, they used an academic formatting tool called LaTeX, though Bezos refused to touch the program, claiming it was unnecessarily complicated. D. E. Shaw was also among the very first Wall Street firms to register its URL. Internet records show that Deshaw.com was claimed in 1992. Goldman Sachs took its domain in 1995, and Morgan Stanley a year after that.

Shaw, who used the Internet and its predecessor, ARPANET, during his years as a professor, was passionate about the commercial and social implications of a single global computer network. Bezos had first encountered the Internet in an astrophysics class at Princeton in 1985 but hadn't thought about its commercial potential until arriving at DESCO. Shaw and Bezos would meet for a few hours each week to brain-storm ideas for this coming technological wave, and then Bezos would take those ideas and investigate their feasibility.[6]

In early 1994, several prescient business plans emerged from the discussions between Bezos and Shaw and others at D. E. Shaw. One was the concept of a free, advertising-supported e-mail service for consumers – the idea behind Gmail and Yahoo Mail. DESCO would develop that idea into a company called Juno, which went public in 1999 and soon after merged with NetZero, a rival.

Another idea was to create a new kind of financial service that allowed Internet users to trade stocks and bonds online. In 1995 Shaw turned that into a subsidiary called FarSight Financial Services, a precursor to companies like E-Trade. He later sold it to Merrill Lynch.

Shaw and Bezos discussed another idea as well. They called it 'the everything store.'

Several executives who worked at DESCO at that time say the idea of the everything store was simple: an Internet company that served as the intermediary between customers and manufacturers and sold nearly every type of product, all over the world. One important element in the early vision was that customers could leave written evaluations of any product, a more egalitarian and credible version of the old Montgomery Ward catalog reviews of its own suppliers. Shaw himself confirmed the Internet-store concept when he told the *New York Times Magazine* in 1999, 'The idea was always that someone would be allowed to make a profit as an intermediary. The key question is: Who will get to be that middleman?'[7]

Intrigued by Shaw's conviction about the inevitable importance of the Internet, Bezos started researching its growth. A Texas-based author and publisher named John Quarterman had recently started the *Matrix News*, a monthly newsletter extolling the Internet and discussing its commercial possibilities. One set of numbers in particular in the February 1994 edition of the newsletter was startling. For the first time, Quarterman broke down the growth of the year-old World Wide Web and pointed out that its simple, friendly interface appealed to a far broader audience than other Internet technologies. In one chart, he showed that the number of bytes – a set of binary digits – transmitted over the Web had increased by a factor of 2,057 between January 1993 and January 1994. Another graphic showed the number of packets – a single unit of data – sent over the Web had jumped by 2,560 in the same span.[8]

Bezos interpolated from this that Web activity overall had gone up that year by a factor of roughly 2,300 – a 230,000 percent increase. 'Things just don't grow that fast,' Bezos later said. 'It's highly unusual, and that started me thinking, What kind of business plan might make sense in the context of that growth?'[9] (Bezos also liked to say in speeches during Amazon's early years that it was the Web's '2,300 percent' annual growth rate that jolted him out of complacency. Which makes for an interesting historical footnote: Amazon began with a math error.)

Bezos concluded that a true everything store would be impractical – at least at the beginning. He made a list of twenty possible product categories, including computer software, office supplies, apparel, and music. The category that eventually jumped out at him as the best option was books. They were pure commodities; a copy of a book in one store was identical to the same book carried in another, so buyers always knew what they were getting. There were two primary distributors of books at that time, Ingram and Baker and Taylor, so a new retailer wouldn't have to approach each of the thousands of book publishers individually. And, most important, there were three million books in print worldwide, far more than a Barnes & Noble or a Borders superstore could ever stock.

If he couldn't build a true everything store right away, he could capture its essence – unlimited selection – in at least one important product category. 'With that huge diversity of products you could build a store online that simply could not exist in any other way,' Bezos said. 'You could build a true superstore with exhaustive selection, and customers value selection.'[10]

In his offices on the fortieth floor of 120 West Forty-Fifth Street, Bezos could hardly contain his enthusiasm. With DESCO's recruiting chief, Charles Ardai, he investigated some of the earliest online bookstore websites, such as Book Stacks Unlimited, located in Cleveland, Ohio, and WordsWorth, in Cambridge, Massachusetts. Ardai still has the record from one purchase they made while testing these early sites. He bought a copy of *Isaac Asimov's Cyberdreams* from the website of the Future Fantasy bookstore in Palo Alto, California. The price was $6.04. When the book appeared, two weeks later, Ardai ripped open the cardboard package and showed it to Bezos. It had become badly tattered in transit. No one had yet figured out how to do a good job selling books over the Internet. As Bezos saw it, this was a huge, untapped opportunity.

Bezos knew it would never really be his company if he pursued the venture inside D. E. Shaw. Indeed, the firm initially owned all of Juno and FarSight, and Shaw acted as chairman of both. If Bezos wanted to be a true owner and entrepreneur, with significant equity in his creation and the potential to achieve the same kind of financial rewards that businessmen like pizza magnate Frank Meeks did, he had to leave his lucrative and comfortable home on Wall Street.

What happened next became one of the founding legends of the Internet. That spring, Bezos spoke to David Shaw and told him he planned to leave the company to create an online bookstore. Shaw suggested they take a walk. They wandered in Central Park for two hours, discussing the venture and the entrepreneurial drive. Shaw said he understood Bezos's impulse and sympathized with it – he had done the same thing when he'd left Morgan Stanley. He also noted that D. E. Shaw was growing quickly and that Bezos already had a great job. He told Bezos that the firm might end up competing with his new venture. The two agreed that Bezos would spend a few days thinking about it.

At the time Bezos was newly married, with a comfortable apartment on the Upper West Side and a well-paying job. While MacKenzie said she would be supportive if he decided to strike out on his own, the decision was not an easy one. Bezos would later describe his thinking process in unusually geeky terms. He says he came up with what he called a 'regret-minimization framework' to decide the next step to take at this juncture of his career.

'When you are in the thick of things, you can get confused by small stuff,' Bezos said a few years later. 'I knew when I was eighty that I would never, for example, think about why I walked away from my 1994 Wall Street bonus right in the middle of the year at the worst possible time. That kind of thing just isn't something you worry about when you're eighty years old. At the same time, I knew that I might sincerely regret not having participated in this thing called the Internet that I thought was going to be a revolutionizing event. When I thought about it that way . . . it was incredibly easy to make the decision.'[11]

Bezos's parents, Mike and Jackie, were nearing the end of a three-year stay in Bogotá, Colombia, where Mike was working for Exxon as a petroleum engineer, when they got the phone call. 'What do you mean, you are going to sell books over the Internet?' was their first reaction, according to Mike Bezos. They had used the early online service Prodigy to correspond with family members and to organize Jeff and MacKenzie's engagement party, so it wasn't naïveté about new technology that unnerved them. Rather, it was seeing their accomplished son leave a well-paying job on Wall Street to pursue an idea that sounded like utter madness. Jackie Bezos suggested to her son that he run his new company at night or on the weekends. 'No, things are changing fast,' Bezos told her. 'I need to move quickly.'

So Jeff Bezos started planning for his journey. He held a party at his Upper West Side apartment to watch the final episode of *Star Trek: The Next Generation*. Then he flew out to Santa Cruz, California, to meet two experienced programmers who had been introduced to him by Peter Laventhol, David Shaw's first employee. Over blueberry pancakes at the Old Sash Mill Café in Santa Cruz, Bezos managed to intrigue one of them, a startup veteran named Shel Kaphan. Bezos 'was inflamed by a lot of the same happening with the Internet,' Kaphan says. They looked at office space together in Santa Cruz, but Bezos later learned of a 1992 Supreme Court decision that upheld a previous ruling that merchants did not have to collect sales tax in states where they did not have physical operations. As a result, mail-order businesses typically avoided locating in populous states like California and New York, and so would Bezos.

Back in New York, Bezos informed his colleagues that he was leaving D. E. Shaw. Bezos and Jeff Holden, a recent graduate of the University of Illinois at Urbana-Champaign who had worked for Bezos as an engineer on the third-market project, went out one night for drinks. The two were close. Holden was from Rochester Hills, Michigan, and as a teenager, under the hacker nom de guerre the Nova, he had grown adept at cracking copy-right protection on software. He was an avid Rollerblader and a fast talker; he spoke so rapidly that Bezos liked to joke that Holden 'taught me to listen faster.'

Now they were sitting across from each other at Virgil's, a barbecue place on Forty-Fourth Street. Bezos had tentatively decided to call his company Cadabra Inc. but was not committed to the name. Holden filled both sides of a piece of notebook paper with alternatives. The one Bezos liked best on the list was MakeItSo.com, after Captain Picard's frequent command in *Star Trek*.

Over beers, Holden told Bezos he wanted to come with him. But Bezos was worried; his contract with D. E. Shaw stipulated that if he left the firm, he couldn't recruit DESCO employees for at least two years. David Shaw was not someone he wanted to cross. 'You're just out of school, you've got debt. And this is risky,' Bezos said. 'Stay here. Build up some net worth and I'll be in touch.'

Later that month, Bezos and MacKenzie packed up the contents of their home and told the movers to just start driving their belongings across the country – they said they would call them on the road the next day with a specific destination. First they flew to Fort Worth, Texas, and borrowed a 1988 Chevy Blazer from Bezos's father. Then they drove northwest, Bezos sitting in the passenger seat, typing revenue projections into an Excel spreadsheet – numbers that would later prove to be radically inaccurate. They tried to check into a Motel 6 in Shamrock, Texas, but it was booked, so they settled for a road motel called the Rambler.[12] When MacKenzie saw the room, she declined to take off her shoes that night. A day later, they stopped at the Grand Canyon and watched the sunrise. He was thirty, she was twenty-four, and together they were writing an entrepreneurial origin story that would be imprinted on the collective imagination of millions of Internet users and hopeful startup founders.

More than a year passed before Jeff Holden heard from his friend again. Bezos had settled in Seattle, and he e-mailed Holden a link to a website. They were now calling it Amazon.com. The site was primitive, mostly text and somewhat unimpressive. Holden bought a few books through the site and offered some feedback. Then another year passed, and finally, a few months after Bezos's do-not-poach agreement with David Shaw expired, Holden's phone rang.

It was Bezos. 'It's time,' he said. 'This is going to work.'

CHAPTER 2
The Book of Bezos

Usenet bulletin-board posting, August 21, 1994:

Well-capitalized start-up seeks extremely talented C/C++/Unix developers to help pioneer commerce on the Internet. You must have experience designing and building large and complex (yet maintainable) systems, and you should be able to do so in about one-third the time that most competent people think possible. You should have a BS, MS, or PhD in Computer Science or the equivalent. Top-notch communication skills are essential. Familiarity with web servers and HTML would be helpful but is not necessary.

Expect talented, motivated, intense, and interesting co-workers. Must be willing to relocate to the Seattle area (we will help cover moving costs).

Your compensation will include meaningful equity ownership.

Send resume and cover letter to Jeff Bezos. US mail: Cadabra, Inc. 10704 N.E. 28th St., Bellevue, WA 98004

We are an equal opportunity employer.

'It's easier to invent the future than to predict it.'
                                        – Alan Kay

In the beginning, they knew they needed a better name. The magical allusions of Cadabra Inc., as Todd Tarbert, Bezos's first lawyer, pointed out after they registered that name with Washington State in July of 1994, were too obscure, and over the phone, people tended to hear the name as *Cadaver*. So later that summer, after renting a three-bedroom ranch house in the East Seattle suburb of Bellevue, Bezos and MacKenzie started brainstorming. Internet records show that during that time, they registered the Web domains Awake.com, Browse.com, and Bookmall.com. Bezos also briefly considered Aard.com, from a Dutch word, as a way to stake a claim at the top of most listings of websites, which at the time were arranged alphabetically.

Bezos and his wife grew fond of another possibility: Relentless.com. Friends suggested that it sounded a bit sinister. But something about it must have captivated Bezos: he registered the URL in September 1994, and he kept it. Type *Relentless.com* into the Web today and it takes you to Amazon.

Bezos chose to start his company in Seattle because of the city's reputation as a technology hub and because the state of Washington had a relatively small population (compared to California, New York, and Texas), which meant that Amazon would have to collect state sales tax from only a minor percentage of customers. While the area was still a remote urban outpost known more for its grunge rock than its business community, Microsoft was hitting its stride in nearby Redmond, and the University of Washington produced a steady stream of computer science graduates. Seattle was also close to one of the two big book distributors: Ingram had a warehouse a six-hour drive away, in Roseburg, Oregon. And local businessman Nick Hanauer, whom Bezos had recently met through a friend, lived there and urged Bezos to give Seattle a try. He would later be pivotal in introducing Bezos to potential investors.

That fall, Shel Kaphan drove a U-Haul full of his belongings up from Santa Cruz and officially joined Bezos and his wife as a founding employee of Amazon and as its primary technical steward. Kaphan had grown up in the San Francisco Bay Area and as a teenage computer enthusiast explored the ARPANET, the U.S. Defense Department-developed predecessor to the Internet. In high school, Kaphan met Stewart Brand, the writer and counterculture organizer, and the summer after he graduated, Kaphan took a job at the Whole Earth Catalog, Brand's seminal guide to the tools and books of the enlightened new information age. Sporting long hippie-ish hair and a bushy beard, Kaphan worked at Brand's Whole Earth Truck Store in Menlo Park, a mobile lending library and roving education service. He tended the cash register, filled subscriptions, and packed books and catalogs for shipment to customers.

After earning a bachelor's degree in mathematics in an on-again, off-again decade at the University of California at Santa Cruz, Kaphan logged time at a number of Bay Area companies, including the ill-fated Apple-IBM joint venture called Kaleida Labs, which developed media-player software for personal computers. He tended to display the disappointment of those experiences in what his friends considered a gloomy countenance. When he got to Seattle, Kaphan, characteristically, had severe doubts that the young startup was going to succeed. He immediately began worrying about the company's name. 'I was once part of a little consultancy called the Symmetry Group, and people always thought we were the Cemetery Group,' says Kaphan. 'When I heard about Cadaver Inc., I thought, *Oh God, not this again.*' But

Kaphan (by now shorn of his long locks and beard, balding, and in his early forties) was inspired by what he saw as Amazon's potential to use the Web to fulfill the vision of the Whole Earth Catalog and make information and tools available around the world.

At first, Kaphan figured he'd write some code and return to Santa Cruz to work remotely, so he left half his belongings at home and stayed with Bezos and MacKenzie in Bellevue for a few days while looking for a place to rent. They set up shop in the converted garage of Bezos's house, an enclosed space without insulation and with a large, black potbellied stove at its center. Bezos built the first two desks out of sixty-dollar blond-wood doors from Home Depot, an endeavor that later carried almost biblical significance at Amazon, like Noah building the ark. In late September, Bezos drove down to Portland, Oregon, to take a four-day course on bookselling sponsored by the American Booksellers Association, a trade organization for independent bookstores. The seminar covered such topics as 'Selecting Opening Inventory' and 'Inventory Management.'[1] At the same time, Kaphan started looking for computers and databases and learning how to code a website – in those days, everything on the Internet had to be custom built.

It was all done on a threadbare budget. At first Bezos backed the company himself with $10,000 in cash, and over the next sixteen months, he would finance the startup with an additional $84,000 in interest-free loans, according to public documents. Kaphan's contract required him to commit to buying $5,000 of stock upon joining the company. He passed on the option to buy an additional $20,000 in shares, since he was already taking a 50 percent pay cut to work at the startup and would, like Bezos, earn only $64,000 a year. 'The whole thing seemed pretty iffy at that stage,' says Kaphan, who some consider an Amazon cofounder. 'There wasn't really anything except for a guy with a barking laugh building desks out of doors in his converted garage, just like he'd seen in my Santa Cruz home office. I was taking a big risk by moving and accepting a low salary and so even though I had some savings, I didn't feel comfortable committing more than I did.'

In early 1995, Bezos's parents, Jackie and Mike Bezos, invested $100,000 in Amazon. Exxon had covered most of the couple's living expenses when Mike worked in Norway, Colombia, and Venezuela, so the couple had a considerable nest egg and were willing to spend a good portion of it on their oldest child. 'We saw the business plan, but all of that went over our heads to a large extent,' says Mike Bezos. 'As corny as it sounds, we were betting on Jeff.' Bezos told his parents there was a 70 percent chance they could lose it all. 'I want you to know what the risks are, because I still want to come home for Thanksgiving if this doesn't work,' he said.

Amazon was a family affair in another way. MacKenzie, an aspiring novelist, became the company's first official accountant, handling the finances, writing the checks, and helping with hiring. For coffee breaks and meetings, the employees would go to a nearby Barnes & Noble, an irony that Bezos later mentioned often in speeches and interviews.

There was little urgency to their efforts, at least at first. Kaphan recalls showing up at the Bellevue house early one morning in October, only to have Bezos declare that they were all going to take the day off to go hiking. 'The weather was changing and the days were getting short,' Kaphan says. 'We were all new to the area and hadn't seen much of it.' Bezos, MacKenzie, and Kaphan drove seventy miles to Mount Rainier and spent the day wandering amid patches of snow on the majestic volcano that, on clear days, dominates the Seattle skyline.

Later that fall, they hired Paul Davis, a British-born programmer who had been on staff at the University of Washington's computer science and engineering department. Davis's colleagues were so dubious of his move to an as-yet-unlaunched online bookstore that they passed around a coffee can to collect a few dollars for him in case it didn't work out. Davis joined Kaphan and Bezos in the garage, working on SPARC-station servers from Sun Microsystems, machines that resembled pizza boxes and drew so much power they repeatedly blew fuses in the home. Eventually they had to run orange extension cords from other rooms to put the computers on different circuits, making it impossible to run a hair dryer or vacuum cleaner in the house.[2]

'At first it didn't really have a lot of the energy one stereotypically associates with a startup,' says Davis, who biked to Bellevue each day wearing Gore-Tex socks over the cuffs of his trousers. 'We were pre-startup. It was just Shel, myself, and Jeff in an office, sitting around a table with a whiteboard and discussing how to divide the programming work.'

One of their driving goals was to create something superior to the existing online bookstores, including Books.com, the website of the Cleveland-based bookstore Book Stacks Unlimited. 'As crazy as it might sound, it did appear that the first challenge was to do something better than these other guys,' Davis says. 'There was competition already. It wasn't as if Jeff was coming up with something completely new.'

During that time, the name Cadabra lived on, serving as a temporary placeholder. But in late October of 1994,

Bezos pored through the A section of the dictionary and had an epiphany when he reached the word *Amazon*. Earth's largest river; Earth's largest bookstore.[3] He walked into the garage one morning and informed his colleagues of the company's new name. He gave the impression that he didn't care to hear anyone's opinion on it, and he registered the new URL on November 1, 1994. 'This is not only the largest river in the world, it's many times larger than the next biggest river. It blows all other rivers away,' Bezos said.

While the original Bellevue garage would come to symbolize a romantic time in Amazon's early history – the kind of modest beginnings that legendary companies like Apple and Hewlett-Packard started with – Amazon was located there for only a few months. With Kaphan and Davis nearing completion of a primitive beta website, Bezos began to think about hiring other employees – and that meant finding a more professional place to work. That spring, they moved to a small office above a Color Tile retail store in the industrial SoDo (for 'south of the Kingdome') district, near downtown Seattle. Amazon had its first official warehouse in part of that building's base-ment: a two-hundred-square-foot windowless room that was once a band practice studio and still had the words *Sonic Jungle* spray-painted on a jet-black door. Soon after, Bezos and MacKenzie left the Bellevue house and, attempting to recapture the urban energy of their New York lives, moved into a nine-hundred-square-foot apart-ment on Vine Street in Seattle's fashionable Belltown neighborhood.

In the spring of 1995, Bezos and Kaphan sent links to the beta website to a few dozen friends, family members, and former colleagues. The site was bare, crammed with text and tuned to the rudimentary browsers and slowpoke Internet connections of the time. 'One million titles, consistently low prices,' that first home page announced in blue underlined text. Next to that was the amateurishly illustrated logo: a giant A set against a marbled blue background with the image of a river snaking through the letter. The site seemed uninviting to literate people who had spent their lives happily browsing the shelves of bookstores and libraries. 'I remember thinking that it was very improbable that people would ever want to do this,' says Susan Benson, whose husband, Eric, was a former colleague of Kaphan's. Both would become early employees at Amazon.

Kaphan invited a former coworker, John Wainwright, to try the service, and Wainwright is credited with making the very first purchase: *Fluid Concepts and Creative Analogies*, a science book by Douglas Hofstadter. His Amazon account history records the date of that inaugural order as April 3, 1995. Today, a building on Amazon's Seattle's campus is named Wainwright.

While the site wasn't much to look at, Kaphan and Davis had accomplished a lot on it in just a few months. There was a virtual shopping basket, a safe way to enter credit card numbers into a Web browser, and a rudimentary search engine that scoured a catalog drawn from the *Books in Print* CD-ROMs, a reference source published by R. R. Bowker, the provider of the standard identifying ISBN numbers for books in the United States. Kaphan and Davis also developed a system that allowed users of early online services like Prodigy and AOL to get information on books and place orders via e-mail alone – though that was never rolled out.

These were all state-of-the-art developments during the gritty initial days of the Web, a time when tools were primitive and techniques were constantly evolving. The

HTML standard itself, the lingua franca of the Web, was barely half a decade old, and modern languages like JavaScript and AJAX were years away. Amazon's first engineers coded in a computer language called C and decided to store the website in an off-the-shelf database called Berkeley DB that had never seen the levels of traffic to which it would soon be exposed.

Each order during those early months brought a thrill to Amazon's employees. When someone made a purchase, a bell would ring on Amazon's computers, and everyone in the office would gather around to see if anyone knew the customer. (It was only a few weeks before it started ringing so often that they had to turn it off.) Amazon would then order the book from one of the two major book distributors, paying the standard wholesale rate of 50 percent off the list price (the advertised price printed on the book jacket).

There was little science to Amazon's earliest distribution methods. The company held no inventory itself at first. When a customer bought a book, Amazon ordered it, the book would arrive within a few days, and Amazon would store it in the basement and then ship it off to the customer. It took Amazon a week to deliver most items to customers, and it could take several weeks or more than a month for scarcer titles.

Even back then, Amazon was making only a slender profit on most sales. It offered up to 40 percent off the list price on bestsellers and books that were included in Spotlight, an early feature on the website that highlighted new titles each day. The company offered 10 percent off the list price on other books; it also charged shipping fees starting at $3.95 for single-book orders.

One early challenge was that the book distributors required retailers to order ten books at a time. Amazon didn't yet have that kind of sales volume, and Bezos later enjoyed telling the story of how he got around it. 'We found a loophole,' he said. 'Their systems were programmed in such a way that you didn't have to *receive* ten books, you only had to *order* ten books. So we found an obscure book about lichens that they had in their system but was out of stock. We began ordering the one book we wanted and nine copies of the lichen book. They would ship out the book we needed and a note that said, 'Sorry, but we're out of the lichen book.'"[4]

In early June, Kaphan added a reviews feature that he'd coded over a single weekend. Bezos believed that if Amazon.com had more user-generated book reviews than any other site, it would give the company a huge advantage; customers would be less inclined to go to other online bookstores. They had discussed whether such unfiltered user-generated content could get the company in trouble. Bezos decided to watch reviews closely for offensive material rather than read everything before it was published.

The early employees and their friends wrote many of the initial reviews themselves. Kaphan himself took a book off the shelf that was meant for a customer, a Chinese memoir called *Bitter Winds: A Memoir of My Years in China's Gulag*. He read it cover to cover and wrote one of the first reviews.

Naturally, some of the reviews were negative. In speeches, Bezos later recalled getting an angry letter from an executive at a book publisher implying that Bezos didn't understand that his business was to sell books, not trash them. 'We saw it very differently,' Bezos said. 'When I read that letter, I thought, we don't make money when we sell things. We make money when we help customers make purchase decisions.'[5]

* * *

The site went live on July 16, 1995, and became visible to all Web users. And as word spread, the small Amazon team saw almost immediately that they had opened a strange window onto human behavior. The Internet's early adopters ordered computer manuals, *Dilbert* comic collections, books on repairing antique musical instruments – and sex guides. (The bestseller on Amazon.com from that first year: *How to Set Up and Maintain a World Wide Web Site: The Guide for Information Providers*, by Lincoln D. Stein.)

There were orders from U.S. troops overseas and from an individual in Ohio who wrote to say he lived fifty miles away from the nearest bookstore and that Amazon.com was a godsend. Someone from the European Southern Observatory in Chile ordered a Carl Sagan book – apparently as a test – and after the order was successful, the customer placed a second order for several dozen copies of the same book. Amazon was getting one of the first glimpses of the 'long tail' – the large number of esoteric items that appeal to relatively few people. Paul Davis once surveyed the odd assortment of books squirreled away on the shelves in the basement and with a sigh called it 'the smallest and most eclectic bookstore in the world.'

No one had been hired yet to pack books, so when volumes rose and the company fell behind on shipping, Bezos, Kaphan, and the others would descend to the basement at night to assemble customer orders. The next day, Bezos, MacKenzie, or an employee would drive the boxes to UPS or the post office.

The packing work was arduous and often lasted well into the night. Employees assembled orders on the floor, wrapping books in a cohesive cardboard that stuck to itself but not anything else. That summer Nicholas Lovejoy, a former D. E. Shaw employee who had left the hedge fund to teach high-school math in Seattle, joined the company part-time and made the obvious suggestion of adding packing tables to the warehouse. That tidy anecdote quickly made the catalog of Jeffisms and was still being repeated twenty years later. 'I thought that was the most brilliant idea I had ever heard in my life,' Bezos said in a speech, finding the story so freshly amusing that he accompanied it with a honking laugh.[6]

Bezos tapped Lovejoy to assist with recruiting and told him to go hire the smartest people he knew – just like David Shaw, Bezos wanted all of his employees to be high-IQ brainiacs. Lovejoy brought in four friends from his alma mater, Reed College, one of whom was Laurel Canan, a twenty-four-year-old carpenter who was planning to return to school to become a Chaucer scholar (it never happened). Canan helped build the much-needed packing tables, and then he formally joined the company and took over operations in the warehouse. (The landlord had finally allowed Amazon to expand out of the Sonic Jungle room and take over the entire basement.) One of the first things Canan did upon being hired was give up coffee. 'You can't do a job like that on caffeine. You have to do it on carbs,' he says.

It was an eclectic team operating under unusual circumstances in a challenging environment, and together they took their first tentative steps into an exotic river called the Internet. To everyone's surprise, they all got swept up in a swift current. The first week after the official launch, they took $12,000 in orders and shipped $846 worth of books, according to Eric Dillon, one of Amazon's original investors. The next week they took $14,000 in orders and shipped $7,000 worth of books. So they were behind from the get-go and scrambling to catch up.

A week after the launch, Jerry Yang and David Filo, Stanford graduate students, wrote them an e-mail and asked if they would like to be featured on a site called Yahoo that listed cool things on the Web. At that time, Yahoo was one of the most highly trafficked sites on the Web and the default home page for many of the Internet's earliest users. Bezos and his employees had of course heard of Yahoo and they sat around eating Chinese food that night and discussing whether they were ready for a wave of new business when they were already drowning in orders. Kaphan thought that it might be like 'taking a sip through a fire hose.'[7] But they decided to do it, and within the first month of their launch they had sold books to people in all fifty states and in forty-five countries.[8]

Every day the number of orders increased, and the tendrils of chaos – the company's constant antagonist over the next several years – began to tighten around the young startup. Bezos insisted that Amazon had to have a customer-friendly thirty-day-return policy, but it had no processes in place to handle returns; it had a line of credit but would regularly max out its account, and MacKenzie would then have to walk down the street to the bank and write a check to reopen it. Tom Schonhoff, who joined that summer after getting a computer science degree at the University of Washington, remembers Bezos bringing a latte to work each morning and sitting down at his disorganized desk. One day, the young CEO grabbed the wrong cup and took a slug of curdled, week-old latte. He spent the rest of the day complaining that he might have to go to the hospital. Everyone was working long days, scrambling to keep up, and not getting enough sleep.

On August 9, 1995, Netscape Communications, the corporate descendant of the pioneering Mosaic Web browser, went public. On the first day, its stock jumped from an initial price of $28 per share to $75, and the eyes of the world opened to the gathering phenomenon that was the World Wide Web.

While he and his employees worked exceedingly long days, Bezos was always thinking about raising money. That summer the Bezos family, using the Gise family trust (Gise was Jackie's maiden name), invested another $145,000 in Amazon.[9] But the company couldn't continue hiring and growing on the Bezos family savings alone. That summer, Nick Hanauer, a garrulous fixture of the Seattle business community whose father had started a successful pillow manufacturing company, helped to line up pitch meetings for Bezos. He canvassed sixty potential investors, seeking to raise $1 million from individual contributions of $50,000 each.[10]

In the meetings, Bezos presented what was, at best, an ambiguous picture of Amazon's future. At the time, it had about $139,000 in assets, $69,000 of which was in cash. The company had lost $52,000 in 1994 and was on track to lose another $300,000 that year.

Against that meager start, Bezos would tell investors he projected $74 million in sales by 2000 if things went moderately well, and $114 million in sales if they went much better than expected. (Actual net sales in 2000: $1.64 billion.) Bezos also predicted the company would be moderately profitable by that time (net loss in 2000: $1.4 billion). He wanted to value the fledgling firm at $6 million – an aggressive valuation that he had seemingly picked out of thin air. And he told investors the same thing he told his parents: the company had a 70 percent chance of failing.

Though they could not have known it, investors were looking at the opportunity of a lifetime. This highly driven, articulate young man talked with conviction about the Internet's potential to deliver a more convenient shopping experience than crowded big-box stores where the staff routinely ignored customers. He predicted the company's eventual ability to personalize a version of the website for each shopper based on his or her previous purchases. And he prophesied what must have seemed like a radical future: that everyone would one day use the Internet at high speeds, not over screeching dial-up modems, and that the infinite shelf space of the Web would enable the fulfillment of the merchandiser's dream of the everything store – a store with infinite selection.

Bezos started his investment tour at the Mercer Island home of Eric Dillon, a tall blond stockbroker and one of Hanauer's best friends. 'He swept me off my feet,' Dillon says. 'He was so convinced that what he was doing was basically the work of God and that somehow the money would materialize. The real wild card was, could he really run a business? That wasn't a gimme. Of course, about two years later I was going, "Holy shit, did we back the right horse!"'

Bezos also pitched Bob Gelfond, a former D. E. Shaw colleague. Gelfond turned for advice to his skeptical father, a man who had had a long career in book publishing and who had experienced the pain of trying to get his company to embrace personal computers. His father recommended against the investment, but Gelfond had watched Bezos smoothly operate in the hedge-fund world and bet on his friend anyway. 'It's one thing to have a good idea, but it's another to have confidence in a person to execute it,' he says.

Many others turned Bezos down. Hanauer and his mother invested, but one of Hanauer's brothers and his father declined. Tom Alberg, a former executive at McCaw Cellular, met Bezos and was dubious because he loved browsing in bookstores. Then a few days later he failed to find a business book for his son at a local shop, and he changed his mind and decided to invest. The attorney who told Alberg about the deal invited Bezos to speak at an investment group that met regularly at Seattle's tony Rainier Club. He thought the valuation was too high and passed.

Bezos later told the online journal of the Wharton School, 'We got the normal comments from well-meaning people who basically didn't believe the business plan; they just didn't think it would work.'[11] Among the concerns was this prediction: 'If you're successful, you're going to need a warehouse the size of the Library of Congress,' one investor told him.

Todd Tarbert, Amazon's first lawyer, sighs heavily when recalling his decision about whether to personally back the company. For the first time in his career, he wanted to invest in a client's firm, and he secured written permission to do so from the Washington State Bar Association. He also talked to his father about taking out a loan against their jointly owned farmhouse. But then Tarbert's son was born prematurely, and he took a month off from work and never got around to writing the $50,000 check. By the time Tarbert returned, Bezos had already raised the $1 million at a slightly-lower-than-hoped-for $5 million valuation.

One day in late 1997, after Amazon's IPO, Tarbert was playing golf with his dad. 'You know that company Amazon that just went public?' his father asked. 'Was that the company we were talking about? What happened with that?'

'Yeah, Dad. You don't want to know,' Tarbert replied.

'Well, what would that be worth today?' his father continued.

'At least a few million,' Tarbert said.

At the end of that summer, Nicholas Lovejoy told Bezos he wanted to move from part-time to full-time. To his surprise, his former D. E. Shaw colleague didn't want to hire him full-time. Lovejoy had been working a modest thirty-five hours a week, playing ultimate Frisbee, kayaking, and hanging out with his girlfriend, and Bezos was imagining a different culture for Amazon, one where employees worked tirelessly for the sake of building a lasting company and increasing the value of their own ownership stakes. Lovejoy pleaded his case, arguing he was ready to sign up for sixty hours a week like everyone else, but he couldn't change Bezos's mind. Bezos even asked him to find a full-time employee to replace himself, which seemed particularly cruel. Eventually Lovejoy gave him a stack of résumés, and he put his own at the top. He also appealed to MacKenzie, Kaphan, and Davis and got them to change the boss's mind. Lovejoy would work a variety of jobs at Amazon over the next few years, writing code and book reviews, ferrying packages to the post office at night, and eventually winding up in finance.

Bezos felt that hiring only the best and brightest was key to Amazon's success. For years he interviewed all potential hires himself and asked them for their SAT scores. 'Every time we hire someone, he or she should raise the bar for the next hire, so that the overall talent pool is always improving,' he said, a recurring Jeffism. That approach caused plenty of friction. As Amazon grew, it badly needed additional man-power, and early employees eagerly recommended their friends, many of whom were as accomplished as they were. Bezos interrogated the applicants, lobbing the kind of improbable questions that were once asked at D. E. Shaw, like 'How many gas stations are in the United States?' It was a test to measure the quality of a candidate's thinking; Bezos wasn't looking for the correct answer, only for the individual to demonstrate creativity by coming up with a sound way to derive a possible solution. And if the potential employees made the mistake of talking about wanting a harmonious balance between work and home life, Bezos rejected them.

Paul Davis was incredulous. Amazon at the time was offering about sixty thousand a year in salary, stock options of questionable value, a meager health plan with a high deductible, and an increasingly frenetic work pace. 'We would look at him and ask, How do you think you're ever going to attract anyone with that kind of background to a company that has no revenue and that is not projected to have any kind of revenue?' Davis said. 'I don't see what the selling point is here!'

Little by little, the CEO with the piercing laugh, thinning hair, and twitchy demeanor revealed his true self to his employees. He was unusually confident, more stubborn than they had originally thought, and he strangely and presumptuously assumed that they would all work tirelessly and perform constant heroics. He seemed to keep his ambitions and plans very close to the vest, not revealing much even to Kaphan.

When his goals did slip out, they were improbably grandiose. Though the startup's focus was clearly on books, Davis recalls Bezos saying he wanted to build 'the next Sears,' a lasting company that was a major force in retail. Lovejoy, a kayaking enthusiast, remembers Bezos telling him that he envisioned a day when the site would sell not only books about kayaks but kayaks themselves, subscriptions to kayaking magazines, and reservations for kayaking trips – everything related to the sport.

'I thought he was a little bit crazy,' says Lovejoy. 'At the time we offered 1.5 million books. Only about 1.2 million of those you could actually order. The database came from Baker and Taylor and we had about forty books in the warehouse.'

Bezos was also proving himself to be something of a spoilsport. That year the engineers rigged a database command, rwerich, to track the number of daily purchases as well as orders throughout the lifetime of the company. They obsessively watched those numbers grow – it was one of their pleasures amid the typically frenetic days. Bezos eventually told them to stop doing it, in part because it was putting too much strain on the servers. And when Amazon had its first five-thousand-dollar-order day and Lovejoy wanted to throw a party, Bezos rejected the idea. 'There are a lot of milestones coming and that's not the way I want to run things,' he said.

By early 1996, the young company was outgrowing its space in the Color Tile building. Employees were jammed into three small rooms, four door-desks in each, and the basement warehouse was overflowing with books. Kaphan, Davis, and Bezos piled into a car and went looking for a larger office in industrial areas around Lake Washington. Bezos emerged from every building to proclaim the space too small, Davis recalls. He wanted to accommodate whatever came for the company down the road.

That March, Amazon finally moved to a larger building with a more spacious warehouse a few blocks away. The new office was next to the Pecos Pit, a popular barbecue stand whose tantalizing aromas would waft into the warehouse each day starting at around ten in the morning.

But one early employee did not move with them. Paul Davis, who later became an advocate for open-source software and a critic of Amazon's enforcing its 1-Click patent, told Bezos he wanted to spend more time with his newborn daughter. Leaving Amazon so early cost him a literal fortune in unclaimed stock options. A few months later, he would punctuate that misstep by slicing off the tip of his thumb with a band saw while preparing his home for sale. Bezos and Tom Schonhoff went to visit him in the hospital.

Somehow Davis, a native Londoner, was immune to the gospel of Jeff. He looked askance at the work-first zealotry, and he noticed that Bezos had changed a clever motivational phrase about choosing among three ways to work. In the old Bellevue house, Bezos had said to Kaphan and Davis, 'You can work long, hard, and smart, but at Amazon.com you can pick only two out of three.' Now the young CEO liked to recite, 'You can work long, you can work hard, you can work smart, but at Amazon you *can't* choose two out of three.'

Davis had a KILL YOUR TV bumper sticker on his Honda Civic, and so to commemorate Davis's departure, Bezos laid down a blue tarp in the parking lot and put an old computer terminal and keyboard on it. He handed Davis a sledgehammer and then filmed him smashing the machine. Afterward, Davis kept the Escape key.

* * *

By the first weeks of 1996, revenues were growing 30 to 40 percent a month, a frenzied rate that undermined attempts at planning and required such a dizzying pace that employees later found gaps in their memory when they tried to recall this formative time. No one had any idea how to deal with that kind of growth, so they all made it up as they went along.

That spring, at the American Association of Publishers annual convention, the chairman of Random House, Alberto Vitale, told a *Wall Street Journal* reporter about the new online bookselling sensation from the Pacific Northwest. A few weeks later, Amazon was featured in a front-page *WSJ* article, 'How Wall Street Whiz Found a Niche Selling Books on the Internet,' and Bezos had his first stippled-and-hatched portrait in the country's largest financial newspaper. The number of orders each day immediately doubled. The world now knew about Amazon.com, and, likely, so did Barnes & Noble and Borders, the nation's largest book chains.

With the influx of the $1 million in fresh capital, the company upgraded its servers and software, and, more important, it hired. Bezos added waves of new employees to customer service, to the warehouse, and to Kaphan's technical team. He started building an editorial group – writers and editors who would craft a literary voice for the site and give customers a reason to keep coming back. The group's mission was to make Amazon the most authoritative online source of information about books and replicate the trustworthy atmosphere of a quirky independent bookstore with refined literary tastes. 'We were asking people to put a credit card into the computer, which at the time was a radical concept,' says Susan Benson, whose job title eventually evolved to editor in chief. Editorial 'was important both in creating a good shopping experience but also in getting people comfortable about the idea that there were people on the other side of the screen that they could trust.'

That summer, the company launched what could be considered its first big innovation: allowing other websites to collect a fee when they sent customers directly to Amazon to buy a book. Amazon gave these approved sites an 8 percent commission for the referral. The Associates program wasn't exactly the first of its kind, but it was the most prominent and it helped spawn a multibillion-dollar-a-year industry called affiliate marketing. It also allowed Amazon, very early on, to extend its reach across the Web to other sites, entrenching it in advance of the looming competition.

By that spring, the company was burning cash hiring and buying equipment and server space, so Bezos decided to raise venture capital. He started negotiating with the Boston-based General Atlantic, whose partners discussed valuing the company at $10 million, eminently reasonable for a startup on track for $15.7 million in sales and $5.8 million in losses that year. Then John Doerr, a prominent partner at the storied Silicon Valley venture-capital firm Kleiner Perkins Caufield and Byers, heard about the company and flew up to Seattle for a visit.

'I walked into the door and this guy with a boisterous laugh who was just exuding energy comes bounding down the steps,' says Doerr, who had backed such winners as Netscape and Intuit. 'In that moment, I wanted to be in business with Jeff.' Bezos introduced him to MacKenzie and Kaphan and took him on a tour of the warehouse, where all the outbound orders were neatly stacked on door-desks. When Doerr asked about the volume of daily transactions, Bezos leaned over a computer and typed a *grep* command next to a UNIX prompt, instantly pulling up the data – and demonstrating his technical fluency. Doerr swooned.

Kleiner and General Atlantic dueled for the next few weeks over the investment, driving Amazon's valuation up to an altitude that Bezos had not imagined possible. He chose Kleiner on the strength of its reputation in the technology community. It invested $8 million, acquiring a

13 percent stake in the company, and valuing it at $60 million. Kleiner wanted to put a junior member of the firm on Amazon's board of directors but, as a condition of the deal, Bezos insisted that Doerr himself take the position. Doerr's direct involvement was a public vote of confidence for any technology startup.

In the circuitry of Bezos's brain, something then flipped. Budding optimism about the Internet in Silicon Valley was creating a unique environment for raising money at a historically low price in ownership. Doerr's optimism about the Web mixed with Bezos's own bullish fervor and sparked an explosion of ambitions and expansion plans. Bezos was going to do more than establish an online bookstore; now he was set on building one of the first lasting Internet companies. 'Jeff was always an expansive thinker, but access to capital was an enabler,' Doerr says. James Marcus, an editorial employee, saw it too, writing in his 2004 memoir *Amazonia* that 'the cash from Kleiner Perkins hit the place like a dose of entrepreneurial steroids, making Jeff more determined than ever.'[12]

Employees soon learned of a new motto: Get Big Fast. The bigger the company got, Bezos explained, the lower the prices it could exact from Ingram and Baker and Taylor, the book wholesalers, and the more distribution capacity it could afford. And the quicker the company grew, the more territory it could capture in what was becoming the race to establish new brands on the digital frontier. Bezos preached urgency: the company that got the lead now would likely keep it, and it could then use that lead to build a superior service for customers.

Of course, that meant everyone at Amazon would have to work even harder. The assumption was that no one would take even a weekend day off. 'Nobody said you couldn't, but nobody thought you would,' says Susan

Benson. Eric Benson adds, 'There were deadlines and death marches.'

In the warehouse, an expanding and eclectic group raced to keep up with the surge of customer orders. An Amazon representative even told a temp agency, 'Send us your freaks.' The bejeweled, tattooed, hair-dyed crew that responded to the call worked day and night in the warehouse next to the Pecos Pit and took turns selecting the music that played on a boom box. Their ranks included a three-hundred-pound baritone who would skip through the room belting out Russian arias.

Christopher Smith, a twenty-three-year-old warehouse temp with tattoos of Chinese characters on his forearms, began working at Amazon, and he would stay with the company in various roles for fourteen years. He started his typical day at four thirty in the morning, biked to work and let in the deliveryman from Ingram at six thirty, and usually stayed past midnight, packing furiously and answering customer e-mails before drinking a few beers in the warehouse and biking back home. 'The dominant image in my mind is just . . . running. And scads of cardboard and packing material flying,' he says.

Smith worked so tirelessly over one span of eight months that he forgot about his light blue Peugeot station wagon that he'd parked near his apartment in Seattle's Capitol Hill neighborhood. The fate of the car would later be revealed in the piles of mail that stacked up inside his front door. When he finally opened the mail in that pile, Smith found, in succession, several parking tickets, a notice that the car had been towed, a few warnings from the towing company, and finally a letter informing him that the vehicle had been sold at auction for seven hundred dollars. He still owed eighteen hundred dollars on his car loan, and the incident dinged his credit rating. He doesn't recall caring much at the time.

'Life just stopped,' Smith says. 'You were stuck in amber. But inside that amber was frenetic activity that no one else could see.'

Eric and Susan Benson didn't come to Amazon alone every day – they brought their dog Rufus, a Welsh corgi. Because the two would be working such long hours, Bezos had promised they could always bring Rufus to the office. That was no problem in the SoDo buildings, but then Amazon moved yet again, late in the summer of 1996, to a building downtown, and the company had to write Rufus into the lease with the new landlord. The dog, an amiable presence who liked to park himself in meetings and occasionally suffered gastric distress from being overfed by employees, became the startup's mascot. There was a superstitious belief that his paw tap on the keyboard was required to launch a new feature, and even today, though Rufus is long gone, there's a building named for him on Amazon's Seattle campus. (Bezos, it seems, has a nostalgic streak; one building is called Fiona, the code name of the original Kindle, and another is Obidos, which is what Shel Kaphan dubbed the company's original computer infrastructure, after a town in Brazil where the tributaries of the Amazon River converge.)

Amazon was now nearing a hundred and fifty full-time employees, less than a third of whom were in the warehouse. A few months later, the warehouse also moved, to a larger, ninety-three-thousand-square-foot facility on Dawson Street in South Seattle (another current Amazon building: Dawson). The new downtown digs weren't exactly high-class. Amazon took over the Columbia Building on Second Avenue in a seedy downtown neighborhood full of strip joints that was two blocks from touristy Pike Place Market. On the day the company moved in, a homeless man who'd been sleeping near the front door showed employees how to use their new key cards to gain access to the lobby.

The building itself was across the street from a needle-exchange program and methadone clinic and a wig store that attracted the transvestite trade. Kay Dangaard, a New Zealander who had moved through careers as a reporter and an advertising executive, joined the company as its first publicist, and from her office in the new building, she could stare out the window across the alley and into the apartment of a prostitute who practiced her trade early every evening under a flickering, low-wattage lamp.

Parking was scarce and expensive. Nicholas Lovejoy suggested to Bezos that the company subsidize bus passes for employees, but Bezos scoffed at the idea. 'He didn't want employees to leave work to catch the bus,' Lovejoy says. 'He wanted them to have their cars there so there was never any pressure to go home.'

That fall, the company focused on customizing the site for each visitor, just as Bezos had promised his original investors it would. Its first attempt relied on software developed by a firm called Firefly Network, an offshoot of the MIT Media Lab. The feature, which Amazon called Bookmatch, required customers to rate a few dozen books and then generated recommendations based on their tastes. The system was slow and crashed frequently, and Amazon found that customers were reluctant to go through the extra effort of evaluating books.

So Bezos suggested that the personalization team develop a much simpler system, one that made recommendations based on books that customers had already bought. Eric Benson took about two weeks to construct a preliminary version that grouped together customers who had similar purchasing histories and then found books that appealed to the people in each group. That feature, called Similarities, immediately yielded a noticeable uptick in sales and allowed Amazon to point customers toward books that they might not otherwise have found. Greg Linden, an engineer who worked on the project, recalls Bezos coming into his office, getting down on his hands and knees, and joking, 'I'm not worthy.'

Similarities eventually displaced Bookmatch and became the seed that would grow into Amazon's formidable personalization effort. Bezos believed that this would be one of the insurmountable advantages of e-commerce over its brick-and-mortar counterparts. 'Great merchants have never had the opportunity to understand their customers in a truly individualized way,' he said. 'E-commerce is going to make that possible.'[13]

As the company and its technologies evolved, one person was having a ridiculously good time: Shel Kaphan. He was forty-three years old and had led the remarkable effort to hack Bezos's vision into existence, completely buying into the gospel of a bookstore with limitless shelf space that spread knowledge to all corners of the earth. He was the mother hen of the technology systems: during the move to the Pecos Pit building, he put the company's two servers, dubbed Bert and Ernie, into the back of his Acura Integra and drove them over there himself.

Kaphan had taped a fortune-cookie message to the PC monitor on his desk. It read *Let no one cause you to alter your code.*

Kaphan and Bezos occasionally took walks around the city to discuss the business and Kaphan's concerns about technical issues and future plans. On one walk, Kaphan asked Bezos why, now that they had accomplished some of their earliest goals, he was so bent on rapid expansion. 'When you are small, someone else that is bigger can always come along and take away what you have,' Bezos told him. 'We have to level the playing field in terms of purchasing power with the established booksellers.'

One thing was bothering Kaphan around that time. He had enough experience with technology startups to know that the arrival of venture capitalists usually coincided with an influx of new, high-powered executives. He walked into Bezos's office that year and wondered aloud, 'We're growing pretty quickly now. Are you going to replace me?'

Bezos didn't waver. 'Shel, the job is yours as long as you want it.'

In early 1997, Mark Breier, a former executive at Cinnabon and one of those new executives Kaphan had anticipated, invited his department to his Bellevue home for a day of meetings. That afternoon, Amazon's marketing vice president introduced employees to a game called broomball. Breier's father had been an engineer at IBM in Bethesda and had seen the game played on ice during trips to IBM's offices in Canada. In Breier's land-based version, players swatted a kickball on the lawn with brooms and other random implements from his garage.

It seemed like goofy fun, but there was an undercurrent of intense competition. In other words, it perfectly expressed the temperament of Jeff Bezos, who stopped by the meeting and threw himself into the inaugural Amazon broomball contest with gusto. At one point, Andy Jassy, then a new recruit from Harvard, made his first significant impression at the company by inadvertently hitting Bezos in the head with a kayak paddle. Later, Bezos dove after the ball into some hedges and tore his blue oxford shirt.

Breier's tenure at Amazon was short and rocky. Bezos wanted to reinvent everything about marketing, suggesting, for example, that they conduct annual reviews of advertising agencies to make them constantly compete for Amazon's business. Breier explained that the advertising industry didn't work that way. He lasted about a year. Over the first decade at Amazon, marketing VPs were the equivalent of the doomed drummers in the satirical band Spinal Tap; Bezos plowed through them at a rapid clip, looking for someone with the same low regard for the usual way of doing things that Bezos himself had. Breier's broomball creation, however, became a regular pastime at Amazon employee picnics and offsite meetings, with employees covering their faces in war paint and Bezos himself getting in on the action.

As Shel Kaphan had suspected, Breier's arrival at Amazon was just the beginning of an influx of experienced business executives. With venture capital in the bank, Bezos fixated on taking the company public with an IPO, and he went on a recruiting spree. With the D. E. Shaw noncompete clause finally expiring, he called Jeff Holden and told him to pack his bags. Holden convinced a few other DESCO employees to come with him, though one, Paul Kotas, put his stuff in Holden's U-Haul and then changed his mind. (Kotas moved to Washington two years later and did become a longtime Amazon executive, though his hesitation would cost him tens of millions of dollars in stock.)

Bezos began filling out the rest of his senior leadership ranks, building a group that would formally become known as the J Team. Amazon recruited executives from Barnes & Noble and Symantec and two from Microsoft – Joel Spiegel, a vice president of engineering, and David Risher, who would eventually take over as head of retail. Risher was swayed by the Amazon founder's aggressive vision. 'If we get this right, we might be a $1 billion company by 2000,' Bezos told him. Risher personally informed Microsoft co-founder Bill Gates of his defection to the bookseller across the lake. Gates, who underestimated the Internet's impact for too long, was stunned. 'I think he was honestly flabbergasted,' Risher says. 'To some extent he was right. It didn't make any sense.'

One of Risher's first tasks was taking over negotiations with crosstown coffee giant Starbucks, which had proposed putting a rack of merchandise from Amazon next to its cash registers in exchange for an ownership stake in the startup. Risher and Bezos visited Starbucks' CEO Howard Schultz in his SoDo headquarters – across from the Pecos Pit – and Schultz told the pair that Amazon had a big problem and that Starbucks could solve it. 'You have no physical presence,' the lanky Starbucks founder said as he brewed coffee for his guests. 'That is going to hold you back.'

Bezos disagreed. He looked right at Schultz and told him, 'We are going to take this thing to the moon.' They decided to work on a deal, but it fell apart a few weeks later when Schultz's executives asked for a 10 percent ownership stake in Amazon and a seat on its board of directors. Bezos had been thinking along the lines of less than 1 percent. Even today, Amazon continues to evaluate the possibility of some kind of retail presence. 'We were always willing to consider that there may be an opportunity there,' says Risher.

Another new arrival was Joy Covey as chief financial officer. Driven and often intimidating to underlings, Covey became an intellectual foil to Bezos and a key architect of Amazon's early expansion. She had an unconventional background. A hyperintelligent but alienated child from San Mateo, California, she had run away from home when she was a sophomore in high school and worked as a grocery-store clerk in Fresno. She entered Cal State, Fresno, at age seventeen, graduated in two years, and then took the exam to become a certified public accountant at age nineteen, notching the second-highest score in the nation without studying. She later earned a joint business and law degree from Harvard. When Bezos found her, she was the thirty-three-year-old chief financial officer for a Silicon Valley digital-audio company called Digidesign.

Over the next few years, Covey remained so intensely focused on executing Bezos's 'get big fast' imperative that everything else in her life became background noise. One morning she parked her car in the office garage and was so distracted that she inadvertently left it running – all day. That evening, she couldn't find her car keys, concluded she had lost them, and went home without her car. The security guard in the garage called her a few hours later and told her that she might want to come back to the office to retrieve her still-idling vehicle.

Covey began working on an IPO a month after joining the company. Amazon did not urgently require the capital of a public offering – it had yet to begin launching new product categories, and its ninety-three-thousand-square-foot warehouse in South Seattle was serving the company's needs. But Bezos believed a public offering could be a global branding event that solidified Amazon in customers' minds. In these days, Bezos took every oppor-tunity to appear in public and tell the story of Amazon.com. (Always Amazon.com, never Amazon; he was as insistent on that as David Shaw had been on the space between the *D*. and the *E*. in his company's name.)

Another reason Bezos pushed to go public was that competition was looming online in the form of the reigning giant of the bookselling business, Barnes & Noble.

The chain store was run by Len Riggio, a tough-as-nails Bronx-born businessman with a taste for expensive suits and for fine art, which he lavishly hung on the walls of his lower Manhattan office. Over two decades, Barnes & Noble had revolutionized bookselling. It introduced discount prices on new releases and, with archrival Borders, spread the concept of the book superstore, driving many mall shops and independents out of business. As a result, between 1991 and 1997, the market share of independent bookstores in the United States dropped from 33 to 17 percent, according to the American Booksellers Association, whose membership dropped from 4,500 to 3,300 stores in that time.

Now Barnes & Noble was faced with what must have seemed like a pipsqueak upstart. Amazon had a measly $16 million in sales in 1996; Barnes & Noble notched $2 billion in sales that same year. Still, after the *Wall Street Journal* article in 1996, Riggio called Bezos and told him he wanted to come to Seattle with his brother Stephen to talk about a deal. Inexperienced at the time in these kinds of discussions, Bezos called investor and board member Tom Alberg and asked him to accompany him to dinner with the Riggios. Beforehand, they decided on a strategy of caution and flattery.

The foursome had a steak dinner at Seattle's famous Dahlia Lounge, on Fourth Avenue near the Columbia Building, an iconic Seattle restaurant with a memorable neon sign of a chef holding a strung-up fish. The Riggios wore suits and came on strong. They told Bezos and Alberg that they were going to launch a website soon and crush Amazon. But they said they admired what

Bezos had done and suggested a number of possible collaborations, such as licensing Amazon's technology or opening a joint website. 'They didn't come right out and offer to buy us. It was not particularly specific,' Alberg says. 'It was a pretty friendly dinner. Other than the threats.'

Afterward, Alberg and Bezos told the Riggios they would think about a partnership. Later Alberg and Bezos spoke on the phone and agreed that such a collaboration was unlikely to work. 'Jeff was always a big believer that disruptive small companies could triumph,' Alberg says. 'It wasn't the end of the world. We knew we had a challenge.'

Rebuffed, the Riggio brothers went home and started work on their own site. According to a person who worked at Barnes & Noble at the time, Len Riggio wanted to call the site the Book Predator but colleagues convinced him that was a bad idea. Barnes & Noble would take many months to back up its threat and spin up its own Web operation, and during that time, Bezos's team accelerated the pace of innovation and expansion.

Joy Covey considered both Morgan Stanley and Goldman Sachs for the role of lead underwriter on the Amazon IPO, but she settled on Deutsche Bank and the tall, mustached founder of its technology practice, Frank Quattrone. Quattrone's lead analyst, a future venture capitalist named Bill Gurley, had covered Amazon for a year and presciently identified it as one of the 'wave riders' that was exploiting the ascendance of the Internet.

That spring, Bezos and Covey traveled the United States and Europe to pitch Amazon to potential investors. With three years of sales data, they now felt they had a unique story. Unlike traditional retailers, Amazon boasted what was called a negative operating cycle.

Customers paid with their credit cards when their books shipped but Amazon settled its accounts with the book distributors only every few months. With every sale, Amazon put more cash in the bank, giving it a steady stream of capital to fund its operations and expansion.[14] The company could also lay claim to a uniquely high return on invested capital. Unlike brick-and-mortar retailers, whose inventories were spread out across hundreds or thousands of stores around the country, Amazon had one website and, at that time, a single warehouse and inventory. Amazon's ratio of fixed costs to revenue was considerably more favorable than that of its offline competitors. In other words, Bezos and Covey argued, a dollar that was plugged into Amazon's infrastructure could lead to exponentially greater returns than a dollar that went into the infrastructure of any other retailer in the world.

At seemingly every stop, investors asked the pair about possible expansion into other categories. Bezos demurred and said he was focused only on books. To burnish their case, they compared their fundamentals to Dell, the high-flying PC maker at the time. But Bezos, characteristically secretive, divulged only the legal minimum and withheld some data, like what it cost Amazon to attract a new user and how much loyal customers typically spent on the site. He wanted capital from an IPO but didn't want to give his rivals a road map to use to follow in his footsteps. 'There was a lot of skepticism on the road show,' says Covey. 'A lot of people said, you are going to fail, Barnes and Noble is going to kill you, and who do you think you are not to share this stuff?'

The IPO process was painful in another way: During the seven-week SEC-mandated 'quiet period,' Bezos was not permitted to talk to the press. 'I can't believe we have to delay our business by seven years,' he complained, equating weeks to years because he believed that the Internet was evolving at such an accelerated rate.

Staying out of the press soon became even more difficult. Three days before Amazon's IPO, Barnes & Noble filed a lawsuit against Amazon in federal court alleging that Amazon was falsely advertising itself to be the Earth's Largest Bookstore. Riggio was appropriately worried about Amazon, but with the lawsuit he ended up giving his smaller competitor more attention. Later that month, the Riggios unveiled their own website, and many seemed ready to see Amazon crushed. The CEO of Forrester Research, a widely followed technology research firm, issued a report in which he called the company 'Amazon.Toast.'

Straining against the regulatory shackles that required him to stay silent, Bezos wanted to send mimes wearing Amazon T-shirts to skulk around the Riggios' launch event. Quattrone put the kibosh on the plan.

Later Bezos recalled speaking at an all-hands meeting called to address the assault by Barnes & Noble. 'Look, you should wake up worried, terrified every morning,' he told his employees. 'But don't be worried about our competitors because they're never going to send us any money anyway. Let's be worried about our customers and stay heads-down focused.'[15]

For the next year, Amazon.com and BarnesandNoble.com competed, each asserting that it had a better selection and lower prices. Barnes & Noble laid claim to a deeper catalog; Amazon ramped up efforts to find rare and out-of-print books, assigning employees to track down books in independent bookshops and at antique-book dealers. In 1998, Barnes & Noble would spin off its dot-com subsidiary with a $200 million investment from German media giant Bertelsmann and later take the company public. Amazon would then outflank the bookseller by rapidly expanding into other product categories like music and DVDs.

Bezos had predicted that the chain retailer would have trouble seriously competing online, and, in the end, he was right. The Riggios were reluctant to lose money on a relatively small part of their business and didn't want to put their most resourceful employees behind an effort that would siphon sales away from the more profitable stores. On top of that, their company's distribution operation was well entrenched and geared toward servicing physical stores by sending out large shipments of books to a set number of locations. The shift from that to mailing small orders to individual customers was long, painful, and full of customer-service errors. For Amazon, that was just daily business.

Amazon's IPO, on May 15, 1997, was a success, though a relatively mild one compared with the debauched dot-com affairs that would come later. Bezos battled his bankers to boost the price of the offering to eighteen dollars a share, and the stock traded underwater – below its IPO price – for more than a month. But the IPO raised $54 million and got widespread attention, propelling the company to a blockbuster year of 900 percent growth in annual revenues. Bezos, his parents, and his brother and sister (who had each bought ten thousand dollars' worth of stock early on) were now officially multimillionaires. And Amazon's original backers and Kleiner Perkins all saw a healthy return on their investments. But even that was peanuts compared to the coming exponential growth in Amazon's stock.

From New York, Bezos called into the Amazon office on the day of the IPO and asked employees not to overcelebrate the moment or obsess over the stock price. Henry Weinhard's beer, an inexpensive local brew, was passed around the Seattle offices and then everyone went back to work, although they all occasionally stole furtive glances at Amazon's stock price.

Later that month, everyone who worked on the IPO received a wooden box containing a bottle of tequila. On the bottle was a label with an invitation to a 'Fiesta Mexicana,' a weekend at the Palmilla Resort in Los Cabos, Mexico, courtesy of Frank Quattrone and Deutsche Bank technology group.

Bezos, MacKenzie, Joy Covey, Shel Kaphan, and Nicholas Lovejoy attended, as did Jeff Blackburn, the Deutsche Bank associate and former Dartmouth College linebacker who would soon join Amazon and become its chief of business development. The weekend included a day cruise, during which Quattrone taught Bezos the Macarena, and the two men, despite a significant height difference, danced next to each other on the ship's deck. One night there was an opulent dinner on the beach, and the bankers showed up in pirate regalia. Toward the end of the evening, storm winds started to gust and the ocean grew choppy. An errant wave came onto the shore and washed over electrical cables, shorting out the stereo equipment and sending a dessert tray crashing to the sand. As the partygoers scurried for shelter, a happy Bezos surveyed the scene, his laugh cutting through the Mexican night.

In early 1997, while Amazon was fending off the world's biggest bookstore chain, Covey and Bezos courted Rick Dalzell, a former U.S. Army Ranger. A native of Georgetown, Kentucky, Dalzell had spent the 1980s as a signal engineer stationed in Fort Gamble and then as a communications officer in West Germany. After returning to civilian life, he eventually went to work in the information-systems division of the most technologically sophisticated retailer in the world: Walmart.

With his cheerful demeanor, southern drawl, and penchant for wearing shorts year-round, Dalzell became one of Amazon's most loved and respected executives. But at first, he turned Bezos and Covey down – repeatedly. When he visited Seattle that spring, the airline lost his luggage, so Dalzell borrowed a coat and tie from the bellman's desk at his hotel. Then he showed up early to the Amazon offices, and no one was there; unlike Walmart's staff, Amazon employees worked late and slept late. When Bezos did get there, he and Dalzell sat down to talk, and the Amazon founder promptly spilled his entire cup of coffee right onto Dalzell's borrowed jacket.

Despite the awkward start, Dalzell left Seattle intrigued with Bezos's vision and geeky charisma. But back in Bentonville, Arkansas, Dalzell was easily turned around by Walmart execs. From the front seat of a golf cart that was zooming through a massive distribution center, Lee Scott, the future Walmart CEO who was then running logistics, told Dalzell that Amazon was a novel idea but that it had limited potential. Don Soderquist, Walmart's chief operating officer, said that because Amazon didn't store its own inventory – at the time, it just ordered it from distributors and then quickly shipped it back out – the model would hit a wall once it got to $100 million in sales. He also said that Dalzell was one of a dozen guys they were betting on, and he added ominously, 'Should you decide to leave, you are no longer a member of the Walmart family.'

Dalzell took that advice to heart. But his infatuation with online retailing wouldn't go away. At that time, early

1997, Walmart and Sam's Club were taking their own first steps into the world of e-commerce, but Dalzell could see the effort did not have the company's full backing.

Bezos didn't give up on Dalzell or the prospect of getting another seasoned engineering executive. He kept looking elsewhere but had Covey call Dalzell's wife, Kathryn, every few weeks and deployed John Doerr to try to exert his charm. At one point, Bezos and Covey flew to Bentonville to surprise Dalzell and invite him out for dinner. After that meal, Dalzell agreed to join Amazon – but then changed his mind. 'It would take an atomic bomb to get my family out of Arkansas,' he said at the time.[16]

But Dalzell couldn't get Amazon out of his head. 'My wife will tell you if I'm passionate about something, I don't stop talking about it,' he says. 'One day she turned to me and said, "Why are you still at Walmart?"' In August, he finally accepted the job, for real this time, and Walmart's CIO stood in Dalzell's office as he collected his belongings and then marched him out the door.

In August 1997, Dalzell started his new job as Amazon's chief information officer and became a key member of the J Team. He was a seasoned manager, adept at hiring quickly and getting large groups to set and meet ambitious objectives. Dalzell regularly sat next to Bezos in meetings and was in charge of putting manpower behind the founder's best ideas. 'It was real easy for Jeff to spout off big ideas faster than anyone could practically do any-thing with them,' says Bruce Jones, a longtime Amazon engineer and Dalzell's friend. 'Rick made sure we got the important stuff done.'

Dalzell's arrival that summer had a big ripple effect, and it magnified the growing anxieties of Shel Kaphan. Before the IPO, Bezos had taken his original partner for a walk, told him the company needed deeper technical management, and then asked him to become chief technology officer of Amazon. It sounded like a promotion, but in reality Kaphan would be playing an advisory role with no budget or direct responsibilities. Kaphan thought about it for a few days and then registered an objection, but according to Kaphan, Bezos said, 'It's done,' and wouldn't talk about it anymore.

Kaphan stayed as CTO for the next few years and remained on the management team, but he was sidelined, since he no longer had any employees reporting to him or any way to influence the distribution of critical resources. And his frustration and feelings of powerlessness grew. He had built Amazon's original systems under battle conditions, with an emphasis on frugality. Now that Amazon was approaching $60 million in sales a year, the infrastructure was a disaster. Kaphan wanted to take the time to carefully rebuild it. Bezos refused to lift his foot off the pedal and wanted all his engineers working on new features, not rewriting old ones. Then he distressed Kaphan further by approving some of Kaphan's projects, like rebuilding Amazon's infrastructure from scratch, but allowing other managers to direct them. Kaphan could only sit and watch.

Bezos no longer entrusted the introverted programmer with any real management responsibility, but he did express an appreciation and a fondness for Kaphan. In the fall of 1998, Bezos told Kaphan to pack his bags and accompany him on a trip to check out a potential acquisition target. Then he surprised Kaphan with what he dubbed the Shelebration, a weekend in Hawaii to celebrate Kaphan's four-year anniversary at Amazon. Bezos flew in colleagues and Kaphan's family and friends and put everyone up for three days in private cabins on a Maui beach. Every attendee received an ornamental tile coaster emblazoned with a picture of Kaphan wearing a goofy *Cat in the Hat* hat.

That weekend spawned a fortuitous relationship for Bezos. One of Kaphan's friends who came on the trip was Stewart Brand, the founder of the Whole Earth Catalog. Brand and his wife, Ryan, bonded with Bezos and MacKenzie, forging a connection that led to Bezos's involvement in the Clock of the Long Now, an aspirational project aimed at building a massive mechanical clock designed to measure time for ten thousand years, a way to promote long-term thinking. A few years later, as a direct result of that weekend, Bezos would become the biggest financial backer of the 10,000-Year Clock and agree to install it on property he owned in Texas.

But Kaphan grimaced through the Hawaii weekend. He says he felt like 'the guy getting the gold watch who has not retired yet.'

Two promises were in conflict with each other. Bezos had pledged to Kaphan that he could keep his job forever. But Amazon's founder also promised the company and his investors that he would always raise the hiring bar and that Amazon would live or die based on its ability to recruit great engineers. Rick Dalzell and Joel Spiegel were adept at the political martial arts that occurred inside big companies. Kaphan was an introverted hacker with an idealistic streak and little intuitive leadership ability; in fact, he had been hopelessly behind on hiring and growing his own department. But he had also quietly and competently led the effort to deliver Amazon to the world back when it was only a set of uncertain predictions on Jeff Bezos's spreadsheets.

Kaphan couldn't imagine himself walking away, but he found himself counting the weeks to his five-year anniversary at the company, when he was scheduled to get the last portion of his stock. He eventually stopped going into the office altogether. He officially stayed at Amazon until the fall of 1999 and then called Bezos one morning from home to say he was quitting. Kaphan recalls that Bezos said he was sorry Kaphan felt that he needed to make that decision and made little effort to persuade him to stay.

Bezos would describe Kaphan as 'the most important person ever in the history of Amazon.com.'[17] But Kaphan felt bitter resentment about his five-year odyssey. He calls Bezos's decision to remove him from active participation in Amazon 'a betrayal of a sacred trust' between people who had started a business together and says that the way he was treated 'was one of the biggest disappointments of my entire life.'

It was a distilled version of the dissatisfaction felt by many early Amazon employees. With his convincing gospel, Bezos had persuaded them all to have faith, and they were richly rewarded as a result. Then the steely-eyed founder replaced them with a new and more experienced group of believers. Watching the company move on without them gave these employees a gnawing sensation, as if their child had left home and moved in with another family. But in the end, as Bezos made abundantly clear to Shel Kaphan, Amazon had only one true parent.

CHAPTER 3
Fever Dreams

In early 1997, Jeff Bezos flew to Boston to give a presentation at the Harvard Business School. He spoke to a class taking a course called Managing the Marketspace, and afterward the graduate students pretended he wasn't there while they dissected the online retailer's prospects. At the end of the hour, they reached a consensus: Amazon was unlikely to survive the wave of established retailers moving online. 'You seem like a really nice guy, so don't take this the wrong way, but you really need to sell to Barnes and Noble and get out now,' one student bluntly informed Bezos.

Brian Birtwistle, a student in the class, recalls that Bezos was humble and circumspect. 'You may be right,' Amazon's founder told the students. 'But I think you might be underestimating the degree to which established brick-and-mortar business, or any company that might be used to doing things a certain way, will find it hard to be nimble or to focus attention on a new channel. I guess we'll see.'

After the class, only a few students went to talk to Bezos, far fewer than the crush that greeted most speakers. One of those students was Jason Kilar (who would spend the next nine years scaling the executive ranks at Amazon before taking over as chief executive of the video site Hulu). By the time Birtwistle got to him, Bezos had to leave for the airport, so the professor of the class suggested that Birtwistle give him a ride. 'Great,' Bezos agreed. 'I can save on cab fare.'

During the fifteen-minute drive, Bezos assumed Birtwistle was interested in a job and started to interview him. 'Why do you want to work at Amazon.com?' he asked.

Birtwistle hadn't prepared for an interview but he played along anyway. 'I'm a student of history,' he said. 'If I'm able to join a company like yours at this early stage, I'd feel like I get to participate in something historic.'

Bezos almost started yelling. 'That is exactly how we think at Amazon.com! You watch. There will be a proliferation of companies in this space and most will die. There will be only a few enduring brands, and we will be one of them.'

After a few moments of silence, Bezos asked, 'So, why are manhole covers round?'

'Jeff, if you want to get to the airport on time, you cannot ask me a question like that.'

Bezos let loose a gunfire burst of laughter, startling Birtwistle, who almost veered off the highway. 'No, seriously,' Bezos said. 'How would you solve that problem?'

'They're round because it makes them easier to roll into place?'

'That is incorrect, but it is not a bad guess,' Bezos said.[1]

When Birtwistle graduated from Harvard, he joined Amazon, along with Kilar and Andy Jassy, who years later would run Amazon's pioneering cloud business. They were among the first business-school graduates hired at

Amazon, which had previously favored local, technical talent. They were also a handy resource for Bezos at a crucial juncture in the company's history.

In early 1998, the doomed broomball pioneer and marketing executive Mark Breier brought Bezos findings from a survey that showed a significant majority of consumers did not use Amazon.com and were unlikely to start simply because they bought very few books. Bezos, Breier says, did not seem overly concerned with the depressing math behind America's literary interests. He told Breier to organize the new Harvard Business School graduates into a 'SWAT team' to research categories of products that had high SKUs (the number of potentially stockable items), were underrepresented in physical stores, and could easily be sent through the mail. This was a key part of Amazon's early strategy: maximizing the Internet's ability to provide a superior selection of products as compared to those available at traditional retail stores. 'I brought him very bad news about our business, and for some reason, he got excited,' Breier says.

Bezos now felt expansion into new categories was urgent. In customers' minds, the Amazon brand meant books only. He wanted it to be more malleable, like Richard Branson's Virgin, which stood for everything from music to airlines to liquor. Bezos also needed Amazon to generate the kind of returns that would allow him to invest in technology and stay ahead of rivals. 'By that time, Jeff had done the math on a legal pad and knew this had to happen. It was go really big or go home,' says Joel Spiegel, a vice president of engineering who had spent time at Microsoft and Apple.

Joy Covey believes that from the beginning, Bezos planned to expand beyond books, but he was looking for the right moment to do it. 'He always had a large appetite,' she says. 'It was just a question of staging the opportunities at the right time.'

So that spring, Jassy researched music, Kilar looked into the home-video market, a former Harvard classmate named Victoria Pickett examined shrink-wrapped software, and the list went on. At a management offsite at the Westin Hotel, the MBAs presented their findings. Amazon executives chose music as the first expansion target, and DVDs as the second. To the discomfort of early employees wedded to the zeal of creating a literary hub on the Web, the mission was now more comprehensive. The motto on the top of the website changed from Earth's Largest Bookstore to Books, Music and More, and, soon after, to Earth's Biggest Selection – the everything store.

Near the end of the daylong offsite, Bezos asked everyone to write down a prediction of the company's revenues in five years. Eugene Wei, a strategic planning analyst who was there to take notes, recalls that Bezos's guess was one of the highest in the group but suspects that no one came close to getting it right. They simply had no idea what was coming down the pike.

To open new categories and build more warehouses, Amazon needed more than a plan: it needed additional capital. So that May, the company raised $326 million in a junk-bond offering, and the following February, another $1.25 billion in what was at the time the largest convertible debt offering in history. With a 4.75 percent interest rate for the latter offering, it was exceedingly cheap capital for the time. To their surprise, Covey and Bezos did not have to head back onto the road to pitch the Amazon story to hidebound institutional shareholders. Investors who had been raised on a steady diet of dot-com hype over the preceding year lined up eagerly to buy the bonds.

Randy Tinsley, Amazon's treasurer and corporate development chief, met finance colleague Tim Stone on a Saturday at an auto-repair shop in Issaquah to sign the promissory notes for the convertible-bond deal. Tinsley was having a car stereo installed in his jeep and he showed the papers to the bewildered attendant behind the desk. 'You want to know what this is?' he bragged. 'This is 1.25 billion dollars.'

The two-year frenzy that followed would come to be known as the dot-com bubble.

In the late 1990s, the Web evolved from the province of geeks to the stuff of front-page newspaper stories, day traders, and regular folks who were venturing for the first time into what was then popularly called cyberspace. The resulting mania for the widely predicted changes to business and society sparked an equity bubble that made rational observers question their own sanity. Yahoo was valued more highly than Disney; Amazon was worth more than storied Sears. In Silicon Valley, entrepreneurs and their backers got drunk on the overflowing optimism and abundant venture capital and threw a two-year-long party. Capital was cheap, opportunities seemed limitless, and pineapple-infused-vodka martinis were everywhere.

During that time, no one placed bigger, bolder bets on the Internet than Jeff Bezos. Bezos believed more than anyone that the Web would change the landscape for companies and customers, so he sprinted ahead without the least hesitation. 'I think our company is undervalued' became another oft-repeated Jeffism. 'The world just doesn't understand what Amazon is going to be.' In those highly carbonated years, from 1998 to early 2000, Amazon raised a breathtaking $2.2 billion in three separate bond offerings. It spent much of that on acquisitions, but even just a few years later, it was difficult to show that any of those deals helped its primary business. It opened five new state-of-the-art distribution centers in the United States and later had to close two of them and lay off hundreds of workers amid the inevitable retrenchment.

During those misadventures, Bezos seemed unperturbed. If anything, the setbacks made him push the company even harder into new territory. He said to Rick Dalzell, the former Army Ranger who'd joined Amazon from Walmart, 'Physically, I'm a chicken. Mentally, I'm bold.' Susan Benson remembers riding up the Columbia Building elevator one morning with Amazon's founder. She had Rufus in tow, and Bezos quietly studied the corgi. 'You are a very sweet dog, Rufus,' he said. Then he looked up at Benson. 'But you know, he is not bold.'

Bezos used that word a lot: *bold*. In the company's first letter to its public shareholders, written collaboratively by Bezos and Joy Covey and typed up by treasurer Russ Grandinetti in early 1998, the word *bold* was used repeatedly. 'We will make bold rather than timid investment decisions where we see a sufficient probability of gaining market leadership advantages,' they wrote. 'Some of these investments will pay off, others will not, and we will have learned another valuable lesson in either case.' The letter also stated that the company would make decisions based on long-term prospects of boosting free cash flow and growing market share rather than on short-term profitability, and one section in particular served as a guidepost for the unorthodox way the company planned to approach Wall Street.

We believe that a fundamental measure of our success will be the shareholder value we create over the long term.

This value will be a direct result of our ability to extend and solidify our current market leadership position. The stronger our market leadership, the more powerful our economic model. Market leadership can translate directly to higher revenue, higher profitability, greater capital velocity, and corrspondingly stronger returns on invested capital.

Our decisions have consistently reflected this focus. We first measure ourselves in terms of the metrics most indicative of our market leadership: customer and revenue growth, the degree to which our customers continue to purchase from us on a repeat basis, and the strength of our brand. We have invested and will continue to invest aggressively to expand and leverage our customer base, brand, and infrastructure as we move to establish an enduring franchise.

Inside Amazon, the shareholder letter became the equivalent of holy scripture. Bezos rereleases the letter each year with the company's annual report, and the company has hewed remarkably close to the promises and philosophies laid out in it.

Amazon started its dot-com-era sprint with what it called its megadeals. It paid tens of millions of dollars in the late 1990s to be the exclusive bookseller on the popular sites of the day like AOL, Yahoo, MSN, and Excite. These sites were called portals, because they were the main entryways to the Web for the new and technically unsophisticated masses. The portals were accustomed to receiving equity stakes for these kinds of deals, but Bezos refused to give that – he was as stingy about handing out stock as he was about allowing employees to fly business-class. Instead, he paid cash and convinced each portal to throw in a freebie: links to Amazon books within search results. For example, if someone searched AOL.com for ski vacations, he would see a link to books about skiing on Amazon.

Bezos enforced strict frugality in Amazon's daily operations; he made employees pay for parking and required all executives to fly coach. But he was surprisingly profligate in some ways. In early 1998, when he hired Randy Tinsley from Intel to become director of corporate development, one of the first things he said to him was 'I am really looking forward to going shopping with you.' Their resulting splurge was epic. Amazon bought the movie database IMDB.com, the British Web bookstore BookPages, the German Web bookstore Telebuch, the online marketplace Exchange.com, the pioneering social-networking service PlanetAll, and a data-collection company called Alexa Internet – among many other purchases. The acquisitions brought in experienced executives, but Amazon was moving too quickly, and was too chaotic internally, to properly integrate the companies and their technology. Most of the executives left after a year or two, repulsed by the frenetic pace, the dreary Seattle weather, or both.

Amazon also veered disastrously into the venture-capital arena. In 1998 Bezos and venture capitalist John Doerr saw an opportunity for an online pharmacy and founded Drugstore.com, recruiting longtime Microsoft executive Peter Neupert to run it. Amazon owned a third of the company. The venture got off to a promising start, so for the next two years, Tinsley and Bezos invested tens of millions of Amazon's cash in a variety of dot-com hopefuls, including Pets.com, Gear.com, Wineshopper.com, Greenlight.com, Home-grocer.com, and the urban delivery service Kozmo.com. In exchange for its cash, Amazon took a minority ownership position and a seat on the board for each, and the company believed it was well positioned for the future if those product categories succeeded on the Internet. The startups believed they had a powerful partner invested in their success. Almost all of them went down in flames, though, during the collapse of the dot-com bubble in 2000, and by then, Bezos had his own problems and possessed neither the temperament nor the time to try to save them. The company lost hundreds of millions on these investments. 'Amazon had to be focused on its own business,' says Tinsley. 'Our biggest mistake was thinking we had the bandwidth to work with all these companies.'

Inside Amazon, employees lived under Bezos's frugal edicts while they watched in awe as he kept pushing more and more chips into the pot. Gene Pope was an early engineer at Apple who reunited at Amazon with his former colleague Joel Spiegel. After watching the wild expansion for a few months, Pope said to Spiegel, 'What we are doing here is building a giant rocket ship, and we're going to light the fuse. Then it's either going to go to the moon or leave a giant smoking crater in the ground. Either way I want to be here when it happens.'

As the company grew, Bezos offered another sign that his ambitions were larger than anyone had suspected. He started hiring more Walmart executives. In early 1998, Amazon pursued one of Rick Dalzell's former colleagues, a retired Walmart vice president of distribution named Jimmy Wright. At Walmart, the abrasive Wright had proven himself so exasperating that once during an argument in his office, Dalzell, the Army Ranger, had lifted Wright entirely off his feet, deposited him outside the office, and slammed the door shut. But Dalzell knew that if anyone could accomplish Bezos's ambitious vision of a rapid build-out of distribution capacity, it was Jimmy Wright. 'I'm not sure anyone else in America could have done it,' Dalzell says.

Bezos courted Wright for months and that summer got him to tour the Dawson Street warehouse. Bezos said he wanted a distribution system that was ten times larger than it currently was, and not just in the United States but in Amazon's new markets in the United Kingdom and Germany. Wright asked Bezos what products they would be shipping. 'He said, "I don't know. Just design something that will handle anything,"' Wright recalls. 'I'm going, You're kidding me, right? And he said, "No, that is the mission." I had to have a solution to handle everything but an aircraft carrier.'

Wright had never experienced a challenge of that magnitude. At Walmart, distribution centers shipped containers of products predictably, once a day, to all the stores in the surrounding area. At Amazon, there were innumerable packages going to countless destinations. And there was no predictability, because Amazon sales were growing by 300 percent a year.

As Wright started planning, Amazon navigated a tumultuous 1998 holiday season. Around Thanksgiving, Joy Covey realized that the gap between the number of orders being placed on the website and the number of packages being shipped to customers was widening, and she raised an alarm. Amazon declared an all-hands-on-deck emergency, and, in a program dubbed Save Santa, every employee from the main office took a graveyard shift on Dawson Street or in a new facility in Delaware. They brought their friends and family, ate burritos and drank coffee from a food cart, and often slept in their cars before going to work the next day. Bezos held contests to see who could pick orders off the shelves fastest. After

Christmas was over, he vowed that Amazon would never again have a shortage of physical capacity to meet customer demand.

Around that time, Wright showed Bezos the blueprints for a new warehouse in Fernley, Nevada, thirty miles east of Reno. The founder's eyes lit up. 'This is beautiful, Jimmy,' Bezos said.

Wright asked who he needed to show the plans to and what kind of return on investment he would have to demonstrate.

'Don't worry about that,' Bezos said. 'Just get it built.'

'Don't I have to get approval to do this?' Wright asked.

'You just did,' Bezos said.

Over the next year, Wright went on a wild $300 million spending spree. He not only built the warehouse in Fernley but purchased and retrofitted existing warehouses, one near Atlanta, two in Kentucky, and one in Kansas. He turned them into real-life versions of an M. C. Escher drawing, automating them to the rafters, with blinking lights on aisles and shelves to guide human workers to the right products, and conveyor belts that ran into and out of massive machines, called Crisplants, that took products from the conveyors and scanned and sorted them into customer orders to be packaged and shipped. These facilities, Wright decreed, would be called not warehouses but distribution centers, as they were in Walmart's internal lexicon.

Wright kept his home and private consulting office in Bentonville, and during his fifteen months at Amazon he shuttled back and forth to Seattle. He did something else in that time as well. In backyard barbecues and at the Bentonville community fitness center, he canvassed his former colleagues and pitched them on joining the online retailer. 'Walmart did not even have Internet in the building back then,' says Kerry Morris, a product buyer who moved from Walmart to Amazon. 'We weren't online. We weren't e-mailing. None of us even knew what he meant by online retail.'

Amazon knew Walmart would react poorly to Amazon's poaching from its ranks. Morris says that her interview process was conducted stealthily. She stayed at a friend's in Seattle rather than at a hotel and interviewed for the job at a Starbucks, not at Amazon's office. Amazon, she says, paid for her expenses with cash. That year, more than a dozen Walmart employees moved to Amazon.

The Walmart transplants created plenty of uncomfortable friction. The Amazon employees were in their twenties and early thirties and full of Bezos-programmed bravado about doing everything differently. The folks from Bentonville were considerably older, in their forties and fifties, and had little patience for the brash youngsters. One notoriously caustic émigré from Walmart, Tom Sharpe, took over as vice president of merchandising and lasted a little more than a year. Birtwistle, the Harvard MBA, remembers a preliminary conversation with Sharpe that went like this.

Sharpe: 'What's your name again?'

Birtwistle: 'It's Brian Birtwistle.'

Sharpe: 'Well, listen, Buttwistle, the grown-ups are here now. We are here to make this thing run like a real business.'

The Walmart transplants created another problem. As part of the Drugstore.com build-out, Bezos and Doerr recruited a Walmart engineer named Kal Raman, and he also began cherry-picking his former colleagues from Bentonville. That was the last straw. Walmart sued Amazon, Kleiner, and Drugstore.com in the Arkansas state court, alleging that they were trying to steal trade secrets. John Doerr joked that he could no longer safely travel to the state.

The case was a symbolic shot across the bow and was ultimately settled with no damages. But it brought the bubbling tensions between the reigning retail champion and the brash online upstart into the open. Some people were unhappy about this. Rick Dalzell's wife, Kathryn, was upset that her new community was now at war with her old one. Dalzell happened to mention that to Bezos, and soon after, Bezos and MacKenzie stopped by Dalzell's home with flowers and a copy of Sam Walton's autobiography, *Sam Walton: Made in America*.

Bezos had imbibed Walton's book thoroughly and wove the Walmart founder's credo about frugality and a 'bias for action' into the cultural fabric of Amazon. In the copy he brought to Kathryn Dalzell, he had underlined one particular passage in which Walton described borrowing the best ideas of his competitors. Bezos's point was that every company in retail stands on the shoulders of the giants that came before it. The book clearly resonated with Amazon's founder. On the last page, a section completed a few weeks before his death, Walton wrote:

Could a Wal-Mart-type story still occur in this day and age? My answer is of course it could happen again. Somewhere out there right now there's someone – probably hundreds of thousands of someones – with good enough ideas to go all the way. It will be done again, over and over, providing that someone wants it badly enough to do what it takes to get there. It's all a matter of attitude and the capacity to constantly study and question the management of the business.

Jeff Bezos embodied the qualities Sam Walton wrote about. He was constitutionally unwilling to watch Amazon succumb to any kind of institutional torpor, and he generated a nonstop flood of ideas on how to improve the experience of the website, make it more compelling for customers, and keep it one step ahead of rivals.

In early 1998, Bezos was closely involved with a department called Personalization and Community, which was geared toward helping customers discover books, music, and movies they might find interesting. That May, he surveyed what was then Amazon's Hot 100 bestseller list and had an epiphany – why not rank everything on the site, not just the top sellers? 'I thought, "Hey, why do we stop at a hundred? This is the Internet! Not some newspaper bestseller list. We can have a list that goes on and on,"' he told the *Washington Post*.[2]

The notion was not only to create a new kind of taxonomy of popularity but also to give authors, artists, and publishers a better idea of how they were doing – and to cater to some of their more neurotic impulses. 'Bezos knew sales rank would be like a drug to authors,' says Greg Linden, an early Amazon engineer. 'He insisted that it change whenever a new order came in.'

That was not a trivial challenge. Amazon's overloaded servers were already stretched to the limit, and its Oracle database software was not designed to handle the increasing loads generated by the swelling audience of the Web. Engineers ended up fudging it, taking snapshots of sales data and pushing new rankings to the website every few minutes. The service, called Amazon Sales Rank, was introduced in June to the consternation of not only authors, who began compulsively checking their rankings at all hours of the day and night, but also their spouses and more than a few wary editors and publishers. 'I understand how addictive it can be, but maybe they could spend their time more productively, like, maybe, writing a new book,' veteran editor John Sterling said.[3]

Around that same time, Amazon filed for a patent on what it called its 1-Click ordering process. The system stemmed from a lunch Bezos had with Shel Kaphan and interface engineer Peri Hartman back in 1997, during which he declared that he wanted to make it as easy as possible for customers to buy things on the site. Hartman, a computer science graduate from the University of Washington, devised a system that preloaded a customer's credit card information and preferred shipping address and then offered the opportunity to execute a purchase with a single press of a button when he or she ordered a product.

By reducing the friction of online buying even marginally, Amazon could reap additional millions in revenue while simultaneously digging a protective moat around its business and hobbling its rivals. The company's nineteen-page patent application for the system, entitled 'Method and System for Placing a Purchase Order Via a Communications Network,' was approved in the fall of 1999. Amazon trademarked the name 1-Click, and a multiyear debate over the wisdom of legally protecting basic business tools began.

Critics charged that the idea behind 1-Click was rudimentary and that its approval by the U.S. patent office was a symptom of lazy bureaucracy and a broken patent process. Bezos didn't altogether disagree – intellectually, he was an advocate for patent reform – but he was determined to exploit the status quo for any possible advantage. He sued Barnes & Noble for infringing on the patent in late 1999 and won a preliminary ruling that forced the bookseller to add an extra step to its checkout process. Amazon licensed the patent to Apple in 2000 for an undisclosed sum and tried to use it, ineffectively, to gain some leverage over a rising and worrisome rival that first showed up on Amazon's radar in mid-1998: eBay.

Jeff Blackburn, the former Dartmouth football player who later would become Amazon's chief of business development, saw eBay coming before almost anyone else at Amazon. The Silicon Valley startup, founded in 1995 as a site called AuctionWeb, made $5.7 million in 1997, $47.4 million in 1998, and $224.7 million in 1999. Blackburn realized that it was growing rapidly, and, even more unsettling – and unlike Amazon – it was profitable. The company had the perfect business model: it took a commission on each sale but had none of the costs of storing inventory and mailing packages. Sellers posted their own products on the site, auctioned them off to the highest bidder, and handled shipping to the customers themselves. The site had started with collectibles like Beanie Babies and baseball cards but it was well on its way to intercepting Bezos's dream of unlimited selection and stealing the mantle of the everything store.

In the summer of 1998, Bezos invited eBay's Iranian American founder, Pierre Omidyar, and its CEO, Meg Whitman, a former Disney executive, to Seattle; eBay had just filed to go public when the two executive teams, whose fates would be intertwined for a decade, met for the first time. Bezos gave the eBay team a tour of the Dawson Street distribution center. Omidyar recalls being impressed by the automation in the facility and startled by the piercings and tattoos of the workers. 'I thought it was all very cool,' Omidyar says. Later Whitman told him, 'Pierre, get over it. This is horrible. The last thing we'd ever want to do is manage warehouses like this.'

During the meeting, the executives discussed different ways of working together. Omidyar and Whitman suggested putting eBay links on Amazon when a customer searched for products it didn't carry, such as Beanie Babies, and they offered to do the same on eBay for the books of popular authors like Tom Wolfe. Bezos suggested the possibility of Amazon investing in eBay. The eBay executives came away with an impression that Bezos was offering to buy eBay for around $600 million – roughly the market capitalization it was pursuing in its IPO, though later Jeff Blackburn didn't recall that any formal proposals were made. In the end, though, it didn't matter; the eBay execs believed that they were pioneering a new type of virtual commerce where supply and demand met to identify the perfect price for any product. They were also put off by Bezos's startling laugh. The venture capitalists backing eBay asked around and heard that one did not work *with* Jeff Bezos; one worked *for* him.

Bezos had not immediately viewed eBay as a direct threat. But as eBay's sales and profits grew, he worried that customers might see eBay as the natural starting point for an online shopping trip. Though Bezos often claimed that Amazon considered itself 'a customer-focused company, not a competitor-focused company,'[4] eBay anxiety spread. Employees exposed to a steady barrage of new economy hokum in newspapers and magazines worried not only that eBay had a better business but that fixed-price retailing itself might become a relic of the past.

Late that year, Bezos initiated a secret auctions project in a sequestered space on the second floor of the Columbia Building, dubbing the effort EBS, for Earth's Biggest Selection (or alternatively, employees joked, for eBay by spring). Bezos did not tell other employees or his directors, particularly since Scott Cook, the founder of Intuit, was on both the Amazon and eBay boards. Joel Spiegel, who led the effort with Jeff Blackburn, had a mandate to replicate eBay in three months.

Bezos was confident he could beat eBay, particularly since well-capitalized Amazon could afford to charge a lower listing fee to sellers and offer free fraud insurance. Foreseeing the need to marry auctions with a seamless way for buyers and sellers to exchange money, he paid $175 million to acquire the six-month-old payment firm Accept.com, which had not yet introduced an actual service but was already in the process of finalizing a deal with eBay when Bezos swooped in.

Bezos went skiing in Aspen that winter with Cook and Doerr and finally told them what was coming. 'He said, "We're going to win, so you probably want to consider whether to stay on the eBay board,"' says Cook. 'He thought it would be the only natural outcome.' Cook said he wanted to wait and see how things played out.

Amazon Auctions launched in March 1999, and though it got off to a slow start, Bezos quickly doubled down. He acquired a company to broadcast auctions live on the Web and signed a deal with the storied auction house Sotheby's to focus on high-end products. But the effort went nowhere. Customers could reach Amazon Auctions only by clicking on a separate tab on the Amazon home page, and it looked like a dingy leftovers bin to people who were accustomed to using Amazon to shop in the traditional way, with predictable prices for each item.

The high-tech community was getting a lesson in the dynamics of network effects – products or services become increasingly valuable as more people use them. In online marketplaces, the network effect was pervasive; sellers stuck around for access to a critical mass of buyers, and vice versa. In the auctions category, eBay already had an insurmountable advantage. Amazon's executives remember this significant failure as painful but strangely uplifting. 'Those days in the nineties were the most intense, fun time I ever had at the company,' Blackburn says. 'We had an insanely talented group of people trying to figure out how to launch a superior auctions site. In the end the network effect mattered. You could say we were naïve, but we built a great product.'

Bezos didn't take the defeat personally. He later cast the mistake as the first step in a series of important experiments to bring third-party sellers onto Amazon. Auctions would evolve into something called zShops, a platform for sellers that allowed them to operate their own fixed-price stores on Amazon.com (zShops, incidentally, was almost called Jeff's Club, à la Walmart's Sam's Club). Regardless, it went nowhere as well. For now, at least, the Web's small sellers were wedded to eBay.

Perhaps the most avid user of Amazon's auction site was Bezos himself, who began to collect various scientific and historical curiosities. Most memorably, he purchased the skeleton of an Ice Age cave bear, complete with an accompanying penis bone, for $40,000. After the company's headquarters moved yet again over the summer, out of the deteriorating Columbia Building and into the Pacific Medical Center building, a 1930s-era art-deco hospital that sat on a hill overlooking the I-5 freeway, Bezos displayed the skeleton in the lobby. Next to it was a sign that read PLEASE DON'T FEED THE BEAR.

Bears — the stock-market kind, pessimists who believe security prices are due to fall — would play no part in what happened next. On December 15, 1998, Oppenheimer analyst Henry Blodget made what became one of the most infamous predictions of the decade, projecting that Amazon's stock price – already riding the wave of dot-com hysteria into the $200s – would hit $400 per share over the next twelve months. The forecast became a self-fulfilling prophecy and signaled the onset of mass delusion. It sent Amazon stock $46 dollars higher that first day alone, and the stock hit the $400 mark just three weeks later (after two subsequent stock splits, it peaked at $107). Nudged along by the breathless reports and rhetoric emanating from Wall Street and the press, investors were beginning to lose their minds.

Bezos claimed he was impervious to the hype, but as the dot-com frenzy intensified, he used the unique climate to hasten Amazon's growth. If there was to be a great Internet landgrab, he reasoned, Amazon should rush to carve out the biggest parcel of territory. 'We don't view ourselves as a bookstore or a music store,' he said that year. 'We want to be the place for someone to find and discover anything they want to buy.'[5]

There were two ways to accomplish this: either slowly, category by category, or all at once. Bezos tried both paths, and some of his ideas were so outlandish that employees called them 'fever dreams.'

One internal initiative from that time was dubbed the Alexandria Project or, informally, Noah's Ark. The idea was to obtain two copies of every book ever printed and store them in the new distribution center in Lexington, Kentucky. That was expensive and inefficient; most books would just sit gathering dust and taking up space, but Bezos wanted customers to be able to find any title on Amazon and get it quickly. Book-buying teams eventually pushed back against the directive, stocking only the most popular books but negotiating deals with select distributors and publishers so they would ship less popular titles directly to any customers who ordered them.

An even more absurd Bezos fever dream was named Project Fargo, after the Coen brothers' film. Bezos wanted to obtain one of every product ever manufactured and store it in a distribution center. 'The over-arching goal was to make Amazon the first place people looked to buy anything,' says Kim Rachmeler, a longtime Amazon executive. 'If you had a rodeo costume in stock, what wouldn't you have?'

Rachmeler says that Project Fargo 'didn't have a lot of support among the rank and file, to put it mildly. It kept getting pushed down the stack and Jeff kept reviving it. I vividly remember a large meeting where Jeff was trying to convince people that Fargo needed to be done. 'This is the most critical project in Amazon's history' is pretty close to a direct quote.' Ultimately, the project faded amid other, more pressing priorities.

It is more evident in the way Amazon operates now that Bezos became absorbed with the challenge of delivering products immediately after customers placed their orders. John Doerr says that 'for many years we were on a journey to figure out if we could get to same-day delivery.' The quest sparked a $60 million investment in Kozmo.com, which delivered everything, from snacks to video games, to a New York City customer's doorstep. (It went bust in 2001.) Bezos even wondered aloud whether Amazon could hire college students on every block in Manhattan and get them to store popular products in their apartments and deliver them on bicycles. Employees were dumbstruck. 'We were like, Aren't we already worried about theft from our distribution center in Atlanta?' says Bruce Jones, an engineer who worked on DC software.

The fever dreams were perhaps best embodied by the 1998 acquisition of a Silicon Valley company called Junglee, founded by three graduates from Stanford's computer science PhD program. Junglee was the first comparison-shopping site on the Web; it collected data from a variety of online retailers and allowed customers to easily compare prices on specific products. A few months after the Amazon IPO, Bezos snatched the startup out of the hands of Yahoo, which was also negotiating to acquire it, for $170 million in Amazon stock. His idea was to incorporate Junglee's listings into the Amazon site and ensure that customers could search for and see information on any conceivable product, even if Amazon did not carry it.

Worried that it would have to start collecting sales tax if it had offices in California, Amazon management insisted that the Junglee employees move to Seattle, where for the next few months they turned their service into a feature on the Amazon site called Shop the Web. When a customer searched for a product on Amazon.com, the Junglee software generated a list of prices and blue links. But the customer would have to click on those links and go to another website to actually buy the items. Many Amazon executives hated the fact that customers were leaving their site to make purchases elsewhere. As a result, Shop the Web lasted on Amazon.com for just a few months and then died a quiet death. Ram Shriram, the chief operating officer of Junglee before he became a business-development executive at Amazon, calls it a 'total tissue rejection. Part of the reason it didn't succeed was that the team didn't buy into it.'

By any measure, the acquisition of Junglee was a failure. All of Junglee's founders and most of its employees left Amazon by the end of 1999 to return to the

Bay Area. But the deal nevertheless produced an extra-ordinarily bounteous outcome – for Bezos. Unbeknownst to the founders of Junglee at the time, Ram Shriram was quietly advising two PhD students at Stanford – Larry Page and Sergey Brin – who were trying to reimagine search on the Internet. In February 1998, Shriram had become one of the first four investors who backed the hopeful little company, Google, with $250,000 each.

Six months after that investment, over the summer of 1998, Bezos and MacKenzie were in the Bay Area for a camping trip with friends, and Bezos told Shriram that he wanted to meet the Google guys. On a Saturday morning, Shriram picked up Bezos and his wife at a local hotel, the Inn at Saratoga, and drove them to his home. Page and Brin met them there for breakfast and demonstrated their modest search engine. Years later, Bezos told journalist Steven Levy that he was impressed by the Google guys' 'healthy stubbornness' as they explained why they would never put advertisements on their home page.[6]

Brin and Page left Shriram's house after breakfast. Revealing once again his utter faith in passionate entrepreneurs' power to harness the Internet, Bezos immediately told Shriram that he wanted to personally invest in Google. Shriram told him the financing round had closed months ago, but Bezos insisted and said he wanted the same deal terms as other early investors. Shriram said he would try to get it done. He later went back to the Google founders and argued that Bezos's insight and budding celebrity could help the fledgling firm, and they agreed. Brin and Page flew to Seattle and spent an hour with Bezos at Amazon's offices talking about technical issues like computer infrastructure. 'Jeff was very helpful in some of those early meetings,' Larry Page says.

Thus did Jeff Bezos become one of the original investors in Google, his company's future rival, and four years after starting Amazon, he minted an entirely separate fortune that today might be worth well over a billion dollars. (Bezos adamantly refuses to discuss whether he kept some or all of his Google holdings after its IPO in 2004.) 'He's so prescient. It's like he can peer into the future,' says Shriram, who left Amazon in 2000 and remains a Google board member and who still marvels at that transaction years later. 'He's also extremely shrewd and self-aware and knows just how far he can push something.'

As Bezos's fever dreams receded in the face of practical concerns inside the company, Amazon pursued a more methodical path to expanding selection. The expansion into selling music and DVDs in 1998 had gone well, with Amazon quickly surpassing the early leaders in each market, including a startup called CDNow.com in music and Reel.com in movies. At first Amazon couldn't get music labels and movie studios to supply it directly. But as in the book business, there were intermediary distributors, like Baker and Taylor, that gave Amazon an initial boost and then allowed it to credibly make its case directly to the big media companies.

At the beginning of 1999, an emboldened Bezos selected toys and electronics as two of the company's primary new targets. To lead the toys rollout, David Risher, the senior VP of retail, chose Harrison Miller, a recent graduate of Stanford's MBA program whose only apparent qualification for the toy job came from his once teaching fifth grade in a New York City school. In other words, Miller knew nothing about toy retailing, but in a pattern that would recur over and over, Bezos didn't care.

He was looking for versatile managers – he called them 'athletes' – who could move fast and get big things done.

Miller was given a single lieutenant, Brian Birtwistle, and just eight months to get a toy business up and running before the holiday crush. A few days after getting the assignment, he and Birtwistle flew to the annual toy fair in New York, passing analyst reports about the toy business back and forth across the airplane aisle. They walked the convention floor that week introducing themselves to wary toy companies that weren't sure if Amazon and e-commerce in general represented an opportunity or a threat. The toy company execs demanded to know how much product the two wanted to buy. The young Amazon executives had no earthly idea.

Toys were fundamentally different than books, music, or movies. This time, there were no third-party distributors to provide any item and take back unsold inventory. The big toy makers carefully weighed how much product they would allocate to each retailer. And the retailers had to predict nearly a year in advance what the next holiday season's most popular items would be, as a majority of their sales occurred within a six-week frenzy of parental indulgence. If the retailers' forecasts were wrong, they were in deep trouble, because after the holidays, unsold toys were nonreturnable and about as desirable as rotten fruit. 'Toys are so fad driven, it's a little like betting on Oscar winners only by looking at movie trailers,' Miller says.

For the first time, Amazon had to prostrate itself to suppliers for the privilege of selling the suppliers' products. In pursuit of Star Wars action figures and other toys from the classic trilogy, Miller, Bezos, and John Doerr went to dinner with Hasbro chief executive Alan Hassenfeld at the Fairmont Hotel in San Francisco and made a pilgrimage to Lucasfilm headquarters in Marin County, north of San Francisco. 'It was our first serious encounter with having to beg and plead to stock an item,' says Miller. 'The whole issue of being an approved supplier suddenly became a huge hill to climb.'

That summer, Harrison Miller and Bezos butted heads in front of the board of directors over the size of the bet on toys. Bezos wanted Miller to plow $120 million into stocking every possible toy, from Barbie dolls to rare German-made wooden trains to cheap plastic beach pails, so that kids and parents would never be disappointed when they searched for an item on Amazon. But a prescient Miller, sensing disaster ahead, pushed to lower his own buy.

'No! No! A hundred and twenty million!' Bezos yelled. 'I want it all. If I have to, I will drive it to the landfill myself!'

'Jeff, you drive a Honda Accord,' Joy Covey pointed out. 'That's going to be a lot of trips.'

Bezos prevailed. And the company would make a sizable contribution to Toys for Tots after the holidays that year. 'That first holiday season was the best of times and the worst of times,' Miller says. 'The store was great for customers and we made our revenue goals, which were big, but other than that everything that could go wrong did. In the aftermath we were sitting on fifty million dollars of toy inventory. I had guys going down the back stairs with 'Vinnie' in New York, selling Digimons off to Mexico at twenty cents on the dollar. You just had to get rid of them, fast.'

The electronics effort faced even greater challenges. To launch that category, David Risher tapped a Dartmouth alum named Chris Payne who had previously worked on Amazon's DVD store. Like Miller, Payne had to plead with suppliers – in this case, Asian consumer-electronics companies like Sony, Toshiba, and Samsung.

He quickly hit a wall. The Japanese electronics giants viewed Internet sellers like Amazon as sketchy discounters. They also had big-box stores like Best Buy and Circuit City whispering in their ears and asking them to take a pass on Amazon. There were middlemen distributors, like Ingram Electronics, but they offered a limited selection. Bezos deployed Doerr to talk to Howard Stringer at Sony America, but he got nowhere.

So Payne had to turn to the secondary distributors – jobbers that exist in an unsanctioned, though not illegal, gray market. Randy Miller, a retail finance director who came to Amazon from Eddie Bauer, equates it to buying from the trunk of someone's car in a dark alley. 'It was not a sustainable inventory model, but if you are desperate to have particular products on your site or in your store, you do what you need to do,' he says.

Buying through these murky middlemen got Payne and his fledgling electronics team part of the way toward stocking Amazon's virtual shelves. But Bezos was unimpressed with the selection and grumpily compared it to shopping in a Russian supermarket during the years of Communist rule. It would take Amazon years to generate enough sales to sway the big Asian brands. For now, the electronics store was sparely furnished. Bezos had asked to see $100 million in electronics sales for the 1999 holiday season; Payne and his crew got about two-thirds of the way there.

Amazon officially announced the new toy and electronics stores that summer, and in September, the company held a press event at the Sheraton in midtown Manhattan to promote the new categories. Someone had the idea that the tables in the conference room at the

Sheraton should have piles of merchandise representing all the new categories, to reinforce the idea of broad selection. Bezos loved it, but when he walked into the room the night before the event, he threw a tantrum: he didn't think the piles were large enough. 'Do you want to hand this business to our competitors?' he barked into his cell phone at his underlings. 'This is pathetic!'

Harrison Miller, Chris Payne, and their colleagues fanned out that night across Manhattan to various stores, splurging on random products and stuffing them in the trunks of taxicabs. Miller spent a thousand dollars alone at a Toys 'R' Us in Herald Square. Payne maxed out his personal credit card and had to call his wife in Seattle to tell her not to use the card for a few days. The piles of products were eventually large enough to satisfy Bezos, but the episode was an early warning. To satisfy customers and their own demanding boss during the upcoming holiday, Amazon executives were going to have to substitute artifice and improvisation for truly comprehensive selection.

In the midst of Amazon's frenzied growth and the crush of the holiday selling season, Bezos kept coming back to the kind of culture he wanted to instill in his young but rapidly growing company. With door-desks and minimal subsidies for employee parking, he was constantly reinforcing the value of frugality. A coffee stand on the first floor of the Pac Med building handed out loyalty cards so a customer could get a free drink after his or her tenth purchase. Bezos, by now a multimillionaire, often made a deliberate show of getting his card punched or handing his free-drink credit to a colleague waiting in line next to him. Around that time, he also started traveling via a private plane, which he subleased from a local businessman. But whenever he flew with colleagues, he invariably declared, 'The company isn't paying for this, I am.'

Amazon's purchase of Telebuch in Germany and BookPages in the UK in 1998 gave Bezos an opportunity to articulate the company's core principles. Alison Allgor, a D. E. Shaw transplant who worked in human resources, pondered Amazon's values with Bezos as he prepared for an introductory conference call with the Telebuch founders. They agreed on five core values and wrote them down on a whiteboard in a conference room: *customer obsession, frugality, bias for action, ownership,* and *high bar for talent*. Later Amazon would add a sixth value, innovation.

Bezos began thinking about ways to inculcate those values in the company beyond hanging the lists on the walls of offices and distribution centers. To reinforce the notion of the high hiring bar, he drew inspiration from nearby Microsoft. As part of its famed recruiting process, Microsoft designated what it referred to as an as-appropriate senior interviewer, who talked to the candidate last and got to make the final judgment on the hire. Assigning an experienced executive to this role helped ensure that Microsoft maintained a consistent hiring standard. Bezos heard about the Microsoft program from Joel Spiegel and David Risher and then crafted Amazon's own version, which he called bar raisers.

Bar raisers at Amazon – the program still exists today – are designated employees who have proven themselves to be intuitive recruiters of talent. Dalzell and Bezos hand-picked the original leaders of the program, one of whom was Shaw veteran Jeff Holden. At least one anointed bar raiser would participate in every interview process and would have the power to veto a candidate who did not meet the goal of raising the company's overall hiring bar. Even the hiring manager was unable to override a bar raiser's veto. 'Many companies as they grow begin to compromise their standards in order to fill their resource needs,' says Dalzell. 'We wanted to make sure that did not happen at Amazon.'

Looking for a way to reinforce Walton's notion of a bias for action, Bezos instituted the Just Do It award – an acknowledgment of an employee who did something notable on his own initiative, typically outside his primary job responsibilities. Even if the action turned out to be an egregious mistake, an employee could still earn the prize as long as he or she had taken risks and shown resourcefulness in the process. Considering his emphasis on frugality, Bezos reasoned that the award could not be something of high monetary value. He would eventually acquire a pair of size 21 Nike sneakers from former Northwestern University basket-ball player Dan Kreft, who worked at Amazon as an engineer. Those ratty shoes, and the successors that Kreft periodically supplied, became the prize.

While employees embraced Amazon's newly articulated values, many resisted the breakneck pace of the work. As Amazon's growth accelerated, Bezos drove employees even harder, calling meetings over the weekends, starting an executive book club that gathered on Saturday mornings, and often repeating his quote about working smart, hard, and long. As a result, the company was not friendly toward families, and some executives left when they wanted to have children. 'Jeff didn't believe in work-life balance,' says Kim Rachmeler. 'He believed in work-life harmony. I guess the idea is you might be able to do everything all at once.'

Evidence of this friction usually emerged during the

question-and-answer sessions at the company's regular all-hands meetings, held for many years at Seattle's oldest playhouse, the Moore Theater. Employees would stand up and pose direct questions to the executive team, and often they inquired about the enormous workload and frenetic pace. During one memorable meeting, a female employee pointedly asked Bezos when Amazon was going to establish a better work-life balance. He didn't take that well. 'The reason we are here is to get stuff done, that is the top priority,' he answered bluntly. 'That is the DNA of Amazon. If you can't excel and put everything into it, this might not be the place for you.'

In Amazon's accounting group, the bean counters were working around the clock, and getting nervous. They tried to rationalize the numbers and forecast the future, but none of it added up to anything other than massive losses as far as they could see. They fretted about opening seven costly distribution centers and even about having gotten so deeply immersed in the muck of distribution in the first place. Bezos insisted the company needed to master anything that touched the hallowed customer experience, and he resisted any efforts to project profitability. 'If you are planning for more than twenty minutes ahead in this kind of environment, you are wasting your time,' he said in meetings.

For two years Wall Street had forgiven Amazon's extravagant spending. On the routine conference calls after its quarterly earnings reports came out, analysts were usually so upbeat and congratulatory that Amazon executives had to prevent themselves from sounding overly arrogant. On the tops of their earnings scripts, they wrote in giant letters *Humble, humble, humble*. A few times they also added *Remember, Meg is listening*, a reference to the eBay CEO and a reminder to remain guarded with company information.

In the spring of 1999, Wall Street's euphoria seemed to diminish. The financial weekly *Barron's* published a seminal article entitled 'Amazon.bomb' that declared, 'Investors are beginning to realize that this story-book stock has problems.'[7] The article overreached, suggesting Walmart and Barnes & Noble would crush the upstart. But it did momentarily moderate the market's exuberance. The next month, Amazon released a typical quarterly earnings report, with significant sales growth and deep losses. This time the reaction was more muted and Amazon stock actually fell slightly. Ominously, there were none of the usual ingratiating offers of congratulations from analysts on the conference call.

Kelyn Brannon, Amazon's chief accounting officer at the time, says that she and Joy Covey pulled Bezos into a meeting to show him a form of financial analysis called common-sizing the income statement; it expressed each part of the balance sheet as a percentage of value to sales. The calculations showed that at its current rate, Amazon wouldn't become profitable for decades. 'It was an aha moment,' Brannon says. Bezos agreed to lift his foot from the accelerator and begin to move the company toward profitability. To mark the occasion, he took a photo of the group with his ever-present point-and-shoot digital camera and later taped the picture to the door of his office.

But the deluge of spending and the widening losses had fueled fear among Amazon's management team – a fear that Bezos, still a young and volatile thirty-five-year-old CEO, needed additional help. And after hearing persistent grumbling from the ranks that Bezos didn't listen to his subordinates, the Amazon board initiated one of the biggest misadventures of the company's first decade.

The board members asked Bezos to search for a chief operating officer.

Bezos eventually warmed to the idea. He believed the company should stockpile as many experienced managers as possible, and he was beginning to contemplate spending more of his time in the pursuit of his other personal passions. Amazon interviewed a number of high-powered executives, including Wall Street veteran Jamie Dimon, who had just been fired from Citibank by chairman Sandy Weill. But they settled on Joe Galli Jr., a flamboyant and aggressive salesman from Black and Decker who had developed the popular line of DeWalt power tools. Bezos, Covey, and John Doerr aggressively pursued Galli and closed the deal with him in June, snatching him away from PepsiCo, where he had tentatively agreed to take a job running its Frito-Lay division just a day earlier.[8]

Bezos himself drew up the unorthodox new reporting structure, according to John Doerr. All Amazon executives now reported to Galli, who in turn reported to Bezos. Galli also joined the Amazon board. The J Team was renamed the S Team (the S stood for 'Senior'). Bezos was free to focus his attention on new products, public relations, his outside interests, and his family. MacKenzie was pregnant with their first child, and earlier that year, the couple had moved out of their apartment in Seattle and into a ten-million-dollar mansion in Medina, on the eastern shores of Lake Washington. 'Jeff was really thinking that he would focus on his philanthropic and other interests, which were diverse, and that he would turn Amazon over more,' Galli says. 'That was exciting to me.'

Galli, the son of an Italian American scrapyard owner from Pittsburgh, fashioned himself a cost-cutter and turn-around artist, and he was eager to make an impact on what was then one of the biggest business stages in the world. He walked the halls imperiously, wearing expensive Brioni suits and carrying a baseball bat for dramatic effect. Bezos seemed to love it, at first. 'I hired Joe to be the adult,' Bezos told employees as he introduced Galli around the company. 'But all I've asked Joe to do was pour more gasoline on the fire.'

Galli hit Amazon like an angry bull let loose on the streets of Pamplona. Everywhere around him, he saw employees operating without the discipline he had learned during his nineteen years at Black and Decker. 'There were all these brilliant kids from Stanford and Harvard running up and down the halls,' Galli says. 'But we lacked operational rigor and control. It was the Wild West.' One of his first moves was to cut a rare office perk, free Advil, which he viewed as an unnecessary expense. It sparked a near insurrection among employees.

Galli was not technical, a significant drawback at a firm whose employees somewhat defensively viewed their workplace as a software-development company, not a retailer. He read his e-mail only after his secretary printed it out for him, and he wanted to change the Amazon culture to favor phone calls instead of e-mail. He was absorbed with the trappings of authority and angled for his own private corporate jet, since he flew often to expand Amazon's business abroad. There were widespread rumors at the company that he had parked his Porsche in a prime visitor's spot one too many times and that a building security guard had finally had it towed. Galli remembers only parking it incorrectly.

In October of 1999, Galli led the acquisition of Tool Crib of the North, a small North Dakota hardware chain, and began preparations to open a tool category on the site. He flew to Cleveland to meet with executives from

Sherwin-Williams to investigate the possibility of adding a paint category, even though paint did not ship easily and colors such as Swiss Coffee did not display well on the Web. Copying one of his successful marketing gimmicks from Black and Decker, he set up what he called swarm teams of black SUVs adorned with the Amazon logo; employees were supposed to drive them around the country and give tutorials on how to use Amazon.com and the Web in general. The effort faded amid other urgent priorities, and for a few months the vehicles sat abandoned in the Pac Med parking lot, a stark contrast with the cost-cutting efforts of the time. 'Most companies have priority lists of forty-five good ideas and triage is easy,' Galli says. 'At Amazon there were a hundred and fifty good ideas all the time and Jeff was capable of developing a new one every day.'

Bezos and Galli's collaboration was troubled from the start. Though Bezos had drawn the new organizational structure himself, he kept his hands firmly on Amazon's steering wheel throughout Galli's tenure, voicing detailed opinions about everything from acquisitions to minute changes in the appearance of the home page. Galli thought he had signed up to run the company, and eventually he began to agitate for more authority. 'Frankly, Joe was disruptive,' says board member Tom Alberg. 'What Joe wanted was to be CEO, but he wasn't hired to do that.' Bezos took some time off after the birth of his first child, Preston, and then returned to find the company in an uproar over Galli's abrasive style. Amazon and its board of directors now had a leadership crisis.

But Galli was also making some important contributions. He turned category leaders like Harrison Miller and Chris Payne into general managers who had control over their own profit-and-loss statements and their costs and profit margins. He had experienced the push-and-pull of Black and Decker's relationship with big-box stores like Home Depot, so he introduced traditional retailing concepts, like the idea of earning cooperative marketing dollars, or co-op, from suppliers in exchange for highlighting their products to customers. Covey was burning out after three years of nonstop work, and Galli helped Amazon hire a new chief financial officer, Warren Jenson from Delta. Galli did not get along with Jimmy Wright, who was commuting from Bentonville, and Wright abruptly resigned, under pressure, right before the 1999 holiday season. Galli was instrumental in snagging a new head of operations, Jeff Wilke from AlliedSignal, and Wilke would play a pivotal role in the years ahead.

Customers flocked to the site over the 1999 holidays. After a year of hearing constant hype about dot-coms, consumers were ready to wade en masse into the alluring waters of the Web. The employees of Amazon held their collective breath.

There were now five distribution centers spread across the United States and two in Europe. Jimmy Wright and many of his Walmart cronies were gone, and a software system originally designed for the shipment of books had to accommodate everything from televisions to children's sandboxes. Chaos, Amazon's old foe, reared its head once again.

Soon after Thanksgiving, predictably, Amazon was failing to keep the most popular toys in stock. Kerry Morris, the buyer who joined Amazon from Walmart, says she organized Amazon employee visits to Costco and Toys 'R' Us stores around the country and had them scoop up supplies of Pokémon toys and Mattel's Walk 'N Wag dog, which were hot that season. She cleaned out the inventory of Pokémon products on the brand-new ToysRUs.com website and had everything shipped to Fernley, exploiting a rival's free-shipping promotion. 'Because they were so new to the e-commerce space that year, they really did not have the tools to alert them to us wiping out their inventory until it was too late,' Morris says.

The rapid growth once again required the company to initiate the Save Santa operation. Employees said goodbye to their families and headed off on two-week shifts to staff the customer-service phone lines or work in distribution centers across the country. Frugal to the bone, Amazon packed them two to a hotel room. To some, it was the greatest experience they had ever had at the company. Others hated it and complained vociferously. 'I won't say they were prima donnas but they weren't used to it, they didn't expect it, and a lot couldn't handle it,' says Bert Wegner, the general manager of the Fernley distribution center.

In Fernley, some employees stayed at the Golden Nugget in Reno, and after they worked the graveyard shift, they met for beers at the casino bar at six a.m. Later, a few swore they had been working alongside furloughed prisoners from a nearby jail, though that is difficult to prove. Early employee Tom Schonhoff was among a group that went to Delaware, where the facility was having problems with the quality of the temporary labor pool. 'There were a lot of temp workers that looked like the rehab center had pushed them out the back door,' he says. He watched one worker get fired for intoxication and then wet himself while he tried to protest.

Schonhoff and his team labored for a week clearing up Delaware's backlog and organizing the staff. 'We worked with sincerity and diligence. Can I say that without sounding like an ass?' he says. 'The goal was to get Christmas out the door and uphold our brand promise. We believed in it.'

A team led by Kim Rachmeler and Joel Spiegel descended on the new eight-hundred-thousand-square-foot distribution center in McDonough, Georgia. The facility was not yet finished, so employees had to wear hard hats. Their group focused on a problem called FUD: fillable, unfilled demand. These were cases where products had been sold on the website but had not yet shipped because they were lost somewhere in the cavernous distribution center. This was a more serious problem than a hundred or so customers not getting their orders for Christmas (which itself was bad enough). During the holiday season, when the sorting machines were operating at absolute peak capacity, any order that didn't successfully ship clogged up a chute and backed up another customer order, which then also wouldn't ship on time. So as the FUD accumulated, it started to stall large parts of the facility. Rachmeler's team worked to clear up the backlog but eventually it became evident that there was one item in particular that was causing the distribution center to go haywire – a missing pallet of Pokémon Jigglypuffs.

The Amazon database insisted that the Jigglypuffs had been delivered to the facility, but if so, they were either misplaced or stolen. Although Rachmeler put together a search team, the task seemed nearly impossible. The group was looking for a single box inside an eight-hundred-thousand-square-foot facility. 'It was very much like that scene at the end of *Raiders of the Lost Ark*,' Rachmeler says. She dashed out to a nearby Walmart to buy a few pairs of binoculars and then passed them out among her group so they could scan the upper levels of the metal shelving.

After three days of exhaustive searching, at two o'clock

in the morning, Rachmeler was sitting, spent and dejected, in a private office. Suddenly, the door flew open. A colleague danced in, and Rachmeler briefly wondered if she was dreaming. Then she noticed that the woman was leading a conga line of other workers and that they were jubilantly holding above their heads the missing box of Jigglypuffs.

When the 1999 holiday season ended, employees and executives of Amazon could finally take a breather. Sales were up 95 percent over the previous year, and the company had attracted three million new customers, exceeding twenty million registered accounts. Jeff Bezos was named *Time*'s Person of the Year, one of the youngest ever, and credited as 'the king of cybercommerce.'[9] It was an incredible validation for Amazon and its mission.

The company had stumbled and would write off $39 million in unsold toys. Still, thanks to herculean efforts up and down the ranks, there were no obvious disasters or disappointments for customers. Meanwhile, the websites of rivals like Toys 'R' Us and Macy's barely survived their first major holiday season and were plagued by customer complaints, bad press, and even an investigation by the Federal Trade Commission into unfulfilled promises made to shoppers.[10]

In January, after everyone recovered and many took well-deserved vacations, Amazon held its annual holiday costume party. Warren Jenson, the new chief financial officer, bought a few dozen Barbie dolls on Amazon and sewed them onto a sweater. He darkly joked that he was dressed as excess inventory. Harrison Miller thought it was only kind of funny.

Amazon had battled chaos and lived to fight another day. But it had come closer to the precipice than anyone knew. Its internal accounting was in disarray; rapid growth had led to misplaced and stolen inventory, which made it impossible to close the books on the company's fourth quarter. Accountant Jason Child was working for Amazon's German operation at the time but was called back to Seattle to take over as comptroller and tackle the problem. 'It was the craziest quarter in Amazon's history,' he says. The company sought outside help and hired a consultant through Ernst and Young. He came in, took a good look at the bedlam for a few weeks, and quit. Child and his colleagues had barely closed the books when the quarter ended in late January.

Now Amazon's board had to deal with the leadership crisis. There were complaints about Galli, who was clearly agitating to be CEO, and Bezos, who many employees felt was not taking the time to cultivate other leaders, listen to their issues, or invest in their personal growth. John Doerr quietly phoned many of the company's senior executives to get their take on the boiling tensions in the management team. To adjudicate the matter, he turned to a Silicon Valley legend, a former Columbia University football coach named Bill Campbell.

An amiable former Apple exec and the chief executive of Intuit in the mid-1990s, Campbell had a reputation for being an astute listener who could parachute into difficult corporate situations and get executives to confront their own shortcomings. Steve Jobs considered him a confidant and got him to join the Apple board when Jobs returned to the helm of that company in 1997. At Amazon, Campbell's stated mission was to help Galli play nicely with others. He commuted between Silicon Valley and Seattle for a few weeks, sitting quietly in executive meetings and talking privately with Amazon managers about the metastasizing leadership problems.

Several Amazon executives from that time believe that Campbell was also given another, more secret mandate by the board: To see if Bezos should be persuaded to step aside and let Galli take over as chief executive. This was consistent with the overall philosophy in Silicon Valley at the time, which was to bring in 'adult supervision' to execute the plans of a visionary founder. Meg Whitman had taken over at eBay; a Motorola executive named Tim Koogle had replaced founder Jerry Yang at Yahoo. The Amazon board saw Amazon's egregious spending and widening losses and heard from other executives that Bezos was impetuous and controlling. They were naturally worried that the goose who laid the golden egg might be about to crack the egg in half.

Board members, including Cook, Doerr, and Alberg, deny they ever seriously considered asking Bezos to step aside, and in any case, it would have been fruitless if Bezos resisted, since he controlled a majority of the company. But Campbell himself revealingly described his role at Amazon this way in an interview with *Forbes* magazine in 2011: 'Jeff Bezos at Amazon – I visited them early on to see if they needed a CEO and I was like, "Why would you ever replace him?" He's out of his mind, so brilliant about what he does.'[11]

Regardless, Campbell concluded Galli was unnaturally focused on issues of compensation and on perks like private planes, and he saw that employees were loyal to Bezos. He sagely recommended to the board members that they stick with their founder.

Galli says that the final decision to leave Amazon was his own. Before he joined the company, he had read the book *Odyssey: Pepsi to Apple*, by John Sculley, who had joined Apple as CEO in the mid-1980s and then ousted Steve Jobs in a boardroom coup. 'Before I went out there,

I promised myself and my family that I would never do to Jeff what Sculley did to Steve Jobs,' Galli says. 'I just felt like Jeff was falling in love more and more with his vision and what the company could be. I could anticipate it was not going to work. He wanted to have a more hands-on role. I'm just not a great number two. It's not in my DNA.'

In July of 2000, Galli left Amazon for the top job at a startup called VerticalNet, which perished soon after in the dot-com bust. Within a few months, he moved over to Newell Rubbermaid, a troubled consumer-goods company, where he managed four turbulent years of layoffs and declining stock prices. He later became CEO of the Asian manufacturer Techtronic Industries, which makes the Dirt Devil and Hoover vacuums. He has since presided over six years of growth.

After Galli left Amazon, the board tried to pair Bezos with another chief operating officer. Peter Neupert, the former Microsoft executive who ran Drugstore.com, sat in on S Team meetings for a few months. But Neupert and Bezos couldn't agree on a way to collaborate permanently, and Bezos was coming to recognize that he enjoyed being needed by colleagues and engaged in the details and that he wanted to be an active chief executive. 'He decided to spend the next umpteen years of his life building the company, as opposed to gradually withdrawing to pursue other interests,' says Tom Alberg.

The Galli experiment and all of the misadventures from that year would leave permanent scars on Amazon. As of this writing, the company has not given another executive the formal title of president or chief operating officer. Amazon wouldn't make another significant acquisition for years, and when it did, Bezos carefully considered the lessons from his reckless binge.

As a new millennium dawned, Amazon stood on the

precipice. It was on track to lose more than a billion dollars in 2000, just as the sunny optimism over the dot-com economy morphed into dark pessimism. As he had been doing over and over since the company's very first days, Bezos would have to persuade everyone that Amazon could survive the cyclone of debt and losses that it had created for itself during a singularly feverish time.

CHAPTER 4
Milliravi

The turmoil in Amazon's management during the company's frenzied years of expansion was only the start of a much longer test of faith. In 2000 and 2001, the years commonly thought of as the dot-com bust, investors, the general public, and many of his employees fell out of love with Bezos. Most observers not only dismissed the company's prospects but also began to doubt its chances of survival. Amazon stock, which since its IPO had moved primarily in one direction – up – topped out at $107 and would head steadily down over the next twenty-one months. It was a stunning fall from grace.

There were several immediate reasons for the stock market's reversal. The excesses of the dot-com boom had begun to wear on investors. Companies without actual business models were raising hundreds of millions of dollars, rushing to go public, and seeing their stock prices roar into the stratosphere despite unsound financial footing. In March of 2000, a critical cover story in *Barron's* pointed out the self-destructive rate at which Web companies like Amazon were burning through their venture capital. The dot-com boom had been built largely on faith that the market would give these young, unprofitable companies plenty of room to mature; the Barron's story reinforced fears that a day of reckoning was coming. The NASDAQ peaked on March 10, then wobbled and began to spiral downward.

The outbreak of negative sentiment toward Internet companies in general would be nudged along by other events over the course of the next two years, like the collapse of Enron and the 9/11 terrorist attacks. But the underlying reality was that many investors decided to doff their rose-colored glasses and look at Internet companies more pragmatically. And those companies included Amazon.

While other dot-coms merged or perished, Amazon survived through a combination of conviction, improvisation, and luck. Early in 2000, Warren Jenson, the fiscally conservative new chief financial officer from Delta and, before that, the NBC division of General Electric, decided that the company needed a stronger cash position as a hedge against the possibility that nervous suppliers might ask to be paid more quickly for the products Amazon sold. Ruth Porat, co-head of Morgan Stanley's global-technology group, advised him to tap into the European market, and so in February, Amazon sold $672 million in convertible bonds to overseas investors. This time, with the stock market fluctuating and the global economy tipping into recession, the process wasn't as easy as the previous fund-raising had been. Amazon was forced to offer a far more generous 6.9 percent interest rate and flexible conversion terms – another sign that times were changing. The deal was completed just a month before the crash of the stock market, after which it became exceedingly difficult for any company to raise money. Without that cushion, Amazon would almost certainly have faced the prospect of insolvency over the next year.

At the same time, rising investor skepticism and the pleadings of nervous senior executives finally convinced Bezos to shift gears. Instead of Get Big Fast, the company adopted a new operating mantra: Get Our House in Order. The watchwords were *discipline*, *efficiency*, and *eliminating waste*. The company had exploded from 1,500 employees in 1998 to 7,600 at the beginning of 2000, and now, even Bezos agreed, it needed to take a breath. The rollout of new product categories slowed, and Amazon shifted its infrastructure to technology based on the free operating system Linux. It also began a concerted effort to improve efficiency in its far-flung distribution centers. 'The company got creative because it had to,' says Warren Jenson.

Yet the dot-com collapse took a heavy toll inside the company. Employees had agreed to work tirelessly and sacrifice holidays with their families in exchange for the possibility of fantastic wealth. The cratering stock price cleaved the company in two. Employees who had joined early were still fabulously rich (though they were also exhausted). Many who had joined more recently held stock options that were now worthless.

Even top managers grew disillusioned. Three senior executives recall meeting privately in a conference room that year to write a list of all of Bezos's successes and failures on a whiteboard. The latter column included Auctions, zShops, the investments in other dot-coms, and most of Amazon's acquisitions. It was far longer than the first column, which at that time appeared to be limited to books, music, and DVDs. The future of the new toys, tools, and electronics categories was still in question.

But through it all, Bezos never showed anxiety or appeared to worry about the wild swings in public sentiment. 'We were all running around the halls with our hair on fire thinking, *What are we going to do?*' says Mark Britto, a senior vice president. But not Jeff. 'I have never seen anyone so calm in the eye of a storm. Ice water runs through his veins,' Britto says.

In the span of the next two turbulent years, Bezos redefined Amazon for the rapidly changing times. During this period, he met with two retailing legends who would focus his attention on the power of everyday low prices. He would start to think differently about conventional advertising and look for a way to mitigate the costs and inconveniences of shipping products through the mail. He would also show what was becoming a characteristic volatility, lashing out at executives who failed to meet his improbably high standards. The Amazon we know today, with all of its attributes and idiosyncrasies, is in many ways a product of the obstacles Bezos and Amazon navigated during the dot-com crash, a response to the widespread lack of faith in the company and its leadership.

In the midst of all this, Bezos burned out many of his top executives and saw a dramatic exodus from the company. But Amazon escaped the downdraft that sucked hundreds of other similarly overcapitalized dot-coms and telecoms to their deaths. He proved a lot of people wrong.

'Up until that point, I had seen Jeff only at one speed, the go-go speed of grow at all costs. I had not seen him drive toward profitability and efficiency,' says Scott Cook, the Intuit founder and an Amazon board member during that time. 'Most execs, particularly first-time CEOs who get good at one thing, can only dance what they know how to dance.

'Frankly, I didn't think he could do it.'

In June of 2000, with Amazon's stock price headed

downward along with the rest of the NASDAQ, Bezos first heard the name Ravi Suria. A native of Madras, India, and the son of a schoolteacher, Suria came to the United States to attend the University of Toledo and earned an MBA from the school of business at Tulane University. At the start of 2000, he was a new and unknown twenty-eight-year-old convertible-bond analyst at the investment bank Lehman Brothers, working in a small office on the fourteenth floor of the World Financial Center.[1] By the end of that year, he was one of the most frequently mentioned analysts on Wall Street and the unlikely nemesis of Jeff Bezos and Amazon.

For the first five years of his career, at Paine Webber and then at Lehman, Suria wrote about esoteric subjects like the overcapitalization of telecommunications companies and biotechnology firms. After raising its third high-profile round of debt and losing Joe Galli, its chief operating officer, Amazon demanded Suria's attention. Working from Amazon's latest quarterly earnings release, Suria analyzed the heavy losses of the previous holiday season and concluded that the company was in trouble, and in a widely disseminated research report, he predicted doom.

'From a bond perspective, we find the credit extremely weak and deteriorating,' he wrote in what would be the first of several scathing reports on Amazon over the next eight months. Suria said that investors should avoid Amazon debt at all costs and that the company had shown an 'exceedingly high degree of ineptitude' in areas like distribution. The haymaker was this: 'We believe that the company will run out of cash within the next four quarters, unless it manages to pull another financing rabbit out of its rather magical hat.'

The prediction generated sensational headlines around

the world (*New York Post*: 'Analyst Finally Tells the Truth about Dot-Coms'[2]). Already freaked by the market's initial decline, investors dropped Amazon, and its stock fell by another 20 percent.

Inside Amazon, Suria's report hit a nerve. Bill Curry, Amazon's chief publicist at the time, called the report 'hogwash.' Bezos expanded on that assessment when he spoke to the *Washington Post*, saying that it was 'pure unadulterated hogwash.'[3]

Suria's analysis was, in the narrowest sense and with the benefit of hindsight, incorrect. With the additional capital from the bond raise in Europe, Amazon had nearly a billion dollars in cash and securities, enough to cover all of its outstanding accounts with suppliers. Moreover, the company's negative-working-capital model would continue to generate cash from sales to fund its operations. Amazon was also well along in the process of cutting costs.

The real danger for Amazon was that the Lehman report might turn into a self-fulfilling prophecy. If Suria's predictions spooked suppliers into going on the equivalent of a bank run and demanding immediate payment from Amazon for their products, Amazon's expenses might rise. If Suria frightened customers and they turned away from Amazon because they believed, from the ubiquitous news coverage, that the Internet was only a fad, Amazon's revenue growth could go down. Then it really could be in trouble. In other words, the danger for Amazon was that in their wrongness, Suria and other Wall Street bears might prove themselves right. 'The most anxiety-inducing thing about it was that the risk was a function of the perception and not the reality,' says Russ Grandinetti, Amazon's treasurer at the time.

Which is why Amazon's damage-control response was unusually emphatic. In early summer, Jenson and

Grandinetti crisscrossed the United States and Europe, meeting with big suppliers and giving presentations on the financial health of the company. 'Even the facts were guilty until proven innocent for a short period of time,' Grandinetti says.

In one trip, Grandinetti and Jenson flew to Nashville to reassure the board of Ingram that Amazon was on sound financial footing. 'Look, we believe in you guys. We like what you're doing,' John Ingram, its president, told the Amazon executives while his mother, Martha Ingram, the company's chairman, looked on. 'But if you go down, we go down. If we're wrong about you, it's not "oh, shucks." We have such a concentration of our receivables from Amazon that we will be in trouble too.'

With Amazon's reputation and brand getting battered in the media, Bezos began a charm offensive. Suddenly, he was everywhere – on CNBC, in interviews with print journalists, talking to investors – asserting that Suria was incorrect and that Amazon's fundamentals were fine. At the time, I was the Silicon Valley reporter for *Newsweek* magazine, and I spoke to both Bezos and Jenson that summer. 'The biggest message here is, his cash flow prediction is wrong. It's just completely wrong,' Bezos told me in the first of our dozen or so conversations over the next decade.

In the transcript of that interview, Bezos seemed, even a decade later, to be full of confidence and conviction, and he was already a steady recycler of tidy Jeffisms. He re-affirmed his commitment to building a lasting company, learning from his mistakes, and developing a brand associated not with books or media but with the 'abstract concept of starting with the customer and working backward.'

But when Bezos addressed Suria's predictions, his comments seemed defensive. 'First of all, for anybody who has followed Amazon.com for any length of time, we've all seen this movie before,' he said, interjecting cavalcades of laughter between his answers. 'I know we live in a period where long term is ten minutes [laugh] but if you take any historical perspective whatsoever ... I mean, let me ask you this question. How much do you think our stock is up over the last three years? The stock is up by a factor of twenty! So this is normal. I always say about Amazon.com we don't seek controversy, but we certainly find it [laugh].'

In fact, times were not normal. The challenge from Suria and the dot-com collapse had changed the financial climate, and Bezos knew it. A few weeks later, Jenson and Bezos sat down to scrutinize Amazon's balance sheet. They came to the conclusion that even if the company showed reasonable growth, its fixed costs – the distribution centers and salary rolls – were simply too big. They would have to cut even more. Bezos announced in an internal memo that Amazon was 'putting a stake in the ground' and would be profitable by the fourth quarter of 2001.[4] Jenson said that the company 'tried to be realistic about what revenues were going to be and everyone was given a target on expenses.'

But the company couldn't catch a break in the press. When Amazon announced this goal publicly later in the year, it was subject to a new round of criticism for specifying that it would measure profitability using the pro forma accounting standard – which ignored certain expenses, like the costs of issuing stock options – instead of more conventional accounting methods.

For the next eight months, Ravi Suria continued to pummel Amazon with negative reports. His research became a litmus test for people's view of the dawning new Internet age. Those who believed in the promise of the

Web and who had bet their livelihoods on it were likely to be skeptical of Suria's negative perspective. But those who felt that the coming wave of changes threatened their businesses, their sense of the natural order, even their identities, were likely to embrace the sentiments of Suria and like-minded analysts and believe that Amazon.com was nothing more than a crazy dream precariously built on an irrationally exuberant stock market.

Perhaps that is why hyperrational Bezos grew so obsessed with the mild-mannered, bespectacled New York analyst. To Bezos, Suria represented a strain of illogical thinking that had infected the broader market: the notion that the Internet revolution and all of the brash re-invention that accompanied it would just go away. According to colleagues from the time, Bezos frequently invoked Suria's analyses in meetings. An executive in the finance group used Suria's name to coin a term for a significant mathematical error of a million dollars or more; Bezos loved it and started using it himself.

The word was *milliravi*.

It is the ambition of every technology company to be worth more than the sum of its parts. It inevitably seeks to offer a set of tools that other companies can use to reach their customers. It wants to become, in the parlance of the industry, a platform.

At the time, Microsoft was the archetype for such a strategy. Software makers tailored their products to run on the ubiquitous Windows operating system. Then Apple's iOS operating system for phones and tablets became a foundation for mobile developers to reach users. Over the years, companies like Intel, Cisco, IBM, and even AT&T built platforms and then reaped the rewards of that advantageous position.

So it was only natural that as early as 1997, executives at Amazon were thinking about how to become a platform and augment the e-commerce efforts of other retailers. Amazon Auctions was the first such attempt, followed by zShops, the service that allowed small retailers to set up their own stores on Amazon.com. Both efforts failed in the face of eBay's insurmountable popularity with mom-and-pop merchants. Nevertheless, by 2000, according to an internal company memo, Bezos was telling colleagues that by the time Amazon got to $200 billion in annual sales, he wanted revenues to be split evenly between sales from products it sold itself and commissions that it collected from other sellers who used Amazon.com.

Ironically, it was the industrywide overreach of 1999 that finally sent Amazon down the path of becoming a platform. Toys 'R' Us, though it had taken a $60 million investment from SoftBank and the private equity firm Mobius Equity Partners to create the Internet subsidiary ToysRUs.com, stumbled badly during the 1999 holidays. The offline retailer suffered a raft of negative publicity from frequent outages of its website and late shipments of orders, which in some cases missed Christmas altogether. The company ended up paying a $350,000 fine to the Federal Trade Commission for failing to fulfill its promises to customers. Amazon, meanwhile, had to write off $39 million in the unsold toy inventory that Bezos had so fervently vowed he would personally drive to the local dump.

One night after the holidays, ToysRUs.com chief financial officer Jon Foster cold-called Bezos in his office, and the Amazon CEO picked up the phone. Foster suggested joining forces; the online retailer could provide the critical infrastructure, and the offline retailer would bring the product expertise and relationships with suppliers like Hasbro. Bezos suggested the Toys 'R' Us execs meet with Harrison Miller, the category manager of the toy business. The companies held a preliminary meeting in Seattle, but at that point Amazon saw little reason to collaborate with a key competitor.

The next spring, Miller and Amazon's operations team studied the problems of stocking and shipping toys and concluded that achieving profitability in the category would require sales of nearly $1 billion. The biggest challenge was selecting and acquiring just the right selection of toys – precisely the kind of thing Toys 'R' Us did well.

A few weeks later, Miller and Mark Britto, who ran Amazon's business-development group, met with ToysRUs.com executives in a tiny conference room at Chicago's O'Hare International Airport and began formal negotiations to combine their toy-selling efforts. 'It was dawning on us how brutal it was to pick Barbies and Digimons, and it was dawning on them how expensive it would be to build a world-class e-commerce infrastructure,' Miller says.

It seemed like a perfect fit. Toys 'R' Us was adept at choosing the right toys for each season and had the necessary clout with manufacturers to get favorable prices and sufficient supplies of the most popular toys. Amazon of course had the expertise to run an online retailing business and get products to customers on time. The negotiations were, as was often the case when Jeff Bezos was involved, long and, according to Jon Foster, 'excruciating.' When both teams met for the first time, Bezos made a big show of keeping one chair open at the conference-room table, 'for the customer,' he explained. Bezos was primarily focused on building comprehensive selection and wanted Toys 'R' Us to commit to putting every available toy on the site. Toys 'R' Us argued that this was impractical and expensive. Meanwhile, it wanted to be the exclusive seller of toys on Amazon.com, which Bezos felt was too constricting.

The companies were at loggerheads for months. To get the deal done, they met somewhere in the murky middle. Toys 'R' Us agreed to sell the few hundred most popular toys, and Amazon reserved the right to complement the Toys 'R' Us selection with less popular items. Neither company got what it wanted, but for the moment, everyone was relieved. In August, the companies announced a ten-year partnership, with Amazon getting a major source of desperately needed cash and some help with its balance-sheet problems. The companies agreed that Toys 'R' Us inventory would be kept in Amazon's distribution centers – the first step toward making the most expensive and complicated part of Amazon's business a platform that other companies could use.

The deal became a template for Amazon. Having out-sourced his job running the toy category to Toys 'R' Us, Harrison Miller assumed a newly created role as head of platform services. With Neil Roseman, a vice president of engineering, he started traveling the country pitching other big retailers on duplicating the Toys 'R' Us deal.

They came close with electronics giant Best Buy, until the chain's founder, Richard Schulze, insisted late in the negotiations during a dramatic Saturday-morning conference call that Amazon give him total exclusivity in the electronics category. Bezos refused. Bed, Bath, and Beyond and Barnes & Noble also balked.

Sony Electronics explored the possibility of using Amazon to bring its Sony Style chain online. As part of the discussions, Howard Stringer, chief of Sony Corporation of America, toured the Amazon fulfillment center in

Fernley and, in a memorable moment, encountered on the warehouse floor a pile of Sony merchandise, which Amazon was technically not supposed to be selling. Stringer and his colleagues started examining the labels and writing down product numbers in an attempt to determine where the merchandise had come from. That deal didn't happen either.

But in early 2001, the effort started to gain traction. Amazon signed a deal with the book chain Borders, which had blundered by building a massive distribution facility outside Nashville for online orders before realizing it needed smaller, geographically dispersed warehouses to get books to customers quickly and inexpensively. A few months later, Amazon agreed to run AOL's shopping channel in return for a much-needed $100 million investment. Amazon also signed a deal to carry the inventory of retailer Circuit City, helping to add additional selection to the sparsely furnished shelves of Amazon's electronics category.

All of these deals improved Amazon's balance sheet in the short term, but in the long run, they were awkward for all parties. By relying on Amazon, the retailers delayed a necessary education on an important new frontier and ceded the loyalty of their customers to an aggressive upstart. That would be one of many problems for Borders and Circuit City, both of which went bankrupt in the depths of the financial crisis that began in 2008.

Bezos never got completely comfortable with these deals or with the idea of outsourcing his prized goal of limitless selection. The Toys 'R' Us arrangement in particular was hugely lucrative, but Bezos grew frustrated as it became more difficult to ensure that Amazon could offer a comprehensive toy selection. That ultimately factored heavily into the outcome of the partnership several years later – dueling lawsuits in federal court.

In the summer of 2000, with Ravi Suria continuing to press his case in public, the slide in Amazon's stock price started to accelerate. In the span of three weeks in June, it dropped from $57 to $33, shedding almost half its value. Employees started to get nervous. Bezos scrawled *I am not my stock price* on the whiteboard in his office and instructed everyone to ignore the mounting pessimism. 'You don't feel thirty percent smarter when the stock goes up by thirty percent, so when the stock goes down you shouldn't feel thirty percent dumber,' he said at an all-hands meeting. He quoted Benjamin Graham, the British-born investor who inspired Warren Buffett: 'In the short term, the stock market is a voting machine. In the long run, it's a weighing machine' that measures a company's true value. If Amazon stayed focused on the customer, Bezos declared, the company would be fine.

As if to prove his singular obsession with customer experience, Bezos placed an expensive bet, hitching Amazon's Quidditch broom to the rising fantasy series Harry Potter. In July, author J. K. Rowling published the fourth book in the series, *Harry Potter and the Goblet of Fire*. Amazon offered a 40 percent discount on the book and express delivery so customers would get it on Saturday, July 8 – the day the book was released – for the cost of regular delivery. Amazon lost a few dollars on each of about 255,000 orders, just the kind of money-losing gambit that frustrated Wall Street. But Bezos refused to see it as anything other than a move to build customer loyalty. 'That either-or mentality, that if you are doing something good for customers it must be bad for shareholders, is very amateurish,' he said in our interview that summer.

The Harry Potter promotion unsettled even the executives working on it. 'I was thinking, *Holy shit, this is a lot of money*,' says Lyn Blake, the Amazon executive in charge of books at the time. She was later inclined to admit that Bezos was right. 'We were able to assess all the good press and heard all these stories from people who were meeting their deliverymen at their front doors. And we got these testimonials back from drivers. It was the best day of their lives.' Amazon was mentioned in some seven hundred stories about the new Harry Potter novel in June and July that year.

Bezos was obsessed with the customer experience, and anyone who didn't have the same single-minded focus or who he felt wasn't demonstrating a capacity for thinking big bore the brunt of his considerable temper. One person who became a frequent target during this time was the vice president in charge of customer service, Bill Price.

A veteran of long-distance provider MCI, Price came to Amazon in 1999. He blundered early by suggesting in a meeting that Amazon executives who traveled frequently should be permitted to fly business-class. Bezos often said he wanted his colleagues to speak their minds, but at times it seemed he did not appreciate being personally challenged. 'You would have thought I was trying to stop the Earth from tilting on its axis,' Price says, recalling that moment with horror years later. 'Jeff slammed his hand on the table and said, "That is not how an owner thinks! That's the dumbest idea I've ever heard."

'Of course everyone else was thinking [executives should be allowed to fly business-class], but I was the exposed nail in the room,' Price says.

The 2000 holidays would be Price's Waterloo. His customer-service department tracked two important metrics: average talk time (the amount of time an employee spent on the phone with a customer) and contacts per order (the number of times a purchase necessitated a customer phone call or e-mail). Bezos demanded that Price reduce both, but that was fundamentally impractical. If a customer-service rep stayed on the phone long enough to fully solve each customer's problem, the number of contacts per order might go down, but the average talk time would go up. If the customer-service rep tried to jump off each call quickly, average talk times would decline, but customers would be more likely to call back.

Bezos didn't care about that simple calculus. He hated when customers called at all, seeing it as a defect in the system, and he believed that customers should be able to solve their problems themselves with the aid of self-help tools.[5] When they did call, Bezos wanted their queries answered promptly and their issues settled conclusively. There were no excuses. Price's only solution was to push his team harder, but since he had limited resources to add new people, employees were burning out.

The denouement came in a new S Team ritual called the war room, a meeting that was held daily during the holiday period to review critical company and customer issues. About thirty senior executives in the company packed into a conference room on the top floor of the Pac Med building that had expansive views of the Puget Sound. With Christmas sales ramping up and hold times on Amazon phone lines once again growing longer, Bezos began the meeting by asking Price what the customer wait times were. Price then violated a cardinal rule at Amazon: he assured Bezos that they were well under a minute but without offering much in the way of proof.

'Really?' Bezos said. 'Let's see.' On the speakerphone in

the middle of the conference table, he called Amazon's 800 number. Incongruously cheerful hold music filled the room. Bezos took his watch off and made a deliberate show of tracking the time. A brutal minute passed, then two. Other execs fidgeted uncomfortably while Price furtively picked up his cell phone and quietly tried to summon his subordinates. Bezos's face grew red; the vein in his forehead, a hurricane warning system, popped out and introduced itself to the room. Around four and a half minutes passed, but according to multiple people at the meeting who related the story, the wait seemed interminable.

Eventually a cheerful voice blurted out, 'Hello, Amazon.com!' Bezos said, 'I'm just calling to check,' and slammed down the phone. Then he tore into Price, accusing him of incompetence and lying.

Price resigned about ten months later.

While Amazon executives were courting large chain retailers, a rival was courting them. CEO of eBay Meg Whitman and one of her top deputies, Jeff Jordan, visited Amazon that fall with a tempting proposal: they wanted to take over Amazon's failing Amazon Auctions business.

Whitman made a convincing case. She highlighted eBay's focus on the unruly community of small sellers and argued that Amazon's core retail business was at fundamental odds with its attempts to host third-party sellers, since both Amazon and these merchants were often competing to sell the same items. However, eBay had no such conflict, since it didn't sell anything itself. Whitman argued that the deal could solve a problem for Amazon while also strengthening eBay's position in its primary area of focus, auctions. It was the classic win-win scenario.

But Bezos declined the offer for the same reason he kept

the ghost towns of Auctions and zShops alive on the Amazon website. He wasn't ready to give up or relinquish Amazon's hopes of becoming a platform for small and midsized retailers. The fact that third-party selling on Amazon wasn't working meant, to Bezos, only that it wasn't working at that particular moment.

The main problem was that Auctions and zShops were siloed on the Amazon website and got little attention from customers. Bezos referred to them as cul-de-sacs on the site. To the extent they enjoyed any traffic at all, it was through a feature called Crosslinks, in which links to third-party auctions appeared on related retail pages. For example, a seller hawking vintage fishing rods could choose to list his auctions via Crosslinks on the pages of books or movies about fly-fishing.[6]

Amazon experimented with using algorithms to analyze specific phrases on product pages and auctions and then automatically matching up similar products. The technology resulted in some memorable miscues. For example, the product page for a novel titled *The Subtle Knife*, the sequel to the young-adult novel *The Golden Compass*, carried links to a variety of survivalist-minded sellers in the auctions category who were hawking switchblades and SS weaponry kits. 'There were some very unhappy results,' says Joel Spiegel. 'The person whose mission in life was to sell children's books would storm into my office yelling, Why the hell do I have Nazi memorabilia listed on my pages?'

One weekend in the fall of 2000, Bezos called various S Team members and executives to a daylong meeting in the basement of his lakefront mansion in Medina so they could examine why the third-party efforts were failing. Despite the problems, the group recognized that Crosslinks on the product pages were generating most of the traffic to Amazon's third-party sellers.

That was an important observation. Traffic on Amazon was oriented around Amazon's reliable product catalog. On eBay, a customer might search for the Hemingway novel *The Sun Also Rises* and get dozens of auctions of new and vintage copies. If a customer searched for the book on Amazon, there was one single page, with a definitive description of the novel, and that's where customers flocked.

Amazon executives reasoned that day that they had the Internet's most authoritative product catalog and that they should exploit it. That, it turned out, was the central insight that not only turned Amazon into a thriving platform for small online merchants but powers a good deal of its success today. If Amazon wanted to host other sellers on its site, it would have to list their wares right alongside its own products on the pages that customers actually visited. 'It was a great meeting,' says Jeff Blackburn. 'By the end of the day we all felt one hundred percent sure that this was the future.'

That fall, Amazon announced a new initiative called Marketplace. The effort started with used books. Other sellers of books were invited to advertise their wares directly within a box on Amazon's own book pages. Customers got to choose whether to purchase the item from Amazon itself or from a third-party seller. If they chose the latter, either because the seller had a lower price or because the product was out of stock at Amazon, the company would lose the sale but collect a small commission. 'Jeff was super clear from the beginning,' says Neil Roseman. 'If somebody else can sell it cheaper than us, we should let them and figure out how they are able to do it.'

Marketplace launched in November 2000 in the books

category and immediately drew protests. Two trade groups, the Association of American Publishers and the Authors Guild, each posted a public letter on its website complaining that Amazon was undermining the sale of new books in favor of used books and in the process taking royalties out of the pockets of authors.[7] 'If your aggressive promotion of used book sales becomes popular among Amazon's customers, this service will cut significantly into sales of new titles, directly harming authors and publishers,' said the letter.

The protest was nothing compared to the consternation over Marketplace inside Amazon. Category managers realized they could now lose a sale to a competitor within the previously safe confines of their own store. Even worse, a customer might have a bad experience with that seller and end up leaving a negative review. And the company's buyers now had to contend with irate publishers and other manufacturers who wanted to know why used products from small, often unauthorized sellers were being sold directly next to their new wares. This debate would play out gradually over the next few years as Amazon expanded the effort and added both new and used products from third-party sellers to each category. Marketplace, in effect, made it more difficult for the retailers inside Amazon to accomplish the lofty goals Bezos himself had set for them.

'Imagine you're the guy on the hook for a zillion dollars' worth of inventory,' says Chris Payne, recalling his initial reaction to Marketplace. 'And this other lunatic comes over putting low-priced crap on your page. You can bet that leads to some squabbles.'

The new strategy would result in years of tension between various divisions, between Amazon and its suppliers, and between industry trade groups and the company. Bezos didn't care about any of that, as long as it offered more choices to customers and, in the process, gave Amazon a greater selection of products. With a single brilliant and nonintuitive strategic move, he managed to upset almost everybody, even his own colleagues. 'As usual,' says Mark Britto, 'it was Jeff against the world.'

One Saturday in early December 2000, Britto and Doug Boake, business-development executives who joined Amazon in the Accept.com acquisition, were in Fernley gift-wrapping packages when Britto got a call on his cell phone. It was Bezos. He told them to meet him that night in Bentonville, Arkansas. They were going to visit Walmart.

Though it sounds unlikely, now that they are archrivals, Amazon was pitching Walmart on the idea of operating its website. Walmart was the undisputed gorilla of retailing, opening hundreds of new stores a year around the world and remaining relatively unharmed by the bear market. Lee Scott, just the third CEO in Walmart history, had personally invited Bezos to his home. Britto and Boake happily put down the gift wrap and headed to the Reno airport.

That evening, the Amazon executives met in Bentonville, where they got a taste of Walmart's brand of frugality. Walmart booked them rooms at a local Days Inn. That night, Bezos, Britto, and Boake had dinner at a nearby Chili's and walked around the historic town square.

The next morning, a procession of three black Chevy Suburbans rolled up to the hotel at the appointed time. The drivers wore earpieces, sunglasses, and steely expressions. The Amazon executives were ushered into the middle car and marveled at the abundance of security. Though he didn't know it, Bezos was glimpsing his own future.

The cars drove to a large house in a gated community off a golf course, and the Amazon execs got out, walked up, and knocked on the front door. Linda Scott, the CEO's wife, opened the door and immediately put them at ease. She told Bezos she was a big fan of his and had watched his appearance on CNBC's *Squawk Box* a few weeks before.

The Amazon execs met Lee Scott and his chief financial officer, Tom Schoewe, in a dining room with big bay windows. For two hours, over pastries and coffee, the CEOs spoke frankly. They talked about the companies' shared culture and the principles Bezos had taken from Sam Walton's autobiography. Bezos spoke generally about Amazon's attempts at personalization and the technology behind collaborative filtering – the algorithms that determined that people who bought one particular kind of product were inclined to purchase another specific set of products.

Scott noted that Walmart had similar techniques. It could measure whether a certain item, such as a globe for children, could lift the sale of another item, like a coloring book, if they were placed next to each other on a store display. Both companies had a deep interest in testing these combinations.

Scott also talked about how Walmart viewed advertising and pricing as two ends on the same spectrum. 'We spend only forty basis points on marketing. Go look at our shareholder statement,' he said. 'Most of that goes to newspapers to inform people about what is in our stores. The rest of our marketing dollars we pour into reducing prices. Our marketing strategy is our pricing strategy, which is everyday low pricing.'

Before the meeting, Rick Dalzell had warned Bezos to be wary of the crafty and astute Walmart chief. But Bezos was sponging up everything the older man said. Amazon had always considered itself an e-commerce company, not a retailer. Now Bezos needed to learn some of the fundamental rules in a professional sport that, up until that point, he had been playing only amateurishly.

After the first hour, the executives got down to business. Scott wanted to know what Amazon had in mind. The execs explained the Toys 'R' Us deal and the nascent effort to operate the websites and handle distribution for other retailers. Scott said noncommittally that it was worth talking about. To conclude the meeting, he leaned forward and said, 'So, is there something deeper and more strategic that we should be considering?'

Bezos said he would think about how to make the proposal more interesting to Walmart. The men shook hands, and the Amazon executives returned to the Suburban waiting out front. As they were being driven to the airport, Britto and Boake agreed that Lee Scott's parting words could be interpreted only as a veiled acquisition offer. 'Really, is that what he meant by that?' Bezos asked.

Of course Bezos wasn't interested in selling his company to Walmart, and Scott ultimately rejected the idea of outsourcing a crucial part of Walmart's online operation to Amazon. The conversation between the two retailers never developed further and the meeting remained a quirk of history, a tantalizing suggestion of what might have been. The two companies would continue on separate paths, which, years later, would converge to produce a fierce rivalry.

In February 2001, Ravi Suria reared his head again. He published another report that questioned Amazon's reserve of capital. With Amazon facing $130 million in annual interest expenses on its debt and given the prospect of its continued losses, Suria predicted that the company would face a cash shortage by the end of the year.

This time, Amazon made it personal. Spokesman Bill Curry retorted in an interview that Suria's report was 'silly.'[8] Warren Jenson paid a personal visit to Lehman vice chairman Howard Clark, and John Doerr called Dick Fuld, chief executive of the investment bank, and implored him to have the firm review Suria's research.

Years later, over cocktails at midtown Manhattan's Trump Bar, with its dim lights and dark, polished wood, Suria complained that Amazon exerted unbearable pressure on him during that time. 'They wanted to fire me. Everyone at Lehman hated my guts during those months,' he says. 'Every time I picked up the phone some-one was screaming at me.'

Suria now helps to run a hedge fund and has a bitter view of his history with the online retailer. 'Amazon was like a high-school bully picking on an elementary-school kid. I was twenty-nine years old. It was a character-defining moment [for them], and as far as I'm concerned, they failed it miserably. It ruined my life for two years.' Suria believes Bezos is 'deranged' and proudly notes that he hasn't bought anything from Amazon since he tangled with the company.

But there's no doubt that investors were keyed into Suria's analysis. The February research report, his last at Lehman Brothers before departing for the hedge fund Duquesne Capital Management, sent Amazon stock roar-ing toward the ignominious land of the single digits. It had another repercussion as well. In regulatory papers filed by his lawyer that month, Bezos revealed intentions to sell a small parcel of stock, worth about $12 million. Since

Lehman had allowed Amazon to see a version of Suria's report before it was published, the timing of the stock sale suggested to the Securities and Exchange Commission that Bezos was deliberately dumping Amazon shares before bad news was made public.

In retrospect, one can see it was the farthest thing from the truth; Bezos remained completely convinced of the eventual success of his venture. But the SEC – which had been hammered by critics for whiffing on the dot-com bubble – announced an investigation into the possibility of insider trading. The investigation went nowhere, but the *New York Times*, among other publications, splashed the news prominently on the front of its business section.[9] 'I don't care who you are or how much chutzpah you have,' says Warren Jenson. 'It's not fun picking up the *Times* and seeing your picture above the fold accused of insider trading. We are all products of what we've been through. This is one of the things that made Jeff the person he is. That scar does not heal easily.'

Now Amazon once again had to come to terms with the practical effects of its deteriorating stock price and its overzealous expansion. That month Amazon repriced the stock options of employees. They could trade three shares at their old stock price for one share at the new price – a move that boosted the morale of employees whose options, with the cratering stock prices, had become worthless. Amazon also announced plans to cut thirteen hundred employees, or about 15 percent of its workforce. The company was accustomed to adding people, not losing them, and the layoffs were brutal. People who had been hired just months before were summarily fired, their careers and personal lives left in tatters. Mitch Berman, a merchandising manager in the DVD group, had previously worked at Coca-Cola in Atlanta and had moved to Seattle for the job. He was employed by Amazon for all of four months and never understood why it didn't work out. 'I had literally picked up my entire life and moved across the country,' he says. 'Obviously, I felt burned. I had to roll up my sleeves and start all over again.' He's now a life coach living in Barcelona, Spain.

Diego Piacentini, a new executive from Apple, was thrust directly into the mess. Bezos hired the suave, Italian-born Piacentini in early 2000 to take the top spot running Amazon's international operations. Piacentini's old boss Steve Jobs had expressed incredulity at the move in his typically strident way. Over lunch in the Apple cafeteria in Cupertino, Jobs asked Piacentini why he would possibly want to go to a boring retailer when Apple was in the process of reinventing computing. Then in the same breath, Jobs suggested that maybe the career move revealed that Piacentini was so dumb that it was a good thing he was leaving Apple.

At first, Piacentini himself wondered why he'd made the move. He had joined Amazon right in the middle of Bezos's conflict with Joe Galli. After his first few weeks, Piacentini called his wife back in Milan and told her not to pack their things for Seattle quite yet. But after Galli left, he grew more comfortable at Amazon. A year later, during the layoffs, he was tasked with closing Amazon's new multilingual call center in The Hague. The facility had been poorly selected. The Hague was a financial and diplomatic hub, and the call center was incongruously located in a marble-floored building that had once been occupied by a bank. It never should have been opened in the first place, but 'people at various levels were making decentralized decisions to move quickly and the process wasn't strong,' Piacentini says.

The center had been open only a few months when

Piacentini arrived to shut it down. With a few colleagues from Seattle, he collected the two hundred and fifty or so employees in the large marble lobby and made a brief speech in English telling everyone the bad news. Employees started howling and shouting, according to one Amazon employee who was there. One woman began sobbing and rolling on the floor.

Inside Amazon's Seattle offices, it seemed like the walls were closing in – at times, literally. On the morning of Wednesday, February 28, Neil Roseman, Rick Dalzell, and an executive named Tom Killalea met with Bezos in his private conference room to brief him on a potentially serious security breach at Amazon's used-book marketplace, Exchange.com. A few minutes into the conversation, the room started to shake.

It started slowly, a rumbling in the floor that passed into the walls and then intensified. The four men looked questioningly at one another and then dove under the side-by-side door-desks at the center of the room. Forty-six miles southwest, the Earth had suddenly shifted, and the Nisqually earthquake, 6.9 on the Richter scale, had begun.

Outside, chunks of brick and mortar were shaken loose from the sixty-eight-year-old Pacific Medical building and rained to the ground. Inside, the sprinklers went off and employees rolled under their mercifully thick door-desks. Bezos's tiny conference room was full of tchotchkes like Star Trek figurines and water guns, many of which noisily rattled to the floor. Also in the room was a twenty-two-pound ball made of the dense metal tungsten, a memento from Stewart Brand and the organizers of the Clock of the Long Now. Halfway through the earthquake, the executives in the room heard the ominous sound of the ball rolling off its stand. 'I was the low man on the totem pole, so my legs were halfway exposed,' says Neil Roseman, only partly in jest. Fortunately, the ball thudded harmlessly to the floor.

As the earthquake progressed, Killalea poked his head out, retrieved his laptop, and checked to see if the Amazon website was still running. (He would win a Just Do It award and get to keep an old ratty sneaker for that bit of bravado.)

The rumbling stopped after forty-five seconds, and employees evacuated the building. In a commanding performance, Bezos donned an item from his collection of oddities, a hard hat shaped like a ten-gallon cowboy hat, scrambled onto the roof of a car in the parking lot, and organized pairs of employees to reenter the building and collect their valuables. The building owner later shut down the tenth and twelfth floors for repairs, and for months plastic tarps covered patches of the façade where bricks had shaken loose.

When I visited Amazon for another *Newsweek* story that March, the stock was hovering around $10 and the city inspector had closed the main lobby. It was an unattractive sight and an unavoidable metaphor for the company's rapid descent. Visitors were ushered into the basement through the back of the building, past a large placard warning of falling bricks.

In early 2001, Amazon's position and future prospects remained dubious. The problem wasn't only its diminishing market capitalization or its overlarded staffing and expansion efforts. Growth, particularly in the oldest category, books – still more than half its business at the time – appeared to be slowing after years of annual double-digit increases. Inside the company, executives were fearful that the slowdown augured an overall decrease in online shopping itself. 'We were scared to death,' says Erich Ringewald, a vice president in charge of Marketplace. 'Books were decelerating, and everyone thought that Walmart.com would start selling books at a loss to keep us from growing.'

Amazon then did something rare in its history. Warren Jenson, pushing to improve margins to meet the company's self-imposed profitability deadline, convinced Bezos to quietly raise prices in the older media categories. Amazon reduced its discounts on bestselling books and started charging more to overseas customers who were buying from the domestic website. Bezos signed off on the increases, but another important meeting quickly made him change his mind.

On a Saturday morning that spring, at the Starbucks inside the Bellevue Barnes & Noble where he had conducted Amazon's very first meetings, Bezos met Jim Sinegal, the founder of Costco. Sinegal was a casual, plain-speaking native of Pittsburgh, a Wilford Brimley look-alike with a bushy white mustache and an amiable countenance that concealed the steely determination of an entrepreneur. Well into retirement age, he showed no interest in slowing down. The two had plenty in common. For years Sinegal, like Bezos, had battled Wall Street analysts who wanted him to raise Costco's prices on clothing, appliances, and packaged foods. Like Bezos, Sinegal had rejected multiple acquisition offers over the years, including one from Sam Walton, and he liked to say he didn't have an exit strategy – he was building a company for the long term.

Bezos had set up the meeting to ask Sinegal about using Costco as a wholesale supplier for products that manufacturers still wouldn't sell to Amazon. That idea never went anywhere, but over the next hour, Bezos listened carefully and once again drew key lessons from a more experienced retail veteran.

Sinegal explained the Costco model to Bezos: it was all about customer loyalty. There are some four thousand products in the average Costco warehouse, including limited-quantity seasonal or trendy products called treasure-hunt items that are spread out around the building. Though the selection of products in individual categories is limited, there are copious quantities of everything there – and it is all dirt cheap. Costco buys in bulk and marks up everything at a standard, across-the-board 14 percent, even when it could charge more. It doesn't advertise at all, and earns most of its gross profit from the annual membership fees.

'The membership fee is a onetime pain, but it's reinforced every time customers walk in and see forty-seven-inch televisions that are two hundred dollars less than anyplace else,' Sinegal said. 'It reinforces the value of the concept. Customers know they will find really cheap stuff at Costco.'[10]

Costco's low prices generated heavy sales volume, and the company then used its significant size to demand the best possible deals from suppliers and raise its per-unit gross profit dollars. Its vendors hadn't been happy about being squeezed but they eventually came around. 'You can fill Safeco Field with the people that don't want to sell to us,' Sinegal said. 'But over a period of time, we generate enough business and prove we are a good customer and pay our bills and keep our promises. Then they say, "Why the hell am I not doing business with these guys. I gotta be stupid. They are a great form of distribution."

'My approach has always been that value trumps everything,' Sinegal continued. 'The reason people are prepared to come to our strange places to shop is that we have value. We deliver on that value constantly. There are no annuities in this business.'

A decade later and finally preparing to retire, Sinegal remembers that conversation well. 'I think Jeff looked at it and thought that was something that would apply to his business as well,' he says. Sinegal doesn't regret educating an entrepreneur who would evolve into a ferocious competitor. 'I've always had the opinion that we have shamelessly stolen any good ideas,' he says.

In 2008, Sinegal bought a Kindle e-reader that turned out to be defective and wrote Bezos a laudatory e-mail after Amazon's customer service replaced his device for free. Bezos wrote back, 'I want you to consider me your personal customer service agent on the Kindle.'

Perhaps Amazon's founder realized he owed Sinegal a debt of gratitude, because he took the lessons he learned during that coffee in 2001 and applied them with a vengeance.

The Monday after the meeting with Sinegal, Bezos opened an S Team meeting by saying he was determined to make a change. The company's pricing strategy, he said, according to several executives who were there, was incoherent. Amazon preached low prices but in some cases its prices were higher than competitors'. Like Walmart and Costco, Bezos said, Amazon should have 'everyday low prices.' The company should look at other large retailers and match their lowest prices, all the time. If Amazon could stay competitive on price, it could win the day on unlimited selection and on the convenience afforded to customers who didn't have to get in the car to go to a store and wait in line.

That July, as a result of the Sinegal meeting, Amazon announced it was cutting prices of books, music, and videos by 20 to 30 percent. 'There are two kinds of retailers: there are those folks who work to figure how to charge more, and there are companies that work to figure how to charge less, and we are going to be the second, full-stop,' he said in that month's quarterly conference call with analysts, coining a new Jeffism to be repeated over and over ad nauseam for years.

Bezos had seemingly made up his mind that he was no longer going to indulge in financial maneuvering as a way to escape the rather large hole Amazon had dug for itself, and it wasn't just through borrowing Sinegal's business plan. At a two-day management and board offsite later that year, Amazon invited business thinker Jim Collins to present the findings from his soon-to-be-published book *Good to Great*. Collins had studied the company and led a series of intense discussions at the offsite. 'You've got to decide what you're great at,' he told the Amazon executives.

Drawing on Collins's concept of a flywheel, or self-reinforcing loop, Bezos and his lieutenants sketched their own virtuous cycle, which they believed powered their business. It went something like this: Lower prices led to more customer visits. More customers increased the volume of sales and attracted more commission-paying third-party sellers to the site. That allowed Amazon to get more out of fixed costs like the fulfillment centers and the servers needed to run the website. This greater efficiency then enabled it to lower prices further. Feed any part of this flywheel, they reasoned, and it should accelerate the loop. Amazon executives were elated; according to several members of the S Team at the time, they felt that, after five years, they finally understood their own business. But when Warren Jenson asked Bezos if he should put the flywheel in his presentations to analysts, Bezos asked him not to. For now, he considered it the secret sauce.

In September 2001, Bezos, Mark Britto, Harrison Miller, and two Amazon publicists flew to Minneapolis to announce a long-planned deal with Target. On the day of the announcement, they arrived just before 8:00 a.m. at the retailer's downtown headquarters and took an elevator to a television studio on the thirty-second floor of Target Plaza South, one of the tallest buildings in the city. As they were in the elevator, Amazon PR chief Bill Curry got a call from a colleague in Seattle. A plane had hit the World Trade Center. When they got upstairs, they asked their Target counterparts to turn on the television.

Together the Amazon and Target executives watched in horror as the second plane hit the World Trade Center. No one had any idea what was going on. Curry, a former publicist for Boeing, observed that the plane looked like a 767. Plans to publicize the partnership with a series of satellite-television interviews were scrubbed. The tragic morning then unfolded before them, as it did for everyone else around the world. The Target building was evacuated and then reopened, and the Amazon and Target executives stood together for much of the day watching a single television.

In the afternoon, Bezos, still on his photography kick, walked around the Target office taking pictures with his Elph digital camera to record the awful, historic day. Someone complained to Dale Nitschke, the Target manager in charge of the Amazon partnership, and he quietly asked Bezos to stop.

The skies were closed to commercial flights for the next seventy-two hours, so the Amazon group couldn't fly back to Seattle. On the morning of September 12, they bought additional clothes and an automobile cell phone charger from a Marshall Field's department store, rented a white Mazda minivan from Hertz at an exorbitant daily rate, and headed west on I-90, a highway that ended in Seattle.[11] Britto drove, Miller sat in the front seat, and they all stewed, shell-shocked, listening to music and their own thoughts. 'Driving through the farmland and thinking about what was next was surreal and cathartic,' Miller says.

While Britto drove, Bezos used his phone and helped to organize a donation drive on the Amazon home page, which in two weeks would raise seven million dollars for the Red Cross. They stopped to stretch their legs in the Badlands and spent the night at a Mount Rushmore hotel that Bezos remembered visiting with his family as a child. Flags were at half-mast at the Mount Rushmore memorial, and the tourists were somber. Some tourists recognized Bezos – not as the Amazon.com founder, but as the CEO who had just appeared in a goofy ad for Taco Bell to raise money for the Special Olympics. Afterward, the executives bought matching navy blue Mount Rushmore windbreakers and ate at the park cafeteria.

The group kept driving west. Later that day, the skies briefly reopened for private flights, and Bezos's plane met them on a small airstrip. Bowing to the gravity of the moment, Bezos did not make his usual announcement that the company was not paying for the flight; they flew to Seattle, and their solemn cross-country odyssey ended.

Bezos may have been famous to some because of his notorious Taco Bell ad, but in fact Amazon had some of the most memorable TV ads of the dot-com era. In the Sweatermen series, created by the San Francisco office of an agency called FCB Worldwide, a campy chorus of men dressed like Mr. Rogers extolled the virtues of unlimited selection on Amazon. The playful, retro shtick reflected the goofy sensibility of Amazon's CEO. But a year into the bust, Bezos was desperately trying to figure out how he could stop advertising altogether.

As usual, Bezos battled his marketing executives. They argued that Amazon had to be on the airwaves to reach new customers. As Amazon's losses mounted, Bezos's opposition hardened. He had the marketing department organize tests, running commercials in only the Minneapolis and Portland media markets and measuring whether they generated an uptick in local purchases. They did – but, Bezos concluded, not enough to justify the investment.[12] 'It was pretty clear afterward that TV advertising wasn't really having an impact,' says Mark Stabingas, a finance vice president who joined the company from Pepsi.

The result was not only the cancellation of all of Amazon's television advertising but another dramatic purge of the marketing department. Alan Brown, a chief marketing officer who came from MasterCard, left after only a year on the job. Centralized marketing at Amazon was shut down and its tasks spread out among the e-mail marketing and worldwide discovery groups led by Andy Jassy and Jeff Holden. Amazon wouldn't advertise on television again for another seven years, not until the introduction of the Kindle. 'There can be only one head of marketing at Amazon, and his name is Jeff,' says Diane Lye, a British senior manager who led Amazon's data-mining department and helped run the advertising tests.

Bezos felt that word of mouth could deliver customers to Amazon. He wanted to funnel the saved marketing dollars into improving the customer experience and accelerating the flywheel. And as it happened, at the time, Amazon was conducting an experiment that was actually working this way – free shipping.

During the 2000 and 2001 holidays, Amazon offered free shipping to customers who placed orders of a hundred dollars or more. The promotion was expensive but clearly boosted sales. Customer surveys showed that shipping costs were one of the biggest hurdles to ordering online. Amazon hadn't yet found a good way to convince customers to shop in multiple categories – to buy books, kitchen appliances, and software, for example, all at the same time. The hundred-dollar threshold motivated buyers to fill their baskets with a variety of items.

In early 2002 late on a Monday night, Bezos called a meeting in Warren Jenson's conference room to talk about how to turn the holiday-season free shipping into a permanent offer. This was one way he could redeploy his marketing budget. Jenson in particular was opposed to this. The CFO worried that free shipping would be expensive and wasteful, since Amazon would be giving discounts to all comers, including those customers who were inclined to place large orders anyway.

Then one of his deputies, a finance vice president named Greg Greeley, mentioned how airlines had segmented their customers into two groups – business people and recreational travelers – by reducing ticket prices for those customers who were willing to stay at their destination through a Saturday night. Greeley suggested doing the equivalent at Amazon. They would make the free-shipping offer permanent, but only for customers who were willing to wait a few extra days for their order. Just like the airlines, Amazon would, in effect, divide its customers into two groups: those whose needs were time sensitive, and everyone else. The company could then reduce the expense of free shipping, because workers in the fulfillment centers could pack those free-shipping orders in the trucks that Amazon sent off to express shippers and the post office whenever the trucks had excess room. Bezos loved it. 'That is exactly what we are going to do,' he said.

Amazon introduced the service, called Free Super Saver Shipping, in January 2002 for orders above $99. In the span of a few months, that number dropped to $49, and then to $25. Super Saver Shipping would set the stage for a variety of new initiatives in the years ahead, including the subscription club Amazon Prime.

Not everyone was happy with this outcome. After that meeting, Warren Jenson took Greeley aside and berated him, in that moment seeing free shipping as nothing but another potential balance-sheet buster.

Over the next year, Amazon executives quit in droves. They left because their stock had been vested or because they no longer believed in the mission or because their comparatively low salaries and the depressed stock price guaranteed that they were not getting wealthy anytime soon. Some were tired and just wanted a change. Others felt Bezos didn't listen to them and that he wasn't about to start. Almost all figured that Amazon's best days were behind it. The company reached incredible levels of attrition in 2002 and 2003. 'The number of employees at that point other than Jeff who thought he could turn it into an eighty-billion-dollar company – that's a short list,' says Doug Boake, who departed for the Silicon Valley startup OpenTable. 'He just never stopped believing. He never blinked once.'

They all had their reasons. David Risher left to teach at the University of Washington's business school. Joel

Spiegel wanted to spend more time with his three teenage kids before they left home. Mark Britto wanted to get back to the Bay Area. Harrison Miller was exhausted and needed a change. Chris Payne left for Microsoft, where he would help launch the Bing search engine, after which he would end up as a top executive at eBay. And on and on.

People left and afterward they took a breath and felt disoriented, like they had escaped a cult. Though they didn't share it openly, many just couldn't take working for Bezos any longer. He demanded more than they could possibly deliver and was extremely stingy with praise. At the same time, many felt a tremendous loyalty to Bezos and would later marvel at how much they accomplished at Amazon. Kim Rachmeler shared a favorite quote she heard from a colleague around that time. 'If you're not good, Jeff will chew you up and spit you out. And if you're good, he will jump on your back and ride you into the ground.'

Bezos never despaired over the mass exodus. One of his gifts, his colleagues said, was being able to drive and motivate his employees without getting overly attached to them personally. But he did usually make time in his calendar for a private meeting with exiting executives. Harrison Miller told Bezos at their parting lunch that the accomplishment at Amazon he was most proud of was the platform-services business with large retailers, which was responsible for a third of Amazon's cash flow in 2002. 'Yeah, but don't forget, you built our first toy store and it was great,' Bezos said, another indication he remained more focused on his long-term goal of unlimited selection than on his short-term revenue-boosting partnerships, however lucrative.

At his going-away meeting, Brian Birtwistle wrote a list on a cocktail napkin of his favorite moments at Amazon.

Bezos and Birtwistle took a picture with the napkin and recalled their drive from Harvard's business school to the Boston airport. 'This whole journey started with a car ride and what a ride it's been,' Bezos said.

Bezos wasn't always so sentimental. Christopher Zyda, Amazon's Chief Financial Officer, defected to eBay, and, in a throwback to Walmart's lawsuit over poaching, Amazon sued Zyda in federal court, alleging that he was violating the noncompete clause in his employment contract. The lawsuit, like the Walmart poaching case against Amazon, was settled with no consequential damages. But if his legal strategy was any guide, Bezos was clearly worried about high-flying eBay, whose market capitalization now exceeded Amazon's by a significant margin.

The elevated competition between the two companies put at least one person in an awkward position: Scott Cook, Intuit's founder, was still on the boards of both companies. Now it was clear he would need to cut ties with one of them. He chose to leave Amazon and stick with eBay. 'Jeff was angry, but not at me,' Cook says. 'He was angry at himself for not stopping me when I said I wanted to join the eBay board in the first place. He doesn't like losing.'

Warren Jenson also left. Amazon's CFO explained that he wanted to return to his wife and children, who were still living in Atlanta, and that the time was right because Amazon was finally clear of its most serious financial challenges. This was almost certainly not the whole story.

Jenson and Bezos were at loggerheads. Jenson had tried to placate angry investors by getting the company to profitability. He raised the last round of capital from European bonds at a critical time and forced Bezos to make tough decisions when the company's runway was getting short. But he also pushed to raise prices and campaigned against free shipping. 'I would never claim to be perfect,' he says. 'I always tried to do what was right for the business.'

Jenson's legacy at Amazon was hotly debated even a decade later. Some thought he was overly political. Others argued that he helped to direct the company away from its path of reckless growth and that he assembled an accomplished finance team that would go on to make significant contributions at Amazon and throughout the technology world. The evidence for the pro-Jenson case is difficult to dismiss. 'Warren was the right CFO for the time,' says Dave Stephenson, a finance exec who worked for him at Amazon. 'He forced hard decisions and hard debates. He would always stand up to Jeff a little bit more directly than anyone else.'

To replace Jenson, Bezos recruited another chief financial officer from General Electric, Tom Szkutak, sealing the deal with an impassioned two-page letter to Szkutak and his wife about the impact they could make at a historic juncture for the Internet. Szkutak was also the right CFO for Amazon at the right time. He would facilitate rather than challenge Bezos's ambitious forays into various new businesses in the years ahead.

Perhaps the most rancorous exits in the company during this time stemmed from the intramural combat between two departments: Amazon's editorial group and its personalization team. The editorial division, which dated back to Amazon's earliest days, was composed of writers and editors who added a human touch to the Amazon home page and to the individual product pages. Bezos originally formed the group to cultivate the literary aura of an independent bookstore and recommend books to customers that they might not have otherwise found.

But over the years, the personalization group started to infringe on the editorial group's turf. P13N, as it was cleverly abbreviated (there are thirteen letters between the *p* and the last *n* in *personalization*), used analytics and algorithms to generate recommendations crafted to appeal to individual customers based on their previous purchases. Over the years, P13N kept getting better. In 2001, Amazon started making suggestions based on the items customers looked at, not just the products they bought.

The juxtaposition between the two approaches was stark. Editorial was handselling products with clever writing and intuitive decisions about what to promote. ('We ain't lion: this adorable Goliath Backpack Pal is a *grrreat* way to scare away those first-day-of-school jitters,' read the home page in 1999, promoting a lion-shaped backpack for kids.) Personalization was skipping the puns and building a store for every customer using cold, hard data to stock the shelves with the items that customers were statistically the most likely to buy.

Bezos did not explicitly favor one group over the other, but he looked at the results of tests. Over time it became clear that the humans couldn't compete. PEOPLE FORGET THAT JOHN HENRY DIED IN THE END, read a sign on the wall of the P13N office, a reference to the folktale of the steel driver who raced to dig a hole in competition with a steam-powered drilling machine; he won the contest but died immediately afterward.

Most editors and writers were reassigned or laid off. Susan Benson – Rufus's owner – took a sabbatical from Amazon. When she returned, Jason Kilar, then the vice president of media, invited her to a meeting that he described ominously in e-mails as an 'editorial game changer.' She knew she was in trouble. 'It had a lot do with how to dismantle editorial and turn it into part of the automated universe,' Benson says. 'I thought, *Yeah, my time here is done.*'

An algorithm called Amabot brought about the downfall of editorial. Amabot replaced the personable, handcrafted sections of the site with automatically generated recommendations in a standardized layout. The system handily won a series of tests and demonstrated it could sell as many products as the human editors. Soon after, an anonymous Amazon employee placed a three-line classified advertisement in the Valentine's Day 2002 edition of the *Stranger*, an independent Seattle newspaper. It read:

DEAREST AMABOT

If you only had a heart to absorb our hatred ...
Thanks for nothing, you jury-rigged rust bucket.
The gorgeous messiness of flesh and blood will prevail!

* * *

In January 2002, Amazon reported its first profitable quarter, posting net income of $5 million, a meager but symbolic penny per share. Marketing costs were down, international revenues from the United Kingdom and Germany were up, and sales from third-party sellers on the vaunted Amazon platform made up 15 percent of the company's orders. The exclamation point on the accomplishment was that Amazon had turned a profit by both controversial pro forma accounting standards and conventional methods.

Amazon had finally shown the world that it wasn't just another doomed dot-com. The stock price immediately jumped 25 percent in after-hours trading, clawing its way out of the single digits. Kathy Savitt, a new Amazon publicist, told Bezos she wanted to frame some of the positive news articles and hang them on the office walls. He told her he would rather frame the negative stories like *Barron's* infamous Amazon.bomb cover. When people wrote or said positive things about Amazon, he wanted employees to remember the *Barron's* article and remain scared.

The company wasn't yet entirely clear of its balance-sheet problems but it was on its way. In the first quarter the following year, Amazon cleared $1 billion in sales for the first time during a non-holiday period, setting the stage for its first profitable year. In a sign of optimism, Amazon said it would prematurely redeem the bonds from its first debt round back in 1998, paying bond holders the full outstanding value of the bonds five years before their maturity date.

As they prepared to make this announcement, someone on the finance team wondered what their old foe Ravi Suria was thinking. That revived the notion of the milliravi, a significant mathematical error. Mark Peek, the chief accounting officer at the time, joked that they should find a way to use the word in their press release. Everyone loved that idea, including Bezos, and they started exchanging suggestions over e-mail. Finally, investor-relations chief Tim Stone asked Bezos if he was serious about actually doing this, and Bezos said that yes, he definitely was.

Thus, on April 24, 2003, in the press release announcing quarterly earnings, shareholders, analysts, and journalists were treated to this inexplicable headline, which doubled as a quotation attributed to Bezos: MEANINGFUL INNOVATION LEADS, LAUNCHES, INSPIRES RELENTLESS AMAZON VISITOR IMPROVEMENTS.

Taking the first letter of each word and putting them together produced *milliravi*. A few of the analysts and reporters following the company scratched their heads over the unartful prose. No one outside Amazon knew what to make of it. But for Jeff Bezos, and for the employees who stuck with their implacably demanding leader through that first critical battle, the message was clear.

They had won.

PART II

Literary Influences

CHAPTER 5
Rocket Boy

Jeff Bezos did more than just refute Ravi Suria and other skeptics during the dot-com bust. He soundly defeated them, and then he surreptitiously encoded his victory for posterity in a press release. Similarly, he did more than just outmaneuver Barnes & Noble in the marketplace – he enjoyed telling the story of how he'd held his first meetings in its coffee shops.

When Bezos's longtime friends and colleagues try to explain his fierce competitive streak and uncommon need to best his adversaries, they often veer into the past – back almost fifty years – to the circumstances of his early child-hood. Bezos grew up in a tight-knit family, with two deeply involved and caring parents, Jackie and Mike, and two close younger siblings, Christina and Mark. Seemingly, there was nothing unusual about it.

Yet for a brief period early in his life, before this ordinary childhood, Bezos lived alone with his mother and grandparents. And before that, he lived with his mother and his biological father, a man named Ted Jorgensen. Bezos himself told *Wired* magazine that he remembered when Jackie and Mike, who is technically his adoptive father, explained this situation to him when he was ten. He learned Mike wasn't his biological father around the same time he learned that he needed glasses. '*That* made me cry,' he said.[1] Years later, as a college student, he confronted his mother and asked her a series of pointed questions about his birth. They both declined to discuss the details of that conversation but afterward Bezos hugged her and said, 'You did a great job, Mom.'[2]

Bezos says that the only time he thinks about Ted Jorgensen is when he's filling out a medical form that asks for his family history. He told *Wired* in 1999 that he had never met the man. Strictly speaking, that is not true; Bezos last saw him when he was three years old.

It is of course unknowable whether the unusual circumstances of his birth helped to create that fecund entrepreneurial mix of intelligence, ambition, and a relentless need to prove himself. Two other technology icons, Steve Jobs and Larry Ellison, were adopted, and the experience is thought by some to have given each a powerful motivation to succeed. In Bezos's case, what is undeniably true is that from his earliest years, his parents and teachers recognized that this child was different – unnaturally gifted, but also unusually driven. His childhood was a launching pad, of sorts, that sent Bezos rocketing toward a life as an entrepreneur. It also instilled in him an abiding interest in the exploration and discovery of space, a fascination that perhaps one day may actually take him there.

Theodore John Jorgensen was a circus performer and in the 1960s was one of Albuquerque's best unicyclists. The archives of local newspapers contain a colorful record of his youthful proficiency. An *Albuquerque Journal* photograph taken in 1961, when he was sixteen, shows him standing on the pedals of his unicycle facing backward, one hand on the seat, the other splayed theatrically to the side, his expression tense with concentration. The caption says he was awarded 'most versatile rider' in the local unicycle club.

That year, Jorgensen and half a dozen other riders traveled widely playing unicycle polo in a team managed by Lloyd Smith, the owner of a local bike shop. Jorgensen's team was victorious in places like Newport Beach, California, and Boulder, Colorado. The newspaper has an account of the Boulder event. Four hundred people turned out in freezing weather to a shopping-center parking lot to watch the teams swivel around in four inches of snow wielding thirty-six-inch-long plastic mallets in pursuit of a small rubber ball, six inches in diameter. Jorgensen's team swept the contest, a doubleheader, three to two and six to five.[3]

In 1963, Jorgensen's troupe resurfaced in newspapers as the Unicycle Wranglers, touring county fairs, sporting events, and circuses. They square-danced, did the jitterbug and the twist, skipped rope, and performed tricks like riding on a high wire. The group practiced constantly, rehearsing three times a week at Lloyd Smith's shop and taking dance classes two times a week. 'It's like balancing on greased lightning and dancing all at the same time,' one member told the *Albuquerque Tribune*.[4] When the Ringling Brothers and Barnum & Bailey Circus came to town, the Wranglers performed under the big top, and in the spring of 1965 they performed in eight local shows of the Rude Brothers Circus. They also went to Hollywood to try out (unsuccessfully, as it happened) for the *Ed Sullivan Show*.

Ted Jorgensen was born in Chicago to a family of Baptists. His father moved the family to Albuquerque when Jorgensen and his younger brother, Gordon, were in elementary school. Ted's father took a job as a purchase agent at Sandia, then the largest nuclear-weapons installation in the country, handling the procurement of supplies at the base. Jorgensen's paternal grandfather, an immigrant from Denmark, was one of the last surviving veterans of the Spanish American War.

In high school Jorgensen started dating Jacklyn Gise, a girl two years his junior whose father also worked at Sandia. Their dads knew each other. Her father, Lawrence Preston Gise, known to friends as Preston and to his family as Pop, ran the local office of the U.S. Atomic Energy Commission, the federal agency that managed the nuclear-weapons program after Truman took it from the military following World War II.

Jorgensen was eighteen and was finishing his senior year in high school when Gise became pregnant. She was sixteen and a sophomore. They were in love and decided to get married. Her parents gave them money to fly to Juárez, Mexico, for a ceremony. A few months later, on July 19, 1963, they married again at the Gises' house. Because Gise was underage, both her mother and Jorgensen's signed the application for a marriage license. The baby was born on January 12, 1964. They named him Jeffrey Preston Jorgensen.

The new parents rented an apartment in the city's Southeast Heights neighborhood and Jackie finished high school. During the day, her mother, Mattie, took care of the baby. The situation was difficult. Jorgensen was perpetually broke, and they had only one car, his cream-colored '55 Chevy. Belonging to a unicycle troupe didn't pay much. The Wranglers divided their fees among all members, with Lloyd Smith taking a generous cut off the top. Eventually Jorgensen got a $1.25-an-hour job at the Globe Department Store, which was part of Walgreen's short-lived foray into the promising discount-retail market being pioneered at the time by Kmart and Walmart. Occasionally Jackie brought the baby to the store to visit.

The parents were young and immature and their marriage was probably doomed from the start. But Jorgensen also had a habit of drinking too much and carousing late at night with friends. He was an inattentive dad and husband. Preston Gise tried to help him; he paid his son-in-law's tuition at the University of New Mexico, but Jorgensen dropped out after a few semesters. Gise then tried to get Jorgensen a job with the New Mexico State Police, but Jorgensen didn't follow through on the opportunity.

Eventually, Jackie took the child and moved back in with her parents on Sandia Base. In June 1965, when the baby was seventeen months old, she filed for divorce. The court ordered Jorgensen to pay forty dollars a month in child support. Court records indicate that his income at the time was a hundred and eighty dollars a month. Over the next few years, Jorgensen visited his son occasionally but missed many of those support payments. He was undependable, and he had no money.

Then Jackie started dating someone. On several occasions when Jorgensen was visiting his son, the other man was there, and they avoided each other. But Jorgensen asked around and heard he was a good guy.

In 1968, Jackie called Ted Jorgensen on the phone and told him she was getting remarried and moving to Houston. He could stop paying child support, but she wanted to give Jeffrey her new husband's surname and let him adopt the boy. She asked Jorgensen not to interfere in their lives. Around the same time, Jackie's father confronted Jorgensen and elicited from him a promise that he would stay away. But Ted's permission was needed for the adoption, and after thinking it over and reasoning that the boy was likely to have a better life as the son of Jackie and her new husband, Jorgensen gave it. After a few years, he lost track of the family, and then he forgot their last name. For decades he wouldn't know what had become of his child, and his own bad choices haunted him.

The Cuban Revolution in 1959 blew apart the comfortable world of Miguel Angel Bezos Perez. Jeff Bezos's future adoptive father had been attending the elite Jesuit private school Colegio de Dolores in Santiago de Cuba, on the south coast of the island, when the Batista government fell. Castro (himself a graduate of Dolores) replaced the schools with socialist youth camps and shut down private companies, including a lumberyard owned by Miguel Bezos's father and uncle where Miguel worked most mornings. Miguel and his friends spent their days on the street, floating around and 'doing things we shouldn't have been doing, like writing anti-Castro slogans,' he says. When his parents heard about his antics, they worried he could get in trouble and, like many other Cuban families with teenage children, started making preparations to send him to the United States.

They waited a year before they got his passport under the auspices of the Catholic Church. Miguel's mother fretted about his moving to the frigid climate of *el norte*, so she and his sister knitted him a sweater from old rags. Miguel wore it to the airport. (The sweater is now framed and hanging on the wall of his home in Aspen.) His mother had to drop him off at the curb and then park in a nearby lot to watch the plane take off. But the family figured this was temporary and would last only until the political situation stabilized and everything reverted to normal. Miguel Bezos arrived in Miami in 1962, sixteen years old and alone. He knew only one word in English: *hamburger*. He was one of the oldest members of Operation Pedro Pan, a rescue program run by the Catholic Church and heavily funded by the U.S. government, that removed thousands of teenagers from Castro's grip in the early 1960s. The Catholic Welfare Bureau brought Bezos to a South Florida camp, called Matecumbe, where he joined four hundred other exiled children. By a stroke of good fortune, the next day his cousin Angel arrived at the same facility. 'Immediately the two of us were joined at the hip,' Miguel says. A few weeks later, they were summoned to the camp's office and given suitcases and heavy jackets – real ones. They were being moved to a group home in Wilmington, Delaware. 'We looked at each other and said, "Boy, we're in trouble,"' Miguel recalls.

Miguel and his cousin joined about two dozen other Pedro Pans in a facility called Casa de Sales under the care of Father James Byrnes, a young priest who spoke fluent Spanish and enjoyed the occasional vodka tonic. They would later learn he was fresh from the seminary, but to his youthful charges, Byrnes was a towering figure of authority. He taught them English, forced them to focus on their studies, and gave them each fifty cents a week after their chores were done so they could attend a Saturday-night dance. 'What he did for us we can never repay,' says Carlos Rubio Albet, Miguel and Angel Bezos's roommate at the facility. 'He took a houseful of exiled teenage boys who didn't speak English and turned it into a real family. That first Christmas I was there, in '62, he made sure everyone had something under that tree.' After the thirteen tension-filled days of the Cuban missile crisis in October of that year, the residents of La Casa, as they called it, knew they weren't going home any time soon.

While the atmosphere at the Casa de Sales was strict, the teenagers enjoyed themselves, and when they later gathered for reunions with Father Byrnes, they remembered their days there as among the happiest of their lives. The young Miguel Bezos had a particular affinity for one practical joke. When someone new arrived at the group home, he would pretend to be a deaf-mute, gesturing and grunting for items at the dinner table. A few days into the routine, he would startle the joke's target, usually by standing up and shouting as an attractive girl passed, 'Man, that's a good-looking woman!' His friends would all sing out, 'It's a miracle!' before everyone collapsed in stitches.

Miguel Bezos left the Casa de Sales after a year and enrolled as an undergraduate in the University of Albuquerque, a now-defunct Catholic college that offered full scholarships for Cuban refugees. To earn extra money, he got a job as a clerk on the overnight shift at the Bank of New Mexico – at the same time as the young, recently divorced Jacklyn Gise Jorgensen started work in the bank's bookkeeping department. Their shifts overlapped by an hour. In his thick Cuban accent and rudimentary English, Bezos asked her out several times; he was repeatedly but politely rejected. Finally, she agreed. On their first date they saw the movie *The Sound of Music*.

Miguel Bezos went on to graduate from the University of New Mexico and married Jackie in April 1968 at the First Congregational Church in Albuquerque. The reception was held at the Coronado Club on Sandia Base. Miguel got a job as a petroleum engineer at Exxon and they moved to Houston, the first stop in a career that would take them to three continents. Four-year-old Jeffrey Preston Jorgensen became Jeffrey Preston Bezos and started calling Miguel Bezos Dad. A year later, they had a daughter, Christina, and then a year after that, another son, Mark.

Jeff and his siblings grew up observing their father's tireless work ethic and his frequent expressions of love for America and its opportunities and freedoms. Miguel Bezos, who later began going by the name Mike, acknowledges that he may have also passed on a libertarian aversion to government intrusion into the private lives and enterprises of citizens. 'Certainly it was something that permeated our home life,' he says, while noting that dinnertime conversations were apolitical and revolved around the kids. 'I cannot stand any kind of totalitarian form of government, from the right or the left or anything in between, and maybe that had some impact.'

Certain moments in the early life of her oldest child took on significance when Jackie Bezos viewed them in retrospect. Like the time three-year-old Jeff disassembled his crib with a screwdriver because he insisted on sleeping in a bed. Or the time she took him to a spinning boat ride in the park and saw that while the other toddlers were waving to their moms, Jeff was looking at the mechanical workings of the cables and pulleys. Teachers at his Montessori preschool reported to his parents that the boy became so engrossed in whatever he was doing that they had to pick his chair up, with him still in it, and move it to the next activity. But Jeff was Jackie's first child; she thought *all* children were like that. 'The term *gifted* was new to the education vocabulary and certainly to me at age twenty-six,' Jackie Bezos says. 'I knew he was precocious and determined and incredibly focused, and you follow that through to now and see that it hasn't changed.'

At age eight, Bezos scored highly on a standardized test, and his parents enrolled him in the Vanguard program at

River Oaks Elementary School, a half-hour drive from their home. Bezos was a standout pupil, and the school's principal trotted him out to speak to visitors like Julie Ray, who was doing research for her book *Turning On Bright Minds*. A local company donated the excess capacity on its mainframe computer to the school, and the young Bezos led a group of friends in connecting to the mainframe via a Teletype machine that sat in the school hallway. They taught themselves how to program, then discovered a primitive Star Trek game on the mainframe and spent countless hours playing it.

At the time, Bezos's parents worried their son might be turning into a bit of an egghead. To ensure he was well rounded and help him 'make friends with his weaknesses,' as Jackie Bezos later put it, they enrolled him in various youth sports. Bezos was a pitcher in baseball, but his aim proved so unpredictable that his mother tied a mattress to the fence and asked him to practice on his own. He also reluctantly played football, barely clearing the league weight limit but getting named defensive captain by the team coach because he could memorize the plays and remembered where everyone on the field was supposed to stand. 'I was dead set against playing football,' he said. 'I had no interest in playing a game where people would tackle me to the ground.' Still, in sports, Bezos revealed a ferocious competitive streak, and when his football team, the Jets, lost the league championship, he broke down in tears.[5]

Playing sports didn't diminish young Jeff Bezos's passion for the nerdier pastimes. *Star Trek* was a fixture in the Bezos household in Houston, and they watched reruns in the afternoon after school. 'We were all Trekkies. It got to the point where Jeff would quote the lines, he was so captivated,' says Jackie Bezos. The program reinforced a budding fascination with space exploration that had begun when he was five and watched the Apollo 11 moon landing on his family's old black-and-white television. His grandfather, who two decades earlier had worked in the military's research and development wing, the Advanced Research Projects Agency, or ARPA (now DARPA), also stoked this obsession, telling stories of rockets, missiles, and the coming wonders of space travel.

In 1968, at age fifty-three, Pop Gise resigned from the U.S. Atomic Energy Commission over a bureaucratic squabble with his bosses in Washington. He and Mattie retired to his wife's family's ranch in Cotulla, Texas. Between the ages of four and sixteen, Jeff Bezos spent every summer with his grandparents, and his grandfather enlisted his help in doing the gritty work of the ranch, which was a hundred miles from the nearest store or hospital.

Gise, who had been a lieutenant commander in the U.S. Navy during World War II, was in many ways Bezos's mentor. He instilled in Bezos the values of self-reliance and resourcefulness, as well as a visceral distaste for inefficiency. 'There was very little he couldn't do himself,' Jackie Bezos says of her father. 'He thought everything was something you could tackle in a garage.' Bezos and Pop Gise repaired windmills and castrated bulls; they attempted to grade dirt roads and built contraptions like an automatic gate opener and a crane to move the heavy parts of a broken-down D6 Caterpillar bulldozer.

Every so often, Pop Gise got carried away with this do-it-yourself impulse. One such occasion occurred when his faithful bird dog Spike injured the tip of his tail in a car door. The nearby veterinarians all specialized in cattle and other large animals, and Gise reasoned that he could perform the necessary amputation himself in his garage. 'I never knew a dog's tail could bleed so much,' he reported afterward.

But it wasn't all amateur surgeries and physical labor; Pop Gise also inspired in his grandson a passion for intellectual pursuits. He brought him to the local Cotulla library, where over successive summers Bezos made his way through a sizable collection of science-fiction books donated by a local resident. He read seminal works by Jules Verne, Isaac Asimov, and Robert Heinlein and fantasized about interstellar travel, deciding that he wanted to grow up to be an astronaut. Pop Gise taught Bezos checkers and then soundly and repeatedly defeated him, despite Jackie's pleading with him to let Jeff win a match. 'He'll beat me when he's ready to,' her father said.[6]

Bezos's grandparents taught him a lesson in compassion that he related decades later, in a 2010 commencement speech at Princeton. Every few years Pop and Mattie Gise hooked an Airstream trailer to their car and caravanned around the country with other Airstream owners, and they sometimes took Jeff with them. On one of these road trips, when Bezos was ten and passing time in the back seat of the car, he took some mortality statistics he had heard on an antismoking public service announcement and calculated that his grandmother's smoking habit would take nine years off her life. When he poked his head into the front seat to matter-of-factly inform her of this, she burst into tears, and Pop Gise pulled over and stopped the car.

In fact, Mattie Gise fought cancer for years and would eventually succumb to it. Bezos described what happened next in his speech at Princeton.

He got out of the car and came around and opened my door and waited for me to follow. Was I in trouble? My grandfather was a highly intelligent, quiet man. He had never said a harsh word to me, and maybe this was to be the first time? Or maybe he would ask that I get back in the car and apologize to my grandmother. I had no experience in this realm with my grandparents and no way to gauge what the consequences might be. We stopped beside the trailer. My grandfather looked at me, and after a bit of silence, he gently and calmly said, 'Jeff, one day you'll understand that it's harder to be kind than clever.'

When Jeff was thirteen, Mike Bezos's job with Exxon took the family to Pensacola, on the Florida Panhandle. Showing the same unwavering resolve that her son would employ later in life, Jackie Bezos prevailed on local school officials to let her son into the middle school's gifted program despite the fact that the program had a strict one-year waiting period. The officials had been reluctant, so she forced them to examine the boy's work, which changed their minds.[7] 'You want to account for Jeff's success, look at Jackie,' says Bezos's childhood friend Joshua Weinstein. 'She's the toughest lady you'll ever meet and also the sweetest and most loyal.'

The former Jackie Gise was just thirty when her oldest child became a teenager, but she understood him well and nurtured his passions. Bezos had dreams of becoming an inventor like Thomas Edison, so his mother patiently shuttled him back and forth and back again to a local Radio Shack to buy parts for a succession of gadgets: homemade robots, hovercrafts, a solar-powered cooker, and devices to keep his siblings out of his room. 'I was constantly booby-trapping the house with various kinds of alarms and some of them were not just audible sounds, but actually like physical booby traps,' Bezos said later. 'I think I occasionally worried my parents that they were going to open the door one day and have thirty pounds of nails drop on their head or something.'[8]

Bezos occasionally watched over his younger sister and brother during these years but his booming, uninhibited laugh occasionally caused problems. 'We would trust Jeff to take them to movies,' Jackie Bezos says, 'but the two of them would come back embarrassed, saying, "Jeff laughs too loud." It would be some Disney movie, and his laughter was drowning out everything.'

After a two-year stop in Pensacola, the family moved again. This time, Mike Bezos's job took them to Miami — a city Mike had first encountered fifteen years before as a penniless immigrant. Now he was an executive at Exxon, and the family bought a four-bedroom house with a back-yard pool in the affluent Palmetto neighborhood in unincorporated Dade County.

Miami at the time was a tumultuous place. The drug wars were in full swing, and in 1980 the Mariel boatlift brought a mass emigration of Cubans fleeing the Communist regime. All the violence and frenetic activ-ity barely registered in the insular worlds of Bezos and his new friends. Jeff enrolled in Miami Palmetto Sen-ior High School, joined the science and chess clubs, drove a blue Ford Falcon station wagon with no air-conditioning, and impressed his classmates with his fierce work ethic. 'He was excruciatingly focused,' says Weinstein, who lived around the corner and became one of Bezos's best friends (the two are still close). 'Not like mad-scientist focused, but he was capable of really focus-ing, in a crazy way, on certain things. He was extremely disciplined, which is how he is able to do all these things.'

The Bezos house was a gathering point for Jeff and his

wide circle of friends. They built the homecoming science-club float in his garage and gathered there for prom after-parties. Jackie Bezos, the youngest of all the moms, commanded the kids' respect and became a fixture in their lives. With Weinstein's mother, she organized a neighborhood watch and conducted its meetings at her home. She could be strict. When a state trooper gave Bezos a ticket on the Dixie Highway, she made him call the friends who had been in the car with him and personally apologize.

The teenage Bezos didn't butt heads only with his mother. When he was a senior in high school, Jackie Bezos remembers, Jeff got into a heated argument with his father over some now-forgotten ideological issue. It was ten at night when they started arguing and each was unwilling to retreat on the substance of the matter. The disagreement evolved into a full-blown quarrel but eventually broke up; Mike retreated to his bedroom and Jeff to the first-floor bathroom, which, like those in many South Florida homes at the time, had a separate door that opened onto the backyard. Jackie let them both stew for an hour and then went to check up on them. 'Mike was still in the bedroom, looking like he had lost his best friend,' she says. She went downstairs and knocked on the bathroom door, but there was no answer. It was locked. She went around to the backyard, opened its outside door – and saw the bathroom was empty. The family cars were still there. 'I was terribly worried,' Jackie says. 'It was midnight on a weekday and he's out there on foot. I thought, *This is not good.*'

While she contemplated her next move, the home phone rang. It was Jeff, calling from the closest, safest place with a pay telephone – a hospital. He didn't want her to worry, he said, but he was not yet ready to come home.

She eventually got him to let her pick him up, and they drove to a nearby all-night diner and talked for hours. He finally agreed to return home, and though it was after three a.m. and he had school that day, Jeff apparently didn't go right to sleep. That morning, when Mike Bezos got to work, he discovered a handwritten letter from his son in his briefcase. He still carries the letter in his brief-case today.

Bezos took a series of odd jobs throughout high school. One summer he famously worked as a fryer at a local McDonald's, learning, among other skills, how to crack an egg with one hand. Less well known was his job helping an eccentric neighbor, who decided one day that she was going to breed and sell hamsters. Bezos cleaned the cages and fed the rodents but soon found he was spending more time listening to the woman's troubles than taking care of the animals. He apparently was a good confidant; she once called him at school and pulled him out of a class to discuss some new personal crisis. When Jackie Bezos found out about it, she put an end to the relationship.

Bezos's high-school friends say he was ridiculously competitive. He collected awards for best science student at his school for three years and best math student for two, and he won a statewide science fair for an entry concern-ing the effects of a zero-gravity environment on the housefly. At some point, he announced to his classmates his intention to become the valedictorian of his 680-student class, and he crammed his schedule with honors courses to bolster his rank. 'The race [for the rest of the students] then became to be number two,' says Josh Weinstein. 'Jeff decided he wanted it and he worked harder than anybody else.'

Ursula Werner, Jeff's high-school girlfriend, says he

was exceedingly creative and quite a romantic. For her eighteenth birthday, he spent days crafting an elaborate scavenger hunt that sent her around Miami on bizarre and embarrassing errands, such as entering a bank to ask a teller for a million pennies and navigating a Home Depot to find a clue that was hidden under a toilet lid.

After his greasy summer at McDonald's, Bezos wanted to avoid another low-wage job, so with Werner he created the DREAM Institute, a ten-day summer school for ten-year-olds that explored such diverse topics as *Gulliver's Travels*, black holes, nuclear deterrence, and the Bezos family's Apple II computer. The class 'emphasizes the use of new ways of thinking in old areas,' according to a flier the young teachers passed out to parents. Werner said that her parents were dismissive of the class and wondered who would possibly sign up. But Bezos's parents cheered the effort and immediately enrolled Mark and Christina. 'I got the sense that Jackie and Mike were the kinds of parents who always encouraged Jeff and nurtured his creativity,' Werner says.

Bezos scored straight As at Miami Palmetto, got early admission to Princeton University, and not only became valedictorian of his high school but won the Silver Knight, a prestigious statewide award sponsored by the *Miami Herald*. According to Weinstein, who was there, when Jeff went to the bank to deposit his award check, the teller looked at it and said, 'Oh, what do you do for the *Miami Herald*?' and Bezos cockily replied, 'I win Silver Knights.'

Bezos wrote out his valedictory speech longhand. His mother typed it up, pausing just long enough to realize that for a high-school senior, Jeff had some wildly out-landish ambitions. She still has a copy, which includes the classic *Star Trek* opening, 'Space, the final frontier,' and discusses his dream of saving humanity by creating permanent human colonies in orbiting space stations while turning the planet into an enormous nature preserve.

These were not pie-in-the-sky ideas. They were personal goals. 'Whatever image he had of his own future, it always involved becoming wealthy,' Ursula Werner says. 'There was no way to get what he wanted without it.' What exactly did he want? 'The reason he's earning so much money,' Werner told journalists who contacted her in the 1990s, seeking to understand the Internet magnate, 'is to get to outer space.'

* * *

In the year 2000, as Amazon was trying to restore order to its balance sheet while fighting the dot-com doubters, Bezos saw his fortune drop precipitously, from $6.1 to $2 billion.[9] Still, it was an enormous sum, and it made him one of the richest people in the world. He had seen first-hand how technology, patience, and long-term thinking could pay off. And so, right at the height of the world's skepticism about the future prospects of Amazon, Bezos secretly started an entirely new company devoted to space exploration and registered it with the state of Washington.

Bezos intended to keep his new space lab a secret. But many of his Amazon colleagues knew about his ambitions. He told Kay Dangaard, Amazon's public relations chief in the 1990s, and she quietly tried to please him by incorporating it into the Amazon brand. She actually set up a product-placement deal to put Amazon billboards on the moon in the Eddie Murphy movie *The Adventures of Pluto Nash*, but canceled the deal after reading the terrible script. In 1999, she tried to get NASA to allow the space shuttle *Discovery* astronauts to order Christmas gifts on Amazon.com from orbit. After tentatively expressing interest, the agency nixed the idea as overly commercial.

Bezos also confided his dreams to Nick Hanauer, the early Amazon investor and an unofficial board member during the company's first five years. 'He absolutely thinks he's going to space,' Hanauer says. 'It's always been one of his goals. It's why he started working out every morning. He's been ridiculously disciplined about it.'

In retrospect, it almost seems like Bezos was taunting the media with his top-secret space plans. He clearly couldn't resist obliquely referencing them. Discussing concerns about the long-term health of the planet with *Wired* magazine in 1999, he told an interviewer, 'I wouldn't mind helping in some way. I do think we have all our eggs in one basket.'[10] He told Fast Company in 2001 that it would be great if the novel *Dune*, in which humanity has colonized other planets, was 'nonfiction.'

In an interview I conducted with Bezos in 2000, I asked him what he was reading. He talked about Robert Zubrin's books *Entering Space: Creating a Spacefaring Civilization* and *The Case for Mars*. At the end of the conversation, I wondered when some brave Silicon Valley entrepreneur would start a private space company (this was two years before PayPal cofounder Elon Musk started his rocket company SpaceX). Bezos's answer seemed particularly convoluted. 'It's a very hard technical problem and I think it's very hard to see how you would generate a return in a reasonable amount of time on that investment,' he said. 'So the answer to your question is probably yes, there probably is somebody doing it, but it's not . . . when you go to venture capital conferences, it never comes up. To say it was a cold topic would be exaggerating how hot it is.'

In 2002, Bezos created a public Wish List of his own on

Amazon, available for anyone to see, specifying some of his reading interests. Among the titles were *The History of Space Vehicles*, by Tim Furniss, and *Rare Earth: Why Complex Life Is Uncommon in the Universe*, by Peter Douglas Ward and Donald Brownlee. Then, in February 2003, I attended a TED conference, an annual gathering devoted to technology and design that was held back then in Monterey, California, and I overheard someone talking about a space company in Seattle called Blue. A month later, Bezos and his attorney suffered minor injuries in a helicopter accident near Alpine in West Texas – a few hundred miles from the middle of nowhere. 'During . . . takeoff the tailboom struck a tree, aircraft rolled to side, ended up in a creek partially submerged,' read the official incident report from the Federal Aviation Administration. 'The three passengers received injuries and were trans-ported to the local hospital. Degree of injuries believed to be nonthreatening.'

Bezos later told *Time* magazine that his overarching thought during the accident was *What a dumb way to die*. It later emerged that he was looking to buy land for a Texas ranch. Bezos wanted to give his kids the same experience he'd had growing up on his grandparents' ranch in Cotulla.

He was also looking for a good place to build a launchpad.

At the time of the helicopter crash, the world knew nothing of Jeff Bezos's space-exploration company. But it all seemed to be adding up to something. After the accident, I searched the Washington State corporate data-base for a company called Blue and found an entry for Blue Operations LLC that had been registered with an address of 1200 Twelfth Avenue South in Seattle – Amazon's headquarters. The company had a mysteriously vague website advertising job openings for aerospace engineers who had expertise in areas like propulsion and avionics. I was a cub reporter for *Newsweek* magazine at the time, and the notion that a famous Internet billionaire was secretly building his own spaceship was too enticing to resist.

On a trip to Seattle in March of 2003, I rented a car and, late at night, drove to another address I had found in the Washington State corporate records for Blue, this one located in an industrial zone south of Seattle along the Duwamish Waterway. At that address was a fifty-three-thousand-square-foot warehouse with a blue awning over the front door imprinted with the words *Blue Origin* in white letters.

Though it was late on a weekend night, the lights were on and a few cars and motorcycles were parked out front. I couldn't see anything through the covered windows and there was no one outside. The air smelled heavily of river water and processed lumber. I sat in the rental car, just wondering, indulging visions of secret spaceships and billionaire-funded missions to Mars. But I had nothing to go on, and it was intensely frustrating. After an hour, I couldn't take it anymore. I got out, walked quietly across the street to a trash can, removed an armful of its contents, walked back to the car, and dumped it in the trunk.

A few weeks later, for *Newsweek* magazine, I wrote the first story about Blue Origin, entitled 'Bezos in Space.'[11] Aided by an extremely convenient discovery I'd made that night – a sheaf of coffee-stained drafts of a Blue Origin mission statement – I reported that the long-term mission of the firm was to create an enduring human presence in space. The company was building a spaceship called *New Shepard*, after Alan Shepard, the pioneering Mercury astronaut, which would take tourists into the upper reaches of the atmosphere. The unique designs called for a vertical takeoff and thrusters to control a vertical landing so that the vehicle could be economically reused. The startup was also funding forward-looking research into new propulsion systems, like wave rotors and rockets powered by ground-based lasers.

A few days after my visit to Blue Origin's warehouse, I e-mailed all these details to Bezos to let him know what would be in the article and to try to elicit a reaction. I've since lost the message I sent, but in my breathless quest I must have implied that he had grown impatient with the progress of manned space travel inside NASA. I kept his reply:

Brad, I'm travelling and responding by Blackberry — maybe you'll get this.

It's way premature for Blue to say anything or comment on anything because we haven't done anything worthy of comment. If you're interested in this topic over the coming years, we'll keep it in mind for when we have anything worth saying. Some of what you have below is right and some is wrong. I will comment on one thing because you touched a nerve, and I think it's hurtful to the people of NASA. There should be a counterpoint.

NASA is a national treasure, and it's total bull that anyone should be frustrated by NASA. The only reason I'm interested in space is because they inspired me when I was five years old. How many government agencies can you think of that inspire five year olds? The work NASA does is technically super-demanding and inherently risky, and they continue to do an outstanding job. The ONLY reason any of these small space companies have a chance of doing ANYTHING is because they get to stand on the shoulders of NASA's accomplishments and ingenuity.

If you want a specific example: consider that all these companies use extremely sophisticated computer codes for analyzing things like structures, heat flows and aerodynamics, which codes were developed (over many years and meticulously tested against physical reality) by NASA!

Jeff

There was a smattering of media coverage after the *Newsweek* article but Blue Origin continued to labor in secret. Bezos acquired his Texas ranch using anonymous corporate entities named after historic explorers (enterprises like James Cook LP and Coronado Ventures) to make generous offers to landowners around Van Horn, Texas, not far from where his helicopter had gone down.[12] By 2005 he owned 290,000 acres – an area about a third of the size of Rhode Island. He announced his intentions to build a spaceport by walking into the office of a local newspaper, the *Van Horn Advocate,* and giving an impromptu interview to its bewildered editor.

In a speech at Carnegie Mellon University in 2011, Bezos said that Blue Origin's goal was to drive down the cost and increase the safety of technology that can get humans into space. The group was 'working to lower the cost of space flight to build a future where we humans can explore the solar system firsthand and in person,' he said. 'Slow steady progress can erode any challenge over time.'

Progress may be slower than Bezos and his rocket scientists first imagined. In 2011, a Blue Origin test vehicle spun out of control at Mach 1.2 and an altitude of 45,000 feet, leaving a spectacular fireball in the sky that reminded Van Horn residents of the space shuttle

Challenger disaster. 'Not the outcome any of us wanted, but we're signed up for this to be hard,' Bezos wrote in a blog post on the Blue Origin website.[13] A year after that, the company successfully tested the spaceship's crew-capsule escape system. It has received two grants from NASA worth more than $25 million to develop technologies related to human space-flight. Internet magnate Elon Musk, with SpaceX, and billionaire Richard Branson, the founder of an enterprise called Virgin Galactic, are pursuing some of the same goals.

Bezos does not allow the public or media to tour his space facilities. In 2006, the company moved to larger headquarters in Kent, Washington, twenty miles south of Seattle. Visitors describe a facility studded with Bezos's space collectibles, like props from *Star Trek*, rocket parts from various spaceships throughout history, and a real cosmonaut suit from the Soviet Union. Engineers zoom around the 280,000-square-foot facility on Segways. In the atrium of the building, there is a full-scale steampunk model of a Victorian-era spaceship as it might have been described in the fiction of Jules Verne, complete with a cockpit, brass controls, and nineteenth-century furnishings. Visitors can venture inside, sit on the velvet-covered seats, and imagine themselves as intrepid explorers in the time of Captain Nemo and Phileas Fogg. 'To an imaginative child, it would look like an artifact,' says Bezos's friend Danny Hillis.

Like other great entrepreneurs, including Walt Disney, Henry Ford, and Steve Jobs, Bezos was turning imagination into reality, the fancies of his youth into actual physical things. 'Space for Jeff is not a year 2000 or a year 2010 opportunity,' says Hillis. 'It's been a dream of humanity's for centuries and it will continue to be one for centuries. Jeff sees himself and Blue Origin as part of that bigger story. It's the next step in what Jules Verne was writing about and what the Apollo missions accomplished.'

Bezos did not hesitate to embrace the responsibilities that came with pursuing this passion. Even as Amazon struggled to maintain orbit, he collected new obligations and hired more employees for Blue Origin and then devised clever ways to divide his time among all his responsibilities in the most efficient manner possible. He gave Blue Origin a coat of arms and a Latin motto, *Gradatim Ferociter*, which translates to 'Step by Step, Ferociously.' The phrase accurately captures Amazon's guiding philosophy as well. Steady progress toward seemingly impossible goals will win the day. Setbacks are temporary. Naysayers are best ignored.

An interviewer once asked Bezos why he was motivated to accomplish so much, considering that he had already amassed an exceedingly large fortune. 'I have realized about myself that I'm very motivated by people counting on me,' he answered. 'I like to be counted on.'[14]

CHAPTER 6
Chaos Theory

Jeff Bezos liked to be counted on, but after Amazon reached profitability during the ebb of the dot-com bust in 2002, he discovered that he himself would need to count on someone. For while Amazon had quieted its most vociferous critics, Bezos needed help taming the growing chaos inside his company's walls.

In every significant way, Amazon was becoming a larger and more complicated business. It had 2,100 employees at the end of 1998, and 9,000 at the end of 2004. And after it survived the worst effects of the dot-com crash, it resumed lurching into new categories, like sporting goods, apparel, and jewelry, and new countries, like Japan and China.

Size bred chaos. All companies hit this critical moment, when their internal structures, like a teenager's old shoes, suddenly don't fit anymore. But Amazon went through a severe form of this rite of passage. The larger and more ambitious it got, the more complicated it became structurally and the harder it was to keep everyone co-ordinated and moving quickly. Bezos wanted to execute several strategies simultaneously, but the company's various interdependent divisions were wasting too much time coordinating with one other.

In the distribution centers, chaos wasn't an ethereal thing but tangible, reflected in frequent system outages that could shut down facilities for hours and in omnipresent piles of products that sat on the floor, ignored by workers. During the early years of frenzied growth, new product categories had been plopped onto Amazon's logistics network with little preparation. Employees remember that when the home and kitchen category was introduced in the fall of 1999, kitchen knives would fly down the conveyor chutes, free of protective packaging. Amazon's internal logistics software didn't properly account for new categories, so the computers would ask workers whether a new toy entering the warehouse was a hardcover or a paperback book.

Amazon once tried to conquer chaos by synchronizing its employees' efforts with broad unifying themes like Get Big Fast and Get Our House in Order. That had gotten everyone paddling in the same direction, but now the company had become too big for that kind of transparent sloganeering.

During these years of its awkward adolescence, Bezos refused to slow down, doubling and tripling his bet on the Internet and on his grand vision for a store that sold everything. To guide his company through this transition, he created an unorthodox organizational structure with a peculiar name. And to quell the turmoil in the distribution centers, he started to rely on a young executive named Jeff Wilke, whose cerebral and occasionally impatient management style mirrored his own. 'They fed off each other,' says Bruce Jones, a supply-chain vice president. 'Bezos wanted to do it and Wilke knew how to do it. It was a hell of a lot of fun, in a very Machiavellian sort of way.'

* * *

Jeff Wilke's job was to fix the mistakes of his predecessor. Jimmy Wright and his cowboy crew from Walmart had designed Amazon's nationwide logistics network in the late nineties and were the best in the world at building large-scale retail distribution. But in moving quickly to satisfy Bezos's open-ended goal to store and ship everything, they had created a system that was expensive, unreliable, and hungry for an emergency influx of employees from Seattle at the end of every year. 'It was a mess,' says Bruce Jones. 'It was pretty much how Walmart did all their distribution centers, which was great if you had to send out five thousand rolls of toilet paper. But it was not well suited to small orders.'

Wilke was from suburban Pittsburgh, the son of an attorney; his parents divorced when he was twelve. He learned he had a talent for mathematics in the sixth grade when to his surprise he placed second in a regional math tournament. When he was fifteen and visiting his grandparents in Las Vegas, he was enthralled by a casino's video-poker machine. He went home and replicated it on his first-generation personal computer, called the Timex Sinclair 1000 (internal memory: 2 KB). Wilke got straight As throughout school but his guidance counselor told him not to apply to Princeton University because no one from Keystone Oaks High School had ever been admitted to the Ivy League. He applied anyway and got in.

Wilke graduated summa cum laude from Princeton in 1989, three years after Bezos. He earned an MBA and an MS from the Massachusetts Institute of Technology's engineering/MBA dual-degree program. Called Leaders for Manufacturing (now it's Leaders for Global Operations), the program is a novel alliance of MIT's business school, its engineering school, and partner companies, like Boeing, created to address emerging global competition. Mark

Mastandrea, an MIT classmate who would follow him to Amazon, says that Wilke 'was one of the smartest people I had ever come across. He got to the answers faster than anyone else.'

Wilke began his career at Andersen Consulting and then joined AlliedSignal, the manufacturing giant, which was later acquired by Honeywell. He quickly climbed the ranks to vice president, reporting directly to CEO Larry Bossidy and running the company's $200-million-a-year pharmaceutical business. In AlliedSignal's headquarters in Morristown, New Jersey, Wilke was immersed in the corporate dogma of Six Sigma, a manufacturing and management philosophy that seeks to increase efficiency by identifying and eliminating defects.

Back in 1999, Scott Pitasky, an Amazon recruiter who later became the head of human resources at Microsoft, was put in charge of finding a replacement for Jimmy Wright. Pitasky had previously worked with Wilke at AlliedSignal, so he thought of his former colleague after concluding that Amazon needed someone who was smart enough to go toe to toe with Jeff Bezos, who delighted in questioning how everything was done.

Pitasky tracked Wilke down on a business trip in Switzerland and pitched him on taking over the critical distribution network at Amazon. He told Wilke that he would have the chance to build a unique distribution network and define a nascent industry, an opportunity that simply didn't exist at AlliedSignal. Working quickly, Pitasky convinced then COO Joe Galli, visiting his children at the time on the East Coast, to meet Wilke at a hotel restaurant near Dulles International Airport as soon as Wilke returned to the States.

All of thirty-two years old at the time, with a toothy smile and unfashionable eyeglasses, Wilke did not immediately present the picture of a dynamic leader. 'He was not a charismatic communicator,' Galli says. 'He was an extremely smart and thoughtful supply-chain expert who relied on fact-based analysis and wanted to zero in and do the right thing.' Over dinner that night, and during a separate trip Galli made to visit Wilke and his wife, Liesl, at their home in New Jersey, the pair bonded. Wilke and Galli were both from Pittsburgh and had similar middle-class roots. Ever the salesman, Galli piqued Wilke's interest in the massive logistics challenges Amazon faced. Wilke then visited Seattle to interview with Bezos and Joy Covey. He joined the company soon after as vice president and general manager of worldwide operations. After his last conversation with Larry Bossidy, who had just announced his retirement from AlliedSignal, the veteran CEO gave him a hug.

Immediately upon moving to Seattle, Wilke set about filling the ranks of Amazon's logistics division with scientists and engineers rather than retail-distribution veterans. He wrote down a list of the ten smartest people he knew and hired them all, including Russell Allgor, a supply-chain engineer at Bayer AG. Wilke had attended Princeton with Allgor and had cribbed from his engineering problem sets. Allgor and his supply-chain algorithms team would become Amazon's secret weapon, devising mathematical answers to questions such as where and when to stock particular products within Amazon's distribution network and how to most efficiently combine various items in a customer's order in a single box.[1]

Wilke recognized that Amazon had a unique problem in its distribution arm: it was extremely difficult for the company to plan ahead from one shipment to the next. The company didn't store and ship a predictable number or type of orders. A customer might order one book, a

DVD, some tools – perhaps gift-wrapped, perhaps not – and that exact combination might never again be repeated. There were an infinite number of permutations. 'We were essentially assembling and fulfilling customer orders. The factory physics were a lot closer to manufacturing and assembly than they were to retail,' Wilke says. So in one of his first moves, Wilke renamed Amazon's shipping facilities to more accurately represent what was happening there. They were no longer to be called warehouses (the original name) or distribution centers (Jimmy Wright's name); forever after, they would be known as fulfillment centers, or FCs.

Before Wilke joined Amazon, the general managers of the fulfillment centers often improvised their strategies, talking on the telephone each morning and gauging which facility was fully operational or had excess capacity, then passing off orders to one another based on those snap judgments. Wilke's algorithms seamlessly matched demand to the correct FC, leveling out backlogs and obviating the need for the morning phone call. He then applied the process-driven doctrine of Six Sigma that he'd learned at AlliedSignal and mixed it with Toyota's lean manufacturing philosophy, which requires a company to rationalize every expense in terms of the value it creates for customers and allows workers (now called associates) to pull a red cord and stop all production on the floor if they find a defect (the manufacturing term for the system is *andon*).

In his first two years, Wilke and his team devised dozens of metrics, and he ordered his general managers to track them carefully, including how many shipments each FC received, how many orders were shipped out, and the per-unit cost of packing and shipping each item. He got rid of the older, sometimes frivolous names for mistakes –

Amazon's term to describe the delivery of the wrong product to a customer was *switcheroo* – and substituted more serious names. And he instilled some basic discipline in the FCs. 'When I joined, I didn't find time clocks,' Wilke says. 'People came in when they felt like it in the morning and then went home when the work was done and the last truck was loaded. It wasn't the kind of rigor I thought would scale.' Wilke promised Bezos that he would reliably generate cost savings each year just by reducing defects and increasing productivity.

Wilke elevated the visibility of his FC managers within Amazon. He brought them to Seattle as often as possible and highlighted the urgency of their technical issues. During the holiday season, in what remains today his personal signature, Wilke wore a flannel shirt every day as a gesture of solidarity with his blue-collar comrades in the field. Wilke 'recognized that a general manager was a difficult job and he made you feel you were in a lifelong club,' says Bert Wegner, who ran the Fernley FC in those years.

Wilke had another tool at his disposal: like Bezos, he had an occasionally volcanic temper. Back in the fall of 2000, the software systems in Amazon's FCs were still incapable of precisely tracking inventory and shipments. So that holiday, Wilke's second one at the company, during the annual race to Christmas that the company internally referred to as the big push, Wilke started a series of daily conference calls with his general managers in the United States and Europe. He told his general managers that on each call, he wanted to know the facts on the ground: how many orders had shipped, how many had not, whether there was a backlog, and, if so, why. As that holiday season ramped up, Wilke also demanded that his managers be prepared to tell him 'what was in their yard'

– the exact number and contents of the trucks waiting outside the FCs to unload products and ferry orders to the post office or UPS.

One recurring trouble spot that year was the fulfillment center in McDonough, Georgia, a working-class city thirty miles south of Atlanta. In the heat of the tumultuous holiday season, McDonough – the source of the infamous Jigglypuff crisis of 1999 – was regularly falling behind schedule. Its general manager, a once and future Walmart executive named Bob Duron, was already skating on thin ice when Wilke surveyed his managers on a conference call and asked them what they had in their yards. When he got to McDonough, Duron apparently hadn't gotten the message and said: 'Hold on a second, Jeff, I can see them outside my window.' Then he leaned back in his chair and started counting aloud on the phone. 'I've got one, two, three, four . . .'

Wilke went off like a bomb. He was calling that day from his home office on Mercer Island, and he started screaming – an oral assault of such intensity and vulgarity that the handsets of the general managers on the call shrieked with feedback. And then, just as abruptly as the outburst began, there was quiet. Wilke had seemingly disappeared.

No one said anything for thirty seconds. Finally Arthur Valdez, the general manager in Campbellsville, said quietly, 'I think he ate the phone.'

There were various interpretations of what actually happened. Some claimed that in his rage, Wilke had inadvertently yanked the phone cord out of the wall. Others speculated that he had thrown the receiver across the room in his fury. A decade later, over lunch at an Italian brasserie near Amazon's offices, Wilke explains that he had actually still been on the line but was simply so angry that he could no longer speak. 'We were just struggling to make it work on a whole host of different levels in McDonough,' he says. 'We were struggling to recruit the right leaders, and struggling to get enough people to work there.'

That spring, with Amazon sprinting toward its profitability goal, Wilke shut down McDonough and fired four hundred and fifty full-time employees. Closing the facility wouldn't solve Amazon's problems; in fact, the reduction in capacity put even more pressure on Amazon's other fulfillment centers. The company was already running at capacity over the holidays and sales were growing at more than 20 percent a year. Now Amazon had no choice but to master the complexity of its own systems and get more out of the investments it had already made.

Wilke had burned a boat in mid-voyage, and for the Amazon armada, there was no turning back. Along the way, he was exhibiting a style – leadership by example, augmented with a healthy dose of impatience – that was positively Bezosian in character. Perhaps not coincidentally, Wilke was promoted to senior vice president a little over a year after joining Amazon. Jeff Bezos had found his chief ally in the war against chaos.

At a management offsite in the late 1990s, a team of well-intentioned junior executives stood up before the company's top brass and gave a presentation on a problem indigenous to all large organizations: the difficulty of coordinating far-flung divisions. The junior executives recommended a variety of different techniques to foster cross-group dialogue and afterward seemed proud of their own ingenuity. Then Jeff Bezos, his face red and the blood vessel in his forehead pulsing, spoke up.

'I understand what you're saying, but you are completely wrong,' he said. 'Communication is a sign of dysfunction. It means people aren't working together in a close, organic way. We should be trying to figure out a way for teams to communicate less with each other, not more.'

That confrontation was widely remembered. 'Jeff has these aha moments,' says David Risher. 'All the blood in his entire body goes to his face. He's incredibly passionate. If he was a table pounder, he would be pounding the table.'

At that meeting and in public speeches afterward, Bezos vowed to run Amazon with an emphasis on decentralization and independent decision-making. 'A hierarchy isn't responsive enough to change,' he said. 'I'm still trying to get people to do occasionally what I ask. And if I was successful, maybe we wouldn't have the right kind of company.'[2]

Bezos's counterintuitive point was that coordination among employees wasted time, and that the people closest to problems were usually in the best position to solve them. That would come to represent something akin to the conventional wisdom in the high-tech industry over the next decade. The companies that embraced this philosophy, like Google, Amazon, and, later, Facebook, were in part drawing lessons from theories about lean and agile software development. In the seminal high-tech book *The Mythical Man-Month*, IBM veteran and computer science professor Frederick Brooks argued that adding manpower to complex software projects actually delayed progress. One reason was that the time and money spent on communication increased in proportion to the number of people on a project.

Bezos and other startup founders were reacting to lessons from previous technology giants. Microsoft took a top-down management approach with layers of middle managers, a system that ended up slowing decisions and stifling innovation. Looking at the muffled and unhappy hierarchy of the software giant across Lake Washington, Amazon executives saw a neon sign warning them exactly what to avoid.

The drive to cut costs also forced Bezos to eliminate any emerging layers of middle management from his company. After the stock market crash in 2000, Amazon went through two rounds of layoffs. But Bezos didn't want to stop recruiting altogether; he just wanted to be more efficient. So he framed the kind of employees he wanted in simple terms. All new hires had to directly improve the outcome of the company. He wanted doers – engineers, developers, perhaps merchandise buyers, but not managers. 'We didn't want to be a monolithic army of program managers, à la Microsoft. We wanted independent teams to be entrepreneurial,' says Neil Roseman. Or, as Roseman also put it: 'Autonomous working units are good. Things to manage working units are bad.'

But as was often the case, no one could anticipate just how far Bezos would venture into these organizational theories in his quest to distill them down to their core ideas. In early 2002, as part of a new personal ritual, he took time after the holidays to think and read. (In this respect, Microsoft's Bill Gates, who also took such annual think weeks, served as a positive example.) Returning to the company after a few weeks, Bezos presented his next big idea to the S Team in the basement of his Medina, Washington, home.

The entire company, he said, would restructure itself around what he called 'two-pizza teams.' Employees would be organized into autonomous groups of fewer than ten people – small enough that, when working late, the team members could be fed with two pizza pies. These teams would be independently set loose on Amazon's biggest problems. They would likely compete with one another for resources and sometimes duplicate their efforts, replicating the Darwinian realities of surviving in nature. Freed from the constraints of intracompany communication, Bezos hoped, these loosely coupled teams could move faster and get features to customers quicker.

There were some head-scratching aspects to Bezos's two-pizza-team concept. Each group was required to propose its own 'fitness function' – a linear equation that it could use to measure its own impact without ambiguity. For example, a two-pizza team in charge of sending advertising e-mails to customers might choose for its fitness function the rate at which these messages were opened multiplied by the average order size those e-mails generated. A group writing software code for the fulfillment centers might home in on decreasing the cost of shipping each type of product and reducing the time that elapsed between a customer's making a purchase and the item leaving the FC in a truck. Bezos wanted to personally approve each equation and track the results over time. It would be his way of guiding a team's evolution.

Bezos was applying a kind of chaos theory to management, acknowledging the complexity of his organization by breaking it down to its most basic parts in the hopes that surprising results might emerge. That, at least, was the high-minded goal; the end result was somewhat disappointing. The two-pizza-team concept took root first in engineering, where it was backed by Rick Dalzell, and over the course of several years, it was somewhat inconsistently applied through the rest of the company.

There was just no reason to organize some departments, such as legal and finance, in this way.

The idea of fitness functions in particular appeared to clash with some fundamental aspects of human nature – it's uncomfortable to have to set the framework for your own evaluation when you might be judged harshly by the end result. Asking groups to define their own fitness functions was a little like asking a condemned man to decide how he'd like to be executed. Teams ended up spending too much time worrying over their formulas and making them ever more complex and abstract. 'Being a two-pizza team was not exactly liberating,' says Kim Rachmeler. 'It was actually kind of a pain in the ass. It did not help you get your job done and consequently the vast majority of engineers and teams flipped the bit on it.'

A year into Jeff Wilke's tenure at Amazon, he called a former teacher of his, Stephen Graves, a professor of management science at MIT, and asked for help. Amazon operated an e-commerce distribution network of unrivaled scale but the company was still struggling to run it efficiently. Its seven fulfillment centers around the world were expensive, their output inconsistent. Bezos wanted the Amazon website to be able to tell customers precisely when their packages would be delivered. For example, a college student ordering a crucial book for a final exam should know that the book would be delivered the following Monday. But the fulfillment centers were not yet reliable enough to make that kind of specific prediction.

Wilke asked Graves if he might meet with Wilke and his colleagues later that month to take a fresh look at their problems. Bezos and Wilke were asking themselves a fundamental question that seems surprising today: Should Amazon even be in the business of storing and distributing its products? The alternative was to shift to the model used by rivals like Buy.com, which took orders online but had products drop-shipped from manufacturers and distributors like Ingram.

That St. Patrick's Day, some of Amazon's biggest brains descended on a drab meeting room at the Fernley, Nevada, fulfillment center. Jeff Bezos and Brewster Kahle, a supercomputer engineer and founder of Alexa Internet, a data-mining company Amazon had acquired, made the two-hour flight from Seattle on Bezos's newly purchased private plane, a Dassault Falcon 900 EX. Stephen Graves flew from Massachusetts to Reno and then drove the dreary thirty-four miles through the desert to Fernley. A few other Amazon engineers were there, as was the facility's senior manager at the time, Bert Wegner. In the morning, the group toured the fulfillment center and listened to a presentation by one of the company's primary contractors, who listed the benefits of additional equipment and software that he could sell them, reflecting the same traditional thinking about distribution that wasn't working in the first place. They then dismissed the surprised contractor for the day and spent the afternoon filling up whiteboards and tackling the question of how everything at the FC might be improved. For lunch, they brought in McDonald's and snacked from the building's vending machines.

For Wegner, the questions being asked that day carried personal resonance. 'We had a key decision to make,' he says. 'Was distribution a commodity or was it a core competency? If it's a commodity, why invest in it? And when we grow, do we continue to do it on our own or do we outsource it?' If Amazon chose to outsource it, Wegner might be out of a job. 'I basically saw my own career flash before my eyes,' he says.

Amazon's problem boiled down to something called, in the esoteric lexicon of manufacturing, batches. The equipment in Amazon's FCs had originally been acquired by Jimmy Wright, and, like the system in Walmart's distribution centers, was designed by its manufacturers to operate in waves – moving from minimum capacity to maximum and then back again. At the start of a wave, a group of workers called pickers fanned out across the stacks of products, each in his or her own zone, to retrieve the items ordered by customers. At the time, Amazon used the common pick-to-light system. Various lights on the aisles and on individual shelves guided pickers to the right products, which they would then deposit into their totes – a cart of the picks from that wave. They then delivered their totes to conveyor belts that fed into the giant sorting machines, which rearranged products into customer orders and sent them off on a new set of conveyor belts to be packed and shipped.

The software required pickers to work individually, but, naturally, some took longer than others, which led to problems. For example, if ninety-nine pickers completed their batches within forty-five minutes but the one hundredth picker took additional half an hour, those ninety-nine pickers had to sit idly and wait. Only when that final tote cleared the chute did the system come fully alive again, with a thunderous roar that rolled through the fulfillment center and indicated that it was again ready to start operating at peak capacity.

Everything in the fulfillment center happened in this episodic manner. For a company trying to maximize its capacity during the big push each holiday season, that was a huge problem. Wilke subscribed to the principles laid out in a seminal book about constraints in manufacturing, Eliyahu M. Goldratt's *The Goal*, published in 1984. The book, cloaked in the guise of an entertaining novel, instructs manufacturers to focus on maximizing the efficiency of their biggest bottlenecks. For Amazon, that was the Crisplant sorting machines, where the products all ended up, but picking in batches limited how fast the sorters could be fed. As a result, the machines were operating at full capacity only during the brief few minutes at the peak of the batch. Wilke's group had experimented with trying to run overlapping waves, but that tended to overload the Crisplant sorters and, in the dramatic terminology of the general managers, 'blow up the building.' It would take hours to clean up that mess and get everything back on track.

In the meeting that day at Fernley, the executives and engineers questioned the prevailing orthodoxies of retail distribution. In the late afternoon, everyone headed back onto the facility floor and watched orders move haltingly through the facility. 'I didn't know Jeff Bezos but I just remember being blown away by the fact that he was there with his sleeves rolled up, climbing around the conveyors with all of us,' says Stephen Graves, the MIT professor. 'We were thinking critically and throwing around some crazy ideas of how we can do this better.'

At the end of the day, Bezos, Wilke, and their colleagues reached a conclusion: the equipment and software from third-party vendors simply wasn't designed for the task at hand. To escape from batches and move toward a continuous and predictable flow of orders through the facility, Amazon would have to rewrite all the software code. Instead of exiting the business of distribution, they had to reinvest in it.

Over the next few years, 'one by one, we unplugged our vendors' modems and we watched as their jaws hit the floor,' says Wegner. 'They couldn't believe we were engineering our own solutions.' When Amazon later opened small facilities in places like Seattle and Las Vegas to handle easily packable items and larger fulfillment centers in Indianapolis, Phoenix, and elsewhere, it would go even further, dispensing with the pick-to-light systems and big Crisplant sorting machines altogether and instead employing a less automated approach that favored invisible algorithms. Employees would bring their totes from the shelves right to the packing stations, their movements carefully coordinated by software. Slowly, Amazon would vanquish wave-based picking, elicit more productivity from its workers, and improve the accuracy and reliability of its fulfillment centers.

Wilke's gradual success in making the logistics network more efficient would offer Amazon innumerable advantages in the years ahead. Tightly controlling distribution allowed the company to make specific promises to customers on when they could expect their purchases to arrive. Amazon's operating all of its own technology, from the supply chain to the website, allowed Russell Allgor and his engineers to create algorithms that modeled countless scenarios for each order so systems could pick the one that would yield the quickest and cheapest delivery. Millions of those decisions could be made every hour, helping Amazon reduce its costs – and thus lower prices and increase volume of sales. The challenge was getting good enough to do this well.

'No matter how hard it is, the consolidation of products within fulfillment centers pays for the inventory and for pieces of the overhead,' says Jeff Wilke, who claims that he never worried that Bezos would abandon the FC model at the Fernley meeting. 'The principles and math were on our side, and I realized early on that this was a company where you can carry the day when you have the principles and math on your side, and you are patient and tenacious.'

Whenever Jeff Bezos roamed a fulfillment center or his own Seattle headquarters, he looked for defects – flaws in the company's systems or even its corporate culture. On an otherwise regular weekday morning in 2003, for example, Bezos walked into an Amazon conference room and was taken aback. Mounted on the wall, in a corner of the room, was a newly installed television meant for video presentations to employees. A TV in a conference room did not by itself seem controversial, yet Bezos was not pleased.

The installations, which he had not known about or authorized, represented to him both a clumsy attempt at interoffice communication and an extravagant expenditure. 'How can anything good be communicated in this way,' he complained.

Bezos had all the new televisions in Amazon's conference rooms immediately removed. But according to Matt Williams, a longtime Amazon manager, Bezos deliberately kept the metal mounts hanging in the conference rooms for many years, even some that were so low on the wall that employees were likely to stand up and hit them. Like a warlord leaving the decapitated heads of his enemies on stakes outside his village walls, he was using the mounts as a symbol, and as an admonition to employees about how not to behave.

The television episode was the foundation of another official award at Amazon, this one presented to an employee who identified an activity that was bureaucratic and wasteful. The suddenly superfluous televisions were given as the prize. When the supply ran out, that commendation morphed into the Door-Desk award, given to an employee who came up with 'a well-built idea that helps us to deliver lower prices to customers' – the prize was a door-desk ornament. Bezos was once again looking for ways to reinforce his values within the company.

Around the same time he was ripping televisions off the walls, Bezos made two significant changes to the corporate culture. As part of his ongoing quest for a better allocation of his own time, he decreed that he would no longer have one-on-one meetings with his subordinates. These meetings tended to be filled with trivial updates and political distractions, rather than problem solving and brainstorming. Even today, Bezos rarely meets alone with an individual colleague.

The other change was also peculiar and perhaps unique in corporate history. Up until that time, Amazon employees had been using Microsoft's PowerPoint and Excel spreadsheet software to present their ideas in meetings. Bezos believed that method concealed lazy thinking. 'PowerPoint is a very imprecise communication mechanism,' says Jeff Holden, Bezos's former D. E. Shaw colleague, who by that point had joined the S Team. 'It is fantastically easy to hide between bullet points. You are never forced to express your thoughts completely.'

Bezos announced that employees could no longer use such corporate crutches and would have to write their presentations in prose, in what he called narratives. The S Team debated with him over the wisdom of scrapping PowerPoint but Bezos insisted. He wanted people thinking deeply and taking the time to express their thoughts cogently. 'I don't want this place to become a country club,' he was fond of saying as he pushed employees harder. 'What we do is hard. This is not where people go to retire.'

There was a period of grumbling adjustment. Meetings no longer started with someone standing up and commanding the floor as they had previously at Amazon and everywhere else throughout the corporate land. Instead, the narratives were passed out and everyone sat quietly reading the document for fifteen minutes – or longer. At the beginning, there was no page limit, an omission that Diego Piacentini recalled as 'painful' and that led to several weeks of employees churning out papers as long as sixty pages. Quickly there was a supplemental decree: a six-page limit on narratives, with additional room for footnotes.

Not everyone embraced the new format. Many employees felt the system was rigged to reward good writers but not necessarily efficient operators or innovative thinkers. Engineers in particular were unhappy to suddenly find themselves crafting essays as if they had been hurled back through time into ninth-grade English. 'Putting everything into a narrative ended up sort of being like describing a spreadsheet,' says Lyn Blake, a vice president relationships with manufacturers at the time. Blake herself suspected the whole thing was a phase. (It wasn't.)

Bezos refined the formula even further. Every time a new feature or product was proposed, he decreed that the narrative should take the shape of a mock press release. The goal was to get employees to distill a pitch into its purest essence, to start from something the customer might see – the public announcement – and work backward. Bezos didn't believe anyone could make a good decision about a feature or a product without knowing precisely how it would be communicated to the world – and what the hallowed customer would make of it.

Steve Jobs was known for the clarity of his insights about what customers wanted, but he was also known for his volatility with coworkers. Apple's founder reportedly fired employees in the elevator and screamed at under-performing executives. Perhaps there is something endemic in the fast-paced technology business that causes this behavior, because such intensity is not exactly rare among its CEOs. Bill Gates used to throw epic tantrums. Steve Ballmer, his successor at Microsoft, had a propensity for throwing chairs. Andy Grove, the longtime CEO of Intel, was known to be so harsh and intimidating that a subordinate once fainted during a performance review.

Jeff Bezos fit comfortably into this mold. His manic drive and boldness trumped other conventional leadership ideals, such as building consensus and promoting civility. While he was charming and capable of great humor in public, in private, Bezos could bite an employee's head right off.

Bezos was prone to melodramatic temper tantrums that some Amazon employees called, privately, nutters. A colleague failing to meet Bezos's exacting standards would predictably set off a nutter. If an employee did not have the right answers, or tried to bluff the right answer, or took credit for someone else's work, or exhibited a whiff of internal politics, or showed any kind of uncertainty or frailty in the heat of battle, the vessel in Bezos's forehead popped out and his filter fell away. He was capable of both hyperbole and cruelty in these moments, and over the years he delivered some devastating rebukes to employees. Among his greatest hits, collected and relayed by Amazon veterans:

'If that's our plan, I don't like our plan.'

'I'm sorry, did I take my stupid pills today?'

'Do I need to go down and get the certificate that says I'm CEO of the company to get you to stop challenging me on this?'

'Are you trying to take credit for something you had nothing to do with?'

'Are you lazy or just incompetent?'

'I trust you to run world-class operations and this is another example of how you are letting me down.'

'If I hear that idea again, I'm gonna have to kill myself.'

'Does it surprise you that you don't know the answer to that question?'

'Why are you ruining my life?'

[After someone presented a proposal.] 'We need to apply some human intelligence to this problem.'

[After reviewing the annual plan from the supply-chain team.] 'I guess supply chain isn't doing anything interesting next year.'

[After reading a narrative.] 'This document was clearly written by the B team. Can someone get me the A team document? I don't want to waste my time with the B team document.'

Some Amazon employees currently advance the theory that Bezos, like Steve Jobs, Bill Gates, and Larry Ellison, lacks a certain degree of empathy and that as a result he treats workers like expendable resources without taking into account their contributions to the company. That in turn allows him to coldly allocate capital and manpower and make hyperrational business decisions while another executive might let emotion and personal relationships intrude. But they also acknowledge that Bezos is primarily consumed with improving the company's performance and customer service, and that personnel issues are secondary. 'This is not somebody who takes pleasure at tearing someone a new asshole. He is not that kind of person,' says Kim Rachmeler. 'Jeff doesn't tolerate stupidity, even accidental stupidity.'

Right or wrong, Bezos's behavior was often easier to accept because he was so frequently on target with his criticisms, to the amazement and often irritation of employees. Bruce Jones, the former Amazon vice president, describes leading a five-engineer team working to create algorithms to optimize pickers' movements in the fulfillment centers while the company was trying to solve the problem of batches. The group spent nine months on the task, then presented their work to Bezos and the S Team. 'We had beautiful documents and everyone was really prepared,' Jones says. Bezos read the paper, said, 'You're all wrong,' stood up, and started writing on the whiteboard.

'He had no background in control theory, no background in operating systems,' Jones says. 'He only had minimum experience in the distribution centers and never spent weeks and months out on the line.' But Bezos laid out his argument on the whiteboard and 'every stinking thing he put down was correct and true,' Jones says. 'It would be easier to stomach if we could prove he was wrong but we couldn't. That was a typical interaction with Jeff. He had this unbelievable ability to be incredibly intelligent about things he had nothing to do with, and he was totally ruthless about communicating it.'

In 2002 Amazon changed the way it accounted for inventory, from a system called last-in first-out, or LIFO, to one called first-in first-out, or FIFO. The change allowed Amazon to better distinguish between its products and the products that were owned and stored in the FCs by partners like Toys 'R' Us and Target.

Jones's supply-chain team was in charge of this complicated effort, and its software, ridden by bugs, created a few difficult days during which Amazon's systems were unable to formally recognize any revenue.

On the third day, Jones was updating the S Team on the transition when Bezos tore into him. 'He called me a "complete fucking idiot" and said he had no idea why he hired idiots like me at the company, and said, "I need you to clean up your organization,"' Jones recalls, years later. 'It was brutal. I almost quit. I was a resource of his that failed. An hour later he would have been the same guy as always and it would have been different. He can compartmentalize like no one I've ever seen.'

As Jones left the FIFO meeting, Jeff Wilke's administrative assistant approached him with a telephone. Wilke was calling from vacation in Arizona, where he'd already heard about the confrontation. 'He said, "Bruce, I want you to know I'm behind you one hundred percent. I'm completely confident in you. If you need anything, I'm on a golf course, and I'll do whatever I can to help."'

Jeff Wilke wasn't always the softer counterbalance to Bezos. The pair visited each fulfillment center every fall in an annual ritual they called the whistle-stop tour. They spent a week on the road, one day in each FC, and used their commanding presence to focus attention on eliminating errors and improving processes. General managers, their palms sweaty and their pulses elevated, would present to the pair, laying out their emergency scenarios and the ways in which they had once again managed to wrangle thousands of temporary workers for the holidays. Wilke and Bezos dug into the details, asking their inhumanly prescient questions. It was both inspiring and terrifying. 'Those guys could be brutal,' says Mark Mastandrea. 'You had to be comfortable saying, "I don't know; I'll get back to you in a couple of hours," and then doing it. You could not ever bullshit or make stuff up. That would be the end.'

T. E. Mullane worked in Amazon's logistics network for years, helping to open and manage new fulfillment centers. He opened a new FC in Chambersburg, Pennsylvania, and hosted Wilke on his first visit to the facility. Wilke, Mullane says, started the tour by quietly walking the inside perimeter of the building. In a corner of the building near the inbound docks, he encountered a disorganized pile of nonconveyable products – too heavy to move on the conveyor belts. For one reason or another, workers had not been able to match the merchandise with order slips and so had left them in a heap.

After the walk, Wilke looked at Mullane and initiated a typical exchange. 'T.E., do you know why I walked the perimeter? Tell me why.'

'To look for errors,' Mullane said.

'So why do the operators leave piles?'

'Because the process isn't correct right now. It's not precise and predictable.'

'Right. So you are going to take care of this?'

'Yes.'

The whistle-stop visits usually occurred midway through the fourth quarter of the year, just as the holiday season was ramping up but before the big shopping days known as Black Friday and Cyber Monday. During the big push itself, Wilke would return to Seattle but stay in touch with subordinates via his grueling daily conference calls.

The pressure during the holidays could get so intense that Wilke instituted a new ritual as a form of therapeutic release: primal screams. When a logistics executive or his team accomplished something significant, Wilke would allow the person or even the entire group to lean back, close their eyes, and yell into the phone at the tops of their lungs. 'It was clearly a great release but the first time it almost blew my phone speaker,' Wilke says.

After the big push was over and the last box had shipped, typically on December 23, 'you got to enjoy Christmas Day more than anybody else on the planet, because you had worked so hard to get there,' says Bert Wegner. Then planning would begin all over again.

In 2002, Jeff Wilke led the first significant effort to use Amazon's now impressive size to exact concessions from a major business partner: the United Parcel Service. That year, Amazon's contract with UPS was up for renewal, and the package-delivery giant, embroiled in a separate standoff with the Teamsters Union, did not appear to be in the mood to grant more-favorable terms to the online upstart. Amazon wasn't using Federal Express in any significant way at the time, and the primary alternative to UPS, the federally managed U.S. Postal Service, was not permitted to negotiate its rates. Amazon, it seemed, had no leverage.

But early that year, sensing an opportunity, Wilke approached Bruce Jones in Operations and asked him to begin cultivating FedEx. Over the course of six months, Jones and a team traveled frequently to FedEx's headquarters in Memphis, integrating their systems and quietly ratcheting up the volume of packages. Amazon also increased its shipment injections with the U.S. Postal Service: company employees drove Amazon's trucks to the post office and inserted packages directly into the flow of federal mail.

Wilke started his negotiations with UPS that summer in Louisville, ahead of a September 1 contract deadline. When UPS was predictably obstinate about deviating from its standard rate card, Wilke threatened to walk. UPS officials thought he was bluffing. Wilke called Jones in Seattle and said, 'Bruce, turn them off.'

'In twelve hours, they went from millions of pieces [from Amazon] a day to a couple a day,' says Jones, who flew to Fernley to watch the fallout. The standoff lasted seventy-two hours and went unnoticed by customers and other outsiders. In Fernley, UPS representatives told Jones they knew Amazon couldn't keep it up and predicted that FedEx would be overwhelmed. They were likely right. But before it came to that, UPS execs caved and gave Amazon discounted rates.

'Yes, we could have operated mostly without them,' Wilke says. 'But it would have been very hard, very painful. They knew that. I didn't want to leave them, I just wanted a fair price.' In the end, he got one, bringing home one of Amazon's first bulk discounts and teaching the company an enduring lesson about the power of scale and the reality of Darwinian survival in the world of big business.

In 2003, Jeff Bezos came up with yet another way to frame his concept of Amazon. This time, it was for a group of buyers who were leading the company's charge into the new hard-lines categories, a group of products that included hardware, sporting goods, and electronics. Amazon, Bezos said, was the unstore.

At the time, Bezos had selected jewelry as the company's next big opportunity. It was a tempting target: the products were small, the prices were high, and shipping was relatively cheap. He tapped retail managers Eric Broussard and Randy Miller to lead the effort. As usual, the executives Bezos chose to head the product's sales had no prior experience selling that product.

Though it seemed alluring, selling jewelry posed some challenges. Expensive baubles were difficult to display in full detail online; also, the products were valuable and tempting to pilfering workers in the company's fulfillment centers. Another issue arose with pricing: The jewelry industry had a simplistic pricing model with generous margins. Retail markup was significant; stores doubled the wholesale cost (a practice known as keystone pricing) or even tripled it (known as triple-keystone pricing). Jewelry manufacturers and retailers clung tightly to that custom, which didn't fit well with Bezos's newly adamant resolve to offer the lowest prices anywhere.

The Amazon jewelry executives decided on an approach similar to the one the company had recently used for its cautious first foray into apparel. They would let other, more experienced retailers sell everything on the site via Amazon's Marketplace, and Amazon would take a commission. Meanwhile, the company could watch and learn. 'That was something we did quite well,' says Randy Miller. 'If you don't know anything about the business, launch it through the Marketplace, bring retailers in, watch what they do and what they sell, understand it, and then get into it.'

Bezos seemed amenable to that plan, at least at first. And then one day, in a meeting with the S Team and the hard-lines group, something set him off. They were discussing the margins in the jewelry business, and one of Randy Miller's colleagues mentioned how the jewelry industry conducted business in the 'traditional way.' 'You're not thinking about this right,' Bezos said, and he excused himself to get something from his office. He was gone a few minutes, then returned with a stack of photocopied documents and handed a page to everyone in the meeting. It had only one paragraph, about ten sentences long. It began with the words *We are the 'Unstore'*.

The document, as Miller and other executives who were there remember it, defined how Bezos saw his own company – and explains why, even years later, so many businesses are unsettled by Amazon's entrance into their markets.

Being an unstore meant, in Bezos's view, that Amazon was not bound by the traditional rules of retail. It had limitless shelf space and personalized itself for every customer. It allowed negative reviews in addition to positive ones, and it placed used products directly next to new ones so that customers could make informed choices. In Bezos's eyes, Amazon offered both everyday low prices and great customer service. It was Walmart *and* Nordstrom's.

Being an unstore also meant that Amazon had to concern itself only with what was best for the customer. The conventions of the jewelry business allowed routine 100 or 200 percent markups, but, well, that just didn't apply to Amazon.

In that meeting, Bezos decreed that Amazon was not in retail, and therefore did not have to kowtow to retail. He suggested that Amazon could ignore the conventions of pricing in the jewelry business and envisioned customers buying a bracelet on the site for $1,200 and then going to get an appraisal and finding out from the local jeweler that the item was actually worth $2,000. 'I know you're retailers and I hired you because you are retailers,' Bezos said. 'But I want you to understand that from this day forward, you are not bound by the old rules.'

Amazon started selling jewelry in the spring of 2004; two-thirds of the selection came from its Marketplace and the other third came directly from Amazon. For months, Bezos was consumed by the design of the elegant wooden jewelry box that Amazon would use. 'The box was everything to him,' says Randy Miller. 'He wanted it to be as iconic as Tiffany's.'

Amazon contracted with celebrity socialite Paris Hilton

to sell her jewelry designs exclusively on the site, and the company spent considerable resources creating a tool to let customers design their own rings on the website. Amazon's new staff jewelers would then craft the rings over an open flame on the mezzanine of the Lexington, Kentucky, fulfillment center. Additionally, Amazon introduced a feature called Diamond Search that let customers look for individual stones based on carat, shape, and color. And in a draconian tactic that further exposed his competitive streak, Bezos instructed Amazon's communication staff to time public announcements in the jewelry category to coincide with the quarterly reports of Seattle-based rival Blue Nile, the leader in online jewelry sales.

Selling jewelry became a modestly profitable business for Amazon, according to employees who worked on the category, but the seeds clearly did not grow into the trees that Bezos had envisioned. Although Amazon's watch business became robust, customers still wanted to go into actual stores to pick out engagement rings. After a while, the ring-designing tool and Diamond Search disappeared from the site. Amazon's attention wandered to new battlefields, such as shoes and apparel. Employees who passed through jewelry later described a grueling experience, with shifting goals, rotating bosses, and endless disputes with suppliers who disliked Amazon's pricing. Being an unstore was evidently not as easy as Bezos had thought. Amazon executives in the hard-lines business during these years had a running joke: 'Why do you think they call them hard?'

* * *

As the hard-lines teams were bringing Amazon into new categories, with varying degrees of success, Jeff Wilke and his group had nearly completed their job morphing Amazon's fulfillment process from a network of haphazardly constructed facilities into something that could more accurately be considered a system of polynomial equations. A customer might place an order for a half a dozen products, and the company's software would quickly examine factors like the address of the customer, the location of the merchandise in the FCs, and the cutoff times for shipping at the various facilities around the country. Then it would take all those variables and calculate both the fastest and the least expensive way to ship the items.

The complete software rewrite of the logistics network was having its desired effect. Cost per unit (the overall expense of fulfilling the order of a particular item) fell, while ship times (how quickly merchandise ordered on the website was loaded onto a truck) shortened. A year after the Fernley meeting, the click-to-ship time for most items in the company's FCs was as minimal as four hours, down from the three days it had taken when Wilke first started at the company. The standard for the rest of the e-commerce industry at the time was twelve hours.

Amazon's ability to ship products efficiently and offer precise delivery times to customers gave the company a competitive edge over its rivals, particularly eBay, which avoided this part of the business altogether. Fulfillment was a lever that Bezos had invested in, and he started using it to guide strategy.

By 2002, the company was offering customers the option, for an extra fee, of overnight, two-day, or three-day shipping. Wilke's team called these fast-track or fast-lane orders and built a separate process around them. On the floor of the FCs, those items were accelerated through the Crisplant sorters and were the first to be delivered to the packers and the trucks waiting in the yard. The company refined this ability gradually, pushing the cutoff time for next-day delivery to forty-five minutes before the last trucks left its fulfillment centers. Expedited shipping was almost prohibitively expensive, for customers and for Amazon, but the website's having the capability was to pay huge strategic dividends.

In 2004, an Amazon engineer named Charlie Ward used an employee-suggestion program called the Idea Tool to make a proposal. Super Saver Shipping, he reasoned, catered to price-conscious customers whose needs were not time sensitive – they were like the airline travelers who paid a lower rate because they stayed at their destinations over a Saturday night. Their orders got placed on the trucks whenever there was room for them, reducing the overall shipping cost. Why not create a service for the opposite type of customer, Ward suggested, a speedy shipping club for consumers whose needs were time sensitive and who weren't price conscious? He suggested that it could work like a music club, with a monthly charge.

That fall, employees showed enough enthusiasm for Ward's proposal that it came to the attention of Bezos. Immediately enchanted by the idea, Bezos asked a group that included Vijay Ravindran, the director of Amazon's ordering systems, to meet him on a Saturday in the boathouse behind his home in Medina. Bezos conveyed a sense of urgency as he began the meeting, saying that the shipping club was now top priority. 'This is a big idea,' he told the gathered engineers. He asked Ravindran and Jeff Holden to put together a SWAT team of a dozen of their best people and told them he wanted the program ready by the next earnings announcement, in February – just weeks away.

Bezos met with the group, which included Charlie Ward and Dorothy Nicholls, who would later go on to become a longtime Kindle executive, weekly over the next two months. They devised the two-day shipping offer, exploiting the ability of Wilke's group to accelerate the handling of individual items in its fulfillment centers. The team proposed several names for the new feature, including Super Saver Platinum, which Bezos rejected because he didn't want people to see the service as a money-saving program. Bing Gordon, Amazon board member and partner at Kleiner Perkins, claims he came up with the name Prime, though some members of the team believe the name was chosen because fast-track pallets were in prime positions in fulfillment centers. Focus groups were brought into Amazon's offices to test the Prime sign-up process. The volunteers found the process confusing, so Holden proposed using a large orange button with the words *Create my Prime account* right inside the button.

Selecting the fee for the service was a challenge; there were no clear financial models because no one knew how many customers would join or how joining would affect their purchasing habits. The group considered several prices, including $49 and $99. Bezos decided on $79 per year, saying it needed to be large enough to matter to consumers but small enough that they would be willing to try it out. 'It was never about the seventy-nine dollars. It was really about changing people's mentality so they wouldn't shop anywhere else,' says Ravindran, who later became chief digital officer for the *Washington Post*.

Bezos was adamant about the February launch date. When the Prime team reported that they needed more time, Bezos delayed the earnings announcement by a week. The team members finished mapping out the details for the service at three o'clock in the morning on the day of the deadline. It was a complex undertaking, but it was achievable because so many of the elements of the program already existed. Wilke's organization had created a system for the expedited picking, packing, and shipping of prioritized items within the FCs. The company's European operation had built a subscription-membership tool for its nascent DVD-by-mail business (a Netflix clone) in Germany and the United Kingdom, and that service, though rudimentary, was quickly improved and pushed into production in the United States to support Prime. 'It was almost like Prime was already there, and we were putting the finishing touches on it,' Holden says.

In many ways, the introduction of Amazon Prime was an act of faith. The company had little concrete idea how the program would affect orders or customers' likelihood to shop in other categories beyond media. If each expedited shipment cost the company $8, and if a shipping-club member placed twenty orders a year, it would cost the company $160 in shipping, far above the $79 fee. The service was expensive to run, and there was no clear way to break even. 'We made this decision even though every single financial analysis said we were completely crazy to give two-day shipping for free,' says Diego Piacentini.

But Bezos was going on gut and experience. He knew that Super Saver Shipping had changed customers' behavior, motivating them to place bigger orders and shop in new categories. He also knew from 1-Click ordering that when friction was removed from online shopping, customers spent more. That accelerated the company's fabled flywheel – the virtuous cycle. When customers spent more, Amazon's volumes increased, so it could lower shipping costs and negotiate new deals with vendors. That saved the company money, which would help pay for Prime and lead back to lower prices.

Prime would eventually justify its existence. The service turned customers into Amazon addicts who gorged on the almost instant gratification of having purchases reliably appear two days after they ordered them. Signing up for Amazon Prime, Jason Kilar said at the time, 'was like going from a dial-up to a broadband Internet connection.' The shipping club also keyed off a faintly irrational human impulse to maximize the benefits of a membership club one has already joined. With the punitive cost of expedited shipping, Amazon lost money on Prime membership, at first. But gradually Wilke's organization got better at combining multiple items from a customer's order into a single box, which saved money and helped drive down Amazon's transportation costs by double-digit percentages each year.

Prime wouldn't reveal itself to the world as a huge success for another few years, and originally it was unpopular inside Amazon. One technology executive griped to Vijay Ravindran that he feared Bezos would now believe that he could commandeer engineers and ram his favorite projects through the system. Other execs were wary because of Prime's estimated losses. Almost alone, Bezos believed fervently in Prime, closely tracking sign-ups each day and intervening every time the retail group dropped promotions for the shipping club from the home page.

But even back in February of 2005, Bezos suspected he had a winner. At Amazon's all-hands meeting that month at the usual location, the classic Moore Theater on Second Avenue, Vijay Ravindran presented Prime to the company, and afterward Bezos led everyone in a round of applause.

* * *

Prime opened up new doors, and the next year Amazon introduced a service called Fulfillment by Amazon, or FBA. The program allowed other merchants to have their products stored and shipped from Amazon's fulfillment centers. As an added benefit, their products qualified for two-day shipping for Prime members, exposing the sellers to Amazon's most active customers. For Wilke's logistics group, it was a proud moment. 'That is when it really hit home,' says Bert Wegner. 'We had built such a good service that people were willing to pay us to use it.'

So when Bezos pulled Wilke out of an operating review in late 2006, Wilke wasn't expecting to hear that that holiday season would be his last in the world of logistics. Bezos wanted Wilke to take over the entire North American retail division, and Wilke was charged with finding his own replacement. Wilke thought that Amazon's progress in its FCs had plateaued, so instead of promoting from within the ranks of Amazon's logistics executives, all of them molded, as he was, by the dogma of Six Sigma, Wilke went looking for someone with a fresh approach and additional international experience.

The search led him to Marc Onetto, a former General Electric executive with a thick French accent and a gift for animated storytelling. Under Onetto's watch, engineers once again rewrote elements of Amazon's logistics software and devised a computer system, called Mechanical Sensei, that simulated all the orders coursing through Amazon's fulfillment centers and predicted where new FCs would most productively be located. Onetto also shifted Amazon's focus toward lean manufacturing, another management philosophy that emanated from Toyota and was directed at eliminating waste and making practical changes on the shop floor. Japanese consultants occasionally came to work with Amazon, and they were so unimpressed and derogatory that Amazon employees gave them a nickname: the insultants.

Though Amazon was intensely focused on its software and systems, there was another key element of its distribution system – the low-wage laborers who actually worked in it. As Amazon grew throughout the decade, it hired tens of thousands of temporary employees each holiday season and usually kept on about 10 to 15 percent of them permanently. These generally low-skilled workers, toiling for ten to twelve dollars an hour in places where there were few other good jobs, could find Amazon to be a somewhat cruel master. Theft was a constant problem, as the FCs were stocked with easily concealable goodies like DVDs and jewelry, so the company outfitted all of its FCs with metal detectors and security cameras and eventually contracted with an outside security firm to patrol the facilities. 'They definitely viewed everyone as someone who could potentially steal from them,' says Randall Krause, an associate who worked at the Fernley FC in 2010. 'I didn't really take it personally because probably a lot of people actually were stealing.'

Amazon tried to combat employee delinquency by using a point system to track how workers performed their jobs. Arriving late cost an employee half a point; failing to show up altogether was three points. Even calling in sick cost a point. An employee who collected six such demerits was let go. 'They laid out their expectations and if you didn't meet them, they had people waiting to take your job,' says Krause. 'They wouldn't give you a second chance.'

Over the years, unions like the Teamsters and the United Food and Commercial Workers tried to organize associates in Amazon's U.S. FCs, passing out flyers in the parking lots and in some cases knocking on the doors of workers' homes. Amazon's logistics executives quickly met these campaigns by engaging with employees and listening to complaints while making it clear that unionizing efforts would not be tolerated. The sheer size of Amazon's workforce and the fact that turnover is so high in the fulfillment centers make it extremely difficult for anyone to organize workers. Most recently, in 2013, workers at two Amazon FCs in Germany went on strike for four days, demanding better pay and benefits. The company refused to negotiate with the union.

The unions themselves say there's another hurdle involved – employees' fear of retribution. In January 2001, the company closed a Seattle customer-service call center, as part of a larger round of cost-cutting measures. Amazon said closing the facility was unrelated to recent union activity there, but the union involved was not so sure. 'The number one thing standing in the way of Amazon unionization is fear,' says Rennie Sawade, a spokesman for the Washington Alliance of Technology Workers. Employees are 'afraid they'll fire you – even though it's technically not legal. You're the one who has to fight to get your job back if they do.'

Amazon often had to contend with something even more unpredictable than stealing, unionization, or truancy in its FCs: the weather. Company managers learned quickly that they had no choice but to install air-conditioning in their first fulfillment centers in Phoenix, where the summers were brutal, but they skimped on what they viewed as an unnecessary expense in colder climates. Instead, fulfillment-center managers developed protocols to deal with heat waves. If temperatures spiked above 100 degrees, which they often did over the summer in the Midwest, five minutes were added to morning and afternoon breaks, which were normally fifteen minutes long, and the company installed fans and handed out free Gatorade.

These moves sound almost comically insufficient, and they were. In 2011, the *Morning Call*, an Allentown newspaper, published an exposé about poor working conditions in Amazon's two Lehigh Valley fulfillment centers during that summer's brutal heat wave. Fifteen workers suffered heat-related symptoms and were taken to a local hospital. An emergency room doctor called federal regulators to report an unsafe working environment. In a detail that struck many readers and Amazon customers as downright cruel, the newspaper noted that Amazon paid a private ambulance company to have paramedics stationed outside the FCs during the heat wave — ready to deal with employees as they dropped.

Jeff Wilke argues that Amazon's overall safety record, as reflected in the low number of incidents reported to the Occupational Safety and Health Administration, or OSHA, demonstrates that it is safer to work in the company's warehouses than in department stores. (The low number of recorded complaints to OSHA regarding Amazon facilities backs up this contention.[3]) In terms of public perception, though, it didn't matter. The report sent shock waves through the media, and the following year, battered by the negative publicity, Amazon announced it was paying $52 million to install air-conditioning in more of its fulfillment centers.[4]

Bezos and Wilke could battle chaos, they could try to out-engineer it, but they could never eradicate it completely. The capricious and unpredictable quirks of human nature always managed to emerge in unexpected ways, like in December of 2010, when a disgruntled employee set a fire in a supply room in Fernley. Employees were

Jeff Bezos, childhood portrait. *(Courtesy of Amazon)*

Jeffrey Preston Bezos, age five, with his grandfather, Lawrence Preston "Pop" Gise, in Cotulla, Texas, in 1969. *(Courtesy of Amazon)*

Bezos in 1982, as a senior at Miami Palmetto High School. *(Seth Poppel/ Yearbook Library)*

MOST VERSATILE RIDER of the Albuquerque Unicycle Club is Ted Jorgensen, who received one of three trophies awarded to club members at the club's third anniversary dinner Tuesday night at the Heights Community Center. Other trophies went to Rachel Westerman, "most creative" rider, and Tony Stanphill, winner of the "anniversary race." New officers of the club are Betty Ross, president; Tommy Ratcliff, vice president; Margaret Bradley, secretary, and Jeanne Baum, treasurer. Club members will travel to Oklahoma City this fall to ride in the community celebration. The group meets each Tuesday at 7:30 in the community

Ted Jorgensen in 1961. *(Photograph courtesy of Ted Jorgensen)*

Ted Jorgensen in his bike shop, the Roadrunner Bike Center, March 27, 2013. *(Photograph by Benjamin Rasmussen)*

Jackie and Mike Bezos at the 29th Annual Aspen Institute Awards in 2012. *(© Patrick McMullan/ Photograph by Patrick McMullan)*

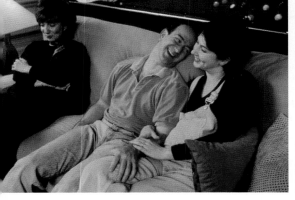

Bezos relaxes at home with MacKenzie and his mother, Jackie. *(© David Burnett/ Contact Press Images)*

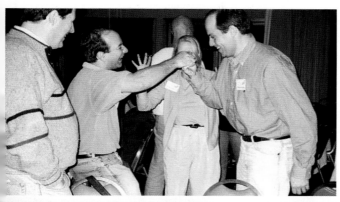

Jeff Bezos and
Amazon
employees.
*(Courtesy of
Laurel Canan)*

'ounding employee Shel Kaphan (left)
vith an early Amazon engineer.
Courtesy of Laurel Canan)

Jeff and MacKenzie Bezos (center)
celebrate with Amazon employees
at a company costume party.
(Courtesy of Amazon)

Amazon and Deutsche Bank employees who worked on Amazon's 1997 IPO
celebrate with family members in Cabo, Mexico. *(Courtesy of J. William Gurley)*

Jeff Bezos with Junglee executives (l-r) Brian Lent, Rakesh Mathur, and Ram Shriram, an early Google investor. *(Photograph courtesy of Brian Lent)*

Bezos helps process toy orders at the short-lived fulfillment center in McDonough, Georgia. *(© David Burnett/Contact Press Images)*

Senior vice president Jeff Wilke, who rebuilt Amazon's fulfillment network. *(© Brian Smale)*

Bezos stands on a Segway in 2002 as the ill-fated electric-powered transporter goes on sale exclusively at Amazon for $5,000. *(Mario Tama/Getty Images)*

Jeff Bezos rings the bell to open the NASDAQ trading session on Friday, September 7, 2001. *(Bloomberg)*

Jeff Bezos demonstrates an educational toy called Gus Gutz to talk-show host Jay Leno during his appearance on *The Tonight Show with Jay Leno* at the NBC studios in Burbank on December 29, 1999. *(Reuters)*

Bezos and tennis pro Anna Kournikova after an exhibition round of tennis at New York's Grand Central Terminal to promote Amazon's new apparel store, August 22, 2003. *(Evan Agostini/Getty Images)*

Jeff Bezos laughs with Google cofounder Sergey Brin at the Allen and Co. conference in Sun Valley, Idaho, in 2007. Bezos was among the original investors in Google. *(Rick Wilking/ Reuters)*

Bezos introduces the original Kindle e-reader at a news conference in New York City on November 19, 2007. *(Mark Lennihan/AP Photo)*

Jeff and MacKenzie Bezos in 2009. *(© Patrick McMullan Photograph by Patrick McMullan)*

Bezos introduces the Kindle Fire tablet in 2011. The device intensified the brewing competition between Amazon and Apple. *(Bloomberg)*

An Amazon employee demonstrates the Kindle Fire to reporters after a news conference. *(EPA/Justin Lane)*

NASA deputy administrator Lori Garver (third from right) takes a tour of the Kent, Washington, headquarters of Blue Origin, Bezos's private space-exploration company. *(Bill Ingalls/NASA)*

An Amazon fulfillment center in Milton Keynes, forty-five miles northwest of London. (*David Levene/Eyevine/Redux*)

In 2013, Amazon proposed radical design for a new headquarters downtown Seattle. (*NBBJ*)

evacuated and had to stand out in the cold shivering for two hours before being sent home, according to two employees who were there. That same year in Fernley, a worker preparing to quit hoisted himself onto a conveyor belt and took a long joyride through the facility. He was subsequently escorted out the door.

Perhaps the best story stems from the busy holiday season of 2006. A temporary employee in the Coffeyville, Kansas, fulfillment center showed up at the start of his shift and left at the end of it, but strangely, he was not logging any actual work in the hours in between. Amazon's time clocks were not yet linked to the system that tracked productivity, so the discrepancy went unnoticed for at least a week.

Finally someone uncovered the scheme. The worker had surreptitiously tunneled out a cavern inside an eight-foot-tall pile of empty wooden pallets in a far corner of the fulfillment center. Inside, completely blocked from view, he had created a cozy den and furnished it with items purloined from Amazon's plentiful shelves. There was food, a comfortable bed, pictures ripped from books adorning the walls – and several pornographic calendars. Brian Calvin, the general manager of the Coffeyville FC, busted the worker in his hovel and marched him out the door. The man left without argument and walked to a nearby bus stop; sheepish, one might imagine, but perhaps also just a little bit triumphant.

CHAPTER 7
A Technology Company, Not a Retailer

On July 30, 2005, Amazon celebrated its tenth anniversary at a gala at Seattle's Benaroya Hall. Authors James Patterson and Jim Collins and screenwriter Lawrence Kasdan spoke to employees and their guests, and Bob Dylan and Norah Jones performed and sang a rare duet, Dylan's 'I Shall Be Released.' The comedian Bill Maher acted as master of ceremonies. Communications vice president Kathy Savitt had persuaded Bezos to splurge on the historic moment, and, characteristically, they organized everything in such a way that it had a benefit for customers: the concert was streamed live on Amazon.com and watched by a million people.

Despite how far Amazon.com had come, it was still often a media afterthought. It was now officially the age of Google, the search-engine star from Silicon Valley. Google cofounders Larry Page and Sergey Brin were rewriting the story of the Internet. Their high-profile ascent, which included an IPO in 2004, was universally watched. Suddenly, clever online business models and experienced CEOs from traditional companies were passé in Silicon Valley, replaced by executives with deep technical competence.

This, it seemed, was to be the era of Stanford computer science PhDs, not Harvard MBAs or hedge-fund whiz kids from Wall Street, and the outside world did not believe Amazon would fare well in this profound shift. In the year leading up to its birthday celebration, Amazon's stock fell 12 percent as Wall Street focused on its slender margins and the superior business models of other Internet companies. Eighteen of the twenty-three financial analysts who covered the company at the time of the anniversary event expressed their skepticism by putting either a hold or a sell rating on Amazon's stock. The market capitalization of eBay, still viewed as a perfect venue for commerce, was three times larger than Amazon's. Google's valuation was more than four times Amazon's, and it had been public for less than a year. Fixed-price on-line retail was simply out of vogue.

Ever since the late 1990s, Bezos had been claiming that Amazon was a technology company pioneering e-commerce, not a retailer. But that sounded like wishful thinking. Amazon still collected a vast majority of its revenues by selling stuff to customers. Despite Bezos's protestations, Amazon looked, smelled, walked, and quacked like a retailer – and not a very profitable one at that.

A week after the tenth-anniversary show, the *New York Times* published a lengthy article on the front page of its Sunday business section that suggested Bezos was no longer the right man for the job.[1] 'It's time for Mr. Bezos to do as the founders of so many other technology companies have done before him: find a professionally trained chief executive with a deep background in operations to take the reins,' said an analyst quoted prominently in the piece.

The rise of Google did more than shift the mind-set of

Wall Street and the media. It posed a new set of challenges to Amazon. Rather than just hopping on Amazon.com and looking for products, Internet users were starting their shopping trips on Google, putting an unwelcome intermediary between Jeff Bezos and his customers. Google had its own e-commerce ambitions and early on opened a comparative shopping engine, dubbed Froogle. Even worse, both Amazon and eBay had to compete with each other to advertise alongside Google results for popular keywords like *flat-screen TV* and *Apple iPod*. They were essentially paying a tax to Google on sales that began with a search. To make this new kind of advertising more efficient, Amazon devised one of the Web's first automated search-ad-buying systems, naming it Urubamba, after a river in Peru, a tributary of the Amazon. But Bezos was wary of helping Google develop tools that it might then extend to Amazon's rivals. 'Treat Google like a mountain. You can climb the mountain, but you can't move it,' he told Blake Scholl, the young developer in charge of Urubamba. 'Use them, but don't make them smarter.'

Google competed with Amazon for both customers and talented engineers. After its IPO, the search giant opened an office in Kirkland, a twenty-minute drive from downtown Seattle. Google offered its employees lavish perks, like free food, office gyms, and day care for their children, not to mention valuable stock options. For its part, Amazon offered a sickly stock price and a combative internal culture, and employees still had to pay for their own parking and meals. Not surprisingly, Google began to suck engineers out of Amazon en masse.

During this time, Bezos relentlessly advocated for taking risks outside of Amazon's core business. Between 2003 and 2005, Amazon started its own search engine and devised a way to allow customers to search for phrases inside books on the site. Bezos also helped to pioneer the modern crowd-sourcing movement with a service called Mechanical Turk and laid the groundwork for Amazon Web Services – a seminal initiative that ushered in the age of cloud computing.

Bezos battled a reaction that he dubbed the institutional no, by which he meant any and all signs of internal resistance to these unorthodox moves. Even strong companies, he said, tended to reflexively push back against moves in unusual directions. At quarterly board meetings, he asked each director to share an example of the institutional no from his or her own past. Bezos was preparing his overseers to approve what would be a series of improbable, expensive, and risky bets. He simply refused to accept Amazon's fate as an unexciting and marginally profitable online retailer. 'There's only one way out of this predicament,' he said repeatedly to employees during this time, 'and that is to invent our way out.'

Bezos was certain that Amazon needed to define itself as a technology company instead of a retailer, so he started hiring technologists and giving them obscure job titles. In 2001, he lured Apple veteran and renowned user-interface expert Larry Tesler to Amazon and called him vice president of shopping experience. The next year, he hired a Stanford-educated machine-learning professor named Andreas Weigend and dubbed him chief scientist. Neither did particularly well under Bezos's demanding tutelage and both quickly grew tired of Seattle. Weigend lasted only sixteen months at Amazon, Tesler a little over three years. Then Bezos found a technologist who thought just as grandly as he did about ways Amazon could branch out in new directions.

Udi Manber was born in Kiryat Haim, a small town in northern Israel, and he earned a PhD in computer science at the University of Washington. In 1989, as a computer science professor at the University of Arizona, he wrote an authoritative book about the problem-solving wonders of complex mathematical formulas called *Introduction to Algorithms: A Creative Approach* that captured the attention of the Silicon Valley cognoscenti. Manber worked at Yahoo during its glory years but quit in disappointment in 2002 after former Warner Brothers CEO Terry Semel took over as CEO and reoriented the Web portal toward becoming a media company.

Rick Dalzell had heard of Manber's book and started courting him while Manber was preparing to leave Yahoo. Dalzell introduced Manber to Bezos, and by all accounts, an intoxicating geek bromance was born. One of the first questions Bezos asked Manber was 'Why don't you describe a new algorithm that you invented?' Manber did and then marveled at Bezos's comprehension. 'He not only fully understood it, but did it faster than most people. I did not expect that from a CEO. It would have taken me a month to explain it to most senior Yahoo people,' he says.

Manber had serious reservations about moving to Seattle. His wife was a professor at Stanford and they had two young daughters in school. But Bezos agreed to let him split his time between Seattle and Silicon Valley. Manber joined Amazon that fall, and Bezos gave him a typically obscure job title: chief algorithms officer. A few months later, he joined the S Team. 'Udi and Jeff had instant chemistry,' says Dalzell.

Manber's mission was a broad one: use technology to improve Amazon's operations and invent new features. He would see Bezos once a week – an exception to the CEO's aversion to one-on-one meetings – to review ongoing projects and brainstorm new ideas. Manber always had Bezos's full attention, even on a day when they met just a few hours before Amazon's quarterly earnings announcement.

One of Manber's first projects at Amazon captured the interest of both the media and the New York publishing establishment for the sheer scope of its ambition. Before Manber joined the company, Amazon had introduced a tool called Look Inside the Book, an effort to match the experience of a physical bookstore by allowing customers to browse through the first few pages of any title. Manber took that idea much further. He proposed a service called Search Inside the Book that would let customers look for specific words or phrases from any book they had purchased. Bezos loved the idea and raised the stakes: he wanted customers to be able to search any book on the site, and he gave Manber a goal of getting one hundred thousand books into the new digital catalog.[2]

'We had a very simple argument' for book publishers, Manber says. 'Think of two bookstores, one where all the books are shrink-wrapped and one where you can sit as long as you want and read any book you want. Which one do you think will sell more books?'

Publishers were concerned that Search Inside the Book might open up the floodgates of online piracy. Most, however, agreed to try it out and gave Amazon physical copies of their titles, which were shipped to a contractor in the Philippines to be scanned. Then Manber's team ran optical character-recognition software over the book files to convert the scanned images into text that Amazon's search algorithms could navigate and index. To reduce the chance that customers would read the books for free, Amazon served up only snippets of content – one or two pages before and after the search term, for example, and only to customers who had credit cards on file. It also dropped a small piece of code, called a cookie, in each customer's computer to ensure he didn't keep coming back to read additional pages without paying.

It was a computationally intensive process, and Amazon did not provide Manber and his team with much in the way of computer resources. Manber almost had to resort to running his software on employee computers at night and on weekends, but one of his employees found a batch of idle PCs that had been set aside for emergencies. He was allowed to commandeer those machines, although with the understanding that they could be taken back at any time.

Amazon introduced Search Inside the Book on October 2003 – and for the first time in three and a half years, there was a feature story on the company in *Wired* magazine, celebrating its significant innovation. The article revived Bezos's vision of the Alexandria Project, that 1990s-era fever dream of a bookstore that stocked every book ever written. Perhaps such a universal library could be digital and thus infinitely more practical? Bezos cautiously told Wired that Search Inside the Book could indeed be such a beginning. 'You have to start somewhere,' he said. 'You climb the top of the first tiny hill and from there you see the next hill.'[3]

As Amazon was adding product categories throughout the 1990s, its executives came to an inevitable conclusion: the company had to become good at product search. Early in its history, Amazon had licensed a now-defunct search engine called Alta Vista, a spinoff of computer maker Digital Equipment Corp., but it had quickly proved insufficient. In the late 1990s, Amazon engineers Dwayne Bowman and Ruben Ortega led the development of an internal product-search tool called Botega (a mash-up of their surnames) that capitalized on Amazon's vast trove of customer data, information the website had been collecting from the moment it officially opened for business. The system identified the top products customers clicked on for a given search term and then positioned those products higher in ensuing searches. That worked, for a time. But as Amazon's catalog grew ever more complicated and Google got exceedingly good at indexing and organizing the Web, Amazon had to confront the awkward truth that one of its chief rivals could search Amazon's site better than its own search engine could.

At that point, several factors led Amazon directly into the broader Web search arena – and into its first head-to-head confrontation with Google. Amazon was having a difficult time luring technical talent to Seattle, and its divisions often found themselves competing for the same engineers. So in late 2003, Jeff Holden, Udi Manber, and several colleagues travelled to Palo Alto to interview potential hires. The trip was so fruitful and the Seattle labor market had grown so challenging that the company decided to open its first North American office outside Seattle.

Bezos and Dalzell came to call these satellite locations remote development centers. The idea was to place the offices in regions with rich pools of technical talent and set teams to work on specific, isolated projects, harnessing the energy and agility of a startup while minimizing the need for communication with the mother ship in Seattle. Amazon's lawyers, concerned that this might require the company to collect state sales tax, signed off on the strategy but only if the offices were set up as independent subsidiaries and stayed away from transactions with customers.

After one year in Seattle, Manber was already tired of his commute, and he was asked to head up the new Palo Alto office. In October 2003, Amazon's first development center was opened on Waverly and Hamilton Streets in downtown Palo Alto. Staying true to his affinity for mathematical abbreviations, Bezos called it A9 – shorthand for *algorithms*. Despite his move, Manber kept up his weekly meetings with Bezos via conference calls and regular trips to headquarters.

They were still thinking big. A9 not only worked on revamping product search on Amazon.com but also, in a direct attack on Google's turf, developed a general Web search engine. The company licensed the Google search index but built on top of it – simultaneously partnering with and challenging Google. 'Search is not a solved problem,' Manber said in April of 2004 when Amazon unveiled a Web search engine at A9.com. 'There are lots more things that can be done. This is just the beginning.'

A9 would give Bezos and Manber a forum to try out some of their more ambitious ideas, most of which had nothing to do with Amazon's core business. In one brainstorming session, they decided the Web presented a natural opportunity to reinvent the Yellow Pages and ginned up a project called Block View that matched street-level photographs of stores and restaurants with their listings in A9's search results. This was two years before Google announced a similar (more successful and ultimately controversial) initiative called Street View.

Google would blanket the country with a fleet of company-owned trucks outfitted with expensive, specialized cameras to get its street views, but Amazon approached the problem with its usual emphasis on frugality. Manber's budget for the project was less than a hundred thousand dollars. A9 flew photographers and portable equipment to twenty major cities and rented vehicles.

By late 2005, with Google gaining in both popularity and market capitalization, the general Web search at A9.com started to look like a noble but failed experiment. Web search, it became apparent, was not something that could be done cheaply or by piggybacking on a rival's search index. Manber had a dozen engineers working on Web search, while Google had several hundred. Still, the A9 development center was showing promise. It made modest improvements to product search on Amazon.com and started work on an advertising service called Clickriver, which would allow advertisers (a television installer, for example) to purchase links within search results on Amazon.com (a search for HDTVs, for instance). Clickriver contained the seeds of a new advertising business, seeds that would later sprout into a healthy source of revenue for the company. Manber's time at Amazon was productive in other ways too: after three years, he had more than twenty patent applications, several of which carried Bezos's name too.

But then a series of conflicts erupted that rocked the S Team, broke up the Bezos-Manber partnership, and sent Bezos all the way back to the drawing board in his ongoing attempts to prove to the world that Amazon was something more than just a boring retailer, or a technology company that had chosen the least inspired business model of a new age.

At ten years old, Amazon could be a deeply unhappy place to work. The stock price was flat, there were strict limits on annual raises, and the pace was unrelenting. Employees felt underpaid and overworked. When the new development centers opened in Palo Alto and elsewhere, the joke inside Amazon was that it was a necessary move because everyone in Seattle was aware of how abjectly miserable employees at the company were.

In the engineering department, employees were constantly trying to fix a technical infrastructure that was now an aging, sprawling mess. The company had outgrown the original framework devised by Shel Kaphan in the 1990s, the monolithic code base dubbed Obidos that for years was held together by what Amazon executive Werner Vogels later called 'duct tape and WD40 engineering.'[4] And when Amazon cloned its clunky code base to run the websites of Target and Borders, those deals were lucrative but they magnified the company's infrastructure problems. Instead of fighting flames emanating from a single building, engineers often had to deal with a neighborhoodwide inferno.

Like a lot of other technology companies at the time, Amazon got an education in the wisdom of moving to a simpler and more flexible technology infrastructure, called service-oriented architecture. In this kind of framework, every feature and service is treated as an independent piece and each can easily be updated or replaced without breaking the whole.

Led by Amazon's chief technology officer at the time, an avid pilot named Al Vermeulen, whom colleagues fondly called Al V., the company rebuilt its technology infrastructure as a series of these independent but interconnected parts. The awkward and extended transition to this new code base, one element of which Amazon called Gurupa (after a section of the Amazon river where the tributaries diverged), took over three years and caused all kinds of excruciating pain among its network engineers, who were forced to carry pagers so they could respond promptly to the numerous problems.

As a result, dozens of these talented technicians left, many of them defecting to Google. Steve Yegge was one such engineer who made the move around this time. He would publish his opinion of his former employer years later by writing a screed on the Google+ social network and accidentally making it public for the entire Internet to read. 'My challenge with Amazon is finding a way to describe it without making me puke,' Yegge wrote. 'But I'll figure something out, eventually. In many ways they're a world-class operation – primarily in ways that matter to their customers; employees, not so much. But I guess in the end it's the customers that matter.'

In late 2004, another window opened on the mood and inner workings of Amazon. Toys 'R' Us sued Amazon in federal court, contending that Amazon had violated the agreement to allow the chain store to be the exclusive seller of the most popular toys on the Amazon website. The issues in the case were numerous and complex and hinged on some of the arcane legal language in the original contract. But they boiled down to a clash of goals and worldviews. Toys 'R' Us thought it was paying Amazon hefty annual fees and a percentage of sales for exclusivity as the seller of the most popular toys on Amazon. But Amazon and its CEO could not abide anything that impeded their drive to give customers the ultimate selection, and Amazon constantly angered its partner by conceiving of new ways to allow other sellers to list competing toys on the site.

The trial was held in September of 2005 in a stuffy courtroom in Paterson, New Jersey. Bezos testified over the course of two days, and from court records, it does not appear that he enjoyed himself. Judge Margaret Mary McVeigh questioned Bezos's inability to recall key decisions and ultimately ruled in favor of Toys 'R' Us, allowing the toy seller to break its contract with Amazon and revive its own website. In her ruling, the judge described Amazon employees as contemptuous toward their offline counterpart and worshipful and apprehensive of their own CEO and his demands. 'It was certainly my perception that nothing major happened at Amazon without Jeff Bezos's approval,' she wrote in her judgment, quoting the testimony of a Toys 'R' Us executive.

Amazon appealed the settlement but lost and was required to pay $51 million to its former partner. The dispute with Toys 'R' Us would become exhibit A in the argument that Amazon was so fixated on catering to its customers and on the mechanics of its own business that the corporation was often hostile to the large companies it partnered with. (At the same time as the Toys 'R' Us suit, another partnership, with travel site Expedia, also dissolved in litigation. That matter was settled out of court.)

With the toy business now in transition after the dissolution of the agreement with Toys 'R' Us, the hard-lines retail division was cast into further disarray. Part of the problem was that categories like electronics and jewelry were not yet profitable but were growing faster than the older media businesses, which dragged down the company's finances. Bezos felt he needed to give the issue specific attention, and so in late 2004, he hired Kal Raman, the former Drugstore.com executive who had played a supporting role in the employee poaching that had led to the Walmart lawsuit in 1998. Overnight, Bezos cleaved in two the domain of Diego Piacentini, then the senior vice president for worldwide retail, and he handed hard lines over to Raman. Bezos announced the move on a Tuesday in an internal e-mail to the company. Almost everyone from that time says the message was a shock not only to them but also to Piacentini (though Piacentini insists that he knew about the change before the e-mail went out).

Raman was a native of a small village in southern India. His father had died when he was fifteen, plunging his family into poverty. He bootstrapped his way to a degree in electrical engineering, then to a job at Tata Consulting Engineers in Mumbai, and then to a consultant gig at Walmart in Texas, where he climbed the ranks of its IT department and met Rick Dalzell.[5] Raman was whip-smart, a tireless worker, and he had a reputation as an exceedingly demanding manager. He also had some memorable habits, including chewing an Indian betel leaf called pan during meetings and spitting into the garbage pails. Diane Lye, who ran Amazon's data warehouse at the time and reported to Raman, sums it up this way: 'Kal was a screamer.'

Applying his experience from Walmart, Raman pushed to build systems that finally realized Bezos's vision of Amazon as a company with data at its heart. His groups created automated tools that allowed buyers to order merchandise based on dozens of variables such as seasonal trends, past purchasing behaviors, and how many customers were searching for a particular product at certain times. Raman's teams also improved the software for pricing bots, which were automated programs that crawled the Web, spied on competitors' prices, and then adjusted Amazon's prices accordingly, ensuring that Bezos's adamant demand that the company always match the lowest price anywhere, offline or online, would be met.

Buyers were held strictly accountable for keeping their products in stock and their prices competitive. If they somehow failed to deliver – if their shelves were suddenly empty or if Amazon's prices were higher than a rival's – then 'Kal was going to personally hunt you down and kill you,' says Diane Lye, who worked for Raman for eighteen months. 'There was so much fighting and yelling at each other. The technology was broken all the time and because the technology was broken, the data was often wrong. We would bring it to Jeff Bezos and it was all contradictory and he would be yelling and screaming at us. Oh, it was horrible.'

Raman spoke fast and had a thick accent, and his malapropisms, dubbed Kalisms, were legendary. 'You all must be smoking cracks!' he yelled. Or 'Can I have some of what you're drinking so I can feel good about your business too?' He lasted at Amazon less than two years, but people at the company still talk about him.

'Kal was brutal,' says Jason Goldberger, a retail director who worked for Raman. 'He's like out of a movie. The year after Katrina, I took over the home-improvement business, and he could not understand why generator business had fallen [compared to the increase that had accompanied the storm]. He's such a driven personality.'

The turbulence caused by all these changes added to the overall dysfunction gripping Amazon at the time. The S Team was beset by a variety of internecine rivalries, perhaps typical for a large company. Raman and Piacentini, uncomfortably splitting ownership of the retail business, did not get along. Raman also battled with Jeff Wilke. At one point, Wilke heard that Raman had spoken negatively about the fulfillment team and he confronted him in a large meeting. 'I heard there's something you want to say to me,' Wilke said. 'Do you want to say it in front of all these people?' Onlookers thought they might come to blows. In addition, Kathy Savitt, the vice president of communications, didn't get along with Piacentini, and Jason Kilar, who had fully imbibed Bezos's principles and mannerisms, had committed to run the video site Hulu but stuck around while he gave Amazon months to find his replacement.

Bezos handled it all poorly; it was as if the personal dramas were happening on a different dimensional plane that he couldn't or didn't want to access. As a result, the S Team, according to several of its members, became a highly combustible forum, a group in which everyone felt the need to be outspoken and curry favor with the boss and where political disputes were allowed to fester.

One of the biggest of those disputes was between Udi Manber and another technical leader of the company, Jeff Holden – Bezos's former colleague at D. E. Shaw, the one-time teenage hacker who had dubbed himself the Nova.

Holden had been at Amazon longer than anyone else on the management team and had the closest personal relationship with Bezos. If members of the S Team were planets revolving around the sun, then Holden was Mercury, occupying a privileged orbit and drawing a fair amount of criticism, partly based on jealousy. Now in his midthirties, Holden remained a fast talker and a prodigious diet soda and Frappuccino drinker who always paced intensely during product meetings. Like Bezos, he was an aggressive manager who wanted to see results fast.

As senior vice president of worldwide discovery, Holden oversaw more than five hundred employees in Personalization, Automated Merchandising, Associates, E-Mail Marketing – and the department in charge of the search engine. It had been partly his idea to have Manber return to Palo Alto and run A9. But after a while, Holden began to feel that Manber's group was too absorbed with the abstract challenges of general search and wasn't focused enough on the practicalities of running the search for the Amazon website and solving nagging problems, such as latency, or the amount of time it took for searches on Amazon.com to generate results. The problem was that Holden retained ownership of the search experience on the website while Manber held responsibility for the search technology; they were basically dependent on each other.

Eventually, after growing increasingly frustrated, Holden concluded the situation was unworkable and, with an engineer named Darren Vengroff, started his own secretive effort in Seattle to rebuild Amazon's search engine using the open-source tools Lucene and Solr. After a few months, Holden demonstrated the prototype to Bezos, who agreed to let them test it. Holden told Bezos he wanted to develop the Solr-based engine further and, if things went well, move search back to Seattle. Bezos said he'd think about it and later ran the proposal by Manber, who felt it was a sneak attack on his turf.

Now everyone was in a difficult spot. Bezos came back and told Holden and Manber to form a joint team to evaluate the new approach. There are various versions of what happened next, but the bottom line is that Manber and Holden didn't like each other and couldn't work well together. After the evaluation period ended, Bezos decided that search should remain the purview of A9. Holden was crestfallen. He argued that his organization had spearheaded the project and was doing the hard work to fix the persistent search problems on the site. Bezos pointed out that those were emotional concerns, not logical ones.

Feeling that Bezos had chosen Manber over him, Holden planned his departure from Amazon. With Vengroff, he would start a mobile search company called Pelago (which Groupon later acquired). Though this was a difficult time in their relationship, Holden and Bezos remained friends, and Bezos invested in Pelago. But when

Holden left, Bezos lost one of his oldest friends at the company and one of Amazon's most versatile innovators. Fortunately, he still had Udi Manber.

And then Manber decided to leave.

Manber said he didn't like running a remote office and felt isolated from the decision-making in Seattle. Privately, he was annoyed that Bezos had allowed Holden's rival search effort to take root in Seattle. He told Bezos and Rick Dalzell that he was considering going back to academia to do research in the science of memory. Bezos pleaded with Manber to stay on as what he called an Amazon Fellow. Manber said he would consider it.

Meanwhile, Urs Hölzle, one of Google's first employees and its vice president of engineering, wanted to relinquish his oversight of search to focus on Google's infrastructure. Hölzle invited Udi Manber to have dinner with him and surprised the Israeli scientist by asking if he was interested in replacing him as Google's head of search engineering. Manber demurred at first, saying he was planning on getting out of the field. Then a few weeks later he changed his mind and decided that he might as well hear Google's offer. Hölzle arranged a dinner that January with Larry Page in a private room of Il Fornaio, a restaurant in downtown Palo Alto. Page and Manber made sure to enter the restaurant separately. In the middle of dinner, Sergey Brin joined them. Google CEO Eric Schmidt showed up for dessert. It was an impressive full-court press.

By February, Manber had received an extraordinarily lucrative offer to run the search team at Google, and he decided to take it. Money aside, for any search engineer at the time, going to Google meant stepping onto the biggest playing field in the world and joining a championship-caliber team. For its part, Google had snagged one of the brightest minds in search and simultaneously decapitated the efforts of a competitor with one swift stroke.

Now Manber had to inform Bezos, right in the midst of so many other defections to Google. He delivered the news over the phone. Amazon employees would describe what happened next as one of Bezos's all-time biggest nutters. Manber anticipated that Bezos would be disappointed and perhaps try to persuade him again to stay. 'That's what I had expected Jeff to do, but that's not what he did,' Manber says. 'He was clearly angry and he was dumping on me. I don't recall now his exact words, but it was something like "No! No! No! You can't do that!" He was blaming me almost like I was a kid who did something very wrong.'

In that moment, Manber felt like he had lost a friend. He pleaded with Bezos that an engineer with his background and interests could not possibly decline the opportunity to run search at Google. Bezos viewed it as a personal betrayal. This time, he couldn't brush away an employee's departure easily. 'He was not mincing words, and I felt horrible. He was always very good to me, the closest to a mentor that I ever had, and I was letting him down,' Manber says. 'I don't know if he ever forgave me, probably not, but I didn't really have a rational choice. I [had] already decided to leave Amazon, so it was between moving to the top of my field or starting from scratch in a new field.'

A few days later Bezos calmed down and tried to get Manber to change his mind, but it was too late. Bezos had now lost his two closest colleagues and technical leaders, and just at the time that Amazon's attempt to break out of retail and embrace an identity as a technology company was faltering. The general search engine at A9.com was a failure and was shut down a year after Manber left. Block

View would be overtaken by Google's Street View. Search Inside the Book was interesting but hardly a game changer, and the world's best engineers were fleeing a poisonous Amazon culture and flocking to Google and other hot Internet companies in Silicon Valley. If Bezos was going to prove to the world that Amazon was indeed the technology company that he so desperately claimed it to be, he needed a dramatic breakthrough.

* * *

In early 2002, Web evangelist and computer book publisher Tim O'Reilly flew to Seattle to bend Jeff Bezos's ear. O'Reilly, who would go on to help create a popular series of Web 2.0 technology conferences and the traveling festival for hardware hobbyists called the Maker Faire, thought that Amazon was acting too much like an isolated Web destination. He wanted the company to make available its sales data that could, for example, allow him and other book publishers to track various trends and help them decide what to publish next.[6] Bezos hadn't considered providing a broad range of such services to the outside world and initially replied that he didn't see how that would benefit Amazon.

Over the years, O'Reilly and Bezos would have a friendly but sometimes adversarial relationship. In February of 2000, O'Reilly had organized an online protest against Amazon when it refused to allow other Internet retailers to use its patented 1-Click system. (Bezos cleverly blunted the campaign by joining in O'Reilly's criticism of the patent system and supporting his idea for an independent company called BountyQuest, which, until it folded, allowed companies to post rewards for documents that undermined patents.[7]) O'Reilly also wrote a blog post urging fans of local bookstores to make their purchases there even if prices were cheaper online, arguing that those merchants would otherwise go away. That missive was taped to the cash registers of more than a few independent bookstores around the country.

But on this particular visit to Bezos in 2002, O'Reilly had a cogent case to make, and Bezos listened. The publisher showed Bezos Amarank, a sophisticated tool his company had created that visited the Amazon website every few hours and copied the rankings of O'Reilly Media books and the books of its competitors. It was a clunky process that relied on a primitive technique called screen scraping, and O'Reilly suggested that Amazon should develop a series of online tools called application programming interfaces, or APIs, that allowed third parties to easily harvest data about its prices, products, and sales rankings. O'Reilly spoke ambitiously about parceling out entire sectors of the Amazon store and allowing other websites to build on top of them. 'Companies need to think not just what they can get for themselves from new tech-nologies but how they can enable others,' he said.[8]

After O'Reilly's visit, Bezos convened a meeting with Rick Dalzell, Neil Roseman, and Colin Bryar, the head of Associates at the time, to talk about the issue. Dalzell pointed out that there was already something like this under way inside the company and told Bezos about a young engineer named Rob Frederick whose mobile commerce startup, Convergence, Amazon had acquired in 1999. Frederick's group was working on APIs that would allow non-PC mobile devices like phones and PalmPilots to access the Amazon store. After that meeting, Bezos invited O'Reilly to speak to a group of engineers, and later at an Amazon all-hands meeting, about lessons from computer history and the importance of becoming a platform. Bezos added Frederick's team to the Associates group under Colin Bryar and tasked them with creating a new set of APIs to let developers plug into the Amazon website. Soon other websites would be able to publish selections from the Amazon catalog, including prices and detailed product descriptions, and use its payment system and shopping cart. Bezos himself bought into the Web's new orthodoxy of openness, preaching inside Amazon over the next few months that they should make these new tools available to developers and 'let them surprise us.' The company held its first developer conference that spring and invited all the outsiders who were trying to hack Amazon's systems. Now developers became another constituency at Amazon, joining customers and third-party sellers. And the new group, run by Colin Bryar and Rob Frederick, was given a formal name: Amazon Web Services.

It was the trailhead of an extremely serendipitous path.

Amazon Web Services, or AWS, is today in the business of selling basic computer infrastructure like storage, databases, and raw computing power. The service is woven into the fabric of daily life in Silicon Valley and the broader technology community. Startups like Pinterest and Instagram rent space and cycles on Amazon's computers and run their operations over the Internet as if the high-powered servers were sitting in the backs of their own offices. Even large companies rely on AWS – Netflix, for example, uses it to stream movies to its customers. AWS helped introduce the ethereal concept known as the cloud, and it is viewed as so vital to the future fortunes of technology startups that venture capitalists often give gift certificates for it to their new entrepreneurs. Various divisions of the U.S. government, such as NASA and the Central Intelligence Agency, are high-profile AWS customers as well. Though Amazon keeps AWS's financial performance and profitability a secret, analysts at Morgan Stanley estimate that in 2012, it brought in $2.2 billion in revenue.

The rise of Amazon Web Services brings up a few obvious questions. How did an online retailer spawn such a completely unrelated business? How did the creature that was originally called Amazon Web Services – the group working on the commerce APIs – evolve into something so radically different, a seller of high-tech infrastructure? Early observers suggested that Amazon's retail business was so seasonal – booming during the holiday months – that Bezos had decided to rent his spare computer capacity during the quieter periods. But that explanation is widely debunked by Amazon insiders, in part because it would require Amazon to kick developers off its servers every fall.

The shift to offering these infrastructure services actually began with the transition to Gurupa and a more reliable technology infrastructure, a process that gathered momentum in 2003. While Amazon's internal systems had been broken down into more durable individual components, Amazon's technical staff was still organized conventionally as a single team, headquartered in a separate office building downtown near Seattle's Union Station. This group strictly controlled who could access Amazon's servers, and various teams inside the company had to plead for resources to try out their new projects and features. The process slowed down and frustrated many Amazon project managers. 'You had a set of folks running these machines who were the priesthood of hardware, and the rest of us were railing against it,' says Chris Brown, a software-development manager at the time. 'We wanted a playground where we could go to freely try things out.'

Bezos was getting annoyed as well. The company had improved on its pick-to-light system in the FCs, and its infrastructure had been successfully recast into component services, but the provisioning of computer resources remained a bottleneck. It got so dysfunctional that project leaders would present the S Team with their six-page narratives and then in the discussion afterward admit they had been unable to actually test their projects. Rick Dalzell recalls a particularly significant meeting when Matt Round, the head of Personalization at the time, complained that he didn't have resources for experimentation. 'Jeff finally just exploded at me,' Dalzell says. 'I always handled Jeff's outbursts pretty well, but to be honest about it, he had a right to be angry. We were stifling the flow of creativity. Even though we were probably faster than ninety-nine percent of companies in the world, we were still too slow.'

At the same time, Bezos became enamored with a book called *Creation*, by Steve Grand, the developer of a 1990s video game called Creatures that allowed players to guide and nurture a seemingly intelligent organism on their computer screens. Grand wrote that his approach to creating intelligent life was to focus on designing simple computational building blocks, called primitives, and then sit back and watch surprising behaviors emerge. Just as electronics are built from basic components like resistors and capacitors, and as living beings spring from genetic building blocks, Grand wrote that sophisticated AI can emerge from cybernetic primitives, and then it's up to the 'ratchet of evolution to change the design.'[9]

The book, though dense and challenging, was widely discussed in the book clubs of Amazon executives at the time and it helped to crystallize the debate over the problems with the company's own infrastructure. If

Amazon wanted to stimulate creativity among its developers, it shouldn't try to guess what kind of services they might want; such guesses would be based on patterns of the past. Instead, it should be creating primitives – the building blocks of computing – and then getting out of the way. In other words, it needed to break its infrastructure down into the smallest, simplest atomic components and allow developers to freely access them with as much flexibility as possible. As Bezos proclaimed at the time, according to numerous employees: 'Developers are alchemists and our job is to do everything we can to get them to do their alchemy.'

Bezos directed groups of engineers in brainstorming possible primitives. Storage, bandwidth, messaging, payments, and processing all made the list. In an informal way – as if the company didn't quite know the insight around primitives was an extraordinary one – Amazon then started building teams to develop the services described on that list.

In late 2004, Chris Pinkham, head of the company's IT infrastructure, told Dalzell that he had decided to return with his family to their native South Africa. At this point, A9 had taken root in Palo Alto, and Dalzell was busy establishing remote developer centers in Scotland and India, among other places. Dalzell suggested to Pinkham that instead of leaving Amazon, he open an office in Cape Town. They brainstormed possible projects and finally settled on trying to build a service that would allow a developer to run any application, regardless of its type, on Amazon's servers. Pinkham and a few colleagues studied the problem and came up with a plan to use a new open-source tool called Xen, a layer of software that made it easier to run numerous applications on a single physical server in a data center.

Pinkham took colleague Chris Brown along with him to South Africa and they set up shop in a nondescript office complex in Constantia, a winemaking region northeast of Cape Town, near a school and a small homeless encampment. Their efforts would become the Elastic Compute Cloud, or EC2 – the service that is at the heart of AWS and that became the engine of the Web 2.0 boom.

EC2 was born in isolation, with Pinkham talking to his colleagues in Seattle only sporadically, at least for the first year. The Constantia office had to make do with two residential-grade DSL lines, and during the hot summer of 2005, one of the country's two nuclear reactors went offline, so engineers worked amid rolling brownouts. Pinkham later said that the solitude was beneficial, as it afforded a comfortable distance from Amazon's intrusive CEO. 'I spent most of my time trying to hide from Bezos,' Pinkham says. 'He was a fun guy to talk to but you did not want to be his pet project. He would love it to distraction.'

The dozen engineers concurrently developing what would become Amazon's Simple Storage Service, or S3, did not have that luxury, despite their best attempts to keep to themselves. They worked in an office on the eighth floor of Pac Med, ate lunch together every day for nearly two years, and often played cards together after work. Neither they nor their manager, Alan Atlas, a veteran of crosstown digital-media startup Real Networks, were able to hide half a world away.

Bezos was deeply interested in the evolution of Web services and often dived into the minutiae of S3, asking for details about how the services would keep up with demand and repeatedly sending engineers back to the drawing board to simplify the S3 architecture. 'It would always start out fun and happy, with Jeff's laugh rebounding against the walls,' Atlas says. 'Then something would happen and the meeting would go south and you would fear for your life. I literally thought I'd get fired after every one of those meetings.'

Atlas said that while working on the S3 project, he frequently had difficulty grasping just how big Bezos was thinking. 'He had this vision of literally tens of thousands of cheap, two-hundred-dollar machines piling up in racks, exploding. And it had to be able to expand forever,' Atlas says. Bezos told him, 'This has to scale to infinity with no planned downtime. Infinity!'

During one meeting, Atlas blundered by suggesting they could figure out how to keep up with any unexpected growth after the service launched. That triggered a Bezos nutter. 'He leaned toward me and said, *"Why are you wasting my life?,"* and went on a tirade about Keystone Cops,' Atlas says. 'That was real anger. I wasn't keeping up with him. There were a number of times like that. He was so far ahead of us.'

For the launch of Simple Storage Service, Atlas had commemorative T-shirts made up for his colleagues; he used the design of Superman's costume but with an S3 rather than an S on the chest. Naturally, he had to pay for the shirts himself.

As their ambitions for Web services expanded between South Africa and Seattle, Bezos and Dalzell began to consider who would lead the effort. Bezos suggested Al Vermeulen, Amazon's chief technology officer, but Al V. commuted to Seattle by plane every day from Corvallis, Oregon, and said he didn't want an administrative job. He demoted himself to an engineer working on S3 with Alan Atlas. So Dalzell recommended Andy Jassy, who had inauspiciously started his career at Amazon so many years ago by hitting Jeff Bezos with a kayak paddle during the company's first game of broomball.

If the new era in high-tech was indeed to be the age of computer science PhDs, then Jassy would prove to be a conspicuous anomaly. A graduate of Harvard Business School with a passion for buffalo wings and New York sports teams, Jassy seemed unlikely to fit in at a geeky technology startup. Perhaps as a result of this, his path at Amazon had been meandering and sometimes difficult. It was Jassy who presented the original business plan in 1998 for Amazon to enter the music business, but then he watched in disappointment as another executive was selected to lead the charge. A few years later, in a companywide reorganization, Jassy was chosen to oversee the personalization group, but then the engineers in that department objected to being led by someone they viewed at the time as nontechnical.

So Jassy was given a unique opportunity. Bezos asked him to become his first official shadow – a new role that would entail Jassy's following around the CEO and sitting with him in every meeting. Other technology companies like Intel and Sun had similar positions, and Bezos had tried this before with executives who were new to the company – including a D. E. Shaw engineer named John Overdeck and Accept.com founder Danny Shader – but it had never been a full-time job, and many of those previous shadows had subsequently left the company. Jassy was conflicted about the proposal. 'I was flattered by the offer to work closely with Jeff but wasn't initially excited about it because I'd seen the way it had gone down before,' he says. 'I asked Jeff what success would look like. He said success would be if I got to know him and he got to know me and we built trust in each other.' Jassy agreed and spent much of the next eighteen months by Bezos's side, traveling with him, discussing the events of each day, and observing the CEO's style and thought process. Jassy would define the shadow role as a quasi chief of staff, and today the position of Bezos's shadow, now formally known as technical adviser, is highly coveted and has broad visibility within the company. For Bezos, having an accomplished assistant on hand to discuss important matters with and ensure that people follow up on certain tasks is another way to extend his reach.

As Jassy's tenure as shadow ended, he became a natural candidate to step in as the new head of AWS. One of his first jobs was to write a vision statement; he had to tinker with the margins to get it under six pages. The paper laid out the expanded AWS mission: 'to enable developers and companies to use Web services to build sophisticated and scalable applications.' The paper listed the primitives that Amazon would subsequently turn into Web services, from storage and computing to database, payments, and messaging. 'We tried to imagine a student in a dorm room who would have at his or her disposal the same infrastructure as the largest companies in the world,' Jassy says. 'We thought it was a great playing-field leveler for startups and smaller companies to have the same cost structure as big companies.'

Jassy, Bezos, and Dalzell presented the plan for the new AWS to the Amazon board, and the institutional no came close to rearing its ugly head. John Doerr, expressing what he would later call a 'healthy skepticism,' asked the obvious question: At a time when Amazon was having difficulty hiring engineers and needed to accelerate its international expansion, 'Why would we go into this business?'

'Because we need it as well,' Bezos replied, suggesting that Amazon's demand for such a service reflected the broader market need. Jassy remembers Doerr telling him after the meeting that he was lucky to work at a company that would invest in something so daring.

Around this time, Bezos was pursuing another project whose origins were shaped by resistance from Amazon's board of directors. When the founders of the comparison-shopping site Junglee had left Amazon in the late 1990s, they had done so on good terms and with the agreement that they would stay in touch with Amazon executives and even coordinate their efforts. Anand Rajaraman and Venky Harinarayan, two of the cofounders, then started their own Internet incubator called Cambrian Ventures, and Bezos wanted Amazon to invest in it. But in a rare act of resistance to Bezos's will, the Amazon board vetoed the move. So Bezos ended up investing personally. The circuitous result of that decision was yet another unlikely Web service from Amazon and another sign that the company was trying to evolve beyond online retailing.

At the time that Cambrian Ventures was starting up in Silicon Valley, the peer-to-peer file-sharing service Napster was dominating headlines and panicking the music business. The Cambrian engineers thought about Napster and the power of networks that linked people who were scattered around the world. Could you do something of value with those distributed networks, they wondered, something better than stealing music? That question became the seed of an initiative they called Project Agreya – the Sanskrit word for 'first.'

The idea was to build software and harness the Internet to coordinate groups of people around the world to work on problems that computers weren't very good at solving. For example, a computer system might have difficulty examining a collection of photos of domestic pets and reliably selecting the ones that depicted cats or dogs. But humans could do that easily. The Cambrian Ventures executives hypothesized that they could build an online service to coordinate low-wage workers around the world and then sell access to this workforce to financial firms and other large companies. In 2001, they filed for a patent for the idea and called it a 'Hybrid machine/human computing arrangement.'[10]

The world would later come to know this idea, and embrace it, as crowd-sourcing. But Project Agreya was ahead of its time, and financial firms didn't know quite what to make of it. The Agreya team was in New York trying to pitch the concept the week of 9/11. Venture capital dried up after the terrorist attacks, so they shut down Project Agreya and moved on.

In 2003 Rajaraman and Harinarayan decided to close Cambrian Ventures to work on a new company called Kosmix, which would develop technology to organize information on the Web by specific topics. As part of winding down Cambrian, they had to deal with Bezos and his investment in the firm. Not surprisingly, Bezos proved to be a tenacious negotiator and a stubborn defender of his own financial interests, even when the stakes were a relatively inconsequential fraction of his net worth. Rajaraman and Harinarayan recall a brutal two-month-long negotiation during which Bezos leveraged the dissolution of Cambrian Ventures into a stake in Kosmix. In the midst of this, they happened to tell Bezos about the Agreya patent, and he was immediately interested and asked for it to be included in the overall deal. Seeing an opportunity to conclude the arrangement, they quickly agreed to sell it to him.

To their surprise, Bezos then actually developed a version of Project Agreya inside Amazon. He renamed it

Mechanical Turk, after an eighteenth-century chess-playing automaton that concealed a diminutive man – a chess master – who hid inside and guided the machine's moves. About two dozen Amazon employees worked on the service from January 2004 to November 2005. It was considered a Jeff project, which meant that the product manager met with Bezos every few weeks and received a constant stream of e-mail from the CEO, usually containing extraordinarily detailed recommendations and frequently arriving late at night.

Amazon started using Mechanical Turk internally in 2005 to have humans do things like review Search Inside the Book scans and check product images uploaded to Amazon by customers to ensure they were not pornographic. The company also used Mechanical Turk to match the images with the corresponding commercial establishments in A9's fledgling Block View tool. Bezos himself became consumed with this task and used it as a way to demonstrate the service.

As the company prepared to introduce Mechanical Turk to the public, Amazon's PR team and a few employees complained they were uncomfortable with the system's reference to the Turkish people. Bezos liked the name for its historical association but agreed to let the communications staff and Mechanical Turk team brainstorm alternatives. They seriously considered Cadabra, an allusion to magic and the original corporate name of Amazon. But in the end, Bezos shrugged off the concerns and said that he personally would bear the responsibility for any backlash.

Mechanical Turk quietly launched in November 2005. Now any Internet user could perform what Amazon called human-intelligence tasks, typically earning a few cents per job. Other companies could list jobs on the

Mechanical Turk website, with Amazon taking a 10 percent cut of the payments.[11] One of the first applications,
from a company called Casting Words, paid workers a few
cents per minute to listen to and transcribe podcasts.

Mechanical Turk gave Bezos another opportunity to
demonstrate Amazon's ability to innovate outside of its
core retail business and show off his own curious attempts
to crystallize abstract concepts. He called Mechanical Turk
'artificial, artificial intelligence' and gave interviews about
the service to the *New York Times* and the *Economist*. The
ethnic reference in the name was never criticized, but
labor activists targeted the service as a 'virtual sweatshop'
and 'the dark side of globalization.'[12]

By 2007 there were a hundred thousand workers on
Mechanical Turk in more than one hundred countries.[13]
But it didn't take off in the way Bezos clearly hoped it
would, or at least it hasn't yet. One obvious reason is that
the exceedingly low wages on Mechanical Turk have the
greatest appeal in less developed countries, yet most
impoverished workers in the third world do not own
Internet-connected PCs. When Amazon's other Web
services unexpectedly took off in the following years,
Bezos devoted considerably more attention and resources
to them. Just as in Amazon's early days, when automated
personalization replaced editorial, machines, not people
hiding inside them, would drive Amazon's long-awaited
big breakthrough.

In March 2006, Amazon introduced the Simple Storage
Service, which allowed other websites and developers to
store computer files like photos, documents, or video-
game player profiles on Amazon's servers. S3 remained
alone and somewhat overlooked, like a section of a fence
that had not yet been finished. A month after the launch,

Alan Atlas recalled, it crashed for nine hours, and hardly anyone in the outside world noticed. Then a few months later, the Elastic Compute Cloud went to public beta, allowing developers to actually run their own programs on Amazon's computers. According to Chris Brown, who returned from South Africa for the launch, Amazon opened the first servers to customers on the East Coast of the United States, and developers rushed in so quickly that the initial batch of computers was taken up before Amazon had a chance to let in folks on the West Coast.

Part of AWS's immediate attraction to startups was its business model. Bezos viewed Web services as similar to an electric utility that allowed customers to pay for only what they used and to increase or decrease their consumption at any time. 'The best analogy that I know is the electric grid,' Bezos said. 'You go back in time a hundred years, if you wanted to have electricity, you had to build your own little electric power plant, and a lot of factories did this. As soon as the electric power grid came online, they dumped their electric power generator, and they started buying power off the grid. It just makes more sense. And that's what is starting to happen with infrastructure computing.'[14]

Bezos wanted AWS to be a utility with discount rates, even if that meant losing money in the short term. Willem van Biljon, who worked with Chris Pinkham on EC2 and stayed for a few months after Pinkham quit in 2006, proposed pricing EC2 instances at fifteen cents an hour, a rate that he believed would allow the company to break even on the service. In an S Team meeting before EC2 launched, Bezos unilaterally revised that to ten cents. 'You realize you could lose money on that for a long time,' van Biljon told him. 'Great,' Bezos said.

Bezos believed his company had a natural advantage in

its cost structure and ability to survive in the thin atmosphere of low-margin businesses. Companies like IBM, Microsoft, and Google, he suspected, would hesitate to get into such markets because it would depress their overall profit margins. Bill Miller, the chief investment officer at Legg Mason Capital Management and a major Amazon shareholder, asked Bezos at the time about the profitability prospects for AWS. Bezos predicted they would be good over the long term but said that he didn't want to repeat 'Steve Jobs's mistake' of pricing the iPhone in a way that was so fantastically profitable that the smartphone market became a magnet for competition.

The comment reflected his distinctive business philosophy. Bezos believed that high margins justified rivals' investments in research and development and attracted more competition, while low margins attracted customers and were more defensible. (He was partly right about the iPhone; its sizable profits did indeed attract a deluge of competition, starting with smartphones running Google's Android operating system. But the pioneering smartphone is also a fantastically lucrative product for Apple and its shareholders in a way that AWS has not been, at least so far.)

Bezos's belief was borne out, and AWS's deliberately low rates had their intended effect; Google chairman Eric Schmidt said it was at least two years before he noticed that the founders of seemingly every startup he visited told him they were building their systems atop Amazon's servers. 'All of the sudden, it was all Amazon,' Schmidt says. 'It's a significant benefit when every interesting fast-growing company starts on your platform.' Microsoft announced a similar cloud initiative called Azure in 2010. In 2012, Google announced its own Compute Engine. 'Let's give them credit,' Schmidt says. 'The book guys got computer science, they figured out the analytics, and they built something significant.'

Just like *Creation* author Steve Grand had predicted, the creatures were evolving in ways that Bezos could not have imagined. It was the combination of EC2 and S3 – storage and compute, two primitives linked together – that transformed both AWS and the technology world. Startups no longer needed to spend their venture capital on buying servers and hiring specialized engineers to run them. Infrastructure costs were variable instead of fixed, and they could grow in direct proportion to revenues. It freed companies to experiment, to change their business models with a minimum of pain, and to keep up with the rapidly growing audiences of erupting social networks like Facebook and Twitter.

All of this took years and required significant effort, and its developers encountered many challenges and setbacks along the way. Andy Jassy, along with technical lieutenants Charlie Bell and Werner Vogels, outpaced rivals by layering additional services like Flexible Payment Services and Amazon CloudSearch alongside of EC2 and S3. Groups within Amazon were told to use AWS while the services were still immature, a demand that led to another round of consternation among its engineers. As startups and even some big companies began to rely heavily on AWS, outages had widespread repercussions, and chronically secretive Amazon found it had to get better at explaining itself and speaking to the public.

But the emergence of Amazon Web Services was transformational in a number of ways. Amazon's inexpensive and easily accessible Web services facilitated the creation of thousands of Internet startups, some of which would not have been possible without it, and it provided larger companies with the ability to rent a supercomputer in the cloud, ushering in a new era of innovation in areas like finance, oil and gas, health, and science. It is not hyperbole to say that AWS, particularly the original services like S3 and EC2, helped lift the entire technology industry out of a prolonged post-dot-com malaise. Amazon also completely outflanked the great hardware makers of the time, like Sun Microsystems and Hewlett-Packard, and defined the next wave of corporate computing.

Perhaps the greatest makeover was of Amazon's own image. AWS enlarged the scope of what it meant to be the everything store and stocked Amazon's shelves with incongruous products like spot instances and storage terabytes. It made Amazon a confusing target for Walmart and other rival retailers and gave the company fresh appeal to the legions of engineers looking to solve the world's most interesting problems. Finally, after years of setbacks and internal rancor, Amazon was unquestionably a technology company, what Bezos had always imagined it to be.

CHAPTER 8

Fiona

Back in the Paleozoic era of the Internet, around the year 1997, an entrepreneur named Martin Eberhard was sitting in a Palo Alto coffee shop with his friend Marc Tarpenning, sipping a latte and pondering the inevitably bright future of mobile computing. The PalmPilot, the pioneering personal digital assistant, had just been introduced, and cell phones were evolving quickly into sleek devices that slid easily into a jacket pocket. Eberhard and Tarpenning worked for a disk-drive manufacturer and had just returned from a conference called DiskCon. In other words, they were bored out of their skulls and looking for something more interesting to do. They both happened to be voracious readers.

Over coffee that day, the friends postulated that it might finally be possible to invent a computer for reading digital books. People had been talking about this for years, ever since Project Gutenberg, a nonprofit founded in the early 1970s in Champaign, Illinois, with a mission to digitize the world's books and make them available on personal computers. Eberhard and Tarpenning had a different idea. They wanted something mobile, so people could take whole libraries of e-books with them in dedicated electronic-reading devices. That spring they started NuvoMedia and developed one of the world's first portable e-readers, which they called the Rocket e-Book, or Rocketbook.

Eberhard had founded a computer-networking company in the 1980s and had been around the Silicon Valley block a few times. (Later he would cofound the electric-car company Tesla.) So he knew that he needed deep-pocketed investors as well as powerful allies to pave his way in the complex and cosseted world of the book-publishing business. Eberhard believed that he needed Jeff Bezos and Amazon.com.

In late 1997, the NuvoMedia founders and their lawyer took a Rocketbook prototype to Seattle and spent three weeks in negotiations with Bezos and his top executives. They stayed at a cheap hotel downtown and made regular trips to the old Columbia Building on Second Avenue to discuss the possibility of an Amazon investment in NuvoMedia. Bezos 'was really intrigued by our device,' Eberhard says. 'He understood that the display technology was finally good enough.'

The prototype itself was crude, with a painted surface and rudimentary software. But it worked, displaying such books as *Alice in Wonderland* and *A Tale of Two Cities* on its glowing transflective LCD screen. The device weighed a little over a pound, heavy by today's standards, but it could be held with one hand, like a paperback book, and its battery lasted twenty hours with the backlight on, which compares favorably to today's mobile devices.

Bezos seemed impressed but had some reservations. To download books, a customer needed to plug the e-reader into his computer. 'We talked about wireless but it was crazily expensive at the time,' says Eberhard. 'It would add an extra four hundred dollars to each unit and the data plans were insane.' The Rocketbook's display wasn't as easy on the eyes as modern e-readers, but Eberhard had checked out low-powered, low-glare alternatives, like E Ink, being developed in the MIT Media Lab, and e-paper, from Xerox, and found the technology was still unreliable and expensive.

After three weeks of intense negotiations, the companies hit a major roadblock. Bezos told Eberhard he was concerned that by backing NuvoMedia and helping it succeed, he might be creating an opportunity for Barnes & Noble to swoop in and buy the startup later. So he demanded exclusivity provisions in any contract between the companies and wanted veto power over future investors. 'If we made a bet on the future of reading, we'd want to help it succeed by introducing it to our customers in a big way,' says David Risher, Amazon's former senior vice president of U.S. retail, who participated in the negotiations. 'But the only way that'd have made sense is if it had been exclusive to us. Otherwise, we'd have been funneling our customers to a potential rival.'

Eberhard couldn't bring himself to agree to limit his future fund-raising opportunities, so Bezos's concerns became a self-fulfilling prophecy. Once it was evident that the companies were at an impasse, Eberhard and Tarpenning got on a plane and flew to New York to meet with Len and Stephen Riggio of Barnes & Noble. They shook hands on a deal within the week. The bookseller and the publishing giant Bertelsmann agreed to invest two million dollars each, and together they owned nearly half of NuvoMedia.

It later became fashionable to say that the Rocketbook and contemporaneous competitors like the SoftBook were ahead of their time and that the world was not yet ready to read digitally. But that is not quite the entire story.

NuvoMedia sold twenty thousand units in its first year and was on track to double that in its second. It negotiated pioneering e-book contracts with all the major book publishers (the Authors Guild condemned the contracts as being unfavorable to authors[1]), and in 1999, Cisco invested in NuvoMedia, giving the company more credibility and another strategically. The reviews of the device were generally favorable. Oprah Winfrey included the Rocketbook among her Ten Favorite Things in the inaugural issue of O magazine, and Wired wrote of the device, 'It's like an object that has tumbled out of the future.'[2]

NuvoMedia had an aggressive road map for rapid development. Eberhard planned to exploit economies of scale and advances in technology to improve the Rocketbook's screen quality and battery life while driving down its price. (Over the 1999 holiday season, the basic model cost $169.) 'Within five years,' he told Newsweek's Steven Levy that December, 'we'll have front-surface technology that doesn't require you to read behind glass.'[3] But NuvoMedia still needed fresh capital, and Eberhard was growing nervous about the unsustainable dot-com bubble and the deteriorating fund-raising climate. In February 2000, he sold NuvoMedia to a Burbank-based interactive TV-guide firm called Gemstar in a stock transaction worth about $187 million. Gemstar also snapped up SoftBook.

It was a terrible move. Gemstar's main corporate objective, it turned out, was exploiting its patent portfolio through litigation. A few months after the sale, Eberhard and Tarpenning exited the firm in disappointment. Gemstar released successors to both Rocketbook and SoftBook, but after slow sales and given its own internal lack of enthusiasm, it pulled them from the market in

2003. Gemstar CEO Henry Yuen, who orchestrated the company's e-book acquisitions, later fled to China amid accusations of accounting fraud.[4]

The Gemstar debacle did more than just demolish the future prospects of the Rocketbook and SoftBook. It seemingly dampened all interest in the very idea of digital reading. BarnesandNoble.com stopped selling e-books altogether after the Rocketbook disappeared, and Palm sold its e-book business at around the same time.[5] E-books seemed like a technological dead-end and a hopeless medium – to almost everyone.

Bezos and Eberhard remained friendly during those years, and Bezos watched the rise and fall of the Rocketbook with more than passing interest. 'I firmly believe that at some point the vast majority of books will be in electronic form,' he said in the late 1990s. 'I also believe that is a long way in the future, many more than ten years in the future.'[6]

Bezos was underestimating the potential, perhaps intentionally. In 2004, seeking a digital strategy for Amazon amid the gathering power of a revived Apple Computer, he started a secretive Silicon Valley skunkworks with the mysterious name Lab126. The hardware hackers at Lab126 were given a difficult job: they were to disrupt Amazon's own successful bookselling business with an e-book device while also meeting the impossibly high standards of Amazon's designer in chief, Bezos himself. In order for Amazon to furnish its new digital library, the company's liaisons to the book world were ordered to push publishers to embrace a seemingly dormant format. It was a nearly impossible mission, and it had to be executed on Amazon's typical shoestring budget. Many mistakes were made, some of which continue to resonate today.

But in 2007, a few weeks after Amazon unveiled the result of all this effort, the first Kindle, Bezos called up Martin Eberhard at his home in Silicon Valley to ask him whether he thought Amazon had finally gotten it right.

Over his years at the helm of Apple, Steve Jobs usually reviled those former colleagues who had defected from his company and abandoned its righteous mission. Though Diego Piacentini left Apple for a startup that Jobs had incredulously dismissed as just a retailer, the two remained unusually cordial, perhaps because Piacentini had given Apple six months to find his replacement as head of European operations. Jobs would occasionally contact Piacentini when he needed something from Amazon, and in early 2003, Piacentini e-mailed his former boss with a request of his own. Amazon wanted to make Apple a proposal.

Piacentini brought Neil Roseman, Rob Frederick and H. B. Siegel, the technologist who'd started the company's fledgling digital-media group, to the meeting that spring on Apple's campus in Cupertino. The Amazon executives did not expect to meet with Jobs himself and were surprised when Apple's cofounder greeted them personally and spent several hours with them that day.

At the time, Apple did not sell music; its iTunes software allowed users to organize and play their music collections on their PCs and transfer songs onto their iPods. Jobs wanted to get iTunes onto as many PCs as possible, and he floated the idea of Amazon distributing CDs to its customers that carried iTunes soft-ware. Piacentini and his colleagues had another plan: they suggested creating a joint music store that would allow iPod owners to buy digital-music files from the Amazon website.

Neither proposal went anywhere. Jobs stood up to illustrate on the conference-room whiteboard his vision of how Apple itself would sell albums and single-tracks directly from iTunes. The Amazon executives countered that surely such a music store should exist on the Web, not inside a piece of clunky desktop software that needed to be regularly updated. But Jobs wanted a consistent, easy-to-use experience that stretched from the music store all the way to the portable media player and was so simple that even unsophisticated users could operate it. 'It was clear that Jobs had disdain for selling on the Web and he didn't think anyone cared about books,' Neil Roseman says. 'He had this vision for a client-application version of the iTunes store and he let us know why it had to be an end-to-end experience.'

Jobs confidently predicted that Apple would quickly overtake Amazon in music sales, and he was right. In April 2003 Apple introduced the iTunes music store, and in just a few years Apple leapfrogged over, in quick succession, Amazon, Best Buy, and Walmart to become the top music retailer in the United States.

At the time of that humbling lesson, Amazon investors 'needed a microscope to find the sales' from all of the company's various digital initiatives, as Bezos later put it.[7] The company sold downloadable e-books in Microsoft's and Adobe's proprietary formats for reading on a PC screen, but the e-book store was well hidden on the Amazon website and yielded few sales. Look Inside the Book and Search Inside the Book were arguably digital-reading efforts, but their purpose was to improve the shopping experience and increase the sales of physical books. As the negotiations with NuvoMedia showed, Bezos was thinking early about the inevitable transition to digital media. But more pressing matters, like fixing the fulfillment centers and improving Amazon's technology infrastructure, always seemed to take precedence.

Over the next few years Apple dominated the music business and helped send chains like Tower Records and Virgin Megastores into the retail dustbin (with a significant assist from Internet piracy). At first Bezos dismissed iTunes, noting that selling single-tracks for ninety-nine cents each wasn't profitable and that Apple's goal was only to increase sales of the iPod. This was true, but as the iPod became ubiquitous, Apple began to exploit iTunes to get into adjacent media such as video, and Amazon took a deeper look. 'We talked a lot about what made the iPod successful in music when nothing else had been,' says Neil Roseman.

Amazon executives spent months considering various digital-music strategies and at one point explored the possibility of preloading iPods sold on Amazon with the music from CDs that customers had bought on the site. When it proved impossible to get the music labels to agree to that, Amazon settled on launching a digital-music service, similar to Rhapsody, which gave monthly subscribers unlimited access to a vast catalog of music. Amazon came close to launching that effort in 2005. It was going to use music encoded with Microsoft's proprietary DRM (digital rights management) anticopying software Janus. But then several members of the team rebelled at what they viewed as a flawed approach, in part because the Janus-encoded music wouldn't play on the iPod, which so many Amazon customers already owned. 'I realized I'd rather die than launch that store,' says Erich Ringewald, a product manager who worked on the initiative. Bezos agreed to scrap the effort and start over. Meanwhile, Apple increased its lead in digital media. Amazon finally introduced the MP3 Store in 2007, featuring songs without DRM that users could freely copy. But Apple quickly negotiated the same agreements and Amazon remained a perennial straggler in music.

Bezos's colleagues and friends often attribute Amazon's tardiness in digital music to Bezos's lack of interest in music of any kind. In high school, Bezos forced himself to memorize the call letters of local Miami radio stations in an effort to fake musical fluency in conversations with his peers.[8] Colleagues remember that on the solemn road trip from Target's offices in Minneapolis after 9/11, Bezos indiscriminately grabbed stacks of CDs from the bargain rack of a convenience store, as if they were all interchangeable.

Steve Jobs, on the other hand, lived and breathed music. He was a notoriously devoted fan of Bob Dylan and the Beatles and had once dated singer Joan Baez. Jobs's personal interests guided Apple's strategy. Bezos's particular passions would have the same defining impact at Amazon. Bezos didn't just love books – he fully imbibed them, methodically processing each detail. Stewart Brand, the author of *How Buildings Learn*, among other works, recalls being startled when Bezos showed him his personal copy of the 1995 book. Each page was filled with Bezos's carefully scribbled notes.

In 2004, Apple's dominance in digital music spawned fresh soul-searching at Amazon. The sales of books, music, and movies accounted for 74 percent of Amazon's annual revenues that year. If those formats were inevitably transitioning to digital, as Apple's accomplishment seemed to demonstrate, then Amazon had to move quickly to protect itself. 'We were freaking out over what the iPod had done to Amazon's music business,' says director John Doerr. 'We feared that there would be another kind of device from Apple or someone else that would go after the core business: books.'

Investor Bill Miller from Legg Mason often discussed the digital transition with Bezos when the two got together. 'I think the thing that blindsided Jeff and helped with the Kindle was the iPod, which overturned the music business faster than he thought,' says Miller. 'He had always understood this stuff was going digital, but he didn't expect to have his CD business eviscerated like that.'

Bezos ultimately concluded that if Amazon was to continue to thrive as a bookseller in a new digital age, it must own the e-book business in the same way that Apple controlled the music business. 'It is far better to cannibalize yourself than have someone else do it,' said Diego Piacentini in a speech at Stanford's Graduate School of Business a few years later. 'We didn't want to be Kodak.' The reference was to the century-old photography giant whose engineers had invented digital cameras in the 1970s but whose profit margins were so healthy that its executives couldn't bear to risk it all on an unproven venture in a less profitable frontier.

Bezos was apparently contemplating a dedicated electronic reader as early as 2003 – around the time Gemstar pulled the Rocketbook from shelves. Andreas Weigend, Amazon's short-lived chief scientist, remembers Bezos speaking to his technical team about such a device and saying, 'It's for one-handed reading.' Upon imagining what the *other* hand might be doing, Weigend started to laugh out loud, and then everyone else in the small conference room did as well. 'Jeff, the good kid that he is, had no idea what one-handed reading could refer to,' Weigend says.

In 2004, Amazon executives were considering shutting down their own fledgling e-bookstore, which featured books in Adobe and Microsoft formats. The store was everything Bezos hated: its selection was small, its prices were high, and the customer experience of downloading titles and reading them on the screen of a PC or PDA was terrible. But Bezos, according to Piacentini, seemed determined. Despite these early flaws, e-books were clearly the future of bookselling.

A few weeks into these discussions, in an S Team meeting, Bezos announced that Amazon would develop its own dedicated electronic reading device for long-form reading. It was a stunning edict. Creating hardware was expensive and complicated. It was also well outside of Amazon's core competency – its litany of obvious skills. There was a chorus of vehement objections. Jeff Wilke in particular had the background in manufacturing to know what challenges lay ahead for the company if it tried to make and sell its own devices. 'I thought it would be difficult and disruptive and I was skeptical that it was the right use of our resources,' he says. 'It turned out that most of the things I predicted would happen actually happened, and we still powered through it because Jeff is not deterred by short-term setbacks.'

Diego Piacentini also protested. He had watched first-hand as Apple struggled through the 1990s with disastrous surpluses of products and massive inventory write-offs. 'It was seen by me and all the small thinkers as a very risky investment,' he says.

Bezos dismissed those objections and insisted that to succeed in books as Apple had in music, Amazon needed to control the entire customer experience, combining sleek hardware with an easy-to-use digital bookstore. 'We are going to hire our way to having the talent,' he told his executives in that meeting. 'I absolutely know it's very hard. We'll learn how to do it.'

Within Amazon there is a term used to describe the top executives who get to implement Jeff Bezos's best ideas:

Jeff Bots. The playfully derisive phrase that undoubtedly hides a little jealousy connotes slavish devotion but also loyalty and effectiveness. Jeff Bots draw fuel from their CEO's ample idea tank and then go out into the world and dutifully execute the best notions. They have completely absorbed Bezos's business philosophy and molded their own worldviews around it, and they recite rote Jeffisms – how they start from the customer and work backward, et cetera – as if these were their prime directives. To interview a Jeff Bot as a journalist is to witness his or her remarkable ability to say absolutely nothing of substance while going on about Amazon's inventiveness and its unmatched, gee-whiz enthusiasm for the customer. Jeff Bots would surely rather chomp down on their cyanide-capsule-implanted molars than address topics that Amazon has programmed them to never publicly discuss – subjects such as the competition and any possible problems with products.

Throughout Amazon history, there was perhaps no more faithful or enterprising Jeff Bot than Steve Kessel, a Boston-born graduate of Dartmouth College and the Stanford University Graduate School of Business. Kessel joined Amazon in the heat of the 1999 expansion after a job consulting for browser pioneer Netscape. In his first few years at the company, he ran the book category at a time when Amazon was cultivating direct relationships with publishers and trying to assuage their fears about third-party merchants selling used books on the site. During this grinding period of Amazon's greatest challenges, Bezos grew to trust him immensely.

One day in 2004, Bezos called Kessel into his office and abruptly took away his impressive job, with all of its responsibilities and subordinates. He said he wanted Kessel to take over Amazon's fledgling digital efforts.

Kessel was skeptical. 'My first reaction was that I already had the best job in the world,' he says. 'Ultimately Jeff talked about building brand-new things, and I got excited by the challenge.' Bezos was adamant that Kessel could not run both the physical and digital-media businesses at the same time. 'If you are running both businesses you will never go after the digital opportunity with tenacity,' he said.

By that time, Bezos and his executives had devoured and raptly discussed another book that would significantly affect the company's strategy: *The Innovator's Dilemma*, by Harvard professor Clayton Christensen. Christensen wrote that great companies fail not because they want to avoid disruptive change but because they are reluctant to embrace promising new markets that might undermine their traditional businesses and that do not appear to satisfy their short-term growth requirements. Sears, for example, failed to move from department stores to discount retailing; IBM couldn't shift from mainframe to minicomputers. The companies that solved the innovator's dilemma, Christensen wrote, succeeded when they 'set up autonomous organizations charged with building new and independent businesses around the disruptive technology.'[9]

Drawing lessons directly from the book, Bezos unshackled Kessel from Amazon's traditional media organization. 'Your job is to kill your own business,' he told him. 'I want you to proceed as if your goal is to put everyone selling physical books out of a job.' Bezos underscored the urgency of the effort. He believed that if Amazon didn't lead the world into the age of digital reading, then Apple or Google would. When Kessel asked Bezos what his deadline was on developing the company's first piece of hardware, an electronic reading device, Bezos told him, 'You are basically already late.'

With no personal knowledge of the hardware business and no internal resources at the company to draw on, Kessel went on a fact-finding mission to Silicon Valley, meeting with hardware experts from Apple and Palm and with executives from the famed industrial design firm Ideo. He learned that Amazon would need not just designers but electrical engineers, mechanical engineers, wireless engineers – the list was endless.

Following Christensen's dictates as if they were instructions in a recipe, Kessel set up another subsidiary in Palo Alto in addition to A9. To take the helm of the new division, he hired Gregg Zehr, an easygoing former vice president of engineering at Palm Computing who kept a jazz guitar in his office. Jateen Parekh, a former engineer at set-top-box maker ReplayTV (an early TiVo rival), became the first employee, and a few others were hired as well. There was no office to report to, so they set up shop in an empty room in the headquarters of A9. Zehr and his colleagues set about furnishing the new division with a name alluring enough to attract the best and brightest engineers from Silicon Valley. They eventually settled on Lab126. The *1* stands for *a*, the *26* for *z*; it's a subtle indication of Bezos's dream to allow customers to buy any book ever published, from *a* to *z*.

They didn't get their marching orders right away, so Zehr and his team spent the first few weeks investigating the possibility of building an Internet-connected set-top box and even an MP3 player. Finally Amazon's new hardware geeks were given their mission: they were to build an electronic reading device. 'We were told to do one great thing with maniacal focus,' says Tom Ryan, a software engineer from Palm whom Zehr brought over that fall. 'The aspiration was to be Apple.'

The group piggybacked on A9's infrastructure for the next year. When the search division moved to the former offices of a law firm on Lytton and Alma in downtown Palo Alto, Lab126 moved with them and took up residence in the old law library. They researched existing e-readers of the time, such as the Sony Libre, which required triple-A batteries and sold poorly. They concluded the market was wide open. 'It was the one thing that wasn't being done well by anyone else out there,' says Parekh.

Lab126 was soon given extensive resources but it also had to contend with the unfettered imagination of Bezos. Amazon's founder wanted his new e-reading device to be so easy to use that a grandmother could operate it, and he argued that configuring devices to work with WiFi networks was too complicated for non-tech-savvy users. He didn't want to force customers to connect the device to a PC, so the only alternative was to build cellular access right into the hardware, the equivalent of embedding a wireless phone in each unit. Nothing like that had been tried before. Bezos insisted that customers should never have to know the wireless connection was there or even pay for access. 'I thought it was insane, I really did,' Parekh says.

In those early months, much of the early direction for the Kindle was set. Zehr and Parekh made the decision to explore the low-powered black-and-white display technology called E Ink that, years before, Martin Eberhard had found too primitive and expensive. It used millions of tiny microcapsules, each about the diameter of a human hair and containing positively charged white particles and negatively charged black particles suspended in a clear fluid. When a positive electric field is applied, positively charged particles move to the top of the microcapsule, making that spot appear white; when a negative electric field is applied, negative particles migrate up, and the spot appears black.

Unlike LCD systems, the technology worked well under direct sunlight, used very little battery power, and was exceedingly easy on the eyes. In a sense, Amazon got lucky. A technology perfectly suited for long-form reading on a device (and terrible for everything else) just happened to be maturing after a decade of development.

In those waning months of 2004, the early Lab126 engineers selected a code name for their new project. On his desk, Zehr had a copy of Neal Stephenson's *The Diamond Age*, a futuristic novel about an engineer who steals a rare interactive textbook to give to his daughter, Fiona. The early Lab126 engineers thought of the fictitious textbook in the novel as a template for what they were creating. Michael Cronan, the San Francisco-based graphic designer and marketing executive who baptized the TiVo, was later hired to officially brand the new dedicated reading device, and he came up with Kindle, which played off the notion of starting a conflagration and worked as both a noun and a verb. But by then Kessel's team was devoted to the name Fiona and the group tried, unsuccessfully, to convince Bezos to keep it. In a sense, the knowledge-starved Fiona of Stephenson's fictional world became Amazon's patron saint in its risky journey into the digital frontier.

While Zehr and his crew at Lab126 worked on software and developed relationships with Asian manufacturers, the early industrial design work on Amazon's new e-reader was contracted out to the San Francisco office of global design firm Pentagram. Zehr had worked with a partner there, Robert Brunner, at Apple in the 1990s, and he introduced Brunner to Steve Kessel with the suggestion that Pentagram could offer a nimbler and perhaps more discrete style of collaboration than larger firms like Ideo. Brunner assigned two of his employees, Tom Hobbs and Symon Whitehorn, to the job.

The Pentagram designers, both British born, began by studying the actual physics of reading – the physical aspects of the pastime, such as how readers turn pages and hold books in their hands. They forced themselves to read on existing e-readers, like the Sony Libre and the old Rocketbook, and on PDAs like the iPaq from Compaq and Palm's Treo. They brought in focus groups, conducted phone interviews, and even went up to Seattle to talk to Bezos himself, trying to deconstruct a process that for many hundreds of years people had taken for granted. 'We were pushing for the subconscious qualities that made it feel like you are reading a book,' says Hobbs. One of the primary conclusions from their research was that a good book disappears in the reader's hands. Bezos later called this the top design objective. 'Kindle also had to get out of the way and disappear so that you could enter the author's world,' he said.[10]

The Pentagram designers worked on the Kindle for nearly two years. They met with Steve Kessel, Greg Zehr, and Charlie Tritschler – another Palm veteran who'd joined Lab126 – every Tuesday morning at A9 in Palo Alto and later at the new Lab126 offices in Mountain View. They periodically traveled to Seattle to update Bezos on their progress, and they had to present to the CEO in the customary Amazon way, with six-page narratives.

The meetings could get tense. Hobbs, Whitehorn, and Brunner wanted to strip out complexity and make the device as streamlined and inconspicuous as possible. Bezos also wanted a simple, iconic design but insisted on adding a keyboard so users could easily search for book titles and make annotations. (He envisioned sitting in a taxi with

Wall Street Journal columnist Walt Mossberg and keying in and downloading an e-book right there in the cab.) Bezos toted around a BlackBerry messaging device at the time and told the designers, 'I want you to join my BlackBerry and my book.'

In one trip to Seattle, the designers stubbornly brought models that left out the keyboard. Bezos gave them a withering look. 'Look, we already talked about this,' he said. 'I might be wrong but at the same time I've got a bit more to stand on than you have.'

'I remember being very silent for the rest of that meeting,' Hobbs says. They complied and designed oblong buttons, based on the style of the BlackBerry, while trying to accommodate the angles that reader's fingers might take moving across the device.

There were similar disputes about wireless connectivity. The Pentagram designers couldn't understand how the economics of the wireless connection could work and assumed Amazon would be asking the user to pay a wireless charge every time he or she bought a book. At one point, they pitched Bezos on a process similar to the iTunes model, which required making the bookstore accessible on a PC. Bezos pushed back. 'Here's my scenario, I'm going to the airport. I need a book to read. I want to enter it into the device and download it right there from my car.'

'But you can't do that,' Hobbs replied.

'I'll decide what I can do,' Bezos said. 'I'll figure this out and it is not going to be a business model you understand. You are the designers, I want you to design this and I'll think about the business model.'

Pentagram worked on Fiona through the middle of 2006, and then Lab126, which by then had hired its own designers, reclaimed the project. The Pentagram designers would feel ambivalent about the device when they finally saw it at the same time as the rest of the world. It was too cluttered with buttons, the design too confusing. After the project, Symon Whitehorn left Pentagram to go work at, of all places, Kodak. He hired Tom Hobbs as a contractor and together they created a unique digital camera that allowed picture-takers to impose on their photos the historical look of classic Kodachrome film. It presaged mobile-phone applications like Instagram, and, naturally, Kodak killed the project before it ever hit the market.

Meanwhile, after Pentagram left the Kindle project, the device seemed nearly ready and close to launching. But a litany of delays followed. E Ink sent displays from Asia, and owing to variable temperatures and humidity, batches would have low contrast or get dimmer with frequent use. Intel sold the family of XScale microprocessor chips that Kindle used to another chip company, Marvell. Qualcomm and Broadcom, two wireless-technology companies that manufactured cellular components to be used in the Kindle, sued each other in 2007, and at one point it seemed like a judge would prevent certain key Kindle parts from entering the United States. Bezos himself brought about repeated delays, finding one fault or another with the device and constantly asking for changes.

The top-secret Kindle effort dragged on for so long that it became the subject of persistent rumors inside Amazon, even though no one was supposed to know of the project's existence. At an all-hands meeting at the Moore Theater in the fall of 2006, someone stood up and asked, 'Can you tell us what Lab126 is?'

Bezos responded brusquely. 'It's a development center in Northern California. Next question.'

* * *

To give the Kindle even a remote chance of succeeding, Amazon needed e-books – lots of them. Bezos had watched the Rocketbook and later saw the Sony Reader hobbled by pitifully limited catalogs. There was simply nothing for owners of the early e-book devices to read. His goal was to have one hundred thousand digital titles, including 90 percent of the *New York Times*' bestsellers, available for download when the device went on sale. At the time, publishers had digitized only their front lists, or about twenty thousand books total. The Kindle store finally offered Bezos another chance to fulfill part of his dream of the everything store, a comprehensively stocked library that was exceedingly convenient for customers, but to get there, Amazon would have to pressure, cajole, and even threaten some of its oldest partners, a group of companies that had come to view Amazon as something other than a faithful friend.

Back in its earliest days, Amazon's relationship with book publishers was uncomplicated and largely symbiotic. The company acquired most of its books from Ingram, Baker and Taylor, and other distributors, and on the rare occasions when the distributors didn't have a title in stock, they bought directly from publishers. There were occasional but insignificant skirmishes during these years. Bezos often said publicly that publishers originally hated the notion of customer reviews, fearing that harsh and often anonymous on-line critiques could hurt sales. Publishers and the Authors Guild also complained about the appearance of third-party sellers hawking used books on the site.[11]

For its part, a young Amazon constantly harangued publishers for more 'metadata,' the books' supplementary information, like author biographies, comprehensive descriptions of the subject matter, and digital images of jacket covers. Still, many publishers viewed Amazon as a savior, a desperately needed counter-balance to Barnes & Noble, Borders, and Waterstones in the United Kingdom, all of which were churning out new superstores and using their size and growth to press for steeper discounts on wholesale prices.

Living in Seattle, a continent away from New York City, Bezos made few friendships in the world of book publishing. One of his rare personal connections was with Larry Kirshbaum, the CEO of the Time Warner Book Group and the high-profile minder of James Patterson and other authors. Kirshbaum believed so deeply in the Amazon mission that he had bought shares in its May 1997 initial public offering. A few months later, on a night of pounding rain in midtown Manhattan, Bezos and Kirshbaum walked six blocks from the Time-Life Building to attend a party that Rupert Murdoch was throwing for Jane Friedman, then the incoming chief executive officer of News Corporation's HarperCollins book division. The luminaries of the publishing business, such as Random House's then CEO Alberto Vitale and literary agent Lynn Nesbit, crowded into the Monkey Bar on Fifty-Fourth Street, with its red-leather booths and murals of gamboling chimps. For a rare night, Bezos socialized amiably with the titans of an industry that Amazon was about to irrevocably change. 'It was one of those moments in your life where you remember everything,' says Kirshbaum, who would join Amazon as the head of its New York publishing division in 2011. 'In fact, I think Bezos still owes me an umbrella.'

When Amazon began its all-consuming pursuit of profitability after the turn of the century, its attitude toward the rest of the book world began to change. By 2004, Amazon sold a large percentage of all books in the

United States. So it aggressively sought more favorable financial terms in its deals with publishers and tried to reap some of the benefits of its growing size and significance in the industry. During these pivotal years, the steward of Amazon's relationship with publishers, Lyn Blake, was herself a veteran of the industry, a former executive of the computer-book division of Macmillan.

Blake joined Amazon in 1999. Her first job was to establish stronger direct relationships with publishers and create standards for how they shipped packages of books to Amazon's fulfillment centers (no Styrofoam packing peanuts, for example). Blake brought more discipline and analytics to Amazon's book-supply chain, overseeing the creation of automated systems that purchased from whichever source – distributor or publisher – had books in stock and offered the best price. She developed Amazon's first co-op programs in the book category, selling prominent placement on the site to publishers who were willing to pay promotional fees. These were customary tactics for any large retailer, and Blake had seen them employed by other retail chains, to profitable effect, from her perch at Macmillan.

Blake was an anomaly at Amazon. She refused to carry a BlackBerry and left the office every day promptly at five to greet her young daughter at home. She could be a tough negotiator, and she knew her way around the Robinson-Patman Act, the 1936 antitrust law that prohibited manufacturers from selling goods to large retailers at a lower price than they sold to their smaller competitors. Having been on the other side of the negotiating table, she was sensitive to the needs of book publishers and was often their advocate inside Amazon. 'My relationship with the largest publishers was very positive,' Blake says. 'Of course I pushed them to do better and work harder, but when they had issues with us, I was willing to address those issues.'

Blake's balancing act soon became difficult. In Bezos's perennial quest to subsidize low prices for customers and finance programs like Super Saver Shipping and Prime, he pushed Blake and her team to establish more favorable financial relationships with book publishers and expand profit margins wherever they could. Bezos believed Amazon should be well compensated for the special benefits it brought to the book industry. The site carried millions of titles, not just the one hundred and fifty thousand or so that appeared on the shelves of a Barnes & Noble superstore. Unlike traditional retailers, Amazon returned few unsold books, often less than 5 percent. The big book chains regularly returned 40 percent of all the books they acquired from publishers, for full refunds, an arrangement that is nearly unique in retail.

By 2004, Amazon's normally placid book-buying department found itself preparing for battle. Buyers received negotiating training and an education on the limits and flexibility of Robinson-Patman. Blake dutifully pushed publishers for compromises while constantly reminding her boss that if publishers rebelled, Amazon could be hurt. 'There was a period of time where inside Amazon, we were scared of how the publishing industry would take all this,' says Erick Goss, a senior manager of the books group. 'Lyn was our ambassador. I credit her for maintaining these relationships.'

Amazon approached large publishers aggressively. It demanded accommodations like steeper discounts on bulk purchases, longer periods to pay its bills, and shipping arrangements that leveraged Amazon's discounts with UPS. To publishers that didn't comply, Amazon threatened to pull their books out of its automated personalization and recommendation systems, meaning that they would no longer be suggested to customers. 'Publishers didn't really understand Amazon. They were very naïve about what was going on with their back catalog,' says Goss. 'Most didn't know their sales were up because their backlist was getting such visibility.'

Amazon had an easy way to demonstrate its market power. When a publisher did not capitulate and the company shut off the recommendation algorithms for its books, the publisher's sales usually fell by as much as 40 percent. 'Typically it was about thirty days before they'd come back and say, Ouch, how do we make this work?' says Christopher Smith, a senior book buyer at the time.

Bezos kept pushing for more. He asked Blake to exact better terms from the smallest publishers, who would go out of business if it weren't for the steady sales of their back catalogs on Amazon. Within the books group, the resulting program was dubbed the Gazelle Project because Bezos suggested to Blake in a meeting that Amazon should approach these small publishers the way a cheetah would pursue a sickly gazelle.

As part of the Gazelle Project, Blake's group categorized publishers in terms of their dependency on Amazon and then opened negotiations with the most vulnerable companies. Three book buyers at the time recall this effort. Blake herself said that Bezos meant the cheetah-and-gazelle analogy as a joke and that it was carried too far. Yet the program clearly represented something real – an emerging realpolitik approach toward book publishers, an attitude whose ruthlessness startled even some Amazon employees. Soon after the Gazelle Project began, Amazon's lawyers heard about the name and insisted it be changed to the less incendiary Small Publisher Negotiation Program.

Publishers were horrified by this. The company they had once viewed as a welcome counterbalance to the book chains was now constantly presenting new demands. The demands were introduced quite persuasively in the form of benefits to be passed on to Amazon's customers, but even that could sound ominous. When Amazon passed on savings to customers in the form of shipping deals or lower prices, it had the effect of increasing the pressure on physical bookstores, including independent bookshops, and adding to Amazon's growing market power.

Around this time, Amazon representatives made the rounds asking publishers to submit titles for its Search Inside the Book program. Meanwhile, Google had begun scanning library books without the permission of copyright owners, part of a massive effort to make the world's literary output available online as a research tool. In 2005, the Authors Guild and the Association of American Publishers filed dual lawsuits against Google in federal court. This was a separate drama with its own convoluted legal backstory, but it amplified some book publishers' growing anxiety: they risked losing control of their own business to the well-capitalized Internet companies on the West Coast, who seemed to approach the cerebral pursuit of bookselling with all the literary nuance one might find in an algorithm.

Lyn Blake left Amazon in early 2005. She had achieved unexpected financial success and wanted to devote more time to her family. She admits that she also saw an approaching rupture in Amazon's relationships with book publishers. 'Maybe I was feeling like it was going to go that way,' she says. 'I like to do business where both parties feel like they are going to get something valuable out of it, which means future negotiations can take place in a civilized way.'

Her successors would not channel the same advocacy for publishers inside Amazon or have the same deft political touch. Before she left, Blake promoted Randy Miller, one of the founders of Amazon's jewelry store, to take over vendor relations in Europe. By his own admission, Miller took an almost sadistic delight in pressuring book publishers to give Amazon more favorable financial terms. He ranked all of the European publishers by their sales and by Amazon's profit margins on their books. Then he and his colleagues persuaded the lagging publishers to alter their deals and give Amazon better terms, once again with the threat of decreased promotion on the site. Miller says he and his colleagues called the program Pay to Play. Once again, Amazon's lawyers caught wind of this and renamed the program Vendor Realignment.

Over the next year, Miller tangled with the European divisions of Random House, Hachette, and Bloomsbury, the publisher of the Harry Potter series. 'I did everything I could to screw with their performance,' he says. He took selections of their catalog to full price and yanked their books from Amazon's recommendation engine; with some titles, like travel books, he promoted comparable books from competitors. Miller's constant search for new points of leverage exploited the anxieties of neurotic authors who obsessively tracked sales rank – the number on Amazon.com that showed an author how well his or her book was doing compared to other products on the site. 'We would constantly meet with authors, so we'd know who would be watching their rankings.' Miller says. 'I knew these people would be on their phones the second they saw their sales numbers drop.'

These tactics were not unique to Amazon. The company had finally learned the tricks of the century-old trade that is modern retail. Profit margin is finite. Better financial terms with suppliers translate directly into a healthier bottom line – and create the foundation on which everyday low prices become possible.

Walmart in particular had mastered this perpetual coercion of suppliers, and it did it with missionary zeal and the belief that it led to the low prices that made products like diapers affordable to lower- and middle-class Americans. Walmart is notorious for demanding that suppliers open offices in Bentonville, Arkansas, and integrate certain technologies, like RFID chips, into their products. The company is also known for specifying just how much it will pay for products and for demanding severe concessions if it believes a supplier's profit margin is too high.

In Amazon's early years, when the likes of Sony and Disney refused to sell directly to the company, Bezos had been on the short end of this Darwinian dynamic. He had learned the game firsthand. Now the balance of power was shifting. Now suppliers needed Amazon more than Amazon needed them.

In the midst of this changing landscape, Amazon started to pitch publishers on the Kindle.

The first two Kindle emissaries to the New York-based publishers presented an unlikely picture. Dan Rose, a longtime Amazon business development executive, led the early effort to bring publishers on board. Rose was of medium height, sported dot-com casual clothes like khakis and royal blue oxford shirts, and spoke easily about the coming opportunities of the digital age. He visited publishers with a former Microsoft product manager named Jeff Steele, an openly homosexual six-foot-four bodybuilder who wore dark suits and ties and cut a menacing figure – but who in reality had an exceedingly gentle temperament.

Their goal, set in the first half of 2006, was to convince jittery publishers to place yet another bet on e-books, despite the many previous failures and false starts in digital publishing. They were handicapped in their mission: Bezos didn't actually permit them to acknowledge the existence of the Kindle, which remained top secret.

So Rose and Steele were forced to approach the topic circuitously, talking up Search Inside the Book and an e-book standard created by the French company Mobipocket, which Amazon acquired in 2005 to jump-start its e-book initiative. Owning Mobi technology allowed Amazon e-books to appear on a variety of different devices, like cell phones and PDAs.

Without any hint of why the prospects for e-books might soon brighten, publishers were reluctant to act. They already encoded their most popular titles in the standards supported by Sony, Adobe, Microsoft, and Palm, yet e-books remained an infinitesimally small part of their business. Digitizing backlist books also presented enormous legal challenges. For titles published prior to the late 1990s, it was sometimes unclear who actually owned the digital rights, and publishers were often loath to revisit the issue with authors and their agents, as they might view it as an opportunity to renegotiate their entire deal.

Rose and Steele's progress was slow. Adding to the pressure, Bezos wanted biweekly reports on their march toward the goal of one hundred thousand e-books. 'I described my job as dragging publishers kicking and screaming into the twenty-first century,' says Jeff Steele. 'We found they really weren't willing to do something interesting.' That summer, the duo finally convinced Bezos they couldn't hide the ball any longer: they had to tell publishers about the Kindle. 'Once they see it, they will get excited about it,' Steele argued. Bezos reluctantly agreed to allow them to show publishers a Kindle prototype, as long as it was within the confines of a strict nondisclosure agreement.

In the fall of 2006, Amazon began showing the device to publishers. At the time, Fiona was unimpressive; it looked like the cream-colored bastard child of a BlackBerry and a calculator, and it froze up as often as it worked. Publishers thought Amazon might be hawking the e-book equivalent of Betamax, the failed Sony home-video format of the 1970s. They saw mostly what wasn't there: no color, no video, no backlight. The early prototypes did not have working wireless access either, though Amazon executives described what the experience might be like while they feebly demonstrated the device by loading SD cards with sample e-books.

During these unproductive months, Amazon developers conceived of a potential shortcut to their goal, which they dubbed Topaz. Topaz was a program to take the scanned digital files from Search Inside the Book and repurpose them in a format suitable for the Kindle. Amazon offered this as an option to publishers, arguing that it would help them decrease the costs of digitizing their catalogs, although the digital file would remain exclusive to the Kindle. Large publishers like Simon and Schuster did not want to create a new dependency on Amazon, but some smaller publishers jumped at the option.

By early 2007, Amazon could demonstrate the Kindle's wireless access, and, finally, some publishers understood its potential. John Sargent, the CEO of Macmillan, and some other executives became converts when they recognized for the first time that giving customers instant gratification – the immediate download of any e-book at any time – might allow Amazon to succeed where Sony and others had failed. Of course, as Bezos had feared, it leaked. *Engadget*, the technology blog, had the first details about Amazon's new e-reading device, and soon after, Victoria Barnsley, the CEO of HarperCollins UK, confirmed at an industry event that she had seen the device and was 'rather impressed.'[12]

The Kindle was supposed to go on sale for the 2006 holidays. But it was delayed another year as Bezos relentlessly pressured Steve Kessel and his team for fixes, new features, and a larger catalog of e-books. By that time, Dan Rose had departed Amazon to join the budding social network Facebook, and Jeff Steele and his group reported directly to Kessel. Steele also worked alongside the merchandising director from the physical books group, Laura Porco.

Porco, a graduate of Ohio State University and one of Lyn Blake's hires, was a blunt and tenacious advocate for Amazon's cause. She channeled the intensity of Bezos, ruthlessly aiming to exact profit margins from Amazon's relationships with its suppliers wherever she could. Prior to joining the Kindle group, she battled with the movie studios, pulling Disney out of Amazon's recommendations in the midst of one negotiation (a tactic that didn't work) and clashing so fiercely with executives at Warner Home Video that the studio famously banned her from its buildings, according to several of Porco's colleagues. One Random House executive called her Amazon's 'battering ram.' Even her colleagues were in awe of her Hyde-like transformation when conducting the company's business. 'Laura can be one of the kindest people, but when it comes to Amazon she wants to drink blood,' says Christopher Smith.

A few years after the original Kindle negotiations, a publishing-industry executive visited Amazon to discuss a job opening at the company. He was interviewed by a series of Amazon book executives, including Porco, who asked only one question: 'What is your negotiation strategy?' The executive replied that he believed a successful negotiation must make both sides happy. Porco's passionate view, according to this executive (who did not get the job), was that this was an 'un-Amazon' response and that one party must always win.

This is not to pick on a particular Amazon executive, but to illustrate a point. Inside the company at the time, the culture was self-perpetuating, and those who couldn't channel Bezos's fervor on behalf of Amazon and its customers didn't stay with the company. Those who could do it stayed and advanced.

Erick Goss, a veteran of the book group, could no longer abide the Jeff Bots, and he moved to Nashville in 2006 to care for his ailing mother. He took a job at a competitor, Magazines.com, and Amazon threatened to sue him for violating his noncompete clause. (The matter was settled privately.) Goss admitted to mixed emotions about Amazon. He was proud of the difficult things he and his colleagues had accomplished. But he also found it increasingly hard to reconcile the company's approach toward its partners with his own Christian values and says that for a year after leaving Amazon, he had post-traumatic stress disorder.

Jeff Steele, the gentle giant who spearheaded Amazon's outreach to the publishers, also grew to dislike Amazon's creeping aggressiveness. 'I didn't like to bully people. Every reasonable business-development deal should involve some sort of compromise, some give-and-take,' he says. 'I just got uncomfortable.' In what became the final straw, Steele quarreled with Kessel over the terms of Amazon's contract with Oxford University Press, which supplied the digital dictionary that was embedded in the Kindle. Kessel wanted to renegotiate the already completed contract to exact more favorable terms from the publisher. Steele bluntly told him that the deal had already been negotiated and that it was unethical to revisit the contract. Soon after, Steele got into a shouting match with Laura Porco and was asked by Kessel to collect his things and leave the company. Porco then took over the Kindle effort.

The next few months were tense. Amazon's inducements to publishers were followed by threats. Publishers that didn't digitize enough of their catalogs, or didn't do it fast enough, were told they faced losing their prominence in Amazon's search results and in its recommendations to customers. Years earlier, the music labels had scampered into the arms of Apple despite their reservations, since they were facing the even more ominous threat of rampant music piracy. But books were not as easily pirated and shared on-line, and book publishers feared no similar bogeyman. So Bezos finally had to turn Amazon into one.

What had started out as Amazon's soliciting publishers for help had evolved into the equivalent of a parent threatening a child. After realizing they did not yet have the Oprah Winfrey book club pick, *One Hundred Years of Solitude* by Gabriel García Márquez, Porco sent an e-mail to Random House's head of sales demanding to know why there was no e-book version available. The note, which came during the middle of the night New York time, was so contemptuous and incendiary that it made the rounds within the publishing company. (Knopf, the Random House imprint that published the book, wouldn't have the digital rights for another year.)

Publishers felt caught up in a schizophrenic assault by Amazon that combined supplication and threats and alternated urgency with delay. Porco and her team presented list after list of books that publishers needed to digitize, then screamed when e-books weren't produced fast enough. Amazon also appealed directly to agents and authors, alienating publishers, who were uncomfortable seeing one of the world's largest retailers speaking with their most prominent authors. 'It seems clear to me that the insanity being directed at us was coming directly from Jeff Bezos, who had some mania about a magic number that needed to be hit about the number of titles available on the Kindle on the word go,' says one publishing executive.

Amazon and its publishing partners now occupied entirely different worlds. The e-book business didn't exist in any meaningful way, so publishers couldn't understand why they were being berated and punished for not embracing it. Amazon executives saw themselves as racing toward the future and fulfilling Bezos's vision of making every book ever printed available for instant digital delivery, but at the same time they were trying desperately to beat Apple and Google to the next vital phase in the evolution of digital media.

And there was one other ingredient in this piquant stew. Bezos decided that the digital versions of the most popular books and new releases would have a flat price of $9.99. There was no research behind that number – it was Bezos's gut call, fashioned after Apple's successful ninety-nine-cent price tag for a digital single in iTunes and based on the assumption that consumers would expect to pay less for an e-book than they did for a traditional book, as an e-book had none of the costs associated with printing and storage. Since Amazon bought e-books from publishers at the same wholesale price as it bought physical books, typically paying around fifteen dollars for a book that would retail at thirty, that meant it would lose money on many of its sales. Bezos was fine with that – he believed publishers would eventually be forced to lower their wholesale prices on e-books to reflect the lower costs of publication. In the meantime, it was just the kind of investment in Amazon's future that he loved. 'Customers are smart, and we felt like they would expect and deserve digital books to be lower priced than physical books,' says Steve Kessel.

Amazon knew quite well that publishers would absolutely hate the $9.99 price. The $9.99 e-books were considerably more appealing to some customers than the more expensive hardcovers, the industry's most profitable format, and the pricing pulled the rug out from under traditional retailers, particularly independent booksellers, who would suddenly find their shelves stocked with what some book buyers might soon view as overly expensive relics. Everyone had watched this precise dynamic play out in music, with disastrous consequences for physical retailers.

So Amazon decided not to let publishers know about the planned $9.99 price, lest they object. This was easily rationalized; retailers have no obligation to tell their suppliers how they plan to price products, and doing so could theoretically raise the specter of vertical price fixing and attract the attention of antitrust authorities. Still, Amazon had approached publishers as a partner, and now it was deliberately withholding a key piece of information. 'We were instructed not to talk about pricing strategy,' Jeff Steele says. 'We knew that if we priced e-books too low, they would fear it would devalue their product. So we just said pricing had not yet been decided.'

Oblivious to the pricing plans, publishers slowly came aboard, digitizing larger parts of their catalog. By the fall of 2007, Amazon had ninety thousand books in the Kindle library, tantalizingly close to Bezos's goal. Kindle owners would have the equivalent of a Barnes & Noble bookstore at their fingertips.

When Bezos finally stopped delaying and set the launch of the first Kindle, executives from all the major book publishers flocked to the press conference. They had been bruised and battered by Amazon over the past few years but they came together as an industry to take a cautious step toward what promised to be the inevitable future of the written word – a future with a major surprise waiting for them.

On November 19, 2007, Jeff Bezos stepped onto a stage at the W Hotel in lower Manhattan to introduce the Kindle. He spoke to an audience of a hundred or so journalists and publishing executives, a relatively small crowd compared to the reverential throngs who gathered for the product rollouts of Apple. Wearing a blue sport coat and khakis, Bezos stated that Amazon's new device was the successor to the five-hundred-and-fifty-year-old invention of blacksmith Johannes Gutenberg, the movable-type printing press. 'Why are books the last bastion of analog?' Bezos asked that day. 'The question is, can you improve upon something as highly evolved and as well suited to its task as the book, and if so, how?'

The original Kindle, priced at $399, was clearly the product of all the compromises and anxieties that had gone into its labored three-year development. It was meant to disappear in the reader's hands, yet it sported a wedge-shaped body with a jumble of angular buttons, an attempt to make a bold design statement while allowing for the easy entry of text. Bezos wanted a device that did one thing extremely well. But the former Palm engineers at Lab126 had watched the PalmPilot get overtaken by more versatile gadgets, so at the last moment they packed the Kindle with other features, like a Web browser and an MP3 player, which were quarantined in an unusual 'experimental' section of the device.

In retrospect, the first Kindle provided an exultant answer to Bezos's question. In many respects, it was superior to its analog predecessor, the physical book. It weighed ten ounces and could carry two hundred titles. The E Ink screen was easy on the eyes. Whispernet, the name Amazon gave to the Kindle's free 3G cellular network, allowed readers to painlessly download books in a flash. 'I think the reason Kindle succeeded while others failed is that we were obsessive, not about trying to build the sexiest gadget in the world, but rather [about building] something that actually fulfilled what people wanted,' says Russ Grandinetti, a faithful Jeff Bot who later joined the Kindle team.

Competitors were caught flat-footed by the success of the Kindle. A few weeks before the W Hotel event, I wrote about the forthcoming launch for the *New York Times* and spoke to Stephen Riggio, then the CEO of Barnes & Noble. Riggio and his brother were still bruised from their early foray into e-reading with the Rocketbook and felt that customers had flatly rejected the idea of e-books. 'The physical value of the book is something that cannot be replicated in digital form,' Riggio told me. 'People love to collect books and to have them in their home and on their shelves. I would say it could never be identically replicated because of the value of books as physical objects in consumers' minds.'[13]

Riggio had heard the rumors about the forthcoming

Kindle but doubted Amazon's prospects. 'Certainly there's an opportunity to get back into the business but we think it's small at this moment and probably will be small for the next couple of years,' he said. 'When the market is there, we'll be there.'

It was an enormous tactical blunder. Barnes & Noble would have to scamper to meet Amazon's challenge in the e-book market. It would follow a very similar blueprint, setting up a development office in Northern California as Amazon had done with Lab126. Ironically, to design the device, the retailer hired Robert Brunner, the former Apple designer who had left Pentagram to start his own agency, Ammunition. Brunner and his employees had battled with Bezos over putting a keyboard on the Kindle, so, perhaps not surprisingly, the new B&N device – dubbed the Nook – would leave out the keyboard in favor of a separate touch-based control pad, and its advertising would sport the tagline 'Books don't have buttons.'

The Kindle wasn't an overnight success, of course, but an avalanche of publicity and its prominent placement at the top of the Amazon website ensured that the company would quickly run through its stock of devices. Steve Kessel had studied the introductions of similar consumer electronics like the iPod and placed a conservative first order of twenty-five thousand units. The original batch sold out in hours. Amazon then discovered that the development of the Kindle had gone on for so long, one of its Taiwanese suppliers had discontinued a key component in the wireless module. The company spent months getting a replacement. When a new batch of Kindles arrived the following fall, Bezos appeared on Oprah Winfrey's talk show, and that blew out the supply once again. 'When we originally made the first manufacturing capacity for the Kindle one, we thought we were being very optimistic,' Bezos said. 'It was just bad planning.'[14]

The shortage led to some internal friction. Even after the device sold out, Bezos wanted to promote it heavily on the Amazon home page to continue educating customers and building the brand. Jeff Wilke, now head of North American retail, thought it was irresponsible to feature a product that wasn't available, and also a waste of Amazon's most precious real estate. Angry e-mails over the issue one day turned into a heated conversation in Bezos's office. 'We were both passionate and within five minutes we were both mad,' says Wilke, who later conceded that Bezos was right and the short-term pain had been worth it to build the Kindle franchise. Bezos won the argument, of course, but Wilke convinced him to at least make it clearer on the site that Amazon did not actually have any Kindles on hand.

Just as Clayton Christensen had predicted in *The Innovator's Dilemma*, technological innovation caused wrenching pain to the company and the broader industry. No one was feeling it more than the book publishers. Amazon had spent much of the last two years cajoling and threatening them to embrace its new digital format. But in all those conversations, the company had clearly withheld a crucial detail that Bezos divulged seventeen minutes into the forty-minute launch speech. '*New York Times* bestsellers and new releases are only nine dollars and ninety-nine cents,' Bezos said almost halfway through his presentation at the W Hotel.

Among the gathered publishing execs at the Kindle press conference, there was confusion. Was the $9.99 price a promotional discount for the launch? Was it only for bestsellers? Even after the event, Amazon executives told their publishing counterparts they didn't know or couldn't say. Soon it was clear to the bookselling industry that the flat price was not transitory at all – Amazon was pushing it as a new standard. Bezos went on a media tour after the Kindle event, appearing on programs like *The Charlie Rose Show*, trumpeting the $9.99 price for new releases and bestsellers and making a persuasive case for change in the book business. 'It is not written anywhere that books shall forever be printed on dead trees,' he told Rose.

Finally the grim reality sank in, and publishing executives kicked themselves for their own gullibility. 'It left an incredibly bad taste in our mouths, that they would slip that one by us after hammering us for months and months with their goddamn lists,' says one executive of a major publishing house. 'I don't think they were doing the wrong thing, but I think the way they handled it was wrong. It was just one more nail in the coffin that no one realized was being closed over [us], even while we were engaged every single day in a conversation about it.'

'I think we were absolutely naïve in agreeing to supply those files without any caveats around them,' says another executive at a big-six publisher, one of the six trade houses with the largest market shares. 'If I could rewrite history I would have said, "Thanks so much, I love the idea of the Kindle, but let's have an agreement that says you will not sell below the cost." I feel like I was asleep at the tiller.'

The new low price for top-selling e-books changed everything. It tilted the playing field in the direction of digital, putting additional pressure on physical retailers, threatening independent bookstores, and giving Amazon even more market power. The publishers had seen over many years what Amazon did with this kind of additional leverage. It exacted more concessions and passed the savings on to customers in the form of lower prices and shipping discounts, which helped it amass even greater market share – and more negotiating leverage. All this would take a few years to sink in, but it became widely understood when the Kindle started gaining real momentum with the introduction of the Kindle 2 in early 2009. The gazelles were wounded, the cheetah was on the loose, and the subsequent high-profile business and legal dramas would shake the book industry to its foundation.

Amazon had grown from a beleaguered dot-com survivor battered by the vicissitudes in the stock market into a diversified company whose products and principles had an impact on local communities, national economies, and the marketplace of ideas. Like all powerful companies, it would now be subject to ongoing scrutiny of its corporate character, a perpetual test of not only how well it served its customers but also how well it treated all of the parties drafted into its whirling ecosystem, including employees, partners, and governments. The development of Fiona set the stage for this new phase in Amazon's history and revealed the company as relentlessly innovative and disruptive, as well as calculating and ruthless. Amazon's behavior was a manifestation of Bezos's own competitive personality and boundless intellect, writ large on the business landscape.

PART III

Missionary or Mercenary?

CHAPTER 9
Liftoff!

The fulfillment center dubbed Phoenix 3 on the east side of Arizona's largest city assaults the senses. It's the physical manifestation of the everything store, a vision that most Amazon customers could never even imagine and will never behold: a 605,000-square-foot temple to the twin gods of efficiency and selection. Products are neatly arranged but seemingly randomly stowed on shelves. Star Wars action figures sit next to sleeping bags; bagel chips next to Xbox video games. In one high-risk-valuables area, monitored by overhead video cameras, a single Impulse Jack Rabbit sex toy is wedged between a Rosetta Stone Spanish CD and an iPod Nano. Amazon stocks dissimilar products next to one another to minimize the possibility of employees selecting the wrong item, but that seems unlikely to happen. Every product, shelving unit, forklift, roller cart, and employee badge has a bar code, and invisible algorithms calculate the most efficient paths for workers through the facility.

The aisles of Phoenix 3 are a bustling hive of activity, yet the cavernous space feels quiet. The prevailing sounds come from 102 humming rooftop air conditioners and a chorus of beeping electric carts. One employee manages to project his voice through this acoustic dead zone. Terry Jones, an inbound support associate making twelve dollars an hour, pushes a cart through aisles with towering stacks of products on each side and shouts his arrival in honeyed tones to everyone in his way: 'Cart coming through. Yu-up! Watch yourself, please!'

Jones says he is making his time at Amazon 'joyful and fun' while complying with the company's rigorous safety rules. And those same warnings could have been shouted to the world's retailers in 2007: Amazon was coming for them.

Wall Street analysts first began to notice changes in the company's financial numbers early that year. Amazon's sales were accelerating while third-party sellers were reporting a surge of activity on the site and a corresponding decrease on rival platforms like eBay. Curiously, Amazon's inventory levels were growing too. The company was keeping more merchandise in places like Phoenix 3, as if it confidently expected customers to start buying more.

Scott Devitt, then an analyst for the investment bank Stifel Nicolaus, spotted these shifts earlier than most and upgraded the stock from hold to buy in January 2007.[1] He changed his rating on the same day a Merrill Lynch adviser offered the far more conventional analysis that Amazon's margins were hopeless and that it could not make any money. 'I was laughed out of portfolio managers' offices,' Devitt says. 'People were ripping apart every component of my investment thesis. At that point, they thought Amazon was some kind of nonprofit scam.'

Inside Amazon, the pain endured over the previous seven years was paying off. Prime, the two-day shipping service, was an engine spinning the company's flywheel ever faster. Amazon customers who joined Prime doubled, on average, their spending on the site, according to a person familiar with the company's internal finances at the time. A Prime member was like a shopper who walked into a Costco warehouse for a case of beer and walked out with the beer plus an armful of DVDs, a nine-pound smoked ham, and a flat-screen television.

Prime members bought more products across more categories, which in turn convinced sellers to let Amazon stock their merchandise and ship their orders from its fulfillment centers, since that meant their products qualified for Prime two-day shipping. Amazon was enjoying what analysts call operating lever-age – it was getting more out of its assets, and its famously microscopic profit margins started to expand. (Although that was temporary – they would shrink again a few years later when Bezos started investing in new areas like tablets and streaming video.)

All of this became dramatically visible to the wider world for the first time on April 24, 2007, when Amazon announced surprisingly strong results from its first quarter. Quarterly sales topped $3 billion for the first time – a 32 percent jump in a year, well above its previously consistent 20-something percent annual growth rate and the 12 percent annual growth rate for the rest of e-commerce. That meant Amazon was stealing customers from other Internet players and likely even from the offline chains. During 2007, as investors came to understand the salubrious effects of Prime, Amazon's stock jumped 240 percent – only to fall all the way back down again in the ensuing financial crisis and global recession.

At the same time that Amazon's flywheel was accelerating, eBay's was flying apart. The appeal of online auctions had faded; a customer wanted the convenience and certainty of a quickly completed purchase, not a seven-day waiting period to see if his aggressively low bid for a set of Cobra golf clubs had won the day.

But eBay's problems went beyond the overripening of the auctions format. Amazon and eBay had taken diametrically opposite paths. Amazon endured the pain of disrupting its own retail business with its eBay-like Amazon Marketplace, which allowed third-party sellers to list their products on the company's single-detail pages; eBay, which had started as a third-party auctions platform, recognized that many of its customers wanted a more Amazon-like fixed-price alternative but failed to self-administer the necessary bitter medicine in a single dose. It spent two years working on a separate destination for fixed-price retail, called eBay Express, which got no traffic when it debuted in 2006 and was quickly shut down. Only then did eBay finally commit to allowing fixed-price sales to share space alongside auctions on the site and in search results on eBay.com.[2]

Meanwhile, Amazon invested heavily in technology, taking aggressive swings with digital initiatives like the Kindle. Amazon also focused on fixing and improving the efficiency of its fulfillment centers. eBay executives searched for high-growth businesses elsewhere, acquiring the calling service Skype in 2005, the online-ticketing site StubHub in 2007, and a series of classified-advertising websites. But it let its primary site wither. Customers became happier over time with the shopping experience on Amazon and progressively more disgruntled with the challenges of finding items on eBay and dealing with sellers who overcharged for shipping. Amazon had battled and mastered chaos; eBay was engulfed by it.

In 2008 Meg Whitman passed eBay's reins to John Donahoe, a tall and gracious onetime Dartmouth College basketball player and a former consultant for Bain and Company. One of Donahoe's first trips in his new capacity was to Seattle, where he went to pay a courtesy visit to Bezos at Amazon's headquarters. The executives talked about innovation, hiring, and how they got enough exercise and dealt with stress. Bezos was now working out regularly and was on a strict lean-protein diet.

At the meeting, Donahoe paid his respects to the e-commerce pioneer. 'I am always going to be less cool than you,' he told Bezos. 'I have huge admiration for what you've done.' Bezos said that he did not view Amazon and eBay as fighting a winner-take-all battle. 'Our job is to grow the e-commerce pie and if we do that there is going to be room for five Amazons and five eBays,' Bezos said. 'I've never said a negative thing about eBay and I never will. I don't want anyone to view this as a zero-sum game.'

That year, eBay's stock lost over half its market value, and in July, Amazon's valuation surpassed eBay's for the first time in nearly a decade. Bezos had now accomplished many of his early goals, like turning Amazon into the primary storefront on the Web. The website was selling more kinds of things – and just generally selling more things – than ever before. Amazon reported $14.8 billion in sales in 2007, which was more than two of its earliest foes combined could boast: Barnes & Noble pulled in $5.4 billion that year, and eBay $7.7 billion.

That meant nothing, of course. Despite the teeming abundance of merchandise at Phoenix 3, Bezos still saw broad gaps in Amazon's product lineup. 'In order to be a two-hundred-billion-dollar company, we've got to learn how to sell clothes and food,' Bezos said frequently to colleagues during this time. That figure was not randomly selected; it referred to the magnitude of Walmart's sales in the middle years of the decade. To lead the new foray into consumable goods, Bezos hired Doug

Herrington, a former executive at Webvan, the failed grocery-delivery business from the dot-com boom. After two years of work, Herrington's group started testing Amazon Fresh, a grocery-delivery service in Amazon's hometown of Seattle.

At the same time that Bezos hired Herrington, he brought in veteran apparel executive Steven Goldsmith and acquired the luxury-goods website Shopbop to help Amazon learn the byzantine ways of the clothing business. Along with Goldsmith, Russ Grandinetti, as head of hard-lines, would lead the renewed charge into apparel.

In the midst of yet another retail expansion at Amazon, Bezos seemed to be trying to modulate his management style and keep his notoriously eviscerating assessments of employees in check. It was said he had hired a leadership coach, though the identity of this counselor was a closely guarded secret. 'You could see the fact that he was getting feedback and taking it seriously,' says Diane Lye, then the director of infrastructure automation. During one memorable meeting, Bezos reprimanded Lye and her colleagues in his customarily devastating way, telling them they were stupid and saying they should 'come back in a week when you figure out what you're doing.' Then he walked a few steps, froze in midstride as if something had suddenly occurred to him, wheeled around, and added, 'But great work, everyone.'

The S Team was working together more smoothly now. Familiarity had bred trust and apparently quelled the acrimony among the Amazon managers. Bezos had at this point worked with executives like Jeff Wilke, Jeff Blackburn, Diego Piacentini, chief financial officer Tom Szkutak, and general counsel Michelle Wilson for the better part of a decade.

But one beloved S Team member was no longer with the company. At an all-hands meeting at the Moore Theater in November of 2007, Jeff Bezos announced to employees that Rick Dalzell, his longtime right-hand man, was retiring. The senior manager of the company's engineers, Dalzell had been trying to exit for a while.

He was fifty years old, he had gained weight, and he was ready to spend more time with his family. After Bezos made the announcement, the two men got emotional and embraced onstage. On Dalzell's last day at work, his colleagues threw him a low-key going-away party at Jillian's bar in South Lake Union.

Four months later, enjoying retirement, Dalzell decided to visit his daughter in college in Oregon. His wife chartered a private plane for her husband, herself, and Dalzell's parents. Strangely, their driver took them not to their usual airport but to a private airfield down the street from Boeing Field. Dalzell finally started to notice something was amiss when the car pulled up to a familiar hangar sheltering a Dassault Falcon. When he walked into the airplane, he found it full of friends, colleagues, and Jeff Bezos, all of whom shouted, 'Surprise!' They were going to Hawaii for a gala given in appreciation of Dalzell's longtime service, just like the Shelebration for Shel Kaphan nine years before. Bezos and MacKenzie invited Andy Jassy and his wife, former colleague Bruce Jones, and a bunch of Dalzell's family friends and army buddies.

They stayed in bungalows on a beach in Kona. Butlers were on call, and a sushi chef appeared at four o'clock every afternoon. Lengthy toasts were proffered over dinners, and one day they took an aerial tour of Volcanoes National Park, but in the jet, not a helicopter. 'Jeff's not a helicopter guy anymore,' says Bruce Jones.

Bezos worked his subordinates to exhaustion, supplied

little in the way of corporate creature comforts, and allowed many key personnel to leave without showing any remorse. But he was also capable of deeply gracious and unexpected expressions of appreciation. Dalzell had performed heroically for a decade and kept the company on track in the gloomy days when the infrastructure was a mess and Google was poaching every other engineer.

Over the next few years, Dalzell watched Amazon from afar and marveled at how Bezos turned himself into one of the world's most admired corporate chiefs. 'Jeff does a couple of things better than anyone I've ever worked for,' Dalzell says. 'He embraces the truth. A lot of people talk about the truth, but they don't engage their decision-making around the best truth at the time.

'The second thing is that he is not tethered by conventional thinking. What is amazing to me is that he is bound only by the laws of physics. He can't change those. Everything else he views as open to discussion.'

Amid this renaissance of sales growth and continued category expansion, Amazon made very few acquisitions. The lessons learned from its early acquisition spree in the late 1990s were still felt inside the company. Amazon had impulsively spent hundreds of millions to buy unproven startups that it could not digest and whose executives almost all left. In the resulting retrenchment, Amazon became uniquely parsimonious in how it approached mergers and acquisitions. Between 2000 and 2008, it acquired just a few companies, among which were the Chinese e-commerce site Joyo (bought in 2004 for $75 million), the print-on-demand upstart BookSurge (bought in 2005 for an undisclosed amount), and audio-book company Audible (bought in 2008 for $300 million). These deals were paltry by the standards of the broader technology industry. During this span of time, for example, Google bought YouTube for $1.65 billion and DoubleClick for $3.1 billion.

Jeff Blackburn, Amazon's chief of business development, said that Amazon's bruises from the 1990s helped to create a 'building culture' there. Every major company faces decisions over whether it should build or buy new capabilities. 'Jeff almost always prefers to build it,' Blackburn says. Bezos had absorbed the lessons of the business bible *Good to Great*, whose author, Jim Collins, counseled companies to acquire other firms only when they had fully mastered their virtuous circles, and then 'as an *accelerator* of fly-wheel momentum, not a creator of it.'[3]

Now that Amazon had finally mastered its flywheel, it was time to splurge. For Bezos and Amazon, the irresistible temptation was Zappos.com, the online footwear and apparel retailer founded in 1999 by a soft-spoken but unnaturally persistent entrepreneur named Nick Swinmurn. By all measures, Swinmurn's unlikely idea – to let people buy shoes over the Web without trying them on first – should have drifted off with the other flotsam in the dot-com bust. But after getting turned away from a dozen venture-capital firms, Swinmurn finally solicited an investment from an equally tenacious entrepreneur named Tony Hsieh, the son of Taiwanese immigrants and a seasoned poker player who had sold his first company, LinkExchange, to Microsoft for $250 million in stock. Hsieh and Alfred Lin, a Harvard classmate and former chief financial officer of LinkExchange, placed a tentative $500,000 bet on the startup Zappos via their investment firm Venture Frogs, and Hsieh later joined it as CEO. In the grip of the dot-com downturn, Hsieh simply refused to let Zappos die, putting in $1.5 million of his own money and selling off some of his personal assets to keep it afloat. He moved the company from San Francisco to Las Vegas to cut costs and to make it easier to find workers for its customer-service call center.

In 2004, Hsieh attracted an investment from Sequoia Capital, the firm that had backed LinkExchange. Sequoia, which had rejected Zappos a few times before coming around, invested a total of $48 million in the startup across several rounds, and a partner, Michael Moritz, joined the board of directors. In Las Vegas, the company finally found its groove, and in the minds of Web shoppers, its name and website became synonymous with the novel idea of buying footwear online.

In many ways, Zappos was the Bizarro World version of Amazon; everything was slightly similar but completely different. Hsieh, like Bezos, nurtured a quirky internal culture and frequently talked about it in public to reinforce the Zappos brand in customers' minds. But he took it even further. New employees were each offered a flat one thousand dollars to quit during the first week on the job, the assumption being that those who took the bounty were not right for the firm anyway. Employees were encouraged to lavishly decorate their cubicles at Zappos headquarters in Henderson, Nevada, and each department would rise in rowdy salute to the visitors who toured the offices. Hsieh felt strongly that everyone, even senior executives, should take below-market compensation to work there because of the great internal culture the company offered.

Like Bezos, Hsieh was obsessed with the customer experience. Zappos promised free five- to seven-day delivery on orders and aimed to surprise customers with two-day delivery in most major urban areas. The website's users could return items at no charge for up to a year after their purchases, allowing a customer to order four pair of shoes, try them all on, and return three of them. Hsieh encouraged his call-center representatives to spend as much time as necessary talking to customers to solve their problems. Bezos, of course, treated phone calls from customers as indications of defects in the Amazon system, and he tried vigorously to reduce the number of customer contacts for each unit sold. In fact, finding the toll-free number on the Amazon website can be something of a scavenger hunt.

Zappos' sales soared from $8.6 million in 2001 to $70 million in 2003 to $370 million in 2005.[4] Hsieh and his cohorts had outflanked Amazon in a key part of the apparel market, establishing Zappos as a strong, flexible presence in customers' minds and forging good relationships with well-known shoe brands like Nike. For the first time in years, Bezos had a reason to admire and closely track an e-commerce upstart that had the potential to expand and take away some of his business.

In August of 2005, Bezos e-mailed Hsieh and told him he was going to be in Las Vegas and would like to pay him a visit. The meeting was held in a conference room at a DoubleTree hotel a few blocks from the Zappos office. Bezos brought Jeff Blackburn. Hsieh brought Nick Swinmurn, Michael Moritz, and Alfred Lin, who had just joined Zappos as chairman and chief operating officer. Playing off Amazon's famous two-pizza-team culture, the Zappos executives served two pizzas, one with pepperoni and one with jalapeño peppers, from a local restaurant. The meeting was brief and awkward. The Zappos executives suggested potential partnership arrangements, but Bezos politely said he would rather own the whole business. Hsieh replied flatly that he was set on building an independent company. Later, Amazon executives got the impression that Zappos could be acquired for around $500 million, but Bezos, who'd become a chronically frugal acquirer, imagined paying only a fraction of that amount.

At this point, the competitive landscape must have looked to Bezos like the chessboards of his youth. The positions of the pieces in this particular game heavily favored his opponent. By law, manufacturers are not allowed to set retail prices, but they can decide whom they want to carry their products, and they make those decisions judiciously. Shoe brands like Nike and Merrell viewed Amazon as a dangerous discounter, a company that would very likely consign their new in-season products to the bargain bin in an effort to garner new customers and gain market share. As a result, the top brands were reluctant to supply Amazon with merchandise, and the website's shoe selection was sparse.

Amazon had other disadvantages in the shoe business. The Amazon website was not well suited to products that had lots of variations, like a shoe that comes in six colors, eighteen sizes, and several widths. Amazon.com listed all these variations on a single shoe as separate products, and customers couldn't perform searches for multiple variables, like both color and size.

Navigating through this complex matrix, Bezos came up with an unlikely gambit. He decided to build an entirely separate website from scratch, devoted solely to the categories of shoes and handbags. Bezos brought that plan to the members of his board, who braced themselves to make another costly and impractical investment at the same time they were betting heavily on the Kindle and Amazon Web Services. 'How much money do you want to spend on this?' asked chief financial officer Tom Szkutak in the board meeting. 'How much do you have?' asked Bezos.

The company worked on the new site for all of 2006, spending some $30 million to design it from scratch using the collection of Web tools known as AJAX, according to an employee who was on the project. Executives came close to calling it Javari.com, but then the owner of that URL reneged on a deal to sell it and demanded more money. The site finally launched in December as Endless.com. On its first day, Endless offered free overnight shipping and free returns. The deal ensured Amazon would lose money on each sale. But it would clearly apply pressure to a certain company in Las Vegas. The Zappos board members considered Amazon's opening maneuver, gritted their teeth, and a week later matched it with free overnight shipping. The difference was that the new Endless.com, unlike its rival, enjoyed almost no traffic or sales volume and so lost little with its overnight-shipping offer; Zappos' profit margins took a direct hit.

Over the next year, Endless made little progress as an independent retail destination. The site attracted brands like Kenneth Cole and Nine West and developed features such as a more flexible search engine and product photos that expanded when customers hovered over them with their cursors. But Amazon was walking an almost impossible precarious tightrope, trying to assuage the fears of brand-name companies with industry-standard pricing while also using Endless as a way to undercut Zappos on price. In early 2007, with apparel brands watching closely for any signs of discounting, Amazon added a five-dollar bonus to its free overnight shipping. In other words, a customer was given five dollars just to buy something on the site. It was a clever but transparent ploy, an effort to inflict further pain on Zappos. Employees who worked on Endless say that, naturally, this was Jeff Bezos's idea. Yet Zappos still continued to grow. Its 2007 gross sales hit $840 million and in 2008 it topped $1 billion. That year, Bezos learned that Zappos was advertising on the bottoms of the plastic bins at airport-security checkpoints. 'They are out-thinking us!' he snapped at a meeting.

But inside Zappos, a big problem had emerged. It had been acquiring inventory with a revolving $100 million line of credit, and the financial crisis, which intensified with the collapse of Lehman Brothers in the fall of 2008, froze the capital markets. With consumer spending declining, Zappos' inventory constrained by new borrowing limits, and the competition with Amazon cutting into the company's profit margins, Zappos' previously spectacular annual growth rate collapsed to a modest 10 percent. The company rolled back its free-overnight-shipping guarantee, and Hsieh reluctantly laid off 8 percent of his workforce.

In his bestselling book *Delivering Happiness: A Path to Profits, Passion, and Purpose*, Hsieh wrote that Amazon continued to make acquisition offers during this time and that Zappos' investors were increasingly interested because they were impatient to see a return on their investment. Michael Moritz has a slightly different take. When he invested in Zappos, he wanted it to become an independent, public company 'that provided every item of clothing for consumers from head to toe.' But he had watched Amazon destroy one of his portfolio companies, eToys, a decade earlier and knew that to compete with Amazon, Zappos needed more engineers and more sophisticated fulfillment capabilities. 'We just didn't move quickly enough,' Moritz says. 'You could sense it was going to be much harder to achieve, and we were squandering the opportunity. The hiring was too slow, the engineering department was not good enough, and the software was inferior to Amazon's. It was very frustrating, and the Las Vegas location, plus an unwillingness to pay competitively, made it even harder to recruit talented people. We were starting to compete with the very best in the business and they had a lot of arrows in their quiver to make life painful. The last thing we wanted to do was to sell. It was mortifying.'

Hsieh wanted to keep going but even he came to acknowledge that Amazon could be a good home for Zappos. One of the factors he considered was that Zappos employees in Las Vegas and near its distribution center in Kentucky lived at ground zero of the housing crisis. Many had seen the value of their homes plummet, and the only valuable thing they owned was Zappos stock. Hsieh saw that the acquisition could offer a sizable payout for employees at a moment when many desperately needed it. The Zappos board ultimately decided to sell to Amazon; the vote was bittersweet but unanimous.

Over the next few months, Alfred Lin negotiated the deal with Peter Krawiec, Amazon's vice president of corporate development. Bezos and Krawiec consummated the deal at Hsieh's house in Southern Highlands, a luxury residential neighborhood built around a golf course. A journey that had started with two pizzas ended with Hsieh cooking burgers on his patio. A few weeks later, Bezos recorded an eight-minute video for Zappos employees while traveling in Europe. 'When given the choice of obsessing over competitors or obsessing over customers, we always obsess over customers,' he said, reciting a well-worn and, considering the past few years of competition with Zappos, credulity-straining Jeffism. 'We pay attention to what our competitors do but it's not where we put our energy.'

Some of Amazon's own executives were now shaking their heads in awe. Bezos had pursued and captured his prey, spending what one Amazon executive estimates was $150 million over two years on projects like Endless.com, which perhaps saved the company money, since it might have been a far more expensive battle or acquisition after the recession. Yet Hsieh, Lin, and Moritz had fought back fiercely, dueling Amazon to what might best be considered a draw. The acquisition price of around $900 million was higher than Bezos originally wanted, and the Zappos board wisely demanded that Amazon pay with equity instead of cash. By the time the deal closed, in November of 2009, the price of Amazon stock was once again zooming into the stratosphere, and Zappos executives, employees, and investors who had held on to their shares were lavishly rewarded. Amazon drew several lessons from its bloody battle with Zappos that it would tenaciously apply to its dealings with e-commerce upstarts in the years ahead.

The great recession that started in December 2007 and lasted until July 2009 was in some ways a gift to Amazon. The crisis not only drove Zappos into Amazon's arms but also significantly damaged the sales of the world's largest offline retail chains, sending executives scurrying into survival mode. Desperate to protect their profit margins, many retailers reacted by firing employees, cutting down their product assortment, and lowering the overall quality of their service, and this just as Bezos was investing in new categories and more rapid distribution. The economic crisis served as a kind of cloaking device, hiding Amazon's evolution into a dangerous diversified competitor. Retailers were scared, but the bogeyman was the reeling global economy and declining consumer spending, not Amazon.

The brutal recession claimed the weakest national retailers and extinguished several historic brands. Circuit City was once the largest electronics retailer in the country. At its peak, the Richmond, Virginia-based chain had more than seven hundred stores and reported $12 billion in sales. Then, in the 1990s, a wave of changes undermined its commission-centered sales model. Companies like Best Buy, Walmart, and Costco ushered in a new age of self-service shopping and big-box stores. Customers could grab a television off the shelf and haul it to the checkout counter, aided (maybe) by an associate being paid a low hourly wage. Circuit City waited too long to drop its commission-based sales force. PCs became a major draw in electronics stores, but Circuit City was reluctant to bring a low-margin product line into its high-margin mix. In addition, its executives were also heavily distracted in the 1990s, spinning off the retail chain CarMax and spending more than a hundred million dollars on a DVD-rental system called DIVX, which quickly failed.

Then Amazon came along with the ultimate self-service model, and again Circuit City was frozen by a disruptive change. Circuit City allowed Amazon to operate its website from 2001 to 2005 but afterward it didn't establish a strong Internet presence. The company had lost touch with what customers wanted and it never embraced, as Rick Dalzell put it with regard to Bezos, 'the best truth at the time.' When the chain needed to finance a turnaround in the midst of the financial crisis, the capital markets were dry. So in 2009, Circuit City, a sixty-year-old company lauded in one of Bezos's favorite books, *Good to Great*, liquidated its operations and laid off thirty-four thousand employees.[5]

A few years later, the book chain Borders traveled down the same dismal path.

Brothers Louis and Tom Borders had founded the

company in Ann Arbor, Michigan, in 1971 after developing a system to track book sales and inventory. The brothers left in 1992 when the company was acquired by Kmart, which later spun it out. All through the 1990s, Borders churned out huge, multistory bookstores in shopping centers around the United States and in Singapore, Australia, and the United Kingdom, among other countries, growing from $224.8 million in sales in 1992 to $3.4 billion by 2002.

But like Circuit City, Borders had a narrow operating philosophy and repeatedly missed the changing tastes of consumers. It was obsessively focused on opening new stores and increasing same-store sales while fighting Barnes & Noble on all fronts and dutifully guiding and meeting Wall Street's quarterly expectations. The Internet didn't fit into this traditional calculus and thus didn't get the company's capital or its most talented executives. Like Circuit City, Borders allowed Amazon to run its online business so it could focus on its physical stores. One long-time Borders executive, who asked for anonymity, says the early perception of Amazon was that it 'was just another catalog – a version of Lands' End.' The executive suggests that this sentiment was now suitable for a bumper sticker.

In the last decade of its life, Borders was battered by rising online book sales, then by the Kindle, and then by the pullback in consumer spending after the financial crisis. Borders, like Circuit City, couldn't cut costs fast enough because it was locked into fifteen- or twenty-year leases on its stores. At the time of its bankruptcy filing, half its stores were still highly profitable, according to its CEO, but the company couldn't raise money to buy out the leases on its bad locations.[6] Borders' decline accelerated during the recession, and it went out of business in 2011, laying off 10,700 employees.[7]

Like some other chain stores, Target, the second-largest retailer in the United States, survived the downturn with layoffs at its Minneapolis headquarters and by closing one of its distribution centers.[8] Target had outsourced its online operations to Amazon in 2001 but the relationship was far from perfect, with joint projects frequently falling behind schedule. 'We had no resources to build infrastructure for Target,' says Faisal Masud, who worked on the Target business at Amazon. 'It was all about Amazon first and Target next.'

But in 2006, Target came to the realization that it did not have the in-house capabilities to develop its own website, and, incredibly, it renewed its agreement with Amazon for another five years. After the new deal was signed, Jeff Bezos returned to Minneapolis to meet with Target executives Robert Ulrich and Gerald Storch and to give a presentation that was open to any Target employee who wanted to attend. Dale Nitschke, the executive running Target.com at the time, recalls that to fill the auditorium, he had to personally implore employees to attend. 'These guys are going to be world-class competitors, you have to keep tracking them,' he told colleagues.

Target knew it had to master its own Web presence and wean itself away from a dangerous dependence on a competitor. In 2009, it belatedly announced it was leaving Amazon, and it finally ended the relationship when the contract expired two years later. It was a rocky breakup. The retailer's new website, built and managed with the help of IBM and Oracle, went down a half a dozen times during the 2011 holiday season, and the president of its online division resigned.

No one had more to lose from Amazon's ascendance than the folks in Bentonville, Arkansas. Despite years of being beaten by Amazon in the realm of e-commerce,

Walmart had smartly resisted the temptation to outsource its website, and yet its Internet operation, established in 1999 in Brisbane, north of Silicon Valley, made little progress cutting into Amazon's lead. After the recession, Walmart too began to view the Internet with renewed urgency.

In September of 2009, I wrote a lengthy story for the *New York Times* entitled 'Can Amazon Be the Wal-Mart of the Web?'[9] The headline apparently hit a nerve in Bentonville. A few weeks after it appeared, Raul Vazquez, then the chief executive of Walmart.com, told the *Wall Street Journal*, 'If there is going to be a 'Wal-Mart of the Web,' it is going to be Walmart.com. Our goal is to be the biggest and most visited retail website.'[10] In the e-commerce equivalent of a preemptive military strike, Walmart then lowered prices on ten new books by high-profile authors, such as Stephen King and Dean Koontz, to ten dollars each. Amazon matched the price on those same books within a few hours. Walmart.com then lowered its prices again, to nine dollars, and Amazon matched it again. It was just the kind of price pressure from Walmart that Amazon executives had always worried about – but it came ten years too late to do Amazon any harm. Now Amazon was large enough that it could easily withstand such losses.

Over the next month, the tit-for-tat price war spread like a brushfire. Target joined the fracas, and all three companies cut prices on DVDs, video-game consoles, mobile phones, and even the humble Easy-Bake Oven, a forty-five-year-old toy from Hasbro known for heating up small cakes, not tensions between billion-dollar corporations.[11] With all three retailers now offering steep discounts on a range of hardcover books, the American Booksellers Association, a trade group of independent bookstores, wrote the U.S. Department of Justice to complain that 'the entire book industry is in danger of becoming collateral damage' in a war among giants.[12]

They hadn't seen anything yet.

* * *

In February 2009, Amazon took over a basement auditorium in New York's Morgan Library and Museum to prepare for the announcement of the Kindle 2. The sequel to Fiona, the Kindle 2 (code-named Turing, after a castle in *The Diamond Age*) sported a thinner profile, a simpler and more intuitive layout, and none of the design excesses of the first device. Amazon had fixed its chronic manufacturing problems, but the company had yet to master the art of the product launch. In tension-filled rehearsals the night before the event, Bezos tore into his communications staff over a number of miscalculations, including the fact that the large screen behind the podium obscured his slides. 'I don't know if you guys don't have high standards or if you just don't know what you're doing,' he said, sighing heavily.

If the original Kindle transformed Amazon and re-positioned it for a digital future, then the Kindle 2 could fairly be considered the device that revolutionized the publishing business and changed the way people around the world read books. With instant brand recognition and broad availability, the new Kindle was coveted by customers and finally fulfilled Bezos's vision of a main-stream electronic reader at an affordable price. With the Nook and the iPad yet to be introduced, Amazon had a commanding 90 percent of the digital reading market in the United States.[13]

For the big book publishers, Amazon's dawning monopoly in e-books was terrifying. As suppliers had learned over the past decade, no matter the category,

Amazon wielded its market power neither lightly nor gracefully, employing every bit of leverage to improve its own margins and pass along savings to its customers. If the company didn't get what it wanted, the reaction could be severe. When the Kindle 2 became available, Amazon UK was no longer selling some of the most popular books of French publishing giant Hachette Livre, part of a protracted and bitter dispute over the terms of the Amazon/Hachette relationship. Customers could buy these Hachette books only from third-party sellers on the Amazon website.[14]

Publishers remained particularly troubled by Amazon's $9.99 price for new releases and bestsellers. They were living the nightmarish reality of every manufacturer – this was the reason that, for example, Nike refused to supply shoes to Endless.com. Amazon, the publishing executives felt, was consigning their in-season products (new books, rather than shoes) to the bargain bin immediately upon their release. The lower price arguably reflected the decreased costs of printing and distributing digital books. But it neglected the new costs publishers faced in making the digital transition and also put enormous pressure on other retailers, particularly independent bookstores, and helped Amazon consolidate its control of the market. Publishers considered several ways to extricate themselves from this mess. In the early fall of 2009, two publishers, HarperCollins and Hachette, experimented with windowing select e-books – that is, delaying e-books' release until the hardcover versions had been out for a few months. But consumers reacted badly and gave these titles withering reviews on Amazon.

There was another reason for publishers' mounting anxieties at the time. That year Amazon introduced the Kindle Digital Text Platform (later renamed KDP), a program that allowed authors to self-publish their works in the U.S. Kindle store. The company would soon expand the effort overseas and grant authors a 70 percent royalty on their sales. The service was widely interpreted as Amazon's first step into publishing; for the moment, it was just unknown writers

Similar efforts from other retailers had worried book publishers in the past. Barnes & Noble had once had its own publishing program too. But Amazon alone had the tools to cut the major houses entirely out of the bookselling process: a dominant position in e-books, via the successful Kindle, and an on-demand publishing unit called CreateSpace that could print a physical book when a customer ordered it on Amazon.com. Amazon seemed to be cultivating its relationships with agents and authors, and the company hired a former Random House executive named David Naggar to join the Kindle team. It all seemed to point toward Jeff Bezos's outsize ambition to control every square on the publishing-industry chess-board. 'Amazon is in a great place to carry out their program to almost any conceivable scale,' blogged Eoin Purcell, a Dublin-based book editor, after the introduction of Amazon Encore, which allowed authors to republish their works on the Kindle. 'Aside from what the author and their agents can grab, Amazon with Encore has successfully placed itself in control of the entire value chain.'[15]

Publishers believed their necks were being fitted for the noose. This view, widely discussed in publishing circles at the time, accounts for what happened next: a sprawling, dramatic, multiyear imbroglio that would be laid bare in the thousands of pages of legal documents and weeks of courtroom testimony resulting from antitrust actions brought against the book publishers and Apple by the European Union and the U.S. Department of Justice.

Over the course of 2009, the chiefs of the six major U.S. publishing houses – Penguin, Hachette, Macmillan, HarperCollins, Random House, and Simon and Schuster – gathered, allegedly to discuss their shared predicament. They communicated over the telephone, via e-mail, and in the private dining rooms of upscale New York City restaurants, and the DOJ later claimed that they took steps to avoid leaving evidence of these discussions, which might be construed as collusion. Publishing executives say the meetings were not held for the purpose of talking about Amazon and that they involved other business issues. But the U.S. government believed the executives were specifically addressing Amazon and its deleterious e-book pricing strategy, or, as the publishers termed it (per the court documents), 'the $9.99 problem.'

According to the Justice Department's filings, the publishing executives believed the only way to alter the balance of power with Amazon was for their industry to act, wielding the leverage that came from producing what amounted to 60 percent of the books Amazon sold. Court documents show that they considered a variety of options, including launching their own joint e-book venture. Then, in the fall of 2009, a white knight appeared in the form of Apple and its cancer-stricken leader, Steve Jobs.

Jobs had his own reasons to combat Amazon. He knew firsthand that Amazon could use its dominance in e-books to transition into other kinds of digital media – Jobs himself had used the iTunes monopoly in digital music to expand into podcasts, television shows, and movies. At the time Apple began reaching out to publishers, Jobs was preparing for the introduction of what would be his final masterstroke: the iPad. For Apple's precious new invention, he wanted every kind of media available – including books.

The publishing executives negotiated that winter with iTunes chief Eddy Cue and a deputy, Keith Moerer (ironically, a former employee of Amazon), and the resulting arrangements with Apple would solve the publishers' $9.99 problem, relieve some of the pressure on physical bookstores, and allow Apple to enter the e-reading space without having to match Amazon's subsidized pricing on bestsellers and new releases. In the new e-book model, publishers themselves would officially become the retailers and could set their own prices, typically in the more comfortable (for them) zone of between thirteen and fifteen dollars. Apple would act as the broker and receive a 30 percent commission, the same arrangement it had for mobile applications on the iPhone. As part of this shift to what was known as the agency model, Apple received a guarantee that other retailers would not undercut it on e-book prices. According to the DOJ, that meant publishers would have to force Amazon to adopt the same model. In his internal e-mails and to his biographer Walter Isaacson, Jobs proudly referred to this as an aikido move.

The CEOs of the publishing houses all said that, independently, each of them considered the costs of Amazon's dominance as well as what was known of the ruthlessness of its corporate character, and then decided to move to the agency model. It was not a painless choice. By giving retailers a 30 percent commission, the publishers would actually make *less* money per e-book than they would if they stuck to the traditional wholesale model, in which they generally collected half of the list price. 'Although agency was more costly in the short term, the strategic advantages were so compelling that we felt – independently – that this was the right way to go,' one publishing chief told me.

There was one holdout: Markus Dohle, chief executive of Random House, worried that the economics of agency pricing were unfavorable and that he would be better off maintaining the status quo. Random House, alone among the six major publishers, decided to stick with the traditional wholesale model for the time being, so Apple declined to sell Random House's books in its newly christened iBookstore.

Apple introduced the iPad on January 27, 2010, at the Yerba Buena Center for the Arts in San Francisco. It was one of Jobs's last public performances and a spellbinding swan song from an iconic entrepreneur – someone Jeff Bezos clearly admired and viewed as a primary rival. After the event, *Wall Street Journal* columnist Walter Mossberg asked Jobs why anyone would buy e-books from Apple when Amazon sold them at a lower price. 'The prices will be the same,' Jobs said, carelessly raising a giant red flag for antitrust regulators by suggesting that the companies had all acted in concert. 'Publishers are actually withholding their books from Amazon because they're not happy.'[16]

While other publishers informed Amazon of their new arrangements via e-mail or phone calls, Macmillan CEO John Sargent flew to Seattle to personally deliver the news of his company's shift to an agency pricing model. In a tense twenty-minute meeting with Kindle executives that included Laura Porco, Russ Grandinetti, and David Naggar, Sargent offered Amazon the right to stick with the old terms and wholesale pricing, but at the cost of getting e-books several months after their publication. That clearly did not go over well. Amazon reacted to the agency move with overwhelming force, pulling the Buy buttons from Macmillan's physical and electronic books on the website. Customers could still buy Macmillan's print books on Amazon, but only from third-party sellers. The Kindle editions completely disappeared and remained unavailable for an entire weekend that January. For those unaware of the tense history between Amazon and publishers – the tortured 'cheetah and gazelle' negotiations and so on – the sudden outbreak of hostility seemed shocking. 'I think everyone thought they were witnessing a knife fight,' Sloan Harris, codirector of the literary department at International Creative Management, said at the time. 'And it looks like we've gone to the nukes.'[17]

A few days later, under a barrage of criticism for making authors and customers collateral damage in the fight, Amazon relented. Bezos and his Kindle team collaborated on a public message, which they posted on an Amazon online forum: 'We have expressed our strong disagreement and the seriousness of our disagreement by temporarily ceasing the sale of all Macmillan titles. We want you to know that ultimately, however, we will have to capitulate and accept Macmillan's terms because Macmillan has a monopoly over their own titles, and we will want to offer them to you even at prices we believe are needlessly high for e-books . . . Kindle is a business for Amazon, and it is also a mission. We never expected it to be easy!'

Ironically, the shift to the agency model made the Kindle business more profitable, since Amazon was forced to charge more for e-books, and Amazon held a near monopoly on e-book sales. That helped Amazon sustain the gradual decrease in the price of the Kindle hardware. Less than two years later, the cheapest Kindle e-reader would cost seventy-nine dollars.

But Amazon wasn't sitting back or letting others dictate their own terms. Over the next year, Amazon responded forcefully in several ways. Russ Grandinetti, who had moved over to Kindle from apparel, and David Naggar, the new hire from Random House, made the rounds of midsize publishers like Houghton Mifflin. According to several executives at those firms, they were warned that they did not have the leverage to move to an agency pricing model and that Amazon would stop selling their books if they did. Amazon also intensified its focus on its own direct-publishing business, which would cause another wave of distress for publishers in the years ahead.

In trying to loosen Amazon's grip on the e-book market, the publishers and Apple created a significant new problem for themselves. A day after the standoff with Macmillan, according to court documents, Amazon sent a white paper to the Federal Trade Commission and the U.S. Department of Justice laying out the chain of events and its suspicion that the publishers and Apple were engaged in an illegal conspiracy to fix e-book prices.

Many publishing executives suspect that Amazon played a major role in provoking the legal brouhaha that resulted. But antitrust investigators likely didn't need much nudging. Incredibly, even though Steve Jobs passed away in the fall of 2011, his earlier comments dug the legal hole deeper for Apple and the five agency publishers. In the biography *Steve Jobs*, Walter Isaacson quoted Jobs as saying, 'Amazon screwed it up . . . Before Apple even got on the scene, some booksellers were starting to withhold books from Amazon. So we told the publishers, "We'll go to the agency model, where you set the price, and we get our 30%, and yes, the customer pays a little more, but that's what you want anyway."'

Jobs's patronizing statement was potentially incriminating. If publishers had engaged in a joint effort to make customers pay 'a little more,' that was the foundation on which antitrust cases were built. The Justice Department sued Apple and the five publishers on April 11, 2012, accusing them of illegally conspiring to raise e-book prices. All the publishers eventually settled without admitting liability while Apple alone held out, claiming that it had done nothing wrong and that its intent was only to expand the market for digital books.

The case against Apple was heard the following June in a Manhattan courtroom and lasted for seventeen days. District judge Denise Cote then found Apple liable, ruling that it had conspired with the book publishers to eliminate price competition and raise e-book prices and had therefore violated Section 1 of the Sherman Antitrust Act. Apple vowed to appeal the verdict. A separate trial on damages was scheduled for 2014 at the time this book went to press.

The e-book battle played out publicly in both the courtroom and the marketplace. But despite the case's visibility in the media, it was a sideshow to the larger rise of Amazon at the time, an ascent interrupted by the great recession that resumed with renewed vigor afterward.

Beginning in 2009, as the fog of the economic crisis lifted, Amazon's quarterly growth rate returned to its pre-recession levels, and over the next two years, the stock climbed 236 percent. The world was broadly recognizing Amazon's potential – the power of Prime and of Amazon's mighty fulfillment network, the promise of AWS, and the steady gains seen in Asia and Europe. In part because of the e-book pricing war, investors began to understand that the Kindle could grab an outsize share of the book business and that the device had the potential to do to bookstores what iTunes had done to record shops. Analysts en masse upgraded their ratings on Amazon's stock, and mutual fund managers added the company to their portfolios. For the first time, *Amazon* was spoken in the same breath as *Google* and *Apple* — not as an afterthought, but as an equal. It had blasted off into high orbit.

CHAPTER 10
Expedient Convictions

The spectacular rise of Amazon's visibility and market power in the wake of the great recession brought the company more frequently into the public eye, but the attention was not always flattering. During the years 2010 and 2011, the company battled a growing chorus of critics over its avoidance of collecting state sales tax, the mechanics behind two of its large acquisitions, its move into the business of publishing books (in competition with its own suppliers), and what appeared to be its systematic disregard for the pricing policies of major manufacturers. Almost overnight, the company that viewed itself as the perennial underdog now seemed to many like a remote and often arrogant giant who was trying to play by his own set of rules.

Bezos (and the few Jeff Bots that Amazon allowed to speak in public) perfected an attitude of bemused perplexity when addressing criticisms. Bezos often said that Amazon had a 'willingness to be misunderstood,' which was an impressive piece of rhetorical jujitsu – the implication being that its opponents just didn't *understand* the company.[1] Bezos also deflected attacks by claiming that Amazon was a missionary company, not a mercenary one.

That dichotomy originated with now former board member John Doerr, who formulated it after reading his partner Randy Komisar's 2001 business-philosophy book *The Monk and the Riddle*. Missionaries have righteous goals and are trying to make the world a better place. Mercenaries are out for money and power and will run over anyone who gets in the way. To Bezos, at least, there was no doubt where Amazon fell. 'I would take a missionary over a mercenary any day,' he liked to say. 'One of those great paradoxes is that it's usually the missionaries who end up making more money anyway.'[2]

Amazon spokespeople approached these controversies with simple, direct points that they repeated over and over, rarely veering into the uncomfortable details of the company's aggressive tactics. The arguments had the advantage of being completely rational while also serving Amazon's strategic interests. And it was these expedient convictions that, to varying degrees, helped steer Amazon through the period of its greatest public scrutiny yet.

While the recession was in many ways a gift to Amazon, the deteriorating finances of local governments in the United States and Europe prompted a new fight over the collection of sales tax – the legal avoidance of which was one of the company's biggest tactical advantages. It was a high-stakes battle where there were more than two sides, no one played it entirely straight, and Amazon's deeply held convictions just happened to be conveniently expedient for its own long-term interests.

Beginning in late 2007, when governor of New York Eliot Spitzer introduced a proposal to raise millions of dollars by expanding the definition of what constituted a taxable presence in his state, Amazon was faced with the disconcerting possibility that its long exemption from adding 5 to 10 percent in sales tax onto the prices of most of its products – which had shaped its earliest decisions about where to conduct operations and place its head-quarters – was about to end.

Spitzer's proposal flopped, at first. He withdrew it the day after introducing it, amid his own slumping approval ratings and a backlash over what his budget director said was concern that residents might consider the bill a tax increase.[3] But New York State had a $4.3 billion budget gap that desperately needed to be filled. The following February, a month before Spitzer's political career imploded in a prostitution scandal, Spitzer reintroduced the bill. David Paterson, his successor, embraced the proposal, and in April it was passed by the state legislature in Albany.

The law cleverly eluded a 1992 Supreme Court ruling, *Quill v. North Carolina*, stipulating that only those merchants who had a physical presence or nexus, like a storefront or an office, in a state had to collect sales tax there. (Technically, the tax was still due for online purchases, but customers were supposed to pay it themselves.) The New York law specified that an affiliate website that took a commission for passing customers on to an online retailer was an agent of that retailer, and thus the retailer officially had a presence in that affiliate's state. By this ruling, if a Yankees-fan website in New York made money every time a visitor clicked a link on its pages and bought former manager Joe Torre's memoir on Amazon.com, then Seattle-based Amazon had an official storefront in New York and so had to collect sales tax on all purchases made in that state.

Amazon was not amused. The New York law went into effect over the summer of 2008 and, along with Overstock.com, another retailer, it sued in state court –

and lost. Publicly, the company complained that state-by-state tax collection was complex and impractical. 'There are currently about seventy-six hundred different jurisdictions in the country that tax, including things like snow-removal and mosquito-abatement districts,' says Paul Misener, Amazon's vice president of global public policy and the public face of its tax battles.

Amazon had avoided sales-tax collection for years with various clever tricks. In states where it had fulfillment centers or other offices, like Lab126, it skirted the definition of what constituted a physical presence by classifying those facilities as wholly owned subsidiaries that earned no revenue. For example, the fulfillment center in Fernley, Nevada, operated as an independent entity called Amazon.com.nvdc, Inc. These arrangements were unlikely to hold up under direct scrutiny, but Amazon had carefully negotiated with each state when opening its facilities, securing hands-off treatment in exchange for the company's generating new jobs and economic activity. Bezos considered his exemption from collecting sales tax to be an enormous strategic advantage and brought a libertarian's earnestness to what he believed was a battle over principle. 'We're not actually benefiting from any services that those states provide locally, so it's not fair that we should be obligated to be their tax collection agent since we're not getting any of the services,' he said at a shareholder meeting in 2008.

Bezos also thought his exemption from collecting sales tax was a big benefit for customers, and the prospect of losing it triggered his apoplectic reaction to raising prices. He had good reason to be worried about the effects of sales-tax collection. When New York passed its Internet sales-tax law, Amazon's sales in New York State dropped 10 percent over the next quarter, according to a person familiar with Amazon's finances at the time.

New York's law spread like a bad cold. Similarly cash-strapped states like Illinois, North Carolina, Hawaii, Rhode Island, and Texas tried the same bank-shot approach of declaring that affiliate websites constituted nexuses. In response, Amazon borrowed a hardnosed tactic that Overstock had used in New York and severed ties with its affiliates in each state. These sites were often run by bloggers and other entrepreneurs who needed their affiliate commissions, and they were angered to find themselves wedged between a cash-starved state government on one side and an online giant belligerently clinging to a blatant tax loophole on the other.

The affiliates were not the only victims at this stage of the sales-tax fight. Vadim Tsypin was an Amazon engineer who often worked from his home in Quebec, Canada. In late 2007, around the time Eliot Spitzer was proposing his tax bill and Amazon's lawyers were growing more anxious, Tsypin's manager showed him the company's restrictive Canada policy, which declared that Amazon had no employees working in that country. His manager allegedly told Tsypin they had to cover up his history of working from home and, according to court documents, said that 'Amazon can have multimillion-dollar problems. If we have even one employee on the ground there, it is a big violation of U.S. and Canadian law.'

Tsypin refused to alter his old time sheets and evaluations, believing that it wouldn't stand up to scrutiny. He claimed that his Amazon bosses then started to harass him into quitting, which led to his getting sick ('constant migraine headaches and frequent seizure-like blackouts') and taking a medical leave of absence. In 2010, he sued Amazon in King County Superior Court for wrongful termination, breach of contract, emotional distress, and negligent hiring – and he lost. The judge acknowledged Tsypin's condition was work related but said the claims were not strong enough to impose a civil liability.

Large companies like Amazon are frequent targets of wrongful-termination claims. But Vadim Tsypin's case was unusual because it grew out of Amazon's own growing sales-tax anxieties and because the discovery phase brought Amazon's extensive tax-avoidance playbook into the public record. Dozens of pages of internal company rulebooks, flowcharts, and maps were filed with the King County Superior Court on Third Avenue in downtown Seattle. Together, they revealed a fascinating portrait of a company desperately contorting itself to accommodate a rapidly shifting tax climate.

The guidelines approached the surreal. Amazon employees had to seek approval to attend trade shows and were told to avoid activities that involved promoting the sale of any products on the Amazon website while on the road. They couldn't blog or talk to the press without permission, had to avoid renting any property on trips, and couldn't place orders on Amazon from the company's computers. They could sign contracts with other companies, such as suppliers who were offering their goods for sale on the site, only in Seattle.

Then the seemingly arbitrary partitions in the company's corporate structure became even more important. Traveling employees working for Amazon's North American retail organization were told to say they worked for a company called Amazon Services, not Amazon.com, and to carry business cards to that effect. According to one document, they were instructed to say, 'I'm with Amazon Services, the operator of the www.amazon.com website and provider of e-commerce solutions and services, and

I'm here to gather information about the latest industry developments and trends,' if they were ever queried by the media regarding their attendance at a trade show.

Color-coded maps were widely distributed to employees at headquarters in Seattle. Travel to green states like Michigan was okay, but orange states like California required special clearance so that the legal department could track the cumulative number of days Amazon employees spent there. Travel to red states, like Texas, New Jersey, and Massachusetts, required employees to complete an intensive seventeen-item questionnaire about the trip that was designed to determine whether they would make the company vulnerable to sales-tax collection efforts (number 16: 'Will you be holding a raffle?'). Amazon lawyers then either nixed the trip altogether or obtained a private letter ruling from that state spelling out its specific treatment of that particular situation.

There was little internal discussion by management on whether it was right or wrong or if it was affecting morale among employees, according to senior employees at the time. It was just strategy, a way to preserve a significant tax advantage that enabled the company to offer comparatively low prices. 'The economic outlook for many states is bleak,' read one early 2010 internal tax memo to employees that was filed in the Vadim Tsypin case record. 'As a result, states are pursuing taxpayers more aggressively than before. Amazon's recent public experiences with New York and Texas provide timely and pertinent examples of the heightened risk. That's why our attention to nexus-related issues are more important than ever.'[4]

That same year, 2010, fully alerted to the urgency of combating the Amazon threat, Walmart, Target, Best

Buy, Home Depot, and Sears put aside their traditional enmities to join forces in an unusual coalition.[5] They jointly backed a new organization called the Alliance for Main Street Fairness, which shrouded itself in populist language and – somehow managing to conceal the dripping irony – touted the importance of pre-serving the vitality of small mom-and-pop retailers. The organization employed a team of well-financed lobbyists who set up a sophisticated website and ran print and television ads around the country. The CEOs of all these big retailers monitored the campaign closely. Mike Duke, Walmart's CEO, requested frequent briefings on the sales-tax fight, according to two lobbyists involved in the battle.

Amazon fought the sales-tax expansion aggressively, soliciting cooperation from politicians by deploying both carrot and stick in the area where they might feel it most – jobs. In Texas in 2011, the legislature passed a bill that would force online retailers with distribution facilities in the state to collect sales tax, and Amazon threatened to close its fulfillment center outside Dallas, fire hundreds of local workers, and scrap plans to build other facilities in the state. Texas governor Rick Perry promptly vetoed the bill. In South Carolina, Amazon won an exemption on a new law by using the same threats, and it agreed to send customers e-mails helpfully reminding them they were supposed to pay sales tax on their own. In Tennessee, legislators agreed to delay a bill when Amazon offered to build three new fulfillment centers in the state.

During these skirmishes, Bezos advocated for a federal bill that simplified the sales tax code and imposed it over the entire e-commerce industry. (This had the advantage of being a highly unlikely scenario, considering the political deadlock gripping Washington, DC, at the time.) 'If I say to customers, "We're not required to collect sales tax, the Constitution is crystal clear that states cannot force out-of-state retailers to collect sales tax and cannot interfere in interstate commerce, but we're going to do it voluntarily anyway," that isn't tenable,' Bezos told me in a 2011 interview. 'Customers would rightly protest. The way this has to work is you either have to amend the Constitution or you have to pass federal legislation.'

The fight came to a dramatic head in 2012. Amazon surrendered in Texas, South Carolina, Pennsylvania, and Tennessee, negotiating accommodations that allowed it to stay tax-free for a few more years in exchange for putting new fulfillment centers in each state. In California, the most populous state, where the company apparently thought it could stave off the inevitable, Amazon girded itself for a fight. After the state legislature passed its sales-tax bill, Amazon engineered a campaign to overturn the law with a ballot measure and spent $5.25 million gathering signatures and running radio advertisements. Observers projected the company would have to spend over $50 million to see the fight through to the end.[6]

It quickly became evident that such a battle would be expensive, bitterly contested – and vicious. The Alliance for Main Street Fairness carpet-bombed the state with anti-Amazon advertisements, and editorial writers and bloggers largely sided with the big-box chains. 'Amazon's attempt to avoid sales tax is one more sad example of the short-term thinking that rules American business,' blogged Web evangelist Tim O'Reilly, knowing just how to push the buttons of Bezos, who prided himself on long-term thinking.[7] Inside Amazon, it was increasingly clear that the company was being fitted for the black hat of the bad guy. At the same time, Amazon was preparing to confront Apple in the high-stakes tablet market with the

Kindle Fire. Colleagues insisted to Bezos that Amazon could not afford to see its brand tarnished at such a critical juncture.

So that fall, Amazon reversed course and reached an agreement with California: the company would drop its ballot measure in exchange for one more tax-free Christmas season, and it promised to build new fulfillment centers outside San Francisco and Los Angeles.[8] Soon after, Paul Misener testified before the Senate Commerce Science and Transportation Committee and reiterated Amazon's support for a federal bill – as did Amazon's unlikely new bedfellows in the sales-tax battle, Best Buy, Target, and Walmart. Now eBay, another combatant in the sales-tax wars, stood alone in trying to protect its smallest merchants, like the stay-at-home mother bringing in extra money by selling handmade mosaics. It advocated that the law should not apply to businesses with fewer than fifty employees or less than $10 million in annual sales, though most of the proposed national sales-tax bills put the exemption at less than $1 million. As of this writing, a national sales-tax-collection bill has not yet passed both houses of Congress.

Amazon was losing a sizable advantage, but Bezos, ever the farsighted chess player, was compensating by cultivating new ones. Amazon's new fulfillment centers would be close to large cities, allowing for the possibility of next-day or same-day delivery and the wider rollout of its grocery business, Amazon Fresh. Amazon also expanded its test of Amazon Lockers – large, orange locked cabinets placed in supermarkets, drugstores, and chains like Radio Shack that customers could have their Amazon packages shipped to if they liked.

As the era of tax-free online purchases was ending in many states, the true architect of Amazon's tax strategy and chief of its eighty-person tax department, an attorney named Robert Comfort, stepped out of the shadows. Comfort, a Princeton alumnus who joined Amazon in 2000, had spent more than a decade employing every trick in the book, and inventing many new ones, to minimize the company's tax burden. He created its controversial tax structure in Europe, funneling sales through entities in Luxembourg, which has a famously low tax rate. In 2012, this arcane tax structure nearly collapsed amid a wave of populist European anger directed at Amazon and other U.S. companies, including Google, who were trying to minimize their overseas tax burden.

Comfort announced his retirement and left Amazon in early 2012, just as the taxman was catching up with the company. (He has since taken a new job – a titular position as Seattle's honorary consul for the Grand Duchy of Luxembourg.)

And for the first time in its history, Amazon would have to fight its offline rivals on a level playing field.

* * *

There is a clandestine group inside Amazon with a name seemingly drawn from a James Bond film: Competitive Intelligence. The group, which since 2007 has operated within the finance department under long-time executives Tim Stone and Jason Warnick, buys large volumes of products from competitors and measures the quality and speed of their services. Its mandate is to investigate whether any rival is doing a better job than Amazon and then present the data to a committee that usually includes Bezos, Jeff Wilke, and Diego Piacentini, who ensure that the company addresses any emerging threat and catches up quickly.

In the late 2000s, Competitive Intelligence began

tracking a rival with a difficult to pronounce name and a strong rapport with female shoppers. Quidsi (*quid si* is Latin for 'what if') was a New Jersey company known for its website Diapers.com. Grammar-school friends Marc Lore and Vinit Bharara founded the startup in 2005 to allow sleep-deprived caregivers to painlessly schedule recurring shipments of vital supplies. By 2008, the company had expanded into selling all of the necessary survival gear for new parents, including baby wipes, infant formula, clothes, and strollers.

Dragging screaming children to the store is a well-known parental hassle, but Amazon didn't start selling diapers until a year after Diapers.com, and neither Walmart.com nor Target.com was investing significantly in the category. Back when the dark clouds of the dot-com bust still hung over the e-commerce industry, retailers felt that they wouldn't make any money shipping big, bulky, low-margin products like jumbo packs of Huggies Snug and Dry to people's front doors.

Lore and Bharara made it work by customizing their distribution system for baby gear. Quidsi's fulfillment centers, designed by former Boeing operations manager Scott Hilton, used software to match every order with the smallest possible shipping box (there were twenty-three sizes available), minimizing excess weight and thus reducing the per-order shipping cost. (Amazon, which had to match box sizes to a much larger selection of products, was not as adept at this.) Quidsi selected warehouses outside major population centers to take advantage of inexpensive ground-shipping rates and was able to promise free overnight shipping in two-thirds of the country. The Quidsi founders studied Amazon closely and idolized Jeff Bezos, referring to him in private conversation as 'sensei.'[9]

Moms got hooked on the seemingly magical appearance

of diapers on their doorsteps and enthusiastically told friends about Diapers.com. Several venture-capital firms, including Accel Partners, a backer of Facebook, bought into the possibility that Lore and Bharara had identified a weakness in Amazon's armor, and they pumped over $50 million into the company. Around this time, Jeff Bezos and his business-development team, as well as Amazon's counterparts at Walmart, started to pay attention.

Executives and official representatives from Amazon, Quidsi, and Walmart have all declined to discuss the ensuing scuffle in detail. Jeff Blackburn, Amazon's mergers and acquisitions chief, said Quidsi was similar to Zappos, a 'stubbornly independent company building an extremely flexible franchise.' He also said that everything Amazon subsequently did in the diapers market was planned beforehand and was unrelated to competing with Quidsi.

The story that follows has been pieced together from the recollections of insiders at all three companies. They spoke anonymously and with a significant amount of trepidation, given the strength of Amazon's and Walmart's strict nondisclosure agreements and the possibility of legal consequences for them for speaking publically about it.

In 2009, Blackburn ominously informed the Quidsi cofounders over an introductory lunch that the e-commerce giant was getting ready to invest in the category and that the startup should think seriously about selling to Amazon. Lore and Bharara replied that they wanted to remain private and build an independent company. Blackburn told the Quidsi founders that they should call him if they ever reconsidered.

Soon after, Quidsi noticed Amazon dropping prices up to 30 percent on diapers and other baby products. As an experiment, Quidsi execs manipulated their prices and then watched as Amazon's website changed its prices accordingly. Amazon's famous pricing bots were lasered in on Diapers.com.

Quidsi fared well under Amazon's assault, at least at first. It didn't try to match Amazon's low prices but capitalized on the strength of its brand and continued to reap the benefits of strong word of mouth. It also used its trusting relationship with customers and its expertise in fulfillment to open two new websites, Soap.com for home goods and BeautyBar.com for makeup. But after a while, the heated competition began to take a toll on the company. Quidsi had grown from nothing to $300 million in annual sales in just a few years, but with Amazon focusing on the category, revenue growth started to slow. Investors were reluctant to furnish Quidsi with additional capital, and the company was not yet mature enough for an IPO. For the first time, Lore and Bharara had to think about selling.

At around this point, Walmart was looking for ways to make up the ground they'd lost to Amazon, and the retailer was shaking up its online division. Walmart vice chairman Eduardo Castro-Wright took over Walmart.com, and one of his first calls was to Marc Lore at Diapers.com to initiate acquisition talks. Lore said that Quidsi wanted a chance to get 'Zappos money' – $900 million, which included bonuses spread out over many years tied to performance goals. Walmart agreed in principle and started due diligence. Mike Duke, Walmart's CEO, even visited a Diapers.com fulfillment center in New Jersey. However, the subsequent formal offer from Bentonville was well under the requested amount.

So Lore picked up the phone and called Amazon. In September 2006, Lore and Bharara traveled to Seattle to pitch Jeff Bezos on acquiring Quidsi. While they were in that early-morning meeting with Bezos, Amazon sent out a press release introducing a new service called Amazon Mom. It was a sweet deal for new parents: they could get up to a year's worth of free two-day Prime shipping (a program that usually cost $79 to join), and there was a wealth of other perks available, including an additional 30 percent off the already-discounted diapers, if they signed up for regular monthly deliveries of diapers as part of a service called Subscribe and Save. Back in New Jersey, Quidsi employees desperately tried to call their founders to discuss a public response to Amazon Mom. It was no accident that they couldn't reach them. They were sitting blithely unaware in a meeting in Amazon's own offices.

Quidsi could now taste its own blood. That month, Diapers.com listed a case of Pampers at forty-five dollars; Amazon priced it at thirty-nine dollars, and Amazon Mom customers with Subscribe and Save could get a case for less than thirty dollars.[10] At one point, Quidsi executives took what they knew about shipping rates, factored in Procter and Gamble's wholesale prices, and calculated that Amazon was on track to lose $100 million over three months in the diapers category alone.

Inside Amazon, Bezos had rationalized these moves as being in the company's long-term interest of delighting its customers and building its consumables business. He told business-development vice president Peter Krawiec not to spend over a certain amount to buy Quidsi but to make sure that Amazon did not, under any circumstances, lose the deal to Walmart.

As a result of Bezos's meeting with Lore and Bharara, Amazon now had an exclusive three-week period to study Quidsi's financial results and come up with a proposal. At the end of that period, Krawiec offered Quidsi $540 million and said that this was a 'stretch price.' Knowing that Walmart hovered on the sidelines, he gave Quidsi a window of forty-eight hours to respond and made it clear that if the founders didn't take the offer, the heightened competition would continue.

Walmart should have had a natural advantage in this fight. Jim Breyer, the managing partner at one of Quidsi's venture-capital backers, Accel, was also on the Walmart board of directors. But Walmart was caught flat-footed. By the time Walmart upped its offer to $600 million, Quidsi had tentatively accepted the Amazon term sheet. Mike Duke called and left messages for several Quidsi board members, imploring them not to sell to Amazon. Those messages were then transcribed and sent to Seattle, since Amazon had stipulated in the preliminary term sheet that Quidsi was required to turn over information about any subsequent offers.

When Amazon executives learned of Walmart's counterbid, they ratcheted up the pressure even further, threatening the Quidsi founders that 'sensei,' being such a furious competitor, would drive diaper prices to zero if they went with Walmart. The Quidsi board convened to discuss the Amazon proposal and the possibility of letting it expire and then resuming negotiations with Walmart. But by then, Bezos's Khrushchev-like willingness to take the e-commerce equivalent of the thermonuclear option in the diaper price war made Quidsi worried that it would be exposed and vulnerable if something went wrong during the consummation of a shotgun marriage to Walmart. So the Quidsi executives stuck with Amazon, largely out of fear. The deal was announced on November 8, 2010.

The money-losing Amazon Mom program was obviously introduced to help dead-end Diapers.com and force a sale, and if anyone at the time had doubts about that, those doubts were quickly dispelled by Amazon's subsequent actions.

A month after it announced the acquisition of Quidsi, Amazon closed the program to new members. But by then the Federal Trade Commission was reviewing the deal, and a few weeks after it closed the program, Amazon reversed course and reopened it, though with much smaller discounts.

The Federal Trade Commission scrutinized the acquisition for four and a half months, going beyond the standard review to the second-request phase, where companies must provide more information about a transaction. The deal raised a host of red flags, according to an FTC official familiar with the review. A significant head-to-head competition and the subsequent merger had led to the demise of a major player in the category. But the deal was eventually approved, in part because it did not result in a monopoly. There was a plethora of other companies, like Costco and Target, that sold diapers both online and offline.

Bezos had won again, neutralizing an incipient competitor and filling another set of shelves in his everything store. Like Zappos, Quidsi was permitted to operate independently within Amazon (from New Jersey), and soon it expanded into pet supplies with Wag.com and toys with Yoyo.com. Walmart had missed the chance to acquire a talented team of entrepreneurs who had gone toe to toe with Amazon in a key product category. And insiders were once again left with their mouths agape, marveling at how Bezos had ruthlessly engineered another acquisition by driving his target off a cliff. Says one observer who had a seat close to the battle, 'They have an absolute willingness to torch the landscape around them to emerge the winner.'

* * *

Anxiety over Amazon isn't restricted to New Jersey, Las Vegas, and other American places. The industrial city of Solingen, Germany, halfway between Düsseldorf and Cologne, is famous for the production of high-quality razors and knives. The local blacksmith trade dates back two millennia, and today the city is the seat of the European knife industry and home to renowned brands like Wüsthof, a two-hundred-year-old firm that's been run by seven successive generations of the Wüsthof family. In the 1960s, Wolfgang Wüsthof introduced the company's high-end products to North America, riding a bus from town to town with a suitcase full of knives. Forty years later, his grandnephew Harald Wüsthof took over the firm and started selling to chains like Williams-Sonoma and Macy's. Then, in the early 2000s, Wüsthof began supplying its wares to Amazon.com.

Over the course of its fifty years in America, Wüsthof has established itself as a premium brand, winning frequent commendations from the likes of *Consumer Reports* and *Cook's Illustrated*. For that reason it can charge a hundred and twenty-five dollars for an eight-inch hollow-ground cook's knife made of high-carbon laser-tested steel, even though similar-size kitchen knives sell for twenty dollars each at Target. Maintaining that lofty price is vital for a company that employs hundreds of skilled artisans in its factory but that competes in a category full of inferior products that, to an untrained eye, all look roughly the same.

Which is why Amazon's five-year association with Wüsthof – like its relationship with so many brands and manufacturers around the world – has been about as bloody as an actual knife fight.

Manufacturers are not allowed to enforce retail prices for their products. But they can decide which retailers to sell to, and one way they wield that power is by setting price floors with a tool called MAP, or minimum advertised price. MAP requires offline retailers like Walmart to stay above a certain price threshold in their circulars and newspaper ads. Online retailers have a higher burden. Their product pages are considered advertisements, so they have to set their promoted prices at or above MAP or else face the manufacturer's wrath and risk the firm's limiting the number of products allocated or withdrawing them altogether.

Over its first few years selling Wüsthof knives, Amazon respected the German firm's pricing wishes. Amazon was a good partner, placing large orders as its traffic grew and settling its bills on time. It quickly became Wüsthof's top online retailer and second-largest U.S. seller overall, after Williams-Sonoma. Then tensions in the relationship emerged. As Amazon pricing-bot software got better at scouring the Web and finding and matching low prices elsewhere, Amazon repeatedly violated Wüsthof's MAP requirements, selling products like the $125 Grand Prix chef's knife for $109. Wüsthof felt it needed MAP to defend the value of its brand and protect the small independent knife shops that were responsible for about a quarter of the company's sales and were not capable of matching such discounts. 'These are the guys that built my brand,' says René Arnold, the CFO of Wüsthof-Trident of America. 'Amazon cannot sell a new knife. They can't explain it like a store.'

Wüsthof finally stopped allocating products to Amazon in 2006. 'It was painful for us,' Arnold says. 'Those were lost sales, at least in the short term. But we believed our product and our brand were stronger than the brand of our distributors.' For the next three years – until 2009, when Wüsthof changed its mind and initiated part two of its tortured relationship with Amazon – Wüsthof knives were absent from the shelves of the everything store.

Companies that make things and companies that sell them have waged versions of this battle for centuries. With its commitment to everyday low prices and the ingenious marriage of direct retail with a third-party marketplace, Amazon has taken these historic tensions to a new level. Like Sam Walton, Bezos sees it as his company's mission to drive inefficiencies out of the supply chain and deliver the lowest possible price to its customers. Amazon executives view MAPs and similar techniques as the last vestiges of an old way of doing business, gimmicks that inefficient companies use to protect their bloated margins. Amazon has come up with countless workarounds, including a technique called hide the price. In some cases, when Amazon breaks MAP, it doesn't list the price on its product page. A customer can see the low price only when he places the item in his shopping cart.

It's an inelegant solution, driven by Amazon's age-old desire to have the lowest prices anywhere and the novel ability of its pricing algorithms to quickly match any major seller that goes lower. 'We know it's in the customer's best interest that we have a cost structure that allows us to match competitors and be known for low prices,' says Jeff Wilke. 'That's our objective.' Wilke acknowledges that not everyone is happy with this approach but says Amazon is consistent about it and that manufacturers should understand that it is the nature of the Internet itself – not just Amazon – that allows customers to easily find the lowest price.

'If vendors or brands leave Amazon, they will eventually come back,' Wilke predicts, because 'customers trust

Amazon to be great providers of information and customer reviews about a vast selection of products. If you have customers ready to buy, and if you have a chance to tell them about your product, what brand ultimately doesn't want that?'

Dyson, the British vacuum maker, is one example of a brand that appears to treat Amazon with caution. It sold on Amazon for years and then an irate Sir James Dyson, its founder, visited Amazon's offices personally to vent his frustrations over repeated violations of MAP. 'Sir James said he trusted us with his brand and we had violated that trust,' says Kerry Morris, a former senior buyer who hosted Dyson on that memorable visit. Dyson pulled its vacuums from Amazon in 2011, though some models are still sold on the Amazon Marketplace by approved third-party merchants. Over the past few years, companies such as Sony and Black and Decker have taken turns yanking various products from the site. Apple in particular keeps Amazon on a tight leash, giving it a limited supply of iPods but no iPads or iPhones.

Amazon's booming marketplace is a primary source of tension between Amazon and other companies. Over the holiday months in 2012, 39 percent of products sold on Amazon were brokered over its third-party marketplace, up from 36 percent the year before. The company said that over two million third-party sellers worldwide used Amazon Marketplace and that they sold 40 percent more products in 2012 than in 2011.[11] The Marketplace business is a profitable one for the company, since it takes a flat 6 to 15 percent commission on each sale and does not bear the expense of buying and holding the inventory.

Some of the retailers who sell via the Amazon Marketplace seem to have a schizophrenic relationship with the company, particularly if they have no unique and sustainable selling point, such as an exclusive on a particular product. Amazon closely monitors what they sell, notices any briskly selling items, and often starts selling those products itself. By paying Amazon commissions and helping it source hot products, retailers on the Amazon Marketplace are in effect aiding their most ferocious competitor.

In 2003, Michael Ross was chief executive of Figleaves.com, a London-based online lingerie and swimwear site that sold popular sports bras made by the British brand Shock Absorber. Figleaves had Amazon's attention early on. To promote the company's debut in the United States on Amazon's Marketplace, Ross helped arrange a lopsided exhibition tennis match between Jeff Bezos and Shock Absorber's celebrity endorser Anna Kournikova.

Figleaves sold its wares on Amazon's Marketplace for a few years but left unhappily at the end of 2008. By then, Amazon.com was carrying a wide assortment of Shock Absorber bras and swimsuits, and Figleaves was selling very little on the site. 'In a world where consumers had limited choice, you needed to compete for locations,' says Ross, who went on to cofound eCommera, a British e-commerce advisory firm. 'But in a world where consumers have unlimited choice, you need to compete for attention. And this requires something more than selling other people's products.'

Even sellers who thrive in Amazon's Marketplace tend to regard it warily. GreenCupboards, a seller of environmentally responsible products, like eco-friendly laundry detergents and pet supplies, has built a sixty-person company almost entirely via Amazon, despite the fact that founder Josh Neblett says that Marketplace enables 'a race to zero.' His company is constantly competing with other sellers and with Amazon's own retail organization to provide the lowest possible price and to capture the 'buy box' – to be the default seller of a particular product on the site. That furious price competition tends to drive prices down and eliminate profit margin. As a result, GreenCupboards has had to get more Amazon-like to survive. Neblett says the company has gotten better at sourcing hot new products, locking up exclusives, and building a lean organization. 'I've just always considered it a game and we are figuring out how to best play it,' he says.

Still, as Wilke says, some of the companies that disavow selling on Amazon ultimately return, irresistibly drawn to its 200 million active customers and brisk sales. Amazon's own employees have compared third-party selling on the site to heroin addiction – sellers get a sudden euphoric rush and a lingering high as sales explode, then progress to addiction and self-destruction when Amazon starts gutting the sellers' margins and undercutting them on price. Sellers 'know they should not be taking the heroin, but they cannot stop taking the heroin,' says Kerry Morris, the former Amazon buyer. 'They push and bitch and complain and threaten until they finally see they have to cut themselves off.'

Wüsthof, the German knife maker, had its relapse in 2009, after an intensive courtship by Amazon that included promises of obedience in regard to the manufacturer's suggested price. The company reallocated product to the online retailer, but the earlier pattern repeated itself; for example, Wüsthof's gourmet twelve-piece knife set, with a MAP of $199, showed up on the site at $179. René Arnold, the CFO, was overwhelmed with complaints from his other retail partners, whose prices remained 10 percent higher. These small shop owners either lost sales to Amazon or were forced by their customers to match Amazon's price. In their angry calls to Arnold, they threatened to lower their retail prices as well, and now it was easy for Arnold and his colleagues to envision a day when all these retailers would start demanding lower wholesale prices on Wüsthof knives, cutting into the company's profit margins. The economics of its traditional-manufacturing operation in Germany would no longer make sense.

When Arnold complained, his counterpart at Amazon, a merchandising manager named Kevin Bates, responded that the company was merely finding and matching lower prices on the Web and in its third-party Marketplace. Arnold argued that many of those sellers were not authorized retailers and urged Amazon not to match them. Bates said that he was required to – Amazon always matched the lowest price.

Arnold was frustrated. He was monitoring Amazon's third-party Marketplace and tracking several unfamiliar low-priced sellers, including one called Great Deals Now Online. This mysterious entity always seemed to have Wüsthof knives for sale, yet Arnold had no idea who they were, and Amazon provided no way to contact them. 'He might know someone who has gotten a hold of surplus product, or he might have someone working at Bed, Bath and Beyond stealing from the distribution center,' says Arnold. 'Customers would never give their credit card to this guy, but because he's on the Amazon platform, they figure he's clean, he must be good.' Arnold felt that Amazon's own Marketplace was enabling the destructive discounting that its retail business was using as an excuse to undercut MAP.

In 2011, Wüsthof decided, again, to end its relationship with Amazon. To help explain to his bosses why Wüsthof was cutting off one of its best sales channels, René Arnold requested a meeting with Amazon and brought Harald Wüsthof over from Germany. Wüsthof, in his mid-forties with wavy, white hair and an avuncular smile, has quite possibly never in his life been photographed without a sharp blade in his hands.

The meeting, at Amazon's offices in Seattle, was tense. Kevin Bates was joined by his boss Dan Joy, a director of hard-line categories like kitchen and dining. Bates and Joy seemed genuinely surprised to hear that Wüsthof was walking away and vowed to acquire Wüsthof knives through the gray market. They also threatened the company, as Arnold recalls, saying that every time a customer searched on Amazon for the Wüsthof brand, Amazon would show advertisements for competitors like J. A. Henckels, another knife company based in Solingen, and Victorinox, maker of Swiss army knives.

Wüsthof and Arnold were shocked by the fierceness of Amazon's stance and held firm on their decision to withdraw. 'Anyone can sell more Wüsthof at half the price. It's easy,' Arnold says. 'But if you start selling at the lower price, maybe you have a heyday for a few years, but within two or three years you drive a two-hundred-year-old family business into a wall. We had to protect our brand. That was the main decision point. So we pulled out.'

At a kitchen-and-bath trade show in Chicago the following spring, Arnold was surprised to receive an outpouring of support from sympathetic vendors who were also tussling with Amazon over issues like MAPs and mysterious third-party sellers. Meanwhile, Amazon followed through on its threats to show ads for Wüsthof rivals. In mid-2012, an enterprising Amazon buyer somehow managed to get someone at Wüsthof headquarters in Germany to ship him a large crate of knives meant to go to Dubai. That supply lasted about six weeks.

By the end of 2012, an Amazon merchandising representative began courting Wüsthof once more, begging the company to reconsider. The knife maker declined. But here's the kicker: Customers can still find a decent selection of Wüsthof knives on Amazon from a handful of third-party sellers and even from Amazon itself. In 2010, Amazon started a unit called Warehouse Deals. The unit buys refurbished and used products and sells them in the Amazon Marketplace and on the Web at Warehousedeals.com. The goal of the project, according to an executive who worked on it, is to become the largest liquidator on the planet. These products are often advertised as 'good as new' – a package of diapers with a tear in the shrink wrap, for example – and Amazon is not required to sell them at MAP.

As of this writing, Warehouse Deals has a selection of more than sixty Wüsthof products at steep discounts. Third-party merchants, mostly other authorized Wüsthof retailers, also sell their knives on Amazon, often through Fulfillment by Amazon, which allows the products to qualify for Prime shipping. So even when partners flee, the groundwork that Amazon has laid ensures that the hallowed shelves of the everything store are never completely bare.

* * *

Back in the anxious years after the dot-com bust, when Wüsthof was still happily selling its knives on Amazon.com, Jeff Bezos was tracking a firm he viewed as a potentially dangerous new rival: Netflix. At the time, Amazon was making a little extra money by inserting paper advertisements into its delivery boxes, and Bezos himself received a package that contained a flyer for the DVD-rental firm. He brought the flyer into a meeting and said irritably of the managers running the advertising program, 'Is it easy for them to ruin the company or do they have to work at it?'

Bezos was clearly nervous about Netflix's gathering momentum. With its recognizable red envelopes and late-fee-slaying DVD-by-mail program, it was forging a bond with customers and a strong brand in movies, a key media category. Bezos's lieutenants met with CEO Reed Hastings several times during Netflix's for-mative years but they always reported back that Hastings was 'painfully uninterested' in selling, according to one Amazon business-development exec. Hastings himself says that Amazon was never truly serious about an acquisition of Netflix because 'the basic operating rhythms' of the DVD-rental space, which required multiple small fulfillment centers to send discs out and then receive them back, were so different from Amazon's core retail business. 'It made no sense for them to be an aggressive bidder because it didn't really leverage their strengths,' he says.

Like everyone else, Amazon executives knew that the days of selling and shipping physical DVDs were numbered, but they wanted to be prepared and well positioned for whatever came next. So Amazon opened DVD-rental services in the United Kingdom and Germany, with the idea that it would learn the rental business and establish its brand in markets that Netflix had not yet entered. But local companies were ahead there too, and the cost to acquire new customers was higher than Amazon had anticipated. In February 2008, Amazon seemingly waved the white flag of surrender, selling those divisions to a larger competitor, Lovefilm, in exchange for about $90 million in stock and a 32 percent ownership position in the European firm. Jeff Blackburn says that by then Amazon suspected there was little future for the rental model and that 'we sold them the DVD business because they seemed to be overvaluing it.'

Lovefilm was a kind of Frankenstein corporate creation, the combination of numerous Netflix clones that had gradually merged with one other and come to control a majority of the British and German rental market. As a result, it had many shareholders (including several prominent venture-capital firms), a large board of directors, and plenty of conflicting internal opinions about its strategic moves. Amazon became the largest shareholder after the deal and later consolidated its grip on the startup when another investor, the European venture-capital firm Arts Alliance, sold the company a 10 percent stake. Greg Greeley, the former finance executive who was running Amazon's European operation, joined the Lovefilm board. As it is wont to do, Amazon watched from the sidelines, learned, and patiently waited for an opening.

By early 2009, the home-video market was inexorably tilting toward streaming movies online and away from sending discs in the mail. Like Netflix, Lovefilm planned to transition to video on demand. It had arranged streaming deals with movie studios like Warner Brothers and put access to its catalog on devices like Sony's PlayStation 3. But the company needed additional capital to execute such a shift in its business, so that year it hired the investment bank Jefferies and started entertaining acquisition and investment offers.

While private equity firms like Silver Lake Partners expressed interest, Google was the most prominent bidder for Lovefilm. The search giant's executive team was developing a plan over the summer of 2009 to acquire both Lovefilm and Netflix and add a significant new focus that was unrelated to its core advertising business. Nikesh Arora and David Lawee, business-development executives at Google, had several meetings with people at both companies that year and produced a preliminary letter of Google's intent to buy Lovefilm for two hundred million pounds (about three hundred million dollars), according to three people with knowledge of the offer. But these efforts ultimately fizzled; there was opposition from Google's YouTube division and fear that the company might be able to acquire one streaming-video business but not the other.

That left Lovefilm still in need of additional capital. So over the summer of 2010, the company's executives decided to pursue an initial public offering. Then Amazon decided it wanted to buy Lovefilm, and everything changed.

Amazon had watched the explosion in popularity of Internet-connected Blu-ray players and video-game consoles in its own electronics store and knew it had to get off the sidelines. Its incipient streaming service, Amazon Video on Demand, was the successor to an overly complicated video download store called Amazon Unbox, which required users to download entire movies to their PCs or TiVo set-top boxes before they could start watching. The streaming service (which did not require downloads) was showing early promise but the company still lagged behind Apple and Hulu in the online-video market. Buying Lovefilm would give it a beachhead in Europe. 'They went from having a financial interest, where they thought they might make a financial return on their investment, to a strategic interest,' says Dharmash Mistry, a former partner at the London venture-capital firm Balderton Capital and a Lovefilm board member. 'They wanted to own the asset.'

Now the Lovefilm board members would witness the same ruthless tactics observed by the founders of Zappos and Quidsi. Amazon pointed out, quite sensibly, that Lovefilm needed to invest hundreds of millions to acquire content and hold off deep-pocketed rivals like the massive cable conglomerate BSkyB and, when it finally entered the European market, Netflix. Amazon also argued that Lovefilm needed to invest in its long-term prospects and should not spend time and money gussying itself up for the conservative public markets in Europe, which would want to see profits before an IPO. The best path forward was for Lovefilm to sell itself to Amazon. It was more Bezos-style expedient conviction – the arguments had the advantage of being completely rational while also serving Amazon's own strategic interests.

In the midst of this debate, Amazon found a technical way to prevent a Lovefilm IPO. If the company was going to free up stock to sell to the public, it needed to amend its own bylaws, or articles of association – and as the largest shareholder, Amazon could block this change. It effectively had a veto over an IPO, and Amazon made it clear that it was not going to authorize or publicly endorse the move, according to multiple board members and people close to the company. This was an enormous problem. Potential investors were likely to balk if the company's biggest shareholder was not visibly showing its support for the offering.

Lovefilm executives had several meetings with attorneys to try to find a way to extricate themselves from the situation. They also attempted to entice other potential acquirers, hoping to spark a bidding war, but without success. Everyone saw that Amazon was squatting over the asset.

Though Lovefilm was a prestigious European company with a strong brand and solid momentum, Amazon offered an opening bid of a hundred and fifty million pounds, the very bottom of Lovefilm's price range. With no alternatives, Lovefilm started negotiating. In the protracted discussions that followed, Amazon characteristically argued every point, such as compensation packages for management and the timing of escrow payments. Lovefilm's attorneys were astonished at the intractable positions taken by Amazon's negotiators. The talks lasted more than seven months, and the acquisition was finally announced in January 2011. Amazon ended up paying close to two hundred million pounds, or about three hundred million dollars – roughly the same amount Google had offered despite the fact that Lovefilm had expanded its subscriber base and its digital catalog of movies in the intervening year and a half.

Amazon now had a strong foothold in the European video market just as it unveiled its most serious play for the living room. A month after it announced the purchase of Lovefilm, the company introduced a video-streaming service for Amazon Prime in the United States. Members of the two-day shipping service could watch for free a selection of movies and television shows, a catalog that would grow steadily over the next few years as Amazon inked deals with content providers such as CBS, NBC Universal, Viacom, and the pay-TV channel Epix.

Inside the company, Bezos rationalized the giveaway by saying that it sustained and even complemented the seventy-nine-dollar fee for Prime at a time when customers were buying fewer DVDs. But Prime Instant Video played another role. Amazon was now providing, as a supplementary perk, something Reed Hastings and his colleagues at Netflix priced at five to eight dollars a month. The service exerted direct pressure on a key rival and worked to prevent it from appropriating an important section of the everything store. Amazon too would offer films and TV shows in any form that customers could possibly want – all with the click of a button.

To Jeff Bezos, perhaps the only thing more sacrosanct than offering customers these kinds of choices was selling them products and services at the lowest possible prices. But in the fractious world of book publishing, Amazon, it seemed in early 2011, was losing its ability to set low prices. That March, Random House, the largest book publisher in the United States, followed the other big publishers and adopted the agency pricing model, which allowed them to set their own price for e-books and remit a 30 percent commission to retailers. Amazon executives had spent considerable time pleading in vain with their Random House counterparts to stick with the wholesale model. Bezos now no longer had control over a key part of the customer experience for some of the biggest books in the world.

With no stark price advantage and increased competition from Barnes & Noble's Nook, Apple's iBook-store, and the Toronto-based startup Kobo, Amazon's e-book market share fell from 90 percent in 2010 to around 60 percent in 2012. 'For the first time, a level playing field was going to get forced on Amazon,' says James Gray, the former chief strategy officer of the Ingram Content Group. Amazon executives 'were basically spitting blood and nails.'

Amazon felt major book publishers were limiting its ability to experiment with new digital formats. For example, the Kindle 2 was introduced with a novel text-to-speech function that read books aloud in a robotic male or female voice. Roy Blount Jr., the president of the Authors Guild, led a protest against the feature, writing an editorial for the *New York Times* that argued authors were not getting paid for audio rights.[12] Amazon backed off and allowed publishers and authors to enable the feature for specific titles; many declined.

Book publishers were refusing to play by Amazon's rules. So Amazon decided to reinvent the rulebook. It started a New York-based publishing imprint with the lofty ambition to publish bestselling books by big-name authors – the bread-and-butter of New York's two-century-old book industry.

In April of 2011, a month after Random House moved to the agency model, an Amazon recruiter sent e-mails to several accomplished editors at New York publishing houses. She was looking for someone to launch and over-see an imprint that 'will focus on the acquisition of original commercially oriented fiction and non-fiction with the goal of becoming bestsellers,' according to the e-mail. 'This imprint will be supported with a large budget and its success will directly impact the success of Amazon's overall business.' Most of the e-mail's recipients politely declined the offer, so Kindle vice president Jeff Belle asked the man who'd been steering him toward possible recruits if he himself might be inter-ested in the job. 'Well, the thought had crossed my mind,' replied Larry Kirshbaum, a literary agent and, before that, the head of Time Warner's book division.

Kirshbaum, sixty-seven at the time, was the ultimate insider, widely known and, until then, almost universally liked. He had a well-honed instinct for big, mass-culture books and an intuitive feel for survival inside large corporations. When AOL acquired Time Warner in 2000, he directed the staff of Warner Books to wear I Heart AOL T-shirts and made a video of everyone standing around a piano singing 'Unforgettable' (the company had just published Natalie Cole's autobiography). He was thinking about e-books – and losing money on them – long before almost anyone else in the industry.

Kirshbaum reentered a very different environment

than the one he had left in 2005 when he departed AOL Time Warner to become an agent. Animosity toward Amazon had become a defining fact of life in the book business. So he was considered by many of his former peers to be a defector, someone who had gone over to the dark side, a sentiment they did not hesitate to express to him, sometimes in pointed terms.

'There have been a few brickbats I've had to duck,' Kirshbaum says, 'but I have a message I really believe in, which is that we're trying to innovate in ways that can help everybody. We are trying to create a tide that will lift all boats.' He points to the industry's similarly negative reaction to Barnes & Noble's acquisition of the publisher Sterling back in 2003, which raised the same fear that a powerful retailer was trying to monopolize the attention of readers. 'We all worried the sun wasn't going to come up the next day, but it did,' he says. Of Amazon, he says, 'We certainly want to be a major player, but there are thousands of publishers and millions of books. I think it's a little bit of a stretch to say we are cornering the market.'

Kirshbaum's bosses in Seattle sounded a similarly conciliatory note. 'Our entire publishing business is an in-house laboratory that allows us to experiment toward the goal of finding new and interesting ways to connect authors and readers,' Jeff Belle told me for a *Businessweek* cover story on Amazon Publishing in early 2012. 'It's not our intention to become Random House or Simon & Schuster or HarperCollins. I think people have a hard time believing that.'[13]

Amazon executives charged that the book publishers were irrationally consumed with the possibility of their own demise and noted that resisting changes, like paperback books and discount superstores, was something of a hallmark for the industry. And when it came to fielding questions on the topic, Amazon executives perfected a sort of passive-aggressive perplexity, insisting that the media was overplaying the issue and giving it undue attention – sometimes with explanations that compounded and confirmed publishers' concerns. 'The iceman was a really important part of weekly American culture for years and his purpose was to keep your food from spoiling,' says Donald Katz, the founder and chief executive of Amazon's Audible subsidiary. 'But when refrigerators were invented, it was not about what the iceman thought, nor did anyone spend a lot of time writing about it.'

Book publishers needed only to listen to Jeff Bezos himself to have their fears stoked. Amazon's founder repeatedly suggested he had little reverence for the old 'gatekeepers' of the media, whose business models were forged during the analogue age and whose function it was to review content and then subjectively decide what the public got to consume. This was to be a new age of creative surplus, where it was easy for anyone to create something, find an audience, and allow the market to determine the proper economic reward. 'Even well meaning gatekeepers slow innovation,' Bezos wrote in his 2011 letter to shareholders. 'When a platform is self-service, even the improbable ideas can get tried, because there's no expert gate-keeper ready to say "that will never work!" And guess what – many of those improbable ideas do work, and society is the beneficiary of that diversity.'

A few weeks after that letter was published, Bezos told Thomas Friedman of the *New York Times*, 'I see the elimination of gatekeepers everywhere.' In case there was any doubt about the nature of Bezos's convictions, Friedman then imagined a publishing world that includes 'just an author, who gets most of the royalties, and Amazon and the reader.'[14]

'At least it's all out in the open now,' one well-known book agent said at the time.

A kind of industrywide immune response then kicked in. The book world rejected Amazon's new publishing efforts en masse. Barnes & Noble and most independent bookstores refused to stock Amazon's books, and New York-based media and publishing executives widely scoffed at the preliminary efforts of Kirshbaum and his fledgling editorial team. Their $800,000 acquisition of a memoir by actress and director Penny Marshall, for example, was targeted for particular ridicule and later sold poorly.

Meanwhile, Amazon continued to experiment with new e-book formats and push the boundaries of publishers' and authors' tolerance. It introduced the Kindle Single, a novella-length e-book format, and the Prime Lending Library, which allowed Prime members who owned a Kindle reading device to borrow one digital book a month for free. But Amazon included the books of many mid-tier publishers in its lending catalog without asking for permission, reasoning that it had purchased those books at wholesale and thus believed it could set any retail price it wished (including, in this case, zero). In the imbroglio that ensued, the Authors Guild called the lending library 'an exercise of brute economic power,' and Amazon backed off.[15]

Bezos and colleagues dismissed the early challenges Kirshbaum's New York division faced and said they would gauge its success over the long term. They were likely positioning their direct-publishing efforts for a future where electronic books made up a majority of the publishing market and where chains like Barnes & Noble might not exist in their present form. In that world, Amazon alone will still be standing, publishing not just scrappy new writers but prominent brand-name authors as well. And Larry Kirshbaum could once again be one of the most popular – and possibly one of the only – publishing guys left in New York City. Even as Kirshbaum announced his departure from Amazon in October 2013, the company vowed to continue building its publishing arm in the very cradle of book publishing – New York City.

* * *

In December of 2011, as if seeking a fitting conclusion to a year filled with controversy over sales tax, acquisitions, MAPs, and the economics of electronic books, Amazon ran a ham-fisted promotion of its price-comparison application for smartphones. The app allowed users to take pictures or scan the bar codes of products in local stores and compare those prices with Amazon's. On December 10, Amazon offered a discount of up to fifteen dollars to anyone who used the application to buy online instead of in a store. Although certain categories, like books, were exempt, the move stirred up an avalanche of criticism.

Senator Olympia Snowe called the promotion 'anti-competitive' and 'an attack on Main Street businesses that employ workers in our communities.' An employee of Powell's Books in Portland, Oregon, created an Occupy Amazon page on Facebook. An Amazon spokesperson noted that the application was meant primarily for comparing the prices of big retail chains, but it didn't matter. The critics piled on, charging that Amazon was using its customers to spy on competitors' prices and was siphoning away the sales of mom-and-pop merchants. 'I first attributed Amazon's price-comparison app to arrogance and malevolence, but there's also something bizarrely clumsy and wrong-footed about it,' wrote the novelist Richard Russo in a scathing editorial for the *New York Times*.[16]

The conflagration over the price-checking app diminished quickly. But it raised larger questions: Would Amazon continue to be viewed as an innovative and value-creating company that existed to serve and delight its customers, or would it increasingly be seen as a monolith that merely transferred dollars out of the accounts of other companies and local communities and into its own gilded coffers?

During these years of conflict, Jeff Bezos sat down to consider this very question. When Amazon became a company with $100 billion in sales, he wondered, how could it be loved and not feared? As he regularly does, Bezos wrote up his thoughts in a memo and distributed it to his top executives at an S Team retreat. I received a copy through a person close to the company who wished to remain anonymous. The memo, which Bezos titled Amazon.love, lays out a vision for how the Amazon founder wants his company to conduct itself and be perceived by the world. It reflects Bezos's values and determination, and perhaps even his blind spots.

'Some big companies develop ardent fan bases, are widely loved by their customers, and are even perceived as cool,' he wrote. 'For different reasons, in different ways and to different degrees, companies like Apple, Nike, Disney, Google, Whole Foods, Costco and even UPS strike me as examples of large companies that are well-liked by their customers.' On the other end of spectrum, he added, companies like Walmart, Microsoft, Goldman Sachs, and ExxonMobil tended to be feared.

Bezos postulated that this second set of companies was viewed, perhaps unfairly, as engaging in exploitative behavior. He wondered why Microsoft's large base of users had never come out in any significant way to defend the company against its critics and speculated that perhaps customers were simply not satisfied with its products. He theorized that UPS, though not particularly inventive, was blessed by having the unsympathetic U.S. Postal Service as a competitor; Walmart had to deal with a 'plethora of sympathetic competitors' in the small downtown stores that competed with it.

But Bezos was dissatisfied with that simplistic conclusion and applied his usual analytical sensibility to parse out why some companies were loved and others feared.

Rudeness is not cool.
Defeating tiny guys is not cool.
Close-following is not cool.
Young is cool.
Risk taking is cool.
Winning is cool.
Polite is cool.
Defeating bigger, unsympathetic guys is cool.
Inventing is cool.
Explorers are cool.
Conquerors are not cool.
Obsessing over competitors is not cool.
Empowering others is cool.
Capturing all the value only for the company is not cool.
Leadership is cool.
Conviction is cool.
Straightforwardness is cool.
Pandering to the crowd is not cool.
Hypocrisy is not cool.
Authenticity is cool.
Thinking big is cool.
The unexpected is cool.
Missionaries are cool.
Mercenaries are not cool.

On an attached spreadsheet, Bezos listed seventeen attributes, including *polite*, *reliable*, *risk taking*, and *thinks big*, and he ranked a dozen companies on each particular characteristic. His methodology was highly subjective, he conceded, but his conclusions, laid out at the end of the Amazon.love memo, were aimed at increasing Amazon's odds of standing out among the loved companies. Being polite and reliable or customer-obsessed was not sufficient. Being perceived as inventive, as an explorer rather than a conqueror, was critically important. 'I actually believe the four "unloved" companies are inventive as a matter of substance. But they are not perceived as inventors and pioneers. It is not enough to be inventive – that pioneering spirit must also come across and be perceivable by the customer base,' he wrote.

'I propose that one outcome from this offsite could be to assign a more thorough analysis of this topic to a thoughtful VP,' Bezos concluded. 'We may be able to find actionable tasks that will increase our odds of being a stand out in that first group of companies. Sounds worthy to me!'

CHAPTER 11
The Kingdom of the Question Mark

As it neared its twentieth anniversary, Amazon had finally come to embody the original vision of the everything store, conceived so long ago by Jeff Bezos and David Shaw and set into motion by Bezos and Shel Kaphan. It sold millions of products both new and used and was continually expanding into new product areas; industrial supplies, high-end apparel, art, and wine were among the new categories introduced in 2012 and 2013. It hosted the storefronts of thousands of other retailers in its bustling Marketplace and the computer infrastructure of thousands of other technology companies, universities, and government labs, part of its flourishing Web Services business. Clearly Jeff Bezos believed there were no limits to the company's mission and to the variety of products that could be sold on the Internet.

If you were to search the world for the polar opposite of this sprawling conglomerate, a store that cultivated not massive selection but an exclusive assortment of high-end products and thrived not on brand loyalty but on the amiable personality of its proprietor, you might just settle on a small bike shop north of Phoenix, in

Glendale, Arizona. It's called the Roadrunner Bike Center.

This somewhat grandiosely named establishment sits in a shoe-box-shaped space in an otherwise ordinary shopping center next to the Hot Cutz Salon and Spa and down a ways from a Walmart grocery store. It offers a small selection of premium BMX and dirt bikes from companies like Giant, Haro, and Redline, brands that carefully select their retail partners and generally do not sell to websites or discount outlets. Many customers have patronized this store for years, even though it has moved three times within the Phoenix area.

'The old guy that runs this is always there and you can tell he loves to fix and sell bikes,' writes one customer in a typically favorable online review of the store. 'When you buy from him he will take care of you. He also is the cheapest place I have ever taken a bike for a service, I think sometimes he runs a special for $30! That's insane!'

A red poster board with the hand-scrawled words *Layaway for the holidays!* leans against an outside window of the store. It is no different than any mom-and-pop shop anywhere in the world that's been carefully tended and nurtured by its owner over the course of thirty years. Except in this case, the store offers more than just a strong contrast to Amazon, and the evidence hangs inside, under the fluorescent lights, next to the front counter. Framed on the wall is a laminated old newspaper clipping with a photograph of a sixteen-year-old boy sporting a flattop haircut and standing up on the pedals of his unicycle, with one hand on the seat and the other flared daringly out to the side.

I found Ted Jorgensen, Jeff Bezos's biological father, behind the counter of his store in late 2012. I had considered a number of ways he might react to my unannounced appearance, but I gave a very low probability to the likelihood of what actually happened: Jorgensen didn't know who Jeff Bezos was or anything at all about a company named Amazon.com. He was utterly confused by what I was telling him and denied being the father of a famous CEO who was one of the wealthiest men in the world.

But then, when I mentioned the names Jacklyn Gise and Jeffrey, the son they had during their brief teenage marriage, the old man's face flushed with recognition and sadness. 'Is he still alive?' he asked, not yet fully comprehending.

'Your son is one of the most successful men on the planet,' I told him. I pulled up some photographs of Bezos from the Internet, and, incredibly, for the first time in forty-five years, Jorgensen saw his biological son, and his eyes filled with emotion and disbelief.

I took Jorgensen and his wife, Linda, to dinner that night at a local steakhouse, and his story tumbled out. When the Bezos family moved from Albuquerque to Houston back in 1968, Jorgensen promised Jackie and her father that he would stay out of their lives. He remained in Albuquerque, performing with his troupe, the Unicycle Wranglers, and taking odd jobs. He drove an ambulance and worked as an installer for Western Electric, a local utility.

In his twenties, he moved to Hollywood to help the Wranglers' manager, Lloyd Smith, start a new bike shop, and then he went to Tucson, looking for work. In 1972 he was mugged outside a convenience store after buying cigarettes. The assailants hit him with a two-by-four and broke his jaw in ten places.

Jorgensen moved to Phoenix in 1974, got remarried,

and quit drinking. By that time he had lost touch with his ex-wife and their child and forgotten their new last name. He had no way to contact his son or follow his progress, and he says he felt constrained by his promise not to interfere in their lives.

In 1980, he put together every cent he had and bought the bike shop from its owner, who wanted to get out of the business. He has run the store ever since, moving it several times, eventually to its current location on the northern edge of the Phoenix metropolitan area, adjacent to the New River Mountains. He divorced his second wife and met Linda, his third, at the bike shop. She stood him up on their first date but showed up the next time he asked her out. They've been married for twenty-five years. Linda says they've talked privately about Jeffrey and replayed Ted's youthful mistakes for years.

Jorgensen has no other children; Linda has four sons from a previous marriage, and they are close with their stepfather, but he never divulged to them that he had another child – he says he didn't think there was any point. He felt it was a 'dead-end street' and was sure he would never see or hear anything about his son again.

Jorgensen is now sixty-nine; he has heart problems, emphysema, and an aversion to the idea of retirement. 'I don't want to sit at home and rot in front of the television,' he says. He is endearingly friendly and, his wife says, deeply compassionate. (Bezos strongly resembles his mother, especially around the eyes, but he has his father's nose and ears.) Jorgensen's store is less than thirty miles from four different Amazon fulfillment centers, but if he ever saw Jeff Bezos on television or read an article about Amazon, he didn't make the connection. 'I didn't know where he was, if he had a good job or not, or if he was alive or dead,' he says. The face of his child, frozen in infancy, has been stuck in his mind for nearly half a century.

Jorgensen says that he always wanted to reconnect with his son – whatever his occupation or station – but he blames himself entirely for the collapse of his first marriage and is ashamed to admit that, all those years ago, he agreed to stay out of his life. 'I wasn't a good father or a husband,' he says. 'It was really all my fault. I don't blame Jackie at all.' Regret, that formidable adversary Jeff Bezos worked so hard to outrun, hangs heavily over the life of his biological father.

When I left Jorgensen and his wife after dinner that night, they were wistful and still in shock and had decided that they weren't going to tell Linda's sons. The story seemed too far-fetched.

But a few months later, in early 2013, I got a phone call from the youngest son, Darin Fala, a senior project manager at Honeywell who also lives in Phoenix and who spent his teenage years living with Jorgensen and his mother.

Jorgensen, Fala told me, had called a family meeting the previous Saturday afternoon. ('I bet he's going to tell us he has a son or daughter out there,' Fala's wife had guessed.) In dramatic fashion, Jorgensen and Linda explained the unlikely situation.

Fala described the gathering as wrenching and tear-filled. 'My wife calls me unemotional because she has never seen me cry,' Fala says. 'Ted is the same way. Saturday was the most emotion I've ever seen out of him, as far as sadness and regret. It was overwhelming.'

Jorgensen had decided he wanted to try to reach out to the Bezos family and reestablish contact, and Fala was helping him craft his letters to Bezos and his mother. They would send those letters via both regular mail and e-mail in February of 2013, and would end up waiting nearly five months for a response. Bezos's silence on the topic of his long-lost biological father is unsurprising: he is far more consumed with pressing forward than looking back.

During the phone call, Fala related a discovery of his own. Curious about Bezos, he had watched several clips on the Internet of the Amazon CEO being interviewed, including one from *The Daily Show with Jon Stewart*. And Fala was startled to hear Bezos's notorious, honking laugh.

It was the same unrestrained guffaw that had once echoed off the walls of Fala's childhood home, though over the past few years it had gradually been inhibited by emphysema. 'He has Ted's laugh!' Fala says in disbelief. 'It's almost exact.'

* * *

Bezos undoubtedly received and read Jorgensen's e-mail — colleagues say that, with his personal assistants, he reviews all the messages sent to his widely known e-mail address, jeff@amazon.com. In fact, many of the more infamous episodes inside Amazon began with unsolicited e-mails from customers that Bezos forwarded to the relevant executives or employees, adding only a question mark at the top of the message. To the recipients of these e-mails, that notation has the effect of a ticking time bomb.

Within Amazon, an official system ranks the severity of its internal emergencies. A Sev-5 is a relatively in consequential technical problem that can be solved by engineers in the course of the workday. A Sev-1 is an urgent problem that sets off a cavalcade of pagers (Amazon still gives them to many engineers). It requires an immediate response, and the entire situation will later be reviewed by a member of Bezos's management council, the S Team.

Then there's an entirely separate kind of crisis, what

some employees have informally dubbed the Sev-B. That's when an e-mail containing the notorious question mark arrives directly from Bezos. When Amazon employees receive one of these missives, they drop everything they are doing and fling themselves at whatever issue the CEO is highlighting. They've typically got a few hours to solve the problem and prepare a thorough explanation for how it occurred in the first place, a response that will be reviewed by a succession of managers before the answer is presented to Bezos himself. The question mark e-mails, often called escalations, are Bezos's way to ensure that potential problems are addressed and that the customer's voice is always heard inside Amazon.

One of the more memorable recent episodes at Amazon began with such an escalation in late 2010. It had come to Bezos's attention that customers who browsed – but didn't buy – in the lubricant section of Amazon's sexual-wellness category were receiving personalized e-mails promoting a variety of gels and other intimacy facilitators. Even though the extent of Bezos's communication to his marketing staff consisted of a single piece of punctuation, they could tell – he was pissed off. Bezos believed the marketing department's e-mails caused customers embarrassment and should not have been sent.

Bezos likes to say that when he's angry, 'just wait five minutes,' and the mood will pass like a tropical squall.[1] When it comes to issues of bungled customer service, though, that is rarely true. The e-mail marketing team knew the topic was delicate and nervously prepared an explanation. Amazon's direct-marketing tool was decentralized, and category managers could generate e-mail campaigns to customers who had looked at certain product categories but did not make purchases. Such e-mails tended to tip vacillating shoppers into buying and were responsible for hundreds of millions of dollars in Amazon's annual sales. In the case of the lubricant e-mail, though, a low-level product manager had clearly overstepped the bounds of propriety. But the marketing team never got to send this explanation. Bezos was demanding a meeting to discuss the issue.

On a weekday morning, Jeff Wilke, Doug Herrington, Steven Shure (the vice president of worldwide marketing and a former executive at Time Inc.), and several other employees gathered and waited solemnly in a conference room. Bezos glided in briskly. He started the meeting with his customary 'Hello, everybody,' and followed that with 'So, Steve Shure is sending out e-mails about lubricants.'

Bezos didn't sit down. He locked eyes with Shure. He was clearly fuming. 'I want you to shut down the channel,' he said. 'We can build a one-hundred-billion-dollar company without sending out a single fucking e-mail.'

There was an animated argument. Amazon's culture is notoriously confrontational, and it begins with Bezos, who believes that truth springs forth when ideas and perspectives are banged against each other, sometimes violently. In the ensuing scrum, Wilke and his colleagues argued that lubricants were available in grocery stores and drugstores and were not, technically, that embarrassing. They also pointed out that Amazon generated a significant volume of sales with such e-mails. Bezos didn't care; no amount of revenue was worth jeopardizing customer trust. It was a revealing – and confirming – moment. He was willing to slay a profitable aspect of his business rather than test Amazon's bond with its customers. 'Who in this room needs to get up and shut down the channel?' he snapped.

Eventually, they compromised. E-mail marketing for

certain categories such as health and personal care was terminated altogether. The company also decided to build a central filtering tool to ensure that category managers could no longer promote sensitive products, so matters of etiquette were not subject to personal taste. E-mail marketing lived to fight another day.

The story highlighted one of the contradictions of life inside Amazon. Long past the era of using the editorial judgment of employees to drive changes to the website, the company relies on metrics to make almost every important decision, such as what features to introduce or kill. Yet random customer anecdotes, the opposite of cold, hard data, also carry tremendous weight and can change Amazon policy. If one customer has a bad experience, Bezos often assumes it reflects a larger problem and escalates the resolution of the matter inside his company with a question mark.

Many Amazon employees are all too familiar with these fire drills and find them disruptive. 'Why are entire teams required to drop everything on a dime to respond to a question mark escalation?' an employee once asked at one of the company's all-hands meetings, which by 2011 were being held in Seattle's KeyArena, a basketball coliseum with more than seventeen thousand seats.

'Every anecdote from a customer matters,' Jeff Wilke answered. 'We research each of them because they tell us something about our metrics and processes. It's an audit that is done for us by our customers. We treat them as precious sources of information.'

Amazon styles itself as highly decentralized and promises that new employees can make decisions independently. But Bezos is capable of stopping any process dead in its tracks if it creates a problem for even a single customer. In the twelve months after the lube crisis,

Bezos made it his personal mission to clean up the e-mail channel. Employees of that department suddenly found themselves in the hottest possible spot at Amazon: under the withering eye of the founder himself.

Despite the scars and occasional bouts of post-traumatic stress disorder, former Amazon employees often consider their time at the company the most productive of their careers. Their colleagues were smart, the work was challenging, and frequent lateral movement between departments offered constant opportunities for learning. 'Everybody knows how hard it is and chooses to be there,' says Faisal Masud, who spent five years in the retail business. 'You are learning constantly and the pace of innovation is thrilling. I filed patents; I innovated. There is a fierce competitiveness in everything you do.'

But some also express anguish about their experience. Bezos says the company attracts a certain kind of person who likes to pioneer and invent, but former employees frequently complain that Amazon has the bureaucracy of a big company with the infrastructure and pace of a startup, with lots of duplicate efforts and poor communication that makes it difficult to get things done. The people who do well at Amazon are often those who thrive in an adversarial atmosphere with almost constant friction. Bezos abhors what he calls 'social cohesion,' the natural impulse to seek consensus. He'd rather his minions battled it out in arguments backed by numbers and passion, and he has codified this approach in one of Amazon's fourteen leadership principles – the company's highly prized values that are often discussed and inculcated into new hires.[2]

Have Backbone; Disagree and Commit
Leaders are obligated to respectfully challenge decisions when they disagree, even when doing so is uncomfortable or exhausting. Leaders have conviction and are tenacious. They do not compromise for the sake of social cohesion. Once a decision is determined, they commit wholly.

Some employees love this confrontational culture and find they can't work effectively anywhere else. The professional networking site LinkedIn is full of executives who left Amazon and then returned. Inside the company, this is referred to as a boomerang.

But other escapees call Amazon's internal environment a 'gladiator culture' and wouldn't think of returning. There are many who last less than two years. 'It's a weird mix of a startup that is trying to be super corporate and a corporation that is trying hard to still be a startup,' says Jenny Dibble, who spent five months there as a marketing manager in 2011, trying, ineffectively, to get the company to use more social-media tools. She found her bosses were not particularly receptive to her ideas and that the long hours were incompatible with raising a family. 'It was not a friendly environment,' she says.

Even leaving Amazon can be a combative process – the company is not above sending letters threatening legal action if an employee takes a similar job at a competitor. It's more evidence of that 'fierce competitiveness' mentioned by Faisal Masud, who left Amazon for eBay in 2010 and received such a legal threat (eBay settled the matter privately). This perpetual exodus of employees hardly seems to hurt Amazon, though. The company, aided by the appeal of its steadily increasing stock price, has become an accomplished recruiter of new talent. In

2012 alone, Amazon's ranks swelled to 88,400 full-time and part-time time employees, up 57 percent from the year before.

The compensation packages at Amazon are designed to minimize the cost to the company and maximize the chances that employees will stick around through the predictable adversity that comes with joining the firm. New hires are given an industry-average base salary, a signing bonus spread over two years, and a grant of restricted stock units over four years. But unlike other technology companies, such as Google and Microsoft, which spread out their stock grants evenly, Amazon backloads the grant toward the end of the four-year period. Employees typically get 5 percent of their shares at the end of their first year, 15 percent their second year, and then 20 percent every six months over the final two years. Ensuing grants vest over two years and are also backloaded, to ensure that employees keep working hard and are never inclined to coast.

Managers in departments of fifty people or more are required to 'top-grade' their subordinates along a curve and must dismiss the least effective performers. As a result of this ongoing examination, many Amazon employees live in perpetual fear. A common experience among Amazon workers is a feeling of genuine surprise when one receives a good performance review. Managers are so parsimonious with compliments that underlings tend to spend their days anticipating their termination.

There is little in the way of perks or unexpected performance bonuses at Amazon, though it has come along since the 1990s, when Bezos refused that early suggestion to give employees bus passes because he didn't want them to feel pressure to leave at a reasonable hour. Employees now get ORCA cards that entitle them to free rides on

Seattle's regional transit system. Parking at the company's offices in South Lake Union costs $220 a month and Amazon reimburses employees – for $180.

Still, evidence of the company's constitutional frugality is everywhere. Conference-room tables are a collection of blond-wood door-desks shoved together side by side. The vending machines take credit cards, and food in the company cafeterias is not subsidized. When a new hire joins the company, he gets a back-pack with a power adapter, a laptop dock, and some orientation materials. When someone resigns, he is asked to hand in all that equipment – including the backpack. The company is constantly searching for ways to reduce costs and pass on those savings to customers in the form of lower prices. This also is embedded in the sacrosanct leadership principles:

Frugality

We try not to spend money on things that don't matter to customers. Frugality breeds resourcefulness, self-sufficiency and invention. There are no extra points for headcount, budget size or fixed expense.

All of this comes from Bezos himself. Amazon's values are his business principles, molded through two decades of surviving in the thin atmosphere of low profit margins and fierce skepticism from the outside world. In a way, the entire company is scaffolding built around his brain – an amplification machine meant to disseminate his ingenuity and drive across the greatest possible radius. 'It's scaffolding to magnify the thinking embodied by Jeff, to the greatest extent possible,' says Jeff Wilke when I bounce that theory off him. 'Jeff was learning as he went along. He learned things from each of us who had expertise and incorporated the best pieces into his mental model. Now everyone is expected to think as much as they can like Jeff.'

Bezos's top executives are always modeling Bezos-like behavior. In the fall of 2012, I had dinner with Diego Piacentini at La Spiga, his favorite Italian restaurant in Seattle's Capitol Hill neighborhood. He graciously insisted on picking up the tab, and after paying, he almost theatrically tore up the receipt. 'The company is not paying for this,' he said.

The rhythms of Amazon are the rhythms of Bezos, and its customs are closely tuned to how he prefers to process information and maximize his time. He personally runs the biannual operating review periods for the entire company, dubbed OP1 (done over the summer) and OP2 (done after the holiday season). Teams work intensely for months preparing for these sessions, drawing up six-page documents that spell out their plans for the year ahead. A few years ago, the company refined this process further to make the narratives more easily digestible for Bezos and other S Team members, who cycle through many topics during these reviews. Now every document includes at the top of the page a list of a few rules, called tenets, the principles for each group that guide the hard decisions and allow them all to move fast, without constant supervision.

Bezos is like a chess master playing countless games simultaneously, with the boards organized in such a way that he can efficiently tend to each match.

Some of these chess games get more attention than others. Bezos spends more time on Amazon's newer businesses, such as Amazon Web Services, the company's streaming-video initiative, and, in particular, the Kindle and Kindle Fire efforts. ('I don't think you can even fart in the Kindle building without Jeff's approval,' quipped one longtime executive.) In these divisions, stress levels are high and any semblance of balance between work and home falls by the wayside.

Once a week, usually on Tuesday, various departments at Amazon meet with their managers to review long spreadsheets of the data important to their business. Customer anecdotes have no place at these meetings. The numbers alone are a proxy for what is working and what is broken, how customers are behaving, and, ultimately, how well the company overall is performing.

The meetings can be intense and intimidating. 'This is what, for employees, is so absolutely scary and impressive about the executive team. They force you to look at the numbers and answer every single question about why specific things happened,' says Dave Cotter, who spent four years at Amazon as a general manager in various divisions. 'Because Amazon has so much volume, it's a way to make very quick decisions and not get into subjective debates. The data doesn't lie.'

The metrics meetings culminate with the weekly business review every Wednesday, one of the most important rituals at Amazon, run by Wilke. Sixty managers in the retail business gather in one room to review their departments, share data about defects and inventory turns, and talk about forecasts and the complex interactions among different parts of the company.

Bezos does not attend these meetings. But he can always make his presence felt anywhere in the company. After the lubricant crisis, for example, e-mail marketing fell squarely under his purview. He carefully monitored efforts to filter the kinds of messages that could be sent to customers and he tried to think about the challenge of e-mail outreach in fresh ways. Then, in late 2011, he had what he considered to be a significant new idea.

Bezos is a fan of e-mail newsletters such as VSL.com, a

daily assortment of cultural tidbits from the Web, and Cool Tools, a compendium of technology tips and product reviews written by Kevin Kelly, a founding editor of *Wired*. Both e-mails are short, well written, and informative. Perhaps, Bezos reasoned, Amazon should be sending a single well-crafted e-mail every week – a short digital magazine – instead of a succession of bland, algorithm-generated marketing pitches. He asked marketing vice president Steve Shure to explore the idea.

Shure formed a team and they spent two months coming up with trial concepts. Bezos gave them little direction, but their broad mandate was to create an entirely new type of e-mail for customers – the kind of personal voice that Amazon had lost more than ten years ago, when it downsized its editorial division after the acrimonious intramural competition with P13N and Amabot.

From late 2011 through early 2012, Shure's group presented a variety of concepts to Bezos, including one that revolved around celebrity Q and As and another that highlighted interesting historical facts about products on the site. The project never progressed – it fared poorly in tests with customers – but several participants remember the process as being particularly excruciating. In one meeting, Bezos quietly thumbed through the mockups, styled in the customary Amazon format of a press release, as everyone waited in tense, edge-of-the-seat silence. Then he tore the documents apart. 'Here's the problem with this, I'm already bored,' he said. He seemed to like the last concept the most, which suggested profiling a selection of products on the site that were suddenly hot, like Guy Fawkes masks and CDs by the Grammy-winning British singer Adele. 'But the headlines need to be punchier,' he told the group, which included the writers of the material. 'And some of this is just bad writing. If you were doing this as a blogger, you would starve.'

Finally he turned his attention to Shure, the marketing vice president, who, like so many other marketing vice presidents throughout the company's history, was a frequent target.

'Steve, why haven't I seen anything on this in three months?'

'Well, I had to find an editor and work through mockups.'

'This is developing too slow. Do you care about this?'

'Yes, Jeff, we care.'

'Strip the design down, it's too complicated. Also, it needs to move faster!'

Faster was one way to describe 2012 and the first half of 2013. Over those months, Amazon's stock rose 60 percent. The company issued a total of 237 press releases – an average of 1.6 announcements for every two weekdays. Since the company was now beginning to collect sales tax in many states, it didn't have to sidestep nexus issues and so opened more than a dozen new fulfillment and customer-service centers around the world. It acquired Kiva Systems, a Boston company building mobile robots meant to one day replace the human pickers in fulfillment centers, for $775 million in cash. It renewed its push into apparel with its dedicated website MyHabit.com and opened a new store for industrial and scientific equipment, Amazon Supply.

Amazon also expanded a service that allowed advertisers to reach Amazon customers on all of the company's websites and devices. Run by business-development chief Jeff Blackburn, advertising at Amazon is a highly profitable side business that helps subsidize free shipping and low prices and funds some of the company's expensive long-term projects, like building its own hardware.

To distinguish its growing digital ecosystem from rival platforms offered by Apple and Google, Amazon spent millions to acquire and create new movies and television shows to add to its free Prime Instant Video catalog, and through Amazon's publishing divisions, it funded the publication of many exclusive books for the Kindle. Amazon's chief rivals, Apple and Google, are arguably better positioned in this burgeoning digital world and have considerably greater resources. So Bezos is hedging his bets; if customers choose Apple iPads or Google tablets, they can still shop on Amazon and play their music collections and read their Kindle books on a variety of applications that have been rolled out for its rivals' devices.

In the fall of 2012, hundreds of journalists turned out at an airplane hangar in Santa Monica to watch Bezos unveil a new line of Kindle Fire tablets, including an iPad-size jumbo version and the $119 Kindle Paperwhite, a dedicated e-reader with a glowing, front-lit screen. 'This achieves our original vision,' Bezos told me in an interview after the event, referring to the latest dedicated reading device. 'I'm sure we'll figure out ways to continue forward, but this is a step-change product.'

Earlier that same week, a federal judge had approved a settlement with three of the major book publishers in the Justice Department's antitrust case over agency pricing. (The other two publishers targeted in the investigation would settle within the next few months.) Amazon was now free to resume discounting new and bestselling e-books. I asked Bezos about it but he didn't care to gloat. 'We are excited to be allowed to lower prices' was all he said.

In December, Amazon held its first conference for

customers of Amazon Web Services at the Sands Expo Center in Las Vegas. Six thousand developers showed up and listened intently as AWS executives Andy Jassy and Werner Vogels discussed the future of cloud computing. The size and passion of the crowd was an emphatic validation of Amazon's unlikely emergence as a pioneer in the field of enterprise computing. On the second day of the conference, Bezos himself took the stage and in a freewheeling discussion with Vogels gave a rare window into his personal projects, like the Clock of the Long Now, that mechanical timepiece designed to last for millennia that engineers are preparing to build inside a remote mountain on Bezos's ranch in Texas. 'The symbol is important for a couple of reasons. If [humans] think long term, we can accomplish things that we wouldn't otherwise accomplish,' Bezos said. 'Time horizons matter, they matter a lot. The other thing I would point out is that we humans are getting awfully sophisticated in technological ways and have a lot of potential to be very dangerous to ourselves. It seems to me that we, as a species, have to start thinking longer term. So this is a symbol. I think symbols can be very powerful.'

On the stage, Bezos then predictably unleashed a steady tide of Jeffisms, about long-term thinking, about a willingness to fail and to be misunderstood, and about that shocking revelation so many years ago, in the very first SoDo warehouse, that it might be a great idea to add – *He's not really going to tell that story again, is he?* – packing tables!

The packing-table anecdote may be showing its age, but Bezos is trying to reinforce the same values. Like the late Steve Jobs, Bezos has gradually worn down employees, investors, and a skeptical public and turned them toward his way of thinking. Any process can be improved. Defects that are invisible to the knowledgeable may be obvious to newcomers. The simplest solutions are the best. Repeating all these anecdotes isn't rote monotony – it's calculated strategy. 'The rest of us try to muddle around with complicated contradictory goals and it makes it harder for people to help us,' says his friend Danny Hillis. 'Jeff is very clear and simple about his goals, and the way he articulates them makes it easy for others, because it's consistent.

'If you look at why Amazon is so different than almost any other company that started early on the Internet, it's because Jeff approached it from the very beginning with that long-term vision,' Hillis continues. 'It was a multi-decade project. The notion that he can accomplish a huge amount with a larger time frame, if he is steady about it, is fundamentally his philosophy.'

* * *

By 2012, Amazon had completed its move to its new office buildings in Seattle's South Lake Union district. Another transition occurred at around this same time, though it was evident only to employees at first. In signs around the new campus, and on the rare tchotchkes like mugs and T-shirts that were available to employees after the move, the company's name was represented as simply Amazon, not Amazon.com. For years Bezos had been adamant about using the longer version, part of an effort to engrave the Web address on customers' minds. Now the company produced so many things, including cloud services and hardware, that the anachronistic original moniker no longer made sense. The name on the website was abbreviated in March of 2012. Few people noticed.

Amazon, it seemed, was a company in constant flux. Yet some things remained the same. On a cold, wet

Tuesday morning in early November 2012 at around nine o'clock, a Honda minivan pulled up to Day One North, on the corner of Terry Avenue and Republican Street in Seattle's South Lake Union neighborhood. Jeff Bezos, sitting in the passenger seat, leaned over to kiss his wife, MacKenzie, good-bye, got out of the car, and walked self-assuredly into the building to start another day.

In many ways, Bezos's life has become as complicated as Lee Scott's was back in 2000 when Bezos visited the former Walmart CEO and marveled at the security around him. Bezos may not get ferried to work in a black sedan, but Amazon still spends $1.6 million per year on personal security for him and his family, according to the company's financial reports.

His small domestic scene with MacKenzie speaks to at least one normal routine he has managed to preserve amid the unimaginable complexity that comes with Amazon's towering success. The family can hire drivers; they can buy limousines and private airplanes. Yet they still own a modest Honda, albeit a larger model than the Accord of a decade ago, and MacKenzie often delivers their four children to school and then drives her husband to work.

There is nothing modest about their wealth, of course. Bezos's fortune is now estimated at $25 billion, making him the twelfth-richest person in the United States.[3]

The family is exceedingly private, yet their lives cannot be completely hidden from view. Their lakefront mansion in the wealthy residential enclave of Medina, near the home of Bill and Melinda Gates, was renovated in 2010 and sits on 5.35 acres. It has 29,000 square feet of living space across two buildings, according to public records, and that's not including a caretaker's cottage and a boathouse – the site where Bezos first organized the team that would build Amazon Prime.[4]

In addition to the primary residence, the Bezos family owns homes in Aspen, Beverly Hills, and New York City, plus the sprawling 290,000-acre ranch in Texas, where Blue Origin has a facility and where its rockets will begin their trips to space. MacKenzie rents a one-bedroom apartment near their home in Medina that she uses as a private office to write. She is the author of two novels, including *Traps*, published in 2012. 'I am definitely a lottery winner of a certain kind,' she told *Vogue* magazine in a rare profile in 2012, referring to her husband's success. 'It makes my life wonderful in many ways, but that's not the lottery I feel defined by. The fact that I got wonderful parents who believed in education and never doubted I could be a writer, the fact that I have a spouse I love, those are the things that define me.'[5]

Bezos and MacKenzie seem to share the skill of efficiently dispersing their time across many personal responsibilities and multiple projects. For Bezos, in addition to his family and Amazon, there's Blue Origin, where he typically spends each Wednesday, and Bezos Expeditions, his personal venture-capital firm, which holds stakes in companies such as Twitter, the taxi service Uber, the news site Business Insider, and the robot firm Rethink Robotics. Since August of 2013, Bezos has owned the *Washington Post* newspaper and has said he wants to apply his passion for invention and experimentation to reviving the storied newspaper. 'He invests in things where information technology can disrupt existing models,' says Rodney Brooks, the MIT robotics professor behind Rethink Robotics, which aims to put inexpensive robots on manufacturing assembly lines. 'He's certainly not hands-on but he has been a good person to talk to when various conundrums come up. When we go ask him questions, it's worth listening to his answers.'

Bezos coordinates closely with the creators of the Clock of the Long Now and oversees its quarterly review sessions, which the clock engineers call Ticks. 'He's hell on the details and in the thick of the design and very strict on where costs are going,' says Stewart Brand, the cochairman of the Long Now Foundation.

Bezos and MacKenzie are personally involved in the Bezos Family Foundation, which doles out education grants and mobilizes students to help other young people in impoverished countries and disaster zones. The foundation is run by Jackie and Mike Bezos, and Christina Bezos Poore and Mark Bezos, Jeff's siblings, are directors. The family has imported a little Amazon-style management to their philanthropy. In the main conference room of the foundation's office, a few blocks from Amazon's headquarters, is a rag doll that they often prop up in an empty chair during meetings. The doll is meant to represent the student they are trying to help – just as Bezos once had a habit of keeping a chair empty in meetings to represent the customer.

The Bezos family is unusually close-knit and focused on the future. But occasionally the past does catch up with them. In June 2013, on a Wednesday evening close to midnight, Jeff Bezos finally responded to the messages sent by Ted Jorgensen, his biological father. In a short but heartfelt e-mail, sent to Jorgensen's stepson because Jorgensen himself does not use the Internet, Bezos tried to put the old man at ease. He wrote that he empathized with the impossibly difficult choices that his teenage parents were forced to make and said that he had enjoyed a happy childhood nonetheless. He said that he harbored no ill will toward Jorgensen at all, and he asked him to cast aside any lingering regret over the circumstances of their lives. And then he wished his long-lost biological father the very best.

* * *

When you have fit yourself snugly into Jeff Bezos's worldview and then evaluated both the successes and failures of Amazon over the past two decades, the future of the company becomes easy to predict. The answer to almost every conceivable question is yes.

Will Amazon move to free next-day and same-day delivery for Prime members? Yes, eventually, when Amazon has so many customers in each urban area that placing a fulfillment center right outside every city becomes practical. Bezos's goal is and always has been to take all the inconvenience out of online shopping and deliver products and services to customers in the most efficient manner possible.

Will Amazon one day run its own delivery trucks? Yes, it already does in cities like San Francisco, Los Angeles and New York. And it will expand its fleet when it has so many customers in other urban areas that operating its own trucks, instead of relying on couriers like UPS and Federal Express, makes economic sense.

Will Amazon roll out its grocery service, Amazon Fresh, beyond Seattle and parts of Los Angeles and San Francisco? Yes, when it has perfected the mechanics of profitable storage and delivery of perishables, like vegetables and fruit. Bezos does not believe Amazon can grow to the scale of Walmart without mastering the science of groceries and apparel.

Will Amazon introduce a mobile phone or an Internet-connected television set-top box? Yes, in fact it did both in 2014 after the initial publication of this book. The company wants to offer its services on all the connected devices that its customers use without having to rely entirely on the hardware of its chief competitors.

Will Amazon expand beyond the ten countries where it currently operates retail websites? Yes, eventually. Bezos's long-term goal is to sell everything, everywhere. As Russia, for example, develops a stronger shipping infrastructure and a more reliable credit card processing system, Amazon will introduce its e-commerce store and digital services there, perhaps by acquiring local companies or by seeding the market with the Kindle and Kindle Fire, as it did in Brazil in 2012 and in India in 2013.

Will Amazon always buy its products from manufacturers? No; at some point it might *print* them right in its fulfillment centers. The evolving technology known as 3-D printing, in which microwave-size machines extrude plastic material to create objects based on digital models, is just the kind of disruptive revolution that fascinates Bezos and could allow him to eliminate more costs from the supply chain. In 2013, Amazon took the first step into this world, opening a site for 3-D printers and supplies.

Will antitrust authorities eventually come to scrutinize Amazon and its market power? Yes, I believe that is likely, because the company is growing increasingly monolithic in markets like books and electronics, and rivals have fallen by the wayside. But as we have seen with the disputes over sales tax and e-book pricing, Amazon is a masterly navigator of the law and is careful to stay on the right side of it. Like Google, it benefits from the example of Microsoft's antitrust debacle in the 1990s, which provided a powerful object lesson of how aggressive monopolistic behavior can nearly ruin a company.

These are not fever dreams. They are near inevitabilities. It's an easy prediction to make – that Jeff Bezos will do what he has always done. He will attempt to move faster, work his employees harder, make bolder bets, and pursue both big inventions and small ones, all to achieve his grand vision for Amazon – that it be not just an everything store, but ultimately an everything company.

Amazon may be the most beguiling company that ever existed, and it is just getting started. It is both missionary *and* mercenary, and throughout the history of business and other human affairs, that has always been a potent combination. 'We don't have a single big advantage,' he once told an old adversary, publisher Tim O'Reilly, back when they were arguing over Amazon protecting its patented 1-Click ordering method from rivals like Barnes & Noble. 'So we have to weave a rope of many small advantages.'

Amazon is still weaving that rope. That is its future, to keep weaving and growing, manifesting the constitutional relentlessness of its founder and his vision. And it will continue to expand until either Jeff Bezos exits the scene or no one is left to stand in his way.

Epilogue

On Thursday, November 21, 2013, at 2:00 p.m. in the afternoon, mourners gathered under the Byzantine-domed ceiling of the Stanford Memorial Church on the lush campus of Stanford University. They were there to say a final goodbye to a cherished friend, colleague, and family member. Two months earlier, Joy Covey, mother, environmentalist, and Amazon.com's first chief financial officer, had been killed in a tragic bicycle accident.

Covey had been riding her bike down wooded Skyline Boulevard, southwest of Palo Alto, when a white Mazda minivan driving in the other direction made a sharp left turn in front of her. Though she was wearing a helmet, she hit the side of the van with tremendous force and died at the scene. In a terrible irony, the minivan was in service for OnTrac[1], a local logistics company that delivers packages for Amazon and other online retailers.

The Stanford ceremony was deeply moving and full of warm, personal tributes. Several of Covey's friends, fellow parents, and neighbors from the nearby suburb of Woodside remembered Covey as a devoted mom, a lover of adventurous pursuits, and an impulsive maker of plans. A teenaged girl, a family friend, sang 'Amazing Grace' and struggled to finish all the verses while fighting back tears. Frances Beinecke, president of the Natural Resources Defense Council, where Covey had worked as treasurer, spoke of harnessing's Covey's limitless well-spring of energy on environmental causes. She said that working with her 'was like stepping into a reality distortion field where those lucky enough to get whisked along, inevitably got the ride of our lives.'

A few speeches centered on Covey's role at Amazon, where she was a key figure in the early years of go-for-broke growth and a partner for Jeff Bezos as he first sought to stock the shelves of the everything store. Mary Meeker, a former Morgan Stanley analyst and now venture capitalist, recalled the time when Covey raised Amazon's first debt offering of $550 million in high-yield junk bonds back in 1998. 'It was a white- knuckle affair,' Meeker said. 'Joy knew it was going to be difficult from the start. She assumed it would be so difficult she made sure Jeff was safely out of the country.'

Bezos himself attended the ceremony with wife MacKenzie and also spoke. Former Amazon executives sometimes wondered whether the focused and driven Bezos even remembered their contributions, but from his speech, it was clear that he valued his three-year collaboration with Covey. 'Joy was substance over optics,' he said. 'Joy was a long-term thinker. Joy was bold.'

Bezos continued, choking up: 'Joy and I talked often about a day in the future when we would sit down together with our grandkids and tell the Amazon story. I still want that to happen.'

The memorial was a bittersweet reunion of sorts. Employees and executives from all the eventful chapters of Amazon's twenty-year odyssey packed into the church. Current S-Team members like Jeff Wilke, Andy Jassy,

Jeff Blackburn, and Russ Grandinetti were there. So were former Amazonians like David Risher, who lead the first expansion into retail in the 1990s; Warren Jenson, Covey's short-lived successor as CFO; and Rick Dalzell, the former Army Ranger who was Amazon's CIO for a decade.

Afterward many attended a private reception at the Stanford Faculty Club, where the group listened to more eulogies and reminisced. The reception was supposed to last until six thirty but stretched well into the evening. Bezos, though typically guarded with his personal time, stayed until the very end, catching up with former employees and surprising many of them with the intensity of his emotion.

One executive, who had departed from Amazon several years before to join a rival e-commerce company, says that at the reception, Bezos approached and embraced him.

The executive's wife, who for years had heard stories of tense senior management meetings at Amazon, was shocked. Afterward, she turned to him and marveled, 'Did Jeff Bezos just give you a hug?'

In January, 2013, eight months before her accident, I received a lengthy e-mail from Joy Covey. She had been generous with her memories and insights as I crafted the first few chapters of this book and was wondering how my writing was progressing. She was reading the Steve Jobs biography by Walter Isaacson and was thinking about how Bezos's leadership style compared to the late Apple cofounder's famously brusque and direct demeanor.

When I rediscovered Covey's email, after her death, I was struck by its thoughtfulness and eloquence. Here it is, lightly edited for clarity.

Hello Brad,

I have been wondering how your writing is coming along. Also, I thought of your project (and Jeff) while beginning the Jobs biography recently.

I found myself thinking about what it takes to accomplish things as big as they both did, when a lot of what you are doing is unconventional. It may very well be that the absolute intensity of drive and focus is essential and incompatible with all of the nice management thought about consensus and gentle demeanor. I think about how effective and quick Jeff was and how important that he didn't slow down too much or modify his ideas to make others feel comfortable.

I think about the early days and the level of clarity, vision, potential and values that Jeff brought. And then I look at Amazon today, and reflect on some conversations I have had with him in the intervening years. It is easy to draw a straight line from the vision he had back then to the Amazon of today. There were a few little wobbles and detours in places, but really I don't know any other company that has created such a juggernaut that is so consistent with the original ideas of the founder. It is almost like he fired an arrow and then followed that arc.

Can we really think of any other company approaching Amazon's size or age that continues to move forward with the boldness, risk-taking, innovation and the long-term perspective that Amazon shows? Jeff's clarity, intensity of focus and ability to prioritize, which has no doubt become ingrained in his key team, is unusual and behind his ability to keep leaping forward versus protecting existing ground.

Seeing the future, he put in place the critical DNA that would help the whole company embody his vision. His focus was on very bright, high growth-potential and fluid-minded people, with the right values as 'builders'. He looked for people that absolutely prioritized customer trust and delight, who at all times were long-term focused and driven to be bold and innovative.

All of this was lived and modeled every day by Jeff and the senior team. Personal wealth was never discussed or really thought about. I see companies these days where thoughts of 'exits' are foremost in the minds of top management and board, and it is so clear that this value will infect the decision-making down to the smallest choice by the most junior employee. Do we create something that is good, or just that seems good and might get us acquired or funded?

At Amazon it was always abundantly clear what the goals and values were, and as I reflect on discussions and decisions throughout my time there, it is easy to imagine how different so many small choices might have been otherwise. Now he has tens of thousands of employees, and I would bet a large sum that the same messages and values are still well understood and driving decisions broadly today. I also reflect on how effective the values were as a screening tool for hiring. People who were highly focused on their titles, traditional status metrics, security, or their own wealth stood out vividly in the process.

We talked a lot about whether Jeff was difficult to work with. Yet Jeff attracted people like me, who really need to work on things they can internalize and adopt as mission, who had to leave the path they thought they were on, and who poured their hearts and souls and best efforts into building Amazon. And he has kept a terrific and close team now for years. We believed in what we were building, and felt that our very best was needed to have a hope of accomplishing the enormous potential ahead of us. Jeff's style always read as completely pure – never a self interest or political dimension, all purely focused on the best outcomes for Amazon and our customers.

As I read the Jobs book I really had to wonder if that (sometimes-harsh) intensity isn't an essential element when so much of what you want to do requires boldness, immediacy, ruthless prioritization and risk. It seems counter-intuitive to everyone who has pursued traditional corporate goals in the past. I even had an insight and question about myself, that maybe I haven't begun to really find my own limits, since I have not, aside from those times of highest stakes and intensity at Amazon, really run free following my own insights and directions without being too accommodating of others.

I think Jeff is one of the most capable and effective founders ever, and I think the Amazon juggernaut is still in its early stages.

Cheers,

Joy[2]

In the immediate months surrounding the publication of this book in October 2013, Amazon and its founder were almost constantly in the headlines. In September, the company introduced a new Kindle e-book reader and several new models of its Kindle Fire tablet. A few weeks later, the company announced it would start delivering packages on Sundays, in partnership with the United States Postal Service. It was an added convenience for customers and a characteristically brilliant tactical move. One way to look at it: Bezos was propping up a weakened Post Office, which serves as a counterweight to two of Amazon's most powerful partners – UPS and FedEx.

In the same blur of company announcements, Amazon expanded Fresh, its grocery delivery service, to Los Angeles and San Francisco. It is now expected to roll out the service throughout the country in competition with grocers like Safeway and Walmart. In November, the company unveiled a program called Amazon Source, which allowed independent booksellers to sell Kindle e-readers and tablets and keep a 10 percent commission on any resulting e-book sales from those devices. Bookshop owners, whose trade has been gradually eroded by Amazon, reacted with predictable suspicion. 'At first glance, this looks like a Faustian bargain,' Bradley Graham, co-owner of Politics & Prose Bookstore in Washington, D.C., told *Publishers Weekly*.[3]

Over the New Year's holiday, Bezos made news for a reason that had nothing to do with his company. On January 4, he was airlifted off a private yacht near the Galapagos Islands by a helicopter from the Ecuadorian Navy, taken to his jet, and flown to the United States. The medical crisis at the root of the emergency: kidney stones. 'Galapagos: five stars. Kidney stones: zero stars,' he wrote in an e-mailed statement to reporters after the incident became public.

Nothing better defined this period in Amazon history than a quixotic interview of Bezos by *60 Minutes*, the CBS News program. In the fifteen-minute segment, which aired on December 1, a day before the online shopping frenzy known as Cyber Monday, Bezos unleashed a flood of earnest *Jeffisms*, those well-worn portions of positivity that he has been reliably meting out for years. 'I would define Amazon by our big ideas, which are customer centricity, putting the customer at the center of everything we do, and invention,' Bezos recited, when interviewer Charlie Rose asked him to define Amazon today.

Later, when asked why there was so much animosity toward Amazon in the book world, Bezos was unapologetic. 'The Internet is disrupting every media industry, Charlie,' he said. 'You know, people can complain about that, but complaining is not a strategy.'

Bezos had promised *60 Minutes* a big surprise, and at the end of the segment, he delivered. Amazon's CEO ushered Rose into a darkened room that housed . . . two aerial drones, each with a set of eight rotors. The idea, Bezos said, was to use these so-called 'octocopters' to ferry packages weighing up to five pounds from fulfillment centers to customers' backyards within thirty minutes. 'I know this looks like science fiction,' Bezos said. 'It's not.'

A video demonstrating Amazon's drone program was later watched fourteen million times on YouTube. Yet skeptics pounced, accusing *60 Minutes* of serving up high-altitude propaganda for Amazon right before the biggest online shopping day of the year. Such drone delivery systems won't be legally or technically plausible for years. Critics imagined drones getting shot out of the sky for sport, dropping onto the heads of unsuspecting neighbors, or even getting felled by inclement winds or rain. 'I guess it could work on nice days,' said Ronald Arkin, director of the mobile robot laboratory at the Georgia Institute of Technology. 'I wish Amazon fair weather in their future endeavors.'

Epilogue

Current and former executives in Amazon's operations group insisted the drone program inside Amazon was real and designed to solve a pressing problem in the company's rapidly growing supply chain. Members of Amazon Prime, the free two-day shipping program, were increasingly indulging their shopping urges and buying a single item at a time. Amazon could no longer rely on efficiently combining products in boxes.

One of Bezos's signature strengths was combining technology and a penchant for bold, risky bets. He did so first in retail, and then in the book publishing industry with the Kindle. An army of unmanned octocopters darkening the skies over major cities could help control Amazon's growing shipping expenses and give Prime members a way to indulge their basest shopping impulses. Drones also promised to take expensive, sometimes dangerous trucks off of congested streets.

Such ambitious dreaming is represented among Amazon's fourteen leadership principles.

> Think Big: Thinking small is a self-fulfilling prophecy. Leaders create and communicate a bold direction that inspires results. They think differently and look around corners for ways to serve customers.

And yes, it was also brilliant PR. As the holiday shopping season kicked into high gear, everyone, it seemed, was talking about Amazon.

One of the new features in Amazon's updated Kindle Fire tablets allowed device owners to see a member of Amazon's customer service team on their screens via a live video-chat. Amazon technicians, talking into their webcams, could access a customer's tablet, draw pictures on the device's screen to demonstrate a point and remotely fix any problems. Reviewers hailed the service, dubbed Mayday, as an innovative feature for customers and a breakthrough in customer service. Amazon highlighted it in ubiquitous television advertisements starring 'Amy', a young, attractive customer service representative whose smiling visage materialized on the screens of male Kindle Fire owners.

Yet for many of the low-wage employees in Amazon's customer service call center in Kennewick, Washington, the story of Mayday was a considerably less happy one.

Kennewick is one of the so-called Tri-Cities in eastern Washington, an agricultural region at the confluence of the Yakima, Snake, and Columbia Rivers. Amazon opened a call center in Kennewick in 2005, taking over an old Walmart building and renovating it with a warren of cubicles and offices. It's home to about five hundred workers during off-peak months and a thousand or more when call volumes spike during and after the holidays.

Employees earn a starting wage of $11 an hour, with part of their salary in small grants of stock that vest over a four-year period. It's intense, exhausting work, taking call after call from the 3 percent or so of Amazon customers who either have serious problems with a service or are just inclined to seek out a friendly voice at the other end of the phone.

Like their blue-collar colleagues in the fulfillment centers, Amazon's customer service associates live under a tyrannical regime. The tyrant is cold, hard data, what workers refer to internally as 'the metrics'. For years, customer service reps were graded on a formula that attempted to measure their productivity, taking into account how many calls they took per hour and the average length of each call. Then Amazon started putting more weight on the most desired outcome: customer satisfaction. Now an associate's job performance is based almost entirely on how customers answer an e-mailed survey they receive after they hang up the phone.

Did I solve your problem?
Yes.   No.

Amazon sets targeted goals for the ratio of yeses and nos and call center employees are ranked based on their number. (Yet associates can not ask customers to answer the survey or click 'yes' – that is a dismissible offense, according to numerous interviews with employees in Kennewick.) If an associate falls into the lowest 15 percent of the rankings, they are placed on a 'PIP' – a performance improvement plan – and can be fired if they don't boost their numbers.

Many customer service representatives describe this system as unfair. They feel like they are penalized for unfixable technology problems that they have nothing to do with, and can find their careers jeopardized by callers who know that clicking 'no' is a way to get additional attention from Amazon's customer service department. 'It's such a stressful environment,' says Trisha Powers, who worked in the Kennewick call center for eight years. 'Their standards are so, so high.'

'I've worked at call centers for Verizon and Qwest. I was never treated the way I was treated at Amazon,' says Troy Eaton, who worked at the center for four and a half years before leaving for another job, and described getting sent home several times for alleged infractions, like hanging up on an a customer, only to be exonerated after an investigation. 'Amazon is an amazing company, but the way that call center was run was a nightmare.'

Some employees contend that Amazon stringently enforces the ranking system to jettison senior employees, particularly after four years of service, when they become eligible for raises and new stock grants. Denise Miner worked at Kennewick for four years and was fired after getting too many 'nos' on customer surveys, getting put on a PIP, and then making a mild minor error – sending a customer an e-mail without authorization. She said that prior to the error, she had 'top performance certificates coming out of my ears.'

Miner believes that Amazon knows it has hundreds of willing applicants and prefers to push senior or otherwise troubled employees out the door instead of promoting them or giving them raises. 'It's kind of funny,' she says. 'Myself and a whole lot of other people, as soon as we reached our four-year mark, it was like getting a target on our backs.'

Workers at Kennewick heard about Mayday only a few days before the rest of the world. It was introduced internally as a clandestine project dubbed 'Secret Squirrel'. The company asked its call center employees for volunteers but didn't explain the details, promising only that employees would 'make history'. There were no volunteers, according to six associates who were there at the time. A few brave souls investigated, than promptly backed out when they learned what it was.

The new tablets were announced in September and set to go on sale in November. Amazon's capacity planners had no idea how many device owners would use Mayday, so after the feature was publicly announced, an edict was handed down from Seattle: everyone in Kennewick and at a new call center in Winchester, Kentucky, had to be Mayday trained. A second computer monitor and a webcam were delivered to each desk in both facilities.

Promotional posters of 'Amy' were hung on the walls, with a caption that read: 'This could be you!'

Employees in Kennewick did not take the news well, according to the associates who were there. They filled the 'Voice of the Associates' whiteboard in the facility with strenuous objections and organized a group to talk to management about their concerns. 'There are certain reasons why a lot of people will take a call center job instead of a face-to-face job,' said Nick McFaddin, a customer service rep who worked at the facility for three years and was among those who complained, without success. 'Either they have anxiety issues or they have a certain lifestyle where they have tattoos or piercings or wear their hair a certain way. It's just easier for them to be a voice on the phone.'

Another call center associate named Sharyn Altshuler perhaps had the worst experience. Altshuler, fifty, has a masters degree in fine arts from Yale University. She says she 'works the phone because I don't want to be seen,' in part because she is overweight and prone to panic attacks, and because her 'face tells every emotion. I don't play poker'.

Altshuler complained to her managers that Mayday posed a health issue for her. They insisted she take the training or use her personal days and not get paid. Meetings with the facility's senior leaders and human resources executives devolved into shouting matches. At one point, Altshuler says, she started popping Xanax in front of her bosses. A kindly human resources manager finally excused her from Mayday duty but by then Altshuler's attitude was poor and she believed she was already being targeted for termination. She lost her job in February, 2014, for an alleged infraction unrelated to Mayday.

She had worked at the company for a little under four years. 'One of their values is "Disagree and Commit," but they don't really like that,' Altshuler says. 'What they really mean is, "Do what we say." If you are my rank, the last thing they really want is for you to have ideas.'

In Jeff Bezos's annual letter to shareholders in March, 2014, Amazon's CEO lauded Mayday, writing that 'Nothing gives us more pleasure at Amazon than *reinventing normal* – creating inventions that customers love and resetting their expectations for what normal should be.' He boasted that Mayday tech advisors had received thirty-five marriage proposals, been serenaded by customers 648 times and asked 109 times for assistance ordering a pizza.

'Pretty cool,' he wrote.

On the corner of 7th Avenue and Westlake Avenue North in Seattle, in an area that locals call 'the Denny Triangle', the future of Amazon is rising from a construction site. The company is building a 3.3-million-square-foot high-rise urban campus it calls Rufus 2.0, after the long-dead Corgi that affectionately patrolled its first offices many years ago. At the center of the new headquarters will be three majestic glass domes, which will be completely transparent and filled with greenery.

Jeff Bezos had been almost religiously frugal with Amazon's offices over the years. Not anymore. When the campus is completed, Amazon will have an iconic headquarters on par with other tech giants like Apple, Facebook, and Google. With Rufus 2.0, it is as if Bezos finally understands that Amazon can no longer hide in plain site.

When visitors and employees encounter the new campus, they will likely be filled with awe at an architectural wonder. But will they be filled with admiration for the company and its founder?

The character of any company is a difficult thing to judge. Amazon has satisfied millions of loyal customers over two decades. As Joy Covey pointed out, it has done so by focusing ferociously on a set of values that stress constant innovation and customer orientation, and then by continuing to refine and distill these values in pursuit of the only things in business that really matter. Was the customer happy? Will they return again? 'Did I solve your problem? Yes or no?'

The approach has worked beyond anyone's wildest dreams. Amazon now employs 124,000 people and by 2015 will likely be the fastest retailer in history to surpass $100 billion in sales. It has over 200 million customers, many of whom love to evangelize about the ease and simplicity of shopping on Amazon. The stock price may occasionally give investors nausea, as it did over the first half of 2014, when shares fell by 20 percent amid concerns over Amazon's anemic profit. But the company's low-margin, low-price approach, and its rapidly growing cloud computer business are still warping the daily reality of nearly every industry all around the world.

Yet there is another side to the Amazon fairy tale. In the spring of 2014, in the midst of fractious negotiations over e-book prices with several major book publishers in the U.S. and Europe (including Hachette, the owner of Little, Brown & Co., the publisher of this book in the U.S.,), Amazon made it more difficult for customers to buy thousands of titles on its website. Amazon said in a statement that it was negotiating on behalf of its customers, but its tactics were criticized by authors and onlookers for punishing readers, the very constituency whose interests Amazon claimed to be protecting.

In its fulfillment centers, Amazon's reputation hasn't fared much better. Workers picketed outside the company's warehouses in Germany in 2013 and 2014, demanding a better wage. In 2013, a group of twenty-seven technicians at a fulfillment center in Middletown, Delaware, tried to join the International Association of Machinists and Aerospace Workers to demand more clarity on hiring and promotions. The workers said they faced intense pressure in mandatory all-hands meetings run by company managers to formally vote against joining the union. 'Our employees have made it clear that they prefer a direct connection with Amazon,' an Amazon spokesperson said, after the technicians voted against joining the union, by a decisive 21–6 margin. 'This direct connection is the most effective way to understand and respond to the wants and needs of our employees.'

Amazon's culture has been engineered to cater obsessively to its customers. The company's loyal patrons enjoy the fruits of that focus every time they interact with it. Suppliers who view Amazon as a bully are perfectly free to sell their wares elsewhere. Employees who feel marginalized or mistreated can leave at any time and many do, sometimes after their first taste of the relentless corporate culture. Yet with so many other retailers in retreat, or tailoring their own operations to get as lean and efficient as Amazon, both suppliers and employees may find their opportunities elsewhere are increasingly limited.

Like it or not, they are living in the age of Amazon. This story is just beginning. And there is no such thing as the last word.

Brad Stone
San Francisco, California
2014

Acknowledgments

For years I talked about writing a book about Amazon. And that's probably what I'd still be doing – talking – if it weren't for the help and support of my wonderful friends, family, and colleagues.

Two years ago, my agent Pilar Queen gently instructed me to stop procrastinating and deliver a book proposal. She then became a tenacious champion for this project. At Little, Brown, executive editor John Parsley gave this book the kind of careful editorial attention that is supposedly going out of style at traditional publishers, at least according to certain critics of the book business. Additional thanks go to Reagan Arthur, Michael Pietsch, Geoff Shandler, Nicole Dewey, Fiona Brown, Pamela Marshall, Tracy Roe, and Malin von Euler-Hogan at Little, Brown for steering this book through the birthing process with professionalism and enthusiasm.

I owe an enormous debt to Craig Berman and Drew Herdener in Amazon's public-relations department. While they were always stubborn advocates for the company, they also saw the need for, and perhaps the inevitability of, a definitive book-length look at Amazon's remarkable rise. I'm grateful to Jeff Wilke, Diego

Piacentini, Andy Jassy, Russ Grandinetti, Jeff Blackburn, and Steve Kessel at Amazon, who all took the time to talk to me, and of course to Jeff Bezos, for approving innumerable interviews with his friends, family, and employees.

Over the course of 2012 and 2013, I spent considerable time in Seattle, and a few families there made me feel especially welcome. Nick and Emily Wingfield put me up in their cozy spare bedroom, and I got to play Trivial Pursuit *Star Wars* over breakfast with their wonderful kids, Beatrice and Miller. Scott Pinizzotto and Ali Frank were great hosts on several occasions.

In Silicon Valley, Jill Hazelbaker, Shernaz Daver, Dani Dudeck, Andrew Kovacs, Christina Lee, Tiffany Spencer, Chris Prouty, and Margit Wennmachers provided helpful connections. Susan Prosser at Domain-Tools helped me to scour the domain-name archives for the early alternatives to Amazon.com. My old Columbia classmate Charles Ardai gave me a head start on untangling the long-ago D. E. Shaw days. Like so many other journalists trying to decipher the modern enigma that is Amazon, I relied heavily on the wisdom of Scott Devitt of Morgan Stanley, Scot Wingo of ChannelAdvisor, and Fiona Dias of ShopRunner.

At *Bloomberg Businessweek*, I've found a comfortable home that not only offers a great platform for serious business journalism but also accommodates ambitious projects like this one. Josh Tyrangiel, Brad Wieners, Romesh Ratnesar, Ellen Pollock, and Norman Pearlstine gave me incredible support and leeway to write this book. My editor Jim Aley provided a careful first read. Diana Suryakusuma helped me assemble the photographs under a tight deadline. My friend and colleague Ashlee Vance proved an invaluable sounding board when I needed to discuss the thornier challenges of telling this story.

I also want to thank fellow journalists Steven Levy, Ethan Watters, Adam Rogers, George Anders, Dan McGinn, Nick Bilton, Claire Cain Miller, Damon Darlin, John Markoff, Jim Brunner, Alan Deutschman, Tom Giles, Doug MacMillan, Adam Satariano, Motoko Rich, and Peter Burrows. Nick Sanchez provided stellar research and reporting assistance for this book, and Morgan Mason from the journalism program at the University of Nevada at Reno assisted with interviews of Amazon associates at the fulfillment center in Fernley, Nevada.

My family was remarkably helpful and patient throughout this process, particularly in taking up the slack when I disappeared into reporting and writing. My parents Robert Stone and Carol Glick have always been wonderfully supportive and nurturing. Josh Krafchin, Miriam Stone, Dave Stone, Monica Stone, Jon Stone, and Steve Stone were great sounding boards. My brothers, Brian Stone and Eric Stone, and Becca Zoller Stone, Luanne Stone, and Jennifer Granick were awesome, as always.

While they were only vaguely aware of a distraction they called 'Daddy's book,' my twin daughters, Calista and Isabella Stone, provided the motivation behind this work. My hope and belief is that it will remain relevant history when they are old enough to find it interesting.

And I couldn't have made it across the finish line without the loving support of Tiffany Fox.

Jeff's Reading List

Books have nurtured Amazon since its creation and shaped its culture and strategy. Here are a dozen books widely read by executives and employees that are integral to understanding the company.

The Remains of the Day, by Kazuo Ishiguro (1989).

Jeff Bezos's favorite novel, about a butler who wistfully recalls his career in service during wartime Great Britain. Bezos has said he learns more from novels than non-fiction.

Sam Walton: Made in America, by Sam Walton with John Huey (1992).

In his autobiography, Walmart's founder expounds on the principles of discount retailing and discusses his core values of frugality and a bias for action – a willingness to try a lot of things and make many mistakes. Bezos included both in Amazon's corporate values.

Memos from the Chairman, by Alan Greenberg (1996).

A collection of memos to employees by the chairman of the now-defunct investment bank Bear Stearns. In his memos, Greenberg is constantly restating the bank's core values, especially modesty and frugality. His repetition of wisdom from a fictional philosopher presages Amazon's annual recycling of its original 1997 letter to shareholders.

The Mythical Man-Month, by Frederick P. Brooks Jr. (1975).

An influential computer scientist makes the counterintuitive argument that small groups of engineers are more effective than larger ones at handling complex software projects. The book lays out the theory behind Amazon's two-pizza teams.

Built to Last: Successful Habits of Visionary Companies, by Jim Collins and Jerry I. Porras (1994).

The famous management book about why certain companies succeed over time. A core ideology guides these firms, and only those employees who embrace the central mission flourish; others are 'expunged like a virus' from the companies.

Good to Great: Why Some Companies Make the Leap . . . and Others Don't, by Jim Collins (2001).

Collins briefed Amazon executives on his seminal management book before its publication. Companies must confront the brutal facts of their business, find out what they are uniquely good at, and master their flywheel, in which each part of the business reinforces and accelerates the other parts.

Creation: Life and How to Make It, by Steve Grand (2001).

A video-game designer argues that intelligent systems can be created from the bottom up if one devises a set of primitive building blocks. The book was influential in the creation of Amazon Web Services, or AWS, the service that popularized the notion of the cloud.

The Innovator's Dilemma: The Revolutionary Book That Will Change the Way You Do Business, by Clayton M. Christensen (1997).

An enormously influential business book whose principles Amazon acted on and that facilitated the creation of the Kindle and AWS. Some companies are reluctant to embrace disruptive technology because it might alienate customers and undermine their core businesses, but Christensen argues that ignoring poten-tial disruption is even costlier.

The Goal: A Process of Ongoing Improvement, by Eliyahu M. Goldratt and Jeff Cox (1984).

An exposition of the science of manufacturing written in the guise of the novel, the book encourages companies to identify the biggest constraints in their operations and then structure their organizations to get the most out of those constraints. *The Goal* was a bible for Jeff Wilke and the team that fixed Amazon's fulfillment network.

Lean Thinking: Banish Waste and Create Wealth in Your Corporation, by James P. Womack and Daniel T. Jones (1996).

The production philosophy pioneered by Toyota calls for a focus on those activities that create value for the customer and the systematic eradication of everything else.

Data-Driven Marketing: The 15 Metrics Everyone in Marketing Should Know, by Mark Jeffery (2010).

A guide to using data to measure everything from customer satisfaction to the effectiveness of marketing. Amazon employees must support all assertions with data, and if the data has a weakness, they must point it out or their colleagues will do it for them.

The Black Swan: The Impact of the Highly Improbable, by Nassim Nicholas Taleb (2007).

The scholar argues that people are wired to see patterns in chaos while remaining blind to unpredictable events, with massive consequences. Experimentation and empiricism trumps the easy and obvious narrative.

Notes

Prologue

1 Jeff Bezos, keynote address at Tepper School of Business graduation, Carnegie Mellon University, May 18, 2008.

Part I
Chapter 1: The House of Quants

1 Jeff Bezos, speech at Lake Forest College, February 26, 1998.
2 Mark Leibovich, *The New Imperialists* (New York: Prentice Hall, 2002), 84.
3 Rebecca Johnson, 'MacKenzie Bezos: Writer, Mother of Four, and High-Profile Wife,' *Vogue*, February 20, 2013.
4 Eerily, here is how Bezos described the third-market opportunity to *Investment Dealers' Digest* on November 15, 1993: 'We wanted something to differentiate our product. We think there is a desire for one stop shopping.'
5 Michael Peltz, 'The Power of Six,' *Institutional Investor* (March 2009). 'David Shaw envisioned D. E. Shaw "as essentially a research lab that happened to invest, and not as a financial firm that happened to have a few people playing with equations."'
6 Leibovich, *The New Imperialists*, 85.
7 Peter de Jonge, 'Riding the Perilous Waters of Amazon.com,' *New York Times Magazine*, March 14, 1999.
8 John Quarterman, *Matrix News*.
9 Jeff Bezos interview, Academy of Achievement, May 4, 2001.
10 Jeff Bezos, speech at Lake Forest College, February 26, 1998.
11 Jeff Bezos, speech to Commonwealth Club of California, July 27, 1998.

12 Jeff Bezos, speech to the American Association of Publishers, March 18, 1999.

Chapter 2: The Book of Bezos

1 Robert Spector, *Amazon.com: Get Big Fast* (New York: HarperCollins, 2000). Spector's book offers a comprehensive account of Amazon's early years.

2 Jeff Bezos, speech to the American Association of Publishers, March 18, 1999.

3 David Sheff, 'The *Playboy* Interview: Jeff Bezos,' *Playboy*, February 1, 2000.

4 Ibid.

5 Adi Ignatius, 'Jeff Bezos on Leading for the Long-Term at Amazon,' *HBR IdeaCast* (blog), *Harvard Business Review*, January 3, 2013, http://blogs.hbr.org/ideacast/2013/01/jeff-bezos-on-leading-for-the.html.

6 Jeff Bezos, speech to the American Association of Publishers, March 18, 1999.

7 Jeff Bezos, speech at Lake Forest College, February 26, 1998.

8 Ibid.

9 Amazon.com Inc. S-1, filed March 24, 1997.

10 Mukul Pandya and Robbie Shell, eds., 'Lasting Leadership: Lessons from the 25 Most Influential Business People of Our Times,' Knowledge@Wharton, October 20, 2004, http://knowledge.wharton.upenn.edu/article.cfm?articleid=1054.

11 Ibid.

12 James Marcus, *Amazonia* (New York: New Press, 2004).

13 Jeff Bezos, speech to Commonwealth Club of California, July 27, 1998.

14 Cynthia Mayer, 'Investing It; Does Amazon = 2 Barnes & Nobles?,' *New York Times*, July 19, 1998.

15 Jeff Bezos, interview by *Charlie Rose*, Charlie Rose, PBS, July 28, 2010.

16 Justin Hibbard, 'Wal-Mart v. Amazon.com: The Inside Story,' *InformationWeek*, February 22, 1999.

17 Jeff Bezos interview, Academy of Achievement, May 4, 2001.

Chapter 3: Fever Dreams

1 One explanation, according to Wikipedia, is that 'a round man-hole cover cannot fall through its circular opening, whereas a square manhole cover may fall in if it were inserted diagonally in the hole.'

2 Ron Suskind, 'Amazon.com Debuts the Mother of All Bestseller Lists,' *Washington Post*, August 26, 1998.

3 Ibid.

4 Jeff Bezos, speech to Commonwealth Club of California, July 27, 1998.

5 Jeff Bezos, speech to the American Association of Publishers, March 18, 1999.

6 Steven Levy, *In the Plex* (New York: Simon and Schuster, 2011), 34.

7 Jacqueline Doherty, 'Amazon.bomb,' *Barron's*, May 31, 1999.

8 George Anders, Nikhil Deogun, and Joann S. Lublin, 'Joseph Galli Will Join Amazon, Reversing Plan to Take Pepsi Job,' *Wall Street Journal*, June 25, 1999.

9 Joshua Cooper Ramo, 'Jeff Bezos: King of the Internet,' *Time*, December 27, 1999.

10 Stefanie Olsen, 'FTC Fines E-Tailers $1.5 Million for Shipping Delays,' CNET, July 26, 2000.

11 Michael Moe, 'Tech Startup Secrets of Bill Campbell, Coach of Silicon Valley,' *Forbes*, July 27, 2011.

Chapter 4: Milliravi

1 Jeremy Kahn, 'The Giant Killer,' *Fortune*, June 11, 2001.

2 Evelyn Nussenbaum, 'Analyst Finally Tells Truth about Dot-Coms,' *New York Post*, June 27, 2000.

3 Mark Leibovich, 'Child Prodigy, Online Pioneer,' *Washington Post*, September 3, 2000.

4 Ibid.

5 Steven Levy, 'Jeff Bezos Owns the Web in More Ways Than You Think,' *Wired*, November 13, 2011.

6 'Amazon.com Auctions Helps Online Sellers Become Effective Marketers,' PR Newswire, August 18, 1999.

7 Scott Hillis, 'Authors Protest Amazon's Practices, Used-Book

Feature Comes under Fire,' Reuters, December 28, 2000.

8   Jennifer Waters, 'Amazon Faces "Creditor Squeeze,"' *CBS MarketWatch*, February 6, 2001.

9   Gretchen Morgenson, 'S.E.C. Is Said to Investigate Amazon Chief,' *New York Times*, March 9, 2001.

10   Sinegal's comments are drawn from my July 2012 interview with Sinegal, the recollections of Amazon executives, and Andrew Bary, 'King of the Jungle,' *Barron's*, March 23, 2009.

11   Monica Soto, 'Terrorist Attacks Overwhelm Amazon's Good News about Deal with Target,' *Seattle Times*, September 27, 2001.

12   Saul Hansell, 'Amazon Decides to Go for a Powerful Form of Advertising: Lower Prices and Word of Mouth,' *New York Times*, February 10, 2003.

Part II
Chapter 5: Rocket Boy

1   Chip Bayers, 'The Inner Bezos,' *Wired*, March 1999.

2   Mark Leibovich, *The New Imperialists* (New York: Prentice Hall, 2002), 79.

3   'Local Team Wins Unicycle Polo Match,' *Albuquerque Tribune*, November 23, 1961.

4   *Albuquerque Tribune*, April 24, 1965.

5   Leibovich, *The New Imperialists*, 73–74.

6   Ibid., 71.

7   Ibid., 74.

8   Jeff Bezos interview, Academy of Achievement, May 4, 2001.

9   'The World's Billionaires,' *Forbes*, July 9, 2001.

10   Bayers, 'The Inner Bezos.'

11   Brad Stone, 'Bezos in Space,' *Newsweek*, May 5, 2003.

12   Mylene Mangalindan, 'Buzz in West Texas Is about Bezos and His Launch Site,' *Wall Street Journal,* November 10, 2006.

13   Jeff Bezos, 'Successful Short Hop, Setback, and Next Vehicle,' Blue Origin website, September 2, 2011.

14   Adam Lashinsky, 'Amazon's Jeff Bezos: The Ultimate Disrupter,' *Fortune*, November 16, 2012.

Chapter 6: Chaos Theory

1   Saul Hansell, 'Listen Up! It's Time for a Profit; a Front-Row Seat as Amazon Gets Serious,' *New York Times*, May 20, 2011.

2   Jeff Bezos, speech to the American Association of Publishers, March 18, 1999.

3   In 2012, my research assistant Nick Sanchez filed a comprehensive FOIA (Freedom of Information Act) request with the U.S. Department of Labor for any complaints or compliance violations for Amazon.com from 1995 through the present day. In addition to the much-publicized heat complaints reviewed by the *Allentown Morning Call*, regional and subregional OSHA offices returned a few dozen employee complaints, including bathroom-break issues at a call center in Washington; forklift horseplay in New Hampshire; improper tornado sheltering in Pennsylvania; and concerns like water-cooler mineral buildup, breakroom mold, inadequate protective headgear, and harmful levels of noise and fumes. In all cases, Amazon responded to OSHA with evidence of compliance or immediately remedied the situation, and it settled the vast majority of concerns without need for OSHA inspection or citation. A $3,000 citation given to an Amazon Fresh center in Washington for not having an adequate emergency evacuation plan to deal with ammonia fumes was the most serious citation we found. But multijurisdiction FOIA requests have to be forwarded by the federal OSHA office to state and regional offices, and it is nearly impossible to obtain all such records for a company with a nationwide footprint as big as Amazon's, even with a year of lead time.

4   In July of 2012, Amazon established its Career Choice tuition-reimbursement program to help fulfillment-center employees with three consecutive years of service return to school to continue their education. Amazon said it would cover up to $2,000 a year in tuition for up to four years for each employee.

Chapter 7: A Technology Company, Not a Retailer

1   Gary Rivlin, 'A Retail Revolution Turns Ten,' *New York Times*, July 27, 2012.

2   Gary Wolf, 'The Great Library of Amazonia,' *Wired*, October 23, 2003.

3   Ibid.

4   Luke Timmerman, 'Amazon's Top Techie, Werner Vogels, on How Web Services Follows the Retail Playbook,' *Xconomy*, September 29, 2010.

5   Shobha Warrier, 'From Studying under the Streetlights to CEO of a U.S. Firm!,' *Rediff*, September 1, 2010.

6   Tim O'Reilly, 'Amazon Web Services API,' July 18, 2002, http://www.oreillynet.com/pub/wlg/1707.

7   Damien Cave, 'Losing the War on Patents,' *Salon*, February 15, 2002.

8   O'Reilly, 'Amazon Web Services API.'

9   Steve Grand, *Creation: Life and How to Make It* (Darby, PA: Diane Publishing, 2000), 132.

10 Hybrid machine/human computing arrangement patent filed October 12, 2001; http://www.google.com/patents/US7197459.

11 'Artificial Artificial Intelligence,' *Economist*, June 10, 2006.

12 Katharine Mieszkowski, 'I Make $1.45 a Week and I Love It,' *Salon*, July 24, 2006.

13 Jason Pontin, 'Artificial Intelligence, with Help from the Humans,' *New York Times*, March 25, 2007.

14 Jeff Bezos, interview by Charlie Rose, *Charlie Rose*, PBS, February 26, 2009.

Chapter 8: Fiona

1   Calvin Reid, 'Authors Guild Shoots Down Rocket eBook Contract,' *Publishers Weekly*, May 10, 1999.

2   Steve Silberman, 'Ex Libris,' *Wired*, July 1998.

3   Steven Levy, 'It's Time to Turn the Last Page,' *Newsweek*, December 31, 1999.

4   Jane Spencer and Kara Scannell, 'As Fraud Case Unravels, Executive Is at Large,' *Wall Street Journal*, April 25, 2007.

5   David Pogue, 'Trying Again to Make Books Obsolete,' *New York Times*, October 12, 2006.

6   Jeff Bezos, speech at Lake Forest College, February 26, 1998.

7   Walt Mossberg, 'The Way We Read,' *Wall Street Journal*, June 9, 2008.

8   Mark Leibovich, 'Child Prodigy, Online Pioneer,' *Washington Post*, September 3, 2000.

9   Clayton Christensen, *The Innovator's Dilemma: When New Technologies Cause Great Firms to Fail* (Boston: Harvard Business Review Press, 1997).

10 Jeff Bezos, interview by Charlie Rose, *Charlie Rose*, PBS, February 26, 2009.

11 David D. Kirkpatrick, 'Online Sales of Used Books Draw Protest,' *New York Times*, April 10, 2002.

12 Graeme Neill, 'Sony and Amazon in e-Books Battle,' *Bookseller*, April 27, 2007.

13 Brad Stone, 'Envisioning the Next Chapter for Electronic Books,' *New York Times*, September 6, 2007.

14 Jeff Bezos, *The Oprah Winfrey Show*, ABC, October 24, 2008.

Part III:
Chapter 9: Liftoff!

1   Ben Charny, 'Amazon Upgrade Leads Internet Stocks Higher,' *MarketWatch*, January 22, 2007.

2   Victoria Barrett, 'Too Smart for Its Own Good,' *Forbes*, October 9, 2008.

3   Jim Collins, Good to Great: *Why Some Companies Make the Leap . . . and Others Don't* (New York: HarperCollins, 2001), 180.

4   Zappos Milestone: Timeline, Zappos.com,http://about. zappos.com/press-center/media-coverage/zappos-milestone-timeline.

5   Parija B. Kavilanz, 'Circuit City to Shut Down,' *CNN Money*, January 16, 2009.

6   Ben Austen, 'The End of Borders and the Future of Books,' *Bloomberg Businessweek*, November 10, 2011.

7   Annie Lowrey, 'Readers Without Borders,' *Slate*, July 20, 2011.

8   Scott Mayerowitz and Alice Gomstyn, 'Target Among the Latest Chain of Grim Layoffs,' ABC News, January 27, 2009.

9   Brad Stone, 'Can Amazon Be the Wal-Mart of the Web?' *New York Times*, September 19, 2009.

10 Miguel Bustillo and Jeffrey A. Trachtenberg, 'Wal-Mart Strafes Amazon in Book War,' *Wall Street Journal*, October 16, 2009.

11 Brad Stone and Stephanie Rosenbloom, 'Price War Brews

Between Amazon and Wal-Mart,' *New York Times*, November 23, 2009.

12   American Booksellers Association, Letter to Justice Department, October 22, 2009.

13   Spencer Wang, Credit Suisse First Boston analyst report, February 16, 2010.

14   Mick Rooney, 'Amazon/Hachette Livre Dispute,' *Independent Publishing Magazine*, June 6, 2008.

15   Eoin Purcell, 'All Your Base Are Belong to Amazon,' *Eoin Purcell's Blog*, May 14, 2009, http://eoinpurcellsblog.com/2009/05/14/all-your-base-are-belong-to-amazon/.

16   According to court testimony, on Jannuary 29, 2010, the general counsel of Simon & Schuster wrote to CEO Carolyn Kroll Reidy that she 'cannot believe that Jobs made the statement' and considered it 'incredibly stupid,'http://www.nysd.uscourts.gov/cases/show.php?db=special&id=306, page 86.

17   Motoko Rich and Brad Stone, 'Publisher Wins Fight with Amazon Over E-Books,' *New York Times*, January 31, 2010.

Chapter 10: Expedient Convictions

1   Jeff Bezos, interview by Charlie Rose, *Charlie Rose*, PBS, July 28, 2010.

2   Fireside Chat with Jeff Bezos and Werner Vogels, Amazon Web Services re: Invent Conference, Las Vegas, November 29, 2012.

3   'Editorial: Spitzer's Latest Flop,' *New York Sun*, November 15, 2007.

4   *Vadim Tsypin and Diana Tsypin v. Amazon.com et al.*, King County Superior Court, case 10-2-12192-7 SEA.

5   Miguel Bustillo and Stu Woo, 'Retailers Push Amazon on Taxes,' *Wall Street Journal,* March 17, 2011.

6   Aaron Glantz, 'Amazon Spends Big to Fight Internet Sales Tax,' *Bay Citizen*, August 27, 2011.

7   Tim O'Reilly, blog post, Google Plus, September 5, 2011, https://plus.google.com/+TimOReilly/posts/QypNDmvJJq7.

8   Zoe Corneli, 'Legislature Approves Amazon Deal,' *Bay Citizen*, September 9, 2011.

9   Bryant Urstadt, 'What Amazon Fears Most: Diapers,' *Bloomberg Businessweek*, October 7, 2010.

10   Nick Saint, 'Amazon Nukes Diapers.com in Price War – May Force Diapers' Founders to Sell Out,' *Business Insider*, November 5, 2010.

11   Amazon, 'Amazon Marketplace Sellers Enjoy High-Growth Holiday Season,' press release, January 2, 2013.

12   Roy Blount Jr., 'The Kindle Swindle?,' *New York Times*, February 24, 2009.

13   Brad Stone, 'Amazon's Hit Man,' *Bloomberg Businessweek*, January 25, 2012.

14   Thomas L. Friedman, 'Do You Want the Good News First?,' *New York Times*, May 19, 2012.

15   'Contracts on Fire: Amazon's Lending Library Mess,' AuthorsGuild.org, November 14, 2011.

16   Richard Russo, 'Amazon's Jungle Logic,' *New York Times*, December 12, 2011.

Chapter 11: The Kingdom of the Question Mark

1   George Anders, 'Inside Amazon's Idea Machine: How Bezos Decodes the Customer,' *Forbes*, April 4, 2012.

2   Amazon's Leadership Principles, http://www.amazon.com/Values-Careers-Homepage/b?ie=UTF8&node=239365011.

3   Luisa Kroll and Kerry A. Dolan, 'The World's Billionaires,' *Forbes*, March 4, 2013.

4   David Dykstra, 'Bezos Completes $28 Million Home Improvement,' Seattle-Mansions.Blogspot.com, October 1, 2010, http://seattle-mansions.blogspot.com/2010/10/bezos-completes-28-million-home.html.

5   Rebecca Johnson, 'MacKenzie Bezos: Writer, Mother of Four, and High-Profile Wife,' *Vogue*, February 20, 2013.

Epilogue

1   David Streitfeld, 'Joy Covey, Top Executive in Amazon.com's Early Days, Dies at 50,' *New York Times*, September 19, 2013, http://bits.blogs.nytimes.com/2013/09/19/former-amazon-executive-dies-in-bicycle-accident.

Notes

2   E-mail from Covey to Stone, January 14, 2013. Reprinted with permission of the Joy Covey estate.

3   Judith Rosen, 'Booksellers Say "No" to Amazon Source,' *Publisher's Weekly*, November 5, 2013, http://www.publishersweekly.com/pw/by-topic/industry-news/bookselling/article/59888-booksellers-say-no-to-selling-kindles.html.

Index

Index

Index

Index

Index

Index

Index

Index

Index

Index

Index

Index

GENA SHOWALTER

THE DARKEST PASSION

HARLEQUIN®MIRA®

Harlequin MIRA is a registered trademark of Harlequin Enterprises Limited, used under licence.

First published in Great Britain 2010. This edition 2014.
Harlequin MIRA, an imprint of Harlequin (UK) Limited,
Eton House, 18-24 Paradise Road,
Richmond, Surrey, TW9 1SR

© 2010 Gena Showalter

ISBN 978-1-848-45348-7

56-0514

Harlequin (UK) Limited's policy is to use papers that are natural, renewable and recyclable products and made from wood grown in sustainable forests. The logging and manufacturing processes conform to the legal environmental regulations of the country of origin.

Printed and bound by
CPI Group (UK) Ltd, Croydon, CR0 4YY